The Classical Age of German Literature 1740–1815

The C

of German Literature 1740–1815

Victor Lange

HM

HOLMES & MEIER PUBLISHERS, INC.
NEW YORK

First published in the United States of America 1982 by
Holmes & Meier Publishers, Inc.
30 Irving Place, New York, N.Y. 10003

Library of Congress Cataloguing in Publication Data

Lange, Victor, 1908–
The classical age of German literature, 1740–1815.
Bibliography: p.
Includes index.
1. German Literature—18th century—History and criticism.
2. Classicism.
I. Title.
PR311.L26 1982 830′.9′006 82–15734

ISBN 0–8419–0853–2
ISBN 0–8419–0854–0 (pbk.)

Text set in 10/11 pt Baskerville Compugraphic
by Colset Private Limited.
Printed and bound in Great Britain

For Frances

From time to time the memory of remarkable human beings and the presence of eminent works of art stir our spirit of reflection. Both are bequests for every generation, the one through their actions and their fame, the other as ineffable objects truly preserved. Every discerning mind knows well enough that only the contemplation of their specific totality can have true value; yet, we try again and again through critical effort and the written word to draw fresh meaning from them.

J.W.v.Goethe *Winckelmann und sein Jahrhundert*

Contents

Preface

A relatively brief survey of the central, the 'classical' period of German literature is an undertaking of considerable challenge. That impressive body of creative and critical writing, heterogeneous but of growing self-assurance and purpose, is not easily described as an achievement in its own right and of consequence for the history of European letters. If any such project is bound to be something of an experiment, this is particularly true of the intricate features and currents of the age under discussion. By forcing the abundance of imaginative effort during the latter half of the eighteenth century into categories derived either from the movement of political events or from a presumed history of ideas, critics have in the past sought to give to the literature of that period at least the semblance of evolutionary logic. Such a taxonomy is no longer adequate; literary historiography, now more than ever an exceedingly problematical enterprise, must justify its legitimacy by specific and clearly envisaged criteria. I have here aimed at recognizing the close interplay in German literature of social and formal impulses and have taken a broadly defined preoccupation with the values of the European Enlightenment as the focus that determines (in assent or protest) the thinking of German writers from Lessing to the end of the Napoleonic campaigns. I have used categories such as 'rococo', 'Sturm und Drang', even 'classical' and 'romantic', with full awareness of their elusive connotations, to indicate attitudes, points of view or formal solutions characterizing the individual work rather than as chronological brackets that can at best aid in placing or classifying it.

Recent scholarship has offered vigorous and at times radical reassessment of the period as a whole and of particular aspects or single figures and has sought to free it of the stubborn accretion of clichés of judgement – national, sentimental or academic. It has made use of a fresh interest in theories of poetics and rhetoric and of the stimulating discourse of the social sciences; it has taken more seriously the importance of the modes of production and reception of literature and has amply documented the role of the writer in a society often enough unresponsive to critical challenges. Much attention has been paid to the awareness of political – and not merely broadly philosophical – pressures upon the work of major or hitherto neglected authors. What has emerged as a topic of literary consequence is the bearing upon German men of letters during the decades immediately preceding and following the American and French Revolutions, of the tensions between the obsolescent values of an entrenched feudal order and those of the increasingly assertive middle class.

Whatever the conclusions of these investigations, they have undoubtedly sharpened our critical judgement of works whose rank has in the past too readily been taken for granted, more often invoked than probed. I have been less intent on celebrating the 'spirit' of the age than on elucidating a succession of memorable works which, like all stirring productions of art, gave shape to experiences felt only indistinctly until they were made intelligible, shared and explored in the act of reading. Instead of providing a catalogue of names, titles and dates I have chosen to deal more fully with a limited number of writers and to place these in relationship to one another. I have been able to touch only in passing on the functioning of literature as an institution, on the largely unexplored ways of patronage, on religious and educational practices or the systems of scientific speculation and enquiry.

It should, perhaps be said that, while I hope that this study may have appeal beyond the specialists' interest, it was written with English and American readers and their critical dispositions in mind.

I acknowledge with much gratitude my indebtedness to the National Endowment of the Humanities for a Senior Fellowship, and to the Humanities Research Centre at the Australian National University for providing the opportunity of uninterrupted reading and writing.

Victor Lange
1981

Introduction

The history of German literature in the second half of the eighteenth century is as rich in individual talent as it is complex in cultural impulses. It is the product of heterogeneous intellectual traditions, of conflicting religious convictions and of stubbornly asserted regional and sectarian forms of life. Without national identity, Germany was a conglomerate of more than 300 principalities and petty states, a multitude of societies held together by the political and administrative authority of provincial courts and by an agrarian economic system largely obsolete in comparison to that of the major European states. Neither the capitals of the two chief powers, Berlin and Vienna, nor the cities in which the mercantile spirit was beginning to create a self-confident citizenry could play anything like the cohesive and representative role of London or Paris. Social and intellectual aspirations were realized only within the opportunities offered by a unique configuration of aristocratic institutions, of secular or ecclesiastical courts, conservative and by no means affluent, but, with few exceptions remarkably cultivated and receptive to the ceaseless European traffic of ideas in which the German men of letters were eager to share.

It is all the more remarkable that such a relatively confined and disparate life should, within two generations, have produced a literature of extraordinary creative genius, of critical energy and philosophical originality that was soon to affect and change the fabric of the European imagination. To describe the memorable features of this historical experience, from the assertion of Prussian power by Frederick the Great to the end of the Napoleonic wars is the purpose of this study.

If that age is here designated as 'classical', the term should first be taken in its most generous sense to characterize an achievement of exceptional scope and consequence. During that half century the German writer becomes aware of his resources and of his public function: he discovers contemporary European categories of taste and judgement which, together with the burden and the strength of separate native traditions, are made to serve his vision of a mature society. Moreover, the literature of the period gives dignity and legitimacy to the aspirations of a diffident middle class. It is in response to the tensions, felt with ever-increasing urgency, between the authority of religious or secular institutions and the counterclaims of an emancipated self, that imaginative and theoretical works of astonishing variety provide social and intellectual resolutions of lasting effect upon European political institutions in the nineteenth century.

The successive stages of this process are not so much discrete movements as modifications of a continuous interaction between indigenous traditions and models of reflection and action offered by the fascinating canon of contemporary English and French thought. However different the social premises of those eagerly received systems of belief and precept may have been, their tenor, at once enlightened and pragmatic, presented far-reaching challenges to German readers. None of the major or minor writers failed to respond to the omnipresent provocations of the Enlightenment, its faith in reason and its hopes for a humane society, tested equally by the defenders of the traditional and the advocates of progress, towards a new order. The thrust of this debate not only lends an enormously diverse character to the period, but establishes its continuity.

German literary historians have in the past been anxious to interpret this 'classical' phase of German letters and culture as a series of efforts to assert a specifically native genius, gradually freeing itself of what was felt to be an alien rationalism of the (French) Enlightenment, and achieving characteristic works of 'natural' poetic force.

The rebellious voices of the 'Sturm und Drang' playwrights are, in this view, the first indicators of a new belief in exuberant creativity against which the 'rococo' sensibility seemed merely mannered, anti-social and obsolete. Herder appears in this design as the magisterial defender of national or populist ideals while the anti-naturalistic postulates of Goethe's and Schiller's 'classicist' programme were regarded as a mistaken effort to reinstitute norms emphatically discredited by the German advocates of spontaneity and passion.

This historical scheme is no longer convincing. The continuity of ideas and postulates of the European tradition of Enlightenment is in Germany far more compelling and striking than the centrifugal tendencies which in literary as well as social postulates challenge its abuses. The fabric of this or any other period cannot be rendered in the speculative perspectives of a history of ideas which are seldom coincidental with those of the history of literary texts. The relationship between a presumed 'climate of opinion' and the intellectual disposition or the performance of a given artist is by no means self-evident. The manner in which a particular poet, or group of poets, deals with received or current ideas and transforms them, often goes counter to prevailing modes of belief. Indeed a writer of consequence necessarily writes against the grain of a society in which he participates effectively only in so far as he confronts it in deliberate critical strategies. Any historical survey must, therefore, pay particular attention to indications in current works of dissociation from, rather than conformity with, ideas and forms widely shared and accepted.

This is not to say that prevalent social and political realities as well as historical memories and imperatives can to any degree be by-passed. During the period under discussion these elements press upon the writer with unparalleled urgency and are constantly tested by the rapidly growing challenges of critical theories coming from England and France. German and European impulses, whatever their tenor, are, far from being categorically antagonistic, palpably interdependent: the traditions of classical learning, of theological argument and aesthetic doctrine are, throughout the period, experienced as living ingredients in what is more and more distinctly recognized as the 'modern' character of life, with inestimable consequences for the functioning of literature and of art throughout Europe.

The German classical age begins with the assertion of a sense of the new in Lessing's incomparable defence of rational pragmatism; it ends with a disavowal of the social instrumentality of reason in the subjective idealism of the romantic doctrine. Wherever, during this period, the cry for 'natural' reasoning is heard, whether in the violent protests of the Sturm und Drang against the inhumanity of absolutism and the atrophy of the imagination, in the testimonials of sectarian piety or in that evocation of the illuminating power of religion by Hamann and Herder – it springs in one form or another from the recognition of a new critical disposition that compels the scrutiny of current philosophical positions and social realities. Broad social concerns rather than narrow literary interests are therefore the links between the several phases of German intellectual life in the late eighteenth century. It is self-evident that literature cannot be adequately assessed by merely pinpointing its social or political subject matter, nor, indeed, should it be reduced to a tool of social historians. Yet, only a sufficient awareness of the concrete preconditions of the literary life enables us to recognize and interpret the efficacy of its propositions, its imaginative force and its formal accomplishments.

The pre-eminent tension from which no writer of the time can isolate himself is that between what are summarily recognized as the traditional values of a feudal ruling caste and the slowly evolving self-testing of the middle class. A clear definition of the range and applicability of the terms 'feudal' and 'middle class' or 'bourgeoisie' is in the German context especially difficult to give. The nobility represented a network of common dynastic and economic interests; their power rested upon landed property and, compared to equivalent groups in England and France, upon relatively modest amounts of ready money. The exercise of power differed widely in spirit and practice from one principality to another. (Weimar, an exceptionally 'liberal' court, was until 1810 governed by administrative statutes issued in 1509; it was in 1816 the first among all German states to introduce a constitution.) The political horizon of the rulers was limited; their decisions were often enough dictated by personal considerations. In each state religious traditions, familial allegiances and the qualities of mind and character of those in power determined the lives of the citizens. Their cultural interests ranged from pointed indifference to the liveliest and most intelligent involvement. Directly as patrons, they could give support to writers, scholars or artists; some were ambitious collectors of art or served as guiding spirits of a court theatre that was often of high quality and open to a growing audience of commoners.

The German middle class, moderately educated and not easily defined by any shared interests or habits of life, depended for its well-being upon a loyal participation in the administrative machinery of the court or of the landed aristocracy. In Prussia the 'bourgeoisie' was systematically mobilized for service in an efficiently stratified society; it remained loyal, disciplined and staunch throughout the revolutionary challenges and provided the ethos of the cultivated, even patrician, class of nineteenth-century German civil servants. Elsewhere in Germany, north or south, the impact of the French Revolution upon communities in which the middle class had previously accepted a deferential symbiosis with the nobility, proved far more radical; it encouraged the 'progressive' hopes of long-dependent citizens for an increasing share in the affairs of government.

Except for a few cities such as Leipzig or Hamburg where a prosperous mercantile society developed a representative if paternalistic form of political conduct, the frame of mind of the provincial middle class was submissive and, with few exceptions, disinclined to entertain extreme alternatives. Not to abolish, or even to diminish, feudal rule, but to liberalize it or to make it more humane was the aim of most German writers, to educate the middle class and to enlarge its economic base so as to make its participation in the political process more effective.

Nothing is more characteristic of the sentiments that motivated those writers who were most emphatically in sympathy with the ideals of the European Enlightenment than the often projected vision of a future society dedicated to the pursuit of universal happiness and human dignity. The achievement of that condition would abolish the divisive distinctions between the classes: 'The term "bürgerlich",' Wieland writes in 1791, 'does not mean a society of inferiors, of *roturiers*, but defines the nature of the political community altogether; every member of the political society, whatever class he may represent, is in this sense a "Bürger".'[1]

It is well to remember that allegiance to the group values of the middle class was in Germany far less firmly developed than the contrary assertion of individual and subjective detachment, that proud weapon of sectarian Protestantism which had, in the northern German states for long served to confront or bypass orthodox or secular authority. The introspective habit and the desire to transcend a monotonous and severely restrictive public life easily induced the German writer to seek satisfaction in utopian speculations or eccentric visions of a community joined in dedication to spiritual rather than political freedom. The degree to which this somewhat abstract commitment is defined, or tempered, by an understanding of the concrete relationship between literature and the social realities, determined during the latter half of the century the manner in which perceptive German men of letters sought to influence and persuade their contemporaries.

The creative artist served, even more than the political journalist, as the eloquent voice, conservative or progressive, of social disquiet; and the literary document, whatever its aesthetic quality, can, after 1770, claim the attention of an audience of increasing discernment. C.M. Wieland is the most resolute defender of literature as a medium of urgent public consequence. It is axiomatic for most responsible German writers of the time, for Lessing and Herder, as well as Goethe and Schiller or the young Romantic critics and poets, that art and literature are exercises not merely of wit or skill or of private articulation, but of a mode of cognition and of judgement indispensable to the proper functioning of the citizen.

It should not surprise us that the limited scope of political participation tended, in Germany more than elsewhere, to encourage oblique forms of communication and, in consequence, the elevation of the aesthetic experience and judgement to a preferred medium of social analysis and change. The presumed efficacy of art and the need of an adequate modern definition of its end and means, the validity of its conventions especially under the disruptive impact of the liberated imagination are, at any rate, the pressing topics that engage every major writer of the age. We may, today, no longer share this lofty estimate of the role of art; for an understanding of the themes and forms of German literature in the late

[1] C.M. Wieland, *Gesammelte Schriften*, (Akademie-Ausgabe), Berlin, Weidmann, 1930, XV, p. 470.

eighteenth century this austere view is of overriding importance.

Nowhere is the implemental character of art more resolutely insisted upon than in the theory of culture that was, during their close association in Weimar between 1794 and 1805, developed and sternly advocated by the most conspicuous German writers, Goethe and Schiller. It is not inappropriate to think of this carefully orchestrated project as a brief but far-reaching interlude in the social and intellectual evolution of the late eighteenth century. The authority of ancient Greek forms of life and thought that was here invoked has persuaded subsequent German critics (not the participants themselves) to speak of this historical moment as 'die Klassik'. While the specifically classical inheritance undoubtedly circumscribes the magnetic field of the Weimar undertaking, the literary and cultural intentions must be clearly distinguished from earlier as well as later European attempts to recover the exemplary strength of Greek convictions.

What Goethe and Schiller envisaged is, of course, part of that historical debate on the relationship between the ancients and the moderns, and as such a reflection of the concern of the late eighteenth century for the recovery of models of belief and action that might inform the hopes of a regenerated society. Yet, the Weimar focus upon classical concepts and propositions has little or nothing to do with the 'classicist' phase of French literature: the social assumptions inspiring its theoretical framework are by no means feudal, its understanding of Greek culture is thoroughly unheroic, it is free of archaeological curiosity, of nostalgia or any faith in mere normative orthodoxy. The cardinal objective of the Weimar enterprise is to make use of the admirably coherent intellectual and aesthetic propositions contained in the art and literature of the Greeks, against which modern convictions, judgements and prospects could be appraised and measured.

The immediate consideration which led Schiller and Goethe to this uncompromising (by no means widely shared) course of action was the fear of radical social changes in Germany brought about abruptly as a consequence of the French Revolution. It is easy to suggest that this concern was the result of reactionary sentiments, of a desire to maintain established forms of life or privilege. There can, indeed, be no doubt that the preservation of a society with clearly differentiated resources and responsibilities seemed to Goethe a goal worth defending, provided the aristocracy could be made aware of its modern, its 'bourgeois' obligations, much as the middle class should increasingly be drawn into the demanding business of government. His poetry and his criticism during that classical decade were, for that reason, consciously directed at the nobility, the class he had come both to respect and to find wanting in seriousness and maturity. This, at least, was his own immediate target.

Schiller on his part, altogether different in his intellectual disposition and background, could not be accused of reactionary attitudes: he was, and remained, the eloquent advocate of freedom in its most categorical form.

The classical project, whatever its initial motive, had, as we shall see, complex reasons and, at the same time, envisioned goals that transcended the aesthetic subject matter with which it seemed so insistently preoccupied. What was obvious to Goethe and Schiller was the fact that the grand heritage of forms and topics which the culture of ancient Greece had developed in such a peerless manner, had been kept alive in the court-oriented feudal civilization of the European Renaissance; the proud commitment to it, which had for long assured institutional stability and public effectiveness to the arts, seemed now, under the pressure of those subjective, instinctual and 'natural' impulses to which the Revolution had given legitimacy, in danger of dissipation. A German middle class could not be expected to perform its responsible role without commanding the immense resources of that cultural legacy. This, and this above all other models, provided the most compelling examples of disciplined critical thinking. Greek life and thought, Greek myths, Greek poetic theory and practice were to provide the guideposts for a future society; the end in view was not an historical 'recovery' of Greek ways, but their rethinking, enriched by, and not in opposition to the tradition of Christianity. To examine and use the central tenets of that heritage, precisely in the light of radically different modern experiences, religious, economic and scientific, was the aim that led to the 'classical' campaign and carried it far beyond the court of Weimar.

Even if that project was more rigorously proclaimed than practiced in their own poetic work, Goethe's and Schiller's view could not have been applauded at a time when the revolutionary armies posed an immediate threat to the security and stability of the German political system, when Jacobin partisans clamoured for radical changes, when the treasured provincial energies – no longer creative in England and France – were threatened by the prospect of untried forms of government. To all these oppressive considerations the Weimar project appeared cruelly indifferent and eventually its sponsors were forced to recognize its failure. While the resistance of the literary establishment at large seemed the result of wrong-headedness, ill will or jealousy, it did not come from obtuse or misguided writers: many of the best were unwilling to subordinate the wealth of recently mobilized native imagination to a severely dogmatic 'classicist' discipline. For Herder, the unfaltering defender of the creative imagination, the Weimar preceptors had by their peremptory manifestos and their static and regressive postulates, betrayed the historical logic of progress towards a humane community of enlightened citizens.

Yet, Goethe and Schiller, whatever their doubts in a teleology of history, knew well enough how deeply indebted they were to that accretion of moral and intellectual maturity which the past half century had brought about. It was clear to them that no reminder of the greatness of Greece could be persuasive without an awareness of the inestimable contributions of the European Enlightenment. In this conviction they were joined for a brief moment of understanding by a number of younger men and women who were captivated precisely by the modern cast of Goethe's thinking. They were soon to move away towards a more radical, a 'romantic', belief in the emancipation of the imagination, of body and mind, from all conventional restraints. The magic of Fichte's idealism and of Schelling's 'Naturphilosophie' had crystallized for them the revolutionary idea that the self must take the responsibility for giving meaning and direction to a future society. But their first encounter with the living substance of Greek culture, as the Weimar project interpreted it, remained decisive for their later thought: 'The end of classical poetry', Friedrich Schlegel jotted down in his Notebook of 1797, 'is the first cycle of the romantic.'[2]

The 'classical' as well as the 'romantic' aspirations, however divergent their means, were links in that unbroken chain of efforts to bring the resources of the modern mind into creative play, a mind strengthened by the dazzling insights of the past half century in science, in political theory, in philosophical reflection, in poetic eloquence. The 'new man' who had been the object of all Enlightenment thought, of Rousseau and Diderot, of Hume and Kant, provides, as metaphor of the prospective citizen, the surpassing theme of German literature in its most critical and inventive age.

[2] Friedrich Schlegel, *Literary Notebooks 1797–1801*, ed. H. Eichner, London, Athlone Press, 1957, p. 105.

1

The Public Uses of Reason

Berlin

In 1786 a young German writer, J.C.F. Schulz, published, in the manner of the age, an account of his visit to the chief centres of literary life between Hamburg and Vienna; he prefaced it by a statement which sums up a conviction that was at the time bound to be shared by readers everywhere: 'Just as Prussia has during the reign of the present king risen in military power and influence upon the political system not only of Germany and the whole of Europe, but of the rest of the world which is now so thoroughly tied in with Europe, so it has made astonishing advances in the arts and sciences.'[1]

It was patriotic pride which prompted these sentiments; yet they reflect an awareness of changes in the constellation of power and in the political and social circumstances of European life that had, within the short span of a generation, radically altered every aspect of experience.

Schulz's *Litterarische Reise durch Deutschland* appeared just after the death of Frederick the Great. For nearly half a century, no ruler in Europe had exercised greater fascination than this master of political and military strategy. Throughout the turbulent years of war and revolution that were to come, the king was to remain a singularly memorable figure who had marshalled the imagination, the sense of historical mission and the humane aspirations of a society that was moving rapidly from feudal forms of life towards ever more effective institutions, eager to translate abstract principles of individual and collective emancipation into social reality.

Enlightened and ambitious, but wilful, nervous and vindictive,

[1] J.C.F. Schulz, *Litterarische Reise durch Deutschland*, Leipzig, Wucherer, 1786, I, p. 2.

Frederick had at an early age outlined in an essay entitled *Anti-Machiavel, ou essai de critique sur 'le Prince' de Machiavel* (edited by Voltaire and published anonymously 1740) his pragmatic philosophy of firm but benevolent rule and his faith in the possibility of a rational social order. Through an almost continuous succession of shrewd military and political manoeuvres he had by 1763 established Prussia as one of the five great European powers. Deeply distrustful of the English, he was an outspoken supporter of the American Revolution. During the last 20 years of his life he instituted social reforms of lasting importance: he created a modern bureaucracy drawn from the landed nobility as well as from the rising middle class of mercantile operators, and introduced a civil code (*Allgemeines Landrecht*) that offered the most advanced system of juridical guarantees in Europe. His energetic policy of colonizing, of industrialization and commercialization achieved the historic transition in Prussia from an agricultural to a market economy. Shortly before his death in 1786, he had succeeded in drawing more than a dozen German states into a loose federation that terminated the long unchallenged leadership of Austria and caused the political and cultural dualism between Berlin and Vienna that was to remain for nearly a century the most persistent element of tension in Europe.

In Austria itself, reforms at least as radical as those in Prussia were decreed by the impulsive and doctrinaire Joseph II, Maria Theresa's eldest son, more even than Frederick the model of an 'enlightened despot', a type of ruler almost entirely unfamiliar in English constitutional history. In 1781, a far-reaching edict of tolerance had been proclaimed, serfdom and torture abolished, religious freedom promised, the ecclesiastical authority curtailed, a more equitable tax-structure and a system of universal education enforced, and German was made the official language of an increasingly centralized multinational and multiracial society. This was the most striking in a series of moves made throughout the century to modernize the vast Habsburg territory that seemed, by its very diversity of language, history, economic condition and social conventions, altogether incapable of being governed successfully. We shall speak more fully of the Vienna scene in a later chapter.

However remarkable the efforts at political stability in both these central European states, their effect upon the social fabric was bound to be disruptive; and no matter how humane and rational the political theories and convictions on which the reforms in the two countries were based, the concrete realities of life were for some time far from promising. Frederick left a loosely organized realm of conquered but not integrated territories, a chaotic fiscal system, and a class of ill-equipped administrators who were tied by traditional and immediate interest to the patriarchal values of the landed aristocracy. Government positions were sold as a means of obtaining much-needed revenue, specialized ministries were unknown, large tracts of uncultivated land made a dependable agricultural economy exceedingly difficult, and industry lacked an over-all organization of the means of production and distribution so urgently needed for the development not only of a modern technology of warfare but of a competitive national product.

In Prussia, Berlin was the only city of substance. Its emergence as a centre of political and cultural energy is one of the most remarkable phenomena of eighteenth-century history. An insignificant provincial town (with 28,000 inhabitants in 1700), it had become one of the most vigorous among European capitals, largely as the result of an uncompromising political concept and the calculated exercise of 'benevolent despotism' over a population whose willingness to obey was no less firm than their ambition. From 1763, the end of the Seven Years' War, to 1800, within little more than one generation, its population expanded from some 100,000 to 175,000. A drab garrison under Frederick William I, the town grew rapidly under Frederick the Great, his successor; it offered extraordinary social opportunities to an assertive but not necessarily sophisticated court society which consisted largely of the representatives of landed Prussian families that had assumed high military and administrative positions. Affluent businessmen were increasingly involved in Frederick's political designs, men whose share in the mercantile system had given them a social standing nearly as commanding, and certainly as committed to the feudal convictions of the court, as the hereditary aristocracy.

More than one-third of the population was almost totally dependent upon the king: in 1783, of 141,000 inhabitants, the military accounted for 33,000, officials for 14,000, and court attendants for 10,000. Most important for the spirit of the capital was the large contingent of first and second-generation French immigrants – some 20,000 in 1750. Ever since the revocation of the Edict of Nantes in 1685, cultivated and highly skilled French Protestants had settled in large numbers throughout Brandenburg; they made Berlin, together with Geneva, London and Amsterdam, one of the centres of French refugee culture, of wealthy, intellectually alert and cosmopolitan businessmen.

The spacious, somewhat mechanical design of the city and an ambitious display of architectural splendour – Frederick planned a *Forum Fridericianum* – provided the setting, sober and commanding at once, for the life of an enlightened and proud community such as the king envisaged. James Boswell, who spent most of the summer of 1764 in

Berlin, thought it 'the finest city I have ever seen'.[2] Five years late[illegible] Friedrich Nicolai, the spirited and indefatigable author and publishe[illegible] gave in 600 crowded pages a detailed description of Potsdam and Berli[illegible] The finest and liveliest of contemporary German engravers, Danie[illegible] Chodowiecki, had come to Berlin in 1743 and was for nearly 60 years th[illegible] meticulous and affectionate recorder of its life.

Institutions such as the Royal Library, several French theatres and [illegible] distinguished French (later German) opera company, a number of book[illegible] stores and two French newspapers testified to the king's cultural ambi[illegible] tions and his respect for the chief figures and tenets of the Enlightenmen[illegible] The Académie Royale des Sciences et Belles-Lettres, founded in 1700 b[illegible] Frederick's father upon the advice of Leibnitz to articulate the 'new[illegible] science within a framework of divine logic, became under Frederick th[illegible] Great a forum without parallel in Europe for the discussion of all areas o[illegible] contemporary knowledge. Frederick himself chose and appointed th[illegible] relatively small circle of about 20 permanent (and a larger group o[illegible] corresponding) members. Few German scholars were thought worthy o[illegible] membership. Its president from 1763 to 1783 was the French mathemati[illegible] cian d'Alembert; among his colleagues were some of the greatest scien[illegible] tists of the age – Maupertuis, Lagrange, Lambert, Euler – all stron[illegible] in their sympathies for Newton's physics and Locke's philosophica[illegible] empiricism. Through lectures and publications formulated, as the kin[illegible] insisted, in clear and intelligible French or German and through th[illegible] award of prizes, the Academy reached a large and receptive audience[illegible] Herder, we may recall, submitted essays on four occasions and won thre[illegible] prizes, the most controversial for his aphoristic and dithyrambic reflec[illegible] tions in *Abhandlung über den Ursprung der Sprache* (1772). Voltair[illegible] was the king's – difficult – guest and chamberlain from 1750 to 175[illegible] and in Berlin completed his *Siècle de Louis XIV*.

Although Berlin was by no means the only important city in German[illegible] – Leipzig and Hamburg were in some respects more lively and self[illegible] confident – it was the conspicuous instrument of Frederick's politica[illegible] and cultural ambitions, French-oriented and therefore especially open t[illegible] the ideas of the sensualist and empirical philosophers. It was, above all[illegible] the one major centre in Germany where, often constrained by roya[illegible] whims, a homogeneous intelligentsia was permitted to test its enlightene[illegible] rationalist convictions in a growing literary establishment that soon afte[illegible] the mid-century developed its unmistakable style and manner o[illegible] discourse.

The role of the Protestant Church, energetically supported b[illegible] Frederick, must be counted as most important: its pronouncements wer[illegible]

[2] *James Boswell On the Grand Tour. Germany and Switzerland 1764*, ed. F.A. Pottle[illegible] New York, McGraw Hill, 1953, p. 33.

critical of any loosening of Christian discipline by 'free spirits' or the emotional faith of pietism, and insistent upon a sober scrutiny of the Biblical dogma by historical and philological evidence. 'Neologists' such as the court-appointed preachers, J.J. Spalding and A.F.W. Sack, were committed to accepting the Bible, intelligently read, as providing 'natural' proof of revelation. Spalding's *Gedanken über die Bestimmung des Menschen* (1748; twelve editions within the next ten years) was directed against the materialism and atheism of J.O. Lamettrie's *L'Homme machine* (1748). Lamettrie lived in Berlin from 1748 till his death three years later, as Frederick's 'physician ordinary' and 'reader' as well as a member of the Academy. The king's *Éloge* was remarkably tolerant towards a philosopher whose mechanistic and hedonistic theories had been the target of furious defamation. Frederick himself held firmly to the deistic concept of a divine architect whose designs were altogether generous and reasonable.

It was within these court-oriented scientific and religious institutions that an emerging middle class, Protestant by tradition, yet open to the various emancipatory challenges of English and French thought, developed its cautiously self-confident convictions and its social effectiveness. Under the impact of Locke and Hume, the optimistic Leibnitzian faith in the metaphysical order of the best of all possible worlds was here openly questioned. A growing group of writers and readers, reasonably (though by no means completely) independent of censorship, joined in Berlin far more vigorously than elsewhere in Germany, the great intellectual debates of the age.

Indeed, Berlin and its climate of rational debate soon became synonymous with a militantly asserted resistance to all forms of orthodoxy, religious and political, within the discrete limits of an autocratically governed society. The king's official support of science and education was motivated by purely political considerations, pragmatic in their aim of building an efficient and loyal machinery of state. The pervasive spirit of benevolent despotism could not easily tolerate public criticism of particular social defects. Lessing's exasperated reflections on the merely abstract provisions of freedom of speech are familiar enough:

> Don't talk to me about Berlin freedom of thought and expression: it is little more than the freedom to bring to market as many foolish notions against religion as you like. But let anyone try to speak freely about other matters, let him try to tell the truth to the noble rabble at court, let a man in Berlin get up who wished to raise his voice for the rights of the subjects and against exploitation and despotism, and you will soon find out which country is to this day the most slavish in Europe.[3]

[3] G.E. Lessing, *Gesammelte Werke*, ed. W. Stammler, Munich, Hanser, 1959, II, p. 1105.

Yet, the intellectual life of the capital was throughout Europe felt t
be more liberal than that of any other major city in Germany, even tha
of Vienna, where the imperial reforms, if only for a short time, ha
expressly granted freedom of speech and publication. This climate
sustained by a sense of the public uses of reason, an awareness of th
responsibility of the man of letters and of literature as an institution wa
one of the most widely admired assets of the Berlin community, givin
encouragement to the scattered and soon intense stirring of Germa
literature in the second half of the eighteenth century.

The articulation of the Berlin frame of mind was in large measure th
work of Friedrich Nicolai, a bookseller, publisher and writer of astonish
ing tenacity, whose lively mind and whose resolute determination t
create a native literary life of cosmopolitan scope, of bourgeois convic
tions and empirical rationalism proved to be of inestimable consequenc
for the social, religious and philosophical discourse of the age.

Nicolai had made a name for himself with a diagnosis of the deplorabl
state of contemporary German writing (*Briefe über den itzigen Zustan der schönen Wissenschaften in Deutschland*, 1755) in which he unequi
vocally defended a didactic view of literature close to that of the Leipzi
critic J.C. Gottsched. His most far-reaching achievement was the editin
and publishing of three resolutely managed and broadly informativ
journals. *Bibliothek der schönen Wissenschaften und der freyen Künst*
(1757–65) was the first German periodical that addressed itself to a
audience of diverse cultural interests who were informed about curren
European letters through reviews by distinguished contributors such a
J.J. Winckelmann, C.F. von Blanckenburg, M.A.v.Thümmel, C. Garve
the musicologist F.W. Marpurg or the Austrian J. Sonnenfels. Togethe
with Moses Mendelssohn and Lessing, Nicolai published *Briefe di neueste Litteratur betreffend* which appeared weekly between 1759 an
1765, ostensibly addressed to a wounded Prussian officer who wished
while recuperating, to be brought up to date on the current state o
literature.

Conservative and monarchical in his politics and an unremitting oppo
nent of all forms of irrationality, whether in orthodox Protestant theolog
or in the rising tide of sentimental fiction and poetry, Nicolai created i
his third journal, *Allgemeine Deutsche Bibliothek* (1765–1806; 22
volumes) the most formidable instrument of the Berlin 'rationalists'
With the help of an army of more than 400 contributors the *AD*
reported on all aspects of contemporary intellectual life, foreign as well a
German. For the period, the journal had an astonishingly wide circu
lation: there were as many as 184 subscribers in Hamburg, 111 i
Frankfurt, 64 in Leipzig, 60 in Nuremberg, 70 in Switzerland and 38 i
Austria. Not only his violent attacks on the young Sturm und Dran

writers (his pamphlet *Freuden des jungen Werthers*, 1775, was one of the first caustic comments upon what seemed to Nicolai the self-indulgent sentimentality of Goethe's novel), but the sustained ridicule and scorn with which he condemned every indication of metaphysical idealism, religious 'enthusiasm' or 'superstition' and, later, the speculative philosophers, Kant and Fichte, earned him the dislike of nearly all major figures of the classical and romantic generation, of Herder and Hamann, of Goethe and Schiller, of Schleiermacher and Friedrich Schlegel. Their chorus of contempt coloured in large measure the later estimation of this stubbornly rational, often cantankerous, but nevertheless remarkably intelligent journalist, undoubtedly the most single-minded defender of enlightened thought. In 'Zur Geschichte der Religion und Philosophie in Deutschland' (1835), Heinrich Heine rightly speaks with admiration of Nicolai as an early fighter in the cause of German liberalism.[4]

If Nicolai's extensive and nearly always polemical oeuvre is insistently preoccupied with religious and theological matters, this indicates not so much a parochial topic as rather the central issue on which the German eighteenth century focused its passionate and critical attention. Religion is the dominant theme of nearly all significant writers from the 1740s – Klopstock and the Swiss critics – until well into the nineteenth century; it is the concern by which, in one form or another, the work of historians and poets, of philosophers and natural scientists, in aesthetic as well as social theory sought to justify itself. Less profound than his fellow citizens Lessing or Mendelssohn, Nicolai can yet take his place in their company as a formidable defender of a 'natural', rational, at times deistic faith, equally opposed to the obsolescent dogmatic puritanism of the Protestants and the anti-institutional cult of the self in German pietism. One of his novels, *Das Leben und die Meinungen des Herrn Magister Sebaldus Nothanker* (1773–76) gives a pointed account of the precarious existence of a country parson who finds his pursuit of moral truth disastrously impeded by a succession of misfortunes and who manages by virtue of his incorruptible sense of decency not only to survive but, despite endless vicissitudes, to complete his critical commentary on the *Apocalypse*. Although not a work of great narrative subtlety, *Nothanker* is one of the early German attempts at social and satirical fiction in the manner of Fielding or Sterne. It was enormously successful, sold 12,000 copies within a few years, and remains one of the least ponderous, most concretely observed and entertaining accounts of German life in mid-century. It is clearly the work of a singularly shrewd and learned mind, attached to the values of his Prussian world, who is a decade later in his informative *Beschreibung einer Reise durch Deutschland und die*

[4] Heinrich Heine, *Sämtliche Werke*, ed. O. Walzel, Leipzig, Insel, 1914, VII, p. 281.

Schweiz, im Jahre 1781 (1783–96), a sceptical reporter of life in the other, the southern, Catholic, Austrian parts of the German-speaking community.

Lessing

Gotthold Ephraim Lessing, not yet 20, had come to Berlin in 1748 from Leipzig where he had studied theology and philology and heard lectures on medicine and the sciences. Having written (and published) half a dozen comedies in the manner of the French classicist theatre (*Der junge Gelehrte*, 1747; *Die alte Jungfer*, 1748; *Die Juden*, 1749; *Der Freigeist* 1749), he was resolved to maintain himself in Berlin, the acknowledged centre of rationalist thought and a place where he might count on a greater freedom of expression than in the conservative Saxon city. From 1752 to 1761 he was a member of the *Montagsclub*, one of the several circles devoted to the discussion of current cultural or literary topics, and there met some of the most influential citizens, writers such as J.G. Sulzer K.W. Ramler, J.J. Engel and J.F. Reichardt, or the celebrated court flutist, J.J. Quantz, the engraver and illustrator J.W. Meil, and the publisher C.F. Voss. As a reviewer for the *Berlinische Privilegirte Zeitung* and later for *Kritische Nachrichten aus dem Reiche der Gelehrsamkeit* Lessing soon established a reputation as a severe critic. Having met Voltaire, the eminent visitor to the court at Potsdam, he translated his shorter historical essays (1751), read Rousseau and Diderot – both sceptical of the social and literary assumptions of the feudal tradition – and became increasingly firm in his opposition to widely held literary notions such as 'imitation', 'genre' or 'genius'. In a style of extraordinary lucidity, of conversational ease and wit, he subjected current literary, philological and theological publications to the sort of scrutiny that clarifies concepts and defines intellectual positions. In these review essays and in his dramatic criticism, he sought to articulate the effect of ideas upon social action, the efficacy of literature and the functioning of contemporary letters in Germany and abroad, towards the strengthening of rational and humane ideals in the middle class.

The most impressive figure among the Berlin intellectuals was Moses Mendelssohn, an uncompromising, enlightened mind, one of the ablest, if critical, followers of Christian Wolff, Leibnitz, Locke and Shaftesbury, an advocate of the relevancy of Jewish thought in the emancipation of the middle class and, above all, a superbly persuasive writer on philosophical and psychological subjects. In 1763 he won, in competition with the young Kant, the Berlin Academy's prize for his *Abhandlung über die Evidenz in den metaphysischen Wissenschaften* (1764). A translation of Rousseau's (second) *Discours sur l'origine et les fondements de l'inégalité parmi les hommes* – profoundly distasteful to Voltaire – which he published in 1765 together with a letter addressed to Lessing, contributed much to the subsequent German fascination with the 'primitive', the 'youthful' and pre-civilized resources of culture; Wieland and Kant, Herder and Hölderlin, each in his manner, were to deal with this immensely influential text. Mendelssohn's *Briefe über die Empfindungen* (1755, amplified 1771) was published at Lessing's instigation, one of the first products of their association. It argues, elegantly, that the aesthetic experience, although located in the 'dark' area between rational and sensual perception, offers in 'Empfindung' a specific mode of knowledge. This concept, and the notion of 'disinterested pleasure', elaborated in Mendelssohn's *Morgenstunden, oder Vorlesungen über das Daseyn Gottes* (1785), became important ingredients of Kant's aesthetic theory in his *Kritik der Urteilskraft* (1790). In an impressive body of philosophical discourse, in letters, essays, reviews and dialogues that were to become models for the German philosophical prose of the classical period, Mendelssohn, a staunch defender of a rational, 'natural' theology, addressed himself to a cultivated audience of intelligent readers.

Unlike many emancipated Jews who found themselves captivated by the growing diversity of German culture, Mendelssohn, with much respect for the German philosophical and literary life, maintained an abiding faith in the Jewish tradition; he was a metaphysician by temperament whose intellectual discipline was directed at explicating a providentially ordered universe which man was able to understand in its awesome logic by an act of free will, the exercise of reason and the use of scientific enquiry. His *Jerusalem, oder Über religiöse Macht und Judentum* (1783) is an historical summary of religious and social views that were to be of great consequence for the later thought of German Jewry.

To the Jews, he argues, was revealed not so much a religion as a Law; they were given the charge to act and not merely to carry the faith. The Law offers a means of access superior to the prophetic books of other creeds, to a rational, theistic order. Jewish faith and rational enquiry are, for Mendelssohn, wholly compatible. Like Lessing and Frederick the Great, he firmly believed in the possibility of a harmonious coexistence of different philosophical convictions and worked consistently for the effective and not merely nominal integration of the Jews in the Christian community ('Über die bürgerliche Verbesserung der Juden', 1781). Mendelssohn's rationalism was challenged by Herder and Hamann, and by J.C. Lavater, whose ecstatic effusions he in turn detested. In 1785 F.H. Jacobi published *Über die Lehre des Spinoza*, a reply to Mendelssohn's *Morgenstunden* that initiated an acrimonious 'Pantheism controversy' by suggesting that even Lessing had in the end accepted certain tenets of Spinoza, who was regarded throughout most of the eighteenth century, especially by Mendelssohn, as the epitome of atheistic materialism.

Goethe's poem 'Prometheus' was here, without the poet's authorization, published for the first time.

Lessing and Mendelssohn were close friends. The first result of their cooperation was an essay, occasioned by but not submitted to the Berlin Academy; it refutes, by examination of Pope's *Essay on Man*, Leibnitz's optimistic doctrine of the best of all conceivable worlds, and, in its published form, *Pope ein Metaphysiker* (1755), asserts the autonomy of poetry against the assumption that it should be the didactic projection of a philosophical system. In a series of letters, Mendelssohn, Lessing and Nicolai engaged (1756–57) in a lively controversy occasioned by Nicolai's 'Abhandlung vom Trauerspiele' (1757). Differing with Mendelssohn and his insistence on the moral efficacy of the dramatic rendering – a view familiar from Baroque and French classicist dramaturgy – of a stoic hero who achieves the admiration of the audience and produces moral elevation by a steadfast display of his perfect integrity, Lessing argued in favour of arousing compassion in a bourgeois audience and heightening in every possible way the capacity for human sympathy. 'The most compassionate is the best human being'[5] – this view based on Lessing's interpretation of Aristotle was later reiterated in modified form in his *Hamburgische Dramaturgie* (1767–69). It was compatible, certainly, with the concept of a 'bourgeois tragedy' which he had realized in his first major play, *Miss Sara Sampson* (1755), and is indicative of his dislike for the formal abstraction of French classicism and of his sympathetic reading of Diderot.

In *Miss Sara Sampson* Lessing does not explicitly question middle-class values; he replaces, rather, the traditional grounding of a tragic action in heroic and courtly ideals by its justification in 'sentimental' terms, through the testing of the 'sensibility' of the middle class. 'Sensibility' was the personal quality that determined the meaning of virtue and moral judgement; yet, 'virtue', Lessing would argue, is a broadly 'human' value and not (like heroism or honour) a concept associated with a specific class. The 'bourgeois' and non-heroic disposition of sensibility was, thus, a means of furthering that goal of achieving a general level of humaneness which was so central to Lessing's ideal of a future culture.

To create 'sensibility' must be the purpose of a 'bourgeois' tragedy, and the means of generating it is the 'compassion' which a tragic action should produce in an audience. Lessing was aware of Aristotle's assertion that tragedy instills fear and terror; yet these seemed to him ultimately subsumed in an attitude of compassion. And it is compassion which in *Miss Sara Sampson* (and even more so in Lessing's later plays) is aroused in the

[5] G.E. Lessing, *Werke*, ed. H. Göpfert, Munich, Hanser, 1973, IV, p. 163. (Henceforth: Lessing *Werke*).

spectator by the actions of 'mixed' characters, neither perfectly good nor evil.

Mellefont has discarded his mistress Marwood and seduced Sara Sampson. In a 'miserable' English inn, the two are confronted by Sara's father and the jealous Marwood, who fails to recapture Mellefont. She poisons Sara, Mellefont kills himself. The play with its simple plot and its somewhat abstract design would have little lasting interest if it were not an attempt to introduce something of the atmosphere and texture of English fiction (in the manner of Richardson) and of the 'sentimental comedy' which, since Steele's *Tender Husband* (1705), had for half a century been popular in England. Lessing's immediate source was Thomas Shadwell's *The Squire of Alsace* (1688), less, probably, Lillo's domestic tragedy *The London Merchant* (1731). All these dealt (in prose) with protagonists from the common ranks, joined in disaster. Sara, the central figure of Lessing's play, is 'pathetic' without any sharply defined moral features; all characters are given scope – to the point of tediousness – to elaborate on their motives, their conflicts, their honorable intentions. Sara recognizes her moral weakness and (like Clarissa) hopes for divine wisdom to lift the fallible soul beyond the dangers of this iniquitous world. Mellefont accepts his guilt, for which he can atone only by his death. This series of more or less accidental events produces no 'tragic' reaction: the play was an experiment pointing forward to Lessing's later reflections, more detailed and critical, on the structure and purpose of dramatic writing.

Miss Sara Sampson was, in any case, Lessing's first major contribution to the German theatre as he envisioned it; it remained for the next 20 years the model of a 'touching' domestic drama. There had been little in his earlier comedies that modified the traditional interplay of figures taken from the Italian and French theatre, nor did his plots offer more than the mechanical clash of moral abstractions. Yet, even in these standard characters we detect something of Lessing's skill in pitting representatives of different points of view against one another and, for the benefit of a German audience as yet amorphous and undiscerning, of using casual, colloquial speech to convey problematical alternatives.

This firm, even passionate, resolution to fashion the German stage into a persuasive instrument of reasoned discourse remains the characteristic impulse of Lessing's work. In the theatre, however undisciplined and irrelevant its present state, he recognized the essential vehicle of his hopes for contemporary German literature as an institution appropriate to the experiences of the middle class. Briefly in 1749–50 he had edited *Beiträge zur Historie und Aufnahme des Theaters*, a short-lived effort – the first in Germany – to strengthen the effectiveness of the theatre by encouraging a discussion of its history. Dramatic theory and questions

of theatrical practice continued to preoccupy him; foreign master
whether of theory or practice, Seneca, Plautus, Dryden, Molière, Bayl
Diderot and soon Shakespeare, served to clarify his critical judgemen
Pierre Bayle's *Dictionnaire historique et critique* (1697; German transla
tion 1741–44) in particular, the canonical source of Enlightenmer
thought, remained decisive for his intellectual development: Bayle
insistence upon a careful weighing of historical sources, his defence c
tolerance and his rejection of all forms of dogmatism became the funda
mental tenets of Lessing's faith.

The products of Lessing's almost seven years in Berlin – poems
letters, philological essays, fables and plays – were collected in six sma
volumes of his *Schriften* (1753–55); they show a mind independent c
any current school or clique, ready to acknowledge indications of nativ
genius (as it seemed to him grandly evident in the first cantos c
Klopstock's *Messias*). He was anxious to draw from the European tradi
tion, French and English as well as the classics, knowledge indispensabl
for a modern bourgeois humanism, rational but without that dogmati
single-mindedness which he felt at times even in his closest Berlin friend
and collaborators, in Mendelssohn or in the poet K.W. Ramler – an
militantly and stubbornly so in Nicolai. Towards Ramler he had stron
admiration: for more than 30 years the teacher of logic at the Militar
Academy, Ramler was equally interested in medicine, theology, philos
ophy and philology; his *Lieder der Deutschen* (1766) and, especially, hi
Oden (1767) were models of poetic skill and taste, his translation i
1756–58 of Batteux' *Cours de belles lettres* (1747–50) gave currency i
Germany to the poetic theory of 'imitating' the 'natural beauty' o
objects. From 1790–96 he was the director of the Berlin Nationa
Theatre.

For Nicolai Lessing wrote more than 50 weekly contributions to *Brief*
die neueste Litteratur betreffend, in an easy style, free of pedantry
aphoristic rather than suggesting any system of critical principles. Her
he passed judgement, at times in defence of his own works, on most o
the popular authors of the time, on Gottsched's purism, on Wieland's, a
he thought, precious sentimentality, on the trivial moralizing of th
popular essayists, on the effusiveness of Klopstock's figures, and the vas
number of quickly produced and often irresponsible translations. Th
most remarkable of these 'Letters' is the seventeenth, in which Lessing
contrasts the dramatic concepts of Sophocles and Shakespeare with thos
of Corneille, Racine and Voltaire. What concerned him here was not s
much the difference between 'French' and 'English' taste, a commo
topic of criticism, as the distinction between courtly or feudal, an
popular theatre: the latter, he insists, cannot confine itself to th
'delicate, the tender, the amorous' but must encompass 'the great, th

terrible and the melancholy'.[6] It is by design that Lessing adds a reference to the old German Faust-play which seemed to him to contain 'scenes that only a Shakespearean genius could have imagined'.[7] In offering a brief excerpt from his own projected but never completed Faust-drama, he concludes: 'What do you say to this scene? You want a German play that has only scenes like this? So do I.'[8]

This enthusiastic apostrophe of Shakespeare, whatever its effect upon his contemporaries, was more a metaphorical expression of his determination to create an affective and 'moving' dramatic literature than a well-considered programmatic reference to a specific model. The 'bourgeois' drama which he endorsed in theory and practice was, at any rate, exemplified less by Shakespeare (a far from middle-class poet) than by English 'domestic' or 'sentimental' tragedies in which the 'private' concerns of the middle class engaged the interest and sympathy of the audience. It is well to remember that public and private life were throughout the eighteenth century, in Germany far more than elsewhere in Europe, spheres of distinctly different social and moral assumptions. The one was the world of the court with its nearly absolute range of privilege and power, the other the non-aristocratic world that lived in 'private' detachment from political concerns but by a moral code assumed to be more severe in its standards of behaviour and judgement that that of the court society. The private seemed valid only in so far as it had public sanction.

There were other significant indications of Lessing's efforts at the time to find antecedents and support for his own critical work in earlier German literature: he had taken an interest in the specimens of Middle High German poetry which the Swiss J.J. Bodmer and J.J. Breitinger had made available in 1753, and he now collaborated with his friend Ramler in a selection of the poetry of Friedrich von Logau (1604–55) which mirrors the agonies of war a century earlier not unlike those of his own time. His introduction was intended to serve as a contribution to the history of German literature which he knew needed to be written; the glossary of unfamiliar Baroque terms which he appended was the first of his several moves towards the project of a German dictionary. No less directed at the formation of a native literary tradition was the essay (1759) on the characteristic features of the fable, still close to the moral presuppositions which the earlier eighteenth century had brought to the discussion of this highly esteemed genre (later attacked as unconvincing by Herder, Jacob Grimm and others) and given special appeal by a

[6] Lessing, *Werke*, V. p. 71.
[7] Ibid., V, p. 72–3.
[8] Ibid., V, p. 73.

number of epigrammatic fables of his own (in prose) that point, far from naively, to some of the social discrepancies and absurdities of the age.

To the form of the epigram he returned frequently. Some two hundred such brief, polished verses are splendid examples of that 'witty' genre which, with its caesura that creates in the reader's mind curiosity and expectation, corresponded to Lessing's own intention of revealing wherever possible, the dramatic tension inherent in an offered idea. In 'Zerstreute Anmerkungen über das Epigramm' he gives (in 1771) an important survey of this type of poetry.

All these were preliminary exercises for the major critical writings which Lessing was to produce in the years to come, *Laokoon: oder Über die Grenzen der Malerei und Poesie* (1766) and *Hamburgische Dramaturgie* (1767–69). Before he left Berlin to serve for nearly five years in Breslau as secretary to the Prussian General Tauentzin, he translated and published (1760) the dramatic and dramaturgical works of Diderot, the liveliest and most congenial of contemporary French writers, who seemed to him altogether the best theoretician since Aristotle.

The years in the Silesian city brought Lessing in close touch with political realities without, however, changing his preference for the detached life of a man of letters beyond involvement in patriotic partisanship: he was, after all, a Saxon in the service of a Prussian general. When he returned to Berlin in 1765 peace had two years earlier concluded the Seven Years' War – Prussia had retained Silesia and assumed its place as a European power.

For Lessing aspects of the political tensions which the fraternal war had created gradually converged in the plan of a play on which he was to work for four years: *Minna von Barnhelm* was finished in 1767 and soon performed on several German stages. It was the first German comedy that dealt with contemporary figures and issues, the first to give to the English and French prototypes (George Farquhar and the comédie larmoyante) a specifically German content. The war has separated a young Saxon lady Minna, from her Prussian fiancé, Major von Tellheim; they meet by coincidence at a Berlin inn. Their union is threatened by a suit brought against Tellheim for accepting a bribe from the Saxon enemy; he had been dismissed by his King, and though innocent, now feels dishonoured and therefore unable to accept Minna's love. His stubbornly maintained sense of honour – this is the point of the comedy – is shown through Minna's admirably and wonderfully human sense of reality, to be a whim, excessive, abstract and blind. Her warmth of feeling and love leads the Prussian officer to a more conciliatory attitude. Moreover, his name is cleared, the King restores his rank, the two can now marry.

The play has immense charm and is, quite properly, a model of a completely satisfactory comedy, a comedy enriched by serious matter and carried by perfectly achieved theatrical figures. Prussian gravity and Saxon urbanity, a stern code of honour and the ready capacity of the heart, class consciousness and mobility, the memory of war and the prospects of peace – all these are the impulses of a dramatic action that produces in the audience generous sensibility and insight. As always, Lessing supports the protagonists by subordinate figures of superb plausibility: the greedy inn-keeper, the Prussian sergeant-major Werner, Tellheim's rough and obedient servant and an energetic lover, and Minna's delicious Saxon maid, Francisca, all contribute to the eventual balancing of the scales.

Minna von Barnhelm is far from being a political statement in any specific sense. It was certainly not, as some have thought, an attack on Frederick the Great and his Prussian regime. Nor is Lessing here or elsewhere inclined to project autobiographical experiences into his work: unlike many of his younger contemporaries, he would not employ his writings as vehicles of self-definition. To put living characters on the stage was always his chief concern. Class differences are not blurred, but they are reconciled, and political ties are made relative. Lessing used the theatre to clarify issues, to urge clear-headedness, to explore the sources of prejudice, to advocate the efficacy of reason.

After his return to Berlin, Lessing hoped to obtain the position of director of the Royal Library, but was repeatedly rejected by Frederick the Great. (The position was, incidentally, offered to Winckelmann, who refused it: the king had decided that, for a German, half the sum Winckelmann proposed as salary should be quite sufficient.) With all his energy he now turned to a large-scale examination – in *Laokoon: oder Über die Grenzen der Malerei und Poesie* – of the differences in procedure between the verbal and the pictorial arts, an issue frequently argued in eighteenth-century aesthetics. He does not fundamentally challenge the validity of Winckelmann's interpretation of the Laocoon statue (as we now know, wrongly dated and wrongly restored) as a projection of the disciplined and Stoic ideal of Greek 'noble simplicity and quiet greatness'; he was mistaken, however, like Winckelmann himself, in regarding the altogether melodramatic and convulsive Laocoon group as an example of high classical composure.

He insisted on the essentially more expressive purpose and character of poetry. Although he enquired ostensibly into the aesthetic difference between a static, space-determined pictorial method and the dynamic, time-related technique of poetry – specifically the Laocoon passage in Virgil's *Aeneid* – he was in fact pleading less for a revision of the *ut-pictura-poesis* theorem than for the stirring kind of effect which only poetry could achieve and which he himself had attempted to produce in *Miss Sara Sampson*.

Not the offering of truth beautified but a representation of truth moving the spectator in its totality and coherence, and therefore 'beautiful', is the task of the sculptor or painter. Sculpture, Lessing was inclined to think in keeping with classicist aesthetics, should affect as a demonstration of order and discipline. Its highest achievements depend, in any case, upon an awareness not so much of principles as of the great models. He recognized the importance and even novelty of J.-B. Dubos's *Réflexions critiques sur la poésie et la peinture* (1719; German 1760–61) which urges the involvement of the viewer and reader in the creative act. Since it is the primary purpose of poetry and art, Dubos maintains, to move us, poems and paintings are successful only to the degree to which they stir and affect us. 'L'art de la poésie et l'art de peinture ne sont jamais plus applaudits que lorsqu'ils ont réussi à nous affliger.'[9] Lessing had little respect for the intellectual equipment of the modern 'artist', of painters or sculptors: artists, he is reported to have said in 1777, 'are the biggest idiots and the most ignorant in everything that has to do with the theory and history of the arts.'[10] Among many of them he had not found a single one who had read the *Aeneid*, much less Homer.

The poet, on the other hand, far from 'painting', should 'evoke'. Only through poetry can the imagination be galvanized and the sensibility led to a confrontation with the most moving issues of experience. Lessing voices a critical topos common to the age: Goethe was later to say, 'No genuine work of art [i.e. painting and sculpture] should attempt to affect the imagination; for that is the task of poetry.'[11] What is here defined is an artistic principle, a mode of rhetorical or poetical communication that is diametrically opposed to the idea of beauty instrumental in the rendering of aristocratic or 'feudal' ideals, but appropriate, rather, to the bourgeois, the humane 'sensibility' which Lessing intended to articulate and mobilize.

It was this faith in the small voice of his critical intelligence that persuaded him in 1767 to accept a position as literary adviser to the newly-established theatre in Hamburg, and for two years to publish his reviews of current offerings as well as critical reflections on the craft of the actor and the dramatist, the available forms of drama and its historical varieties. These pieces, *Hamburgische Dramaturgie*, first published serially, were not intended to offer a coherent theory. They are in fact models of Lessing's characteristic 'dialectical' procedure: he unfolds his ideas before the reader as they occur in the act of thinking, and in such

[9] Jean-Baptiste Dubos, *Réflexions critiques sur la poésie et la peinture*, Slatkine Reprints, Geneva, 1967, p. 7.

[10] R. Daunicht, *Lessing im Gespräch*, Munich, Fink, 1971, p. 441.

[11] J.W. Goethe, *Gedenkausgabe der Werke, Briefe und Gespräche*, ed. E. Beutler, Zürich, Artemis, 1948–71, XIII, p. 119.

dramatized discourse, he hopes to encourage the reader himself to act as a thinking being.

Here, as elsewhere, Lessing is interested primarily in the effect which a given scene or dramatic design has on a receptive mind; this is to say that, against his great German predecessor Gottsched, he rejects all rigidly normative poetics in favour of criteria which relate a poetic intention to a perception present or to be created in the spectator. Accepting the critical categories still maintained by the eighteenth century, he examines the expectations in the audience that bring about tragedy and comedy, the two cardinal dramatic genres, and enquires into the validity of contemporary modifications of the traditional Aristotelian definitions. He tends to deplore the rigid observance of formal rules by the French classicists, suggests the superior value of an 'inner law' and suspects altogether the adequacy of mere 'wit' for readers who should have learned – from Shaftesbury and the English novelists – to explore and mobilize the energies of the heart in the productions of 'genius'.

Shakespeare remains for Lessing the embodiment of dramatic inspiration and ingenuity, not, of course, the eruptive force which the Sturm und Drang writers recognized in his superhuman figures, but a master of character drawing whose indifference to Aristotelian rules may easily be forgiven. Indeed, Shakespeare, Lessing was inclined to think, achieves in his way that purging of passions which Aristotle demanded of tragedy but, unlike Corneille and Racine, he affects the spectator not by causing admiration for an heroic sort of nobility but by a show of feelings that would produce 'virtuous capacities' in the audience. The creation of this moral sensibility, of friendship, discretion, mutual respect or compassion, is for Lessing the very purpose of the theatre and, most significantly, of tragedy. 'Compassion', that central theme of Lessing's theory of tragedy, means the capacity to be struck and moved by the fortunes and vicissitudes, by the dilemmas, challenges and errors of another's life. To this purpose the rendering of reality must be attuned: drama (indeed, all art) is no mere representation of actuality but a carefully constructed model of possible actions and events; it must offer interpreted reality. The task of a critic such as Lessing himself hoped to be is to interpret the degree to which the dramatic effort has succeeded in making a coherent statement about the feelings and thoughts of characters in a given historical context – not, that is to say, the extent to which fixed norms or rules have been either observed or violated.

It was in two more plays, *Emilia Galotti* and *Nathan der Weise*, that Lessing brought together his critical theory and his skill as a dramatist in the service of an enlightened social philosophy. In *Emilia Galotti* (planned since 1757 and completed in 1772), the sense of 'fear' which the *Hamburgische Dramaturgie* had so firmly linked to 'compassion' as a response to be induced in the spectator, was to be produced by the introduction of figures who were reasonably free agents, yet attached to the moral code of their class. The play is not, like so many Sturm und Drang works that were influenced by Lessing's tragedy, an attack on the abuses of power but an acknowledgement of an overriding instinct for a paternalistic system of order and of a demonstrated will to morality. His figures are here, as in all his other plays, of a certain rank, never the outcasts that were soon to make the Sturm und Drang drama so shocking and discomforting.

The argument of *Emilia Galotti* is based on an incident in Roman history in which the wrong done by a patrician to Virginia, the daughter of a plebian, is publicly condoned, whereupon her father kills her and, inciting soldiers and citizens to rebellion, forces the restoration of a less class-determined system of justice. The political implications of the episode were of no, or relatively little, interest to Lessing: political passion seemed to him in any case unsuitable for the dramatic purpose; it was not likely to produce compassion or fear. He proposed to offer the story of a 'bourgeois' Virginia, deliberately set not in contemporary Germany but in a small autocratic court in Italy. Yet, in keeping with Diderot's notion (which Lessing had argued in detail in letters 84–88 of the *Hamburgische Dramaturgie*) that the theatre should represent not merely set characters but the attitudes and convictions of social classes, the audience was led to recognize its own conditions in the actions on the stage. 'Bourgeois' here suggests, as it did in Lessing's previous plays, a 'human' disposition beyond class prejudices and free of those assumptions of 'heroic' or 'courtly' qualities which the traditional tragedy required.

Lessing's plot is, again, a manoeuvre among fairly stereotyped figures. On the morning of Emilia Galotti's marriage to Count Appiani, the Prince, enamoured of Emilia, is persuaded by a scheming courtier, Marinelli, to postpone the wedding and to appoint Appiani to a foreign embassy. When Appiani refuses, the Prince has the wedding carriage attacked by hired thugs. Appiani is killed and Emilia is brought to the Prince's castle. Confronted later by her father, she reminds him of the ancient paternal duty to prevent dishonour by killing his daughter. This the father performs.

What makes the chess game of this action fascinating is the speed and consequence with which each move compels the next. There is little here of the elaborate sentimental reasoning and rhetoric of *Miss Sara Sampson*. Whatever happens seems to provoke events beyond the control of figures who become implicated against their better judgement and without a full understanding of the logic from which they cannot escape. The conclusion has not been easy to accept: it asserts, in one sense, the patriarchal code of the family against despotism; but it may, in another

:ey, suggest that the temptations which Emilia fears and against which he knows herself to be powerless, are not the private designs of the 'rince, but the temptations, biblically speaking, of the world. As she sees no 'retreat' where she can be immune from worldly seductions, she accepts her death as the only means of maintaining her inviolability. The nding remains, nevertheless, problematical and artificial; and it is the omewhat mechanical perfection of the play that has troubled most :ritics: Friedrich Schlegel thought it a 'grand example of dramatic algebra'.[12]

During the last decade of his life, Lessing appeared to his visitors lispirited, melancholy and increasingly fatalistic. His advocacy of a permanent national theatre in Hamburg and his hopes in the effective-ness of literary and theatrical criticism had been sadly disappointed: What a generous hope to create a national theatre for the Germans when ve Germans are not yet a nation! I am not talking about a political consti-ution but simply about moral character: one might almost say that it is heir character not to want to have one. . . .'[13] At any rate, the actors had proved unmanageable, the financial supporters of the theatre exercised an intolerable control over artistic matters, a competing French troupe had proved far more appealing, the public, whose judgement he so fer-ently wished to strengthen, remained indifferent to any serious dis-ourse. 'The French', he had said in the 81st of his *Briefe die neueste Litteratur betreffend*,

> have at least a stage; the Germans barely sheds. The French stage gives pleasure to a large capital while in the German cities that shed is merely the mob's object of ridicule. The French can at least boast of entertaining their monarch, a splendid court society and the most eminent and worthy men of the realm . . .; the German writer must be satisfied if a few respectable private citizens who have sneaked into the shed are willing to listen to him.[14]

Now, having accepted the position of ducal librarian in the small town of Wolfenbüttel, he felt isolated and, except for a brief journey to the German capitals and, for one year (1775–76), to Vienna and Italy, he ived far from the stimulating centres of cultural life. When in 1771, he joined the Hamburg – and later the Braunschweig – lodge of the Freemasons, it was not so much for personal reasons as because he valued that institution as a potential opportunity for a free exchange of ideas. The goals of this supra-religious organization were the spread of a

[12] *Kritische Friedrich-Schlegel-Ausgabe*, ed. E. Behler, Munich, Schöningh, 1967, (Henceforth: Schlegel *KA*). Vol. II, ed. H. Eichner, p. 116.

[13] Lessing, *Werke*, IV, p. 698.

[14] Ibid., V, p. 260.

humanitarian morality, love of fellow-men, tolerance, truthfulness and respect for the supreme Being. It was founded in London in 1717 and had major lodges in Hamburg (1737) and Berlin (1740); in Germany, it had assumed an increasingly important social and political function in response to the peculiarly rigid structure of the absolutist regimes. The lodges bridged the antagonism, fundamental to the political philosophy of absolutism, between the 'state' and 'society'. Members of the middle class as well as of the aristocracy and the court could here meet under the equalizing protection of a secret ritual and could engage in discussions of the sort that were in England openly conducted in coffee houses and in France in the salons. Freemasonic lodges became fashionable institutions: Montesquieu, Voltaire and Benjamin Franklin belonged, 53 of the 56 signers of the American Declaration of Independence were members; in Germany Frederick the Great, Klopstock, Wieland, Claudius, Bürger, Herder, Goethe and many others were active participants.

In his lodge, Lessing was troubled by a sharp discrepancy between Masonic ideals and the social practice of its members; in the five dialogues of *Ernst und Falk* (1778, 1780) he examines the benefits of freemasonry for the enlightened social order he envisioned. At its best, he argues, the unencumbered exchange of a wide range of points of view, sentiments and beliefs should produce mature, responsible and, therefore, happy citizens. And what else could possibly be the aim of a well-ordered state? Not revolution but a gradual modification in the view of the moral capabilities of the individual would bring about more equitable forms of political life. In *Die Erziehung des Menschengeschlechts* (1780), a collection of 100 brief theses, he insists on a clear distinction between religion and philosophy, between revelation and reason; he formulates in his terms the utopia of freedom and anticipates the fulfilment of this historic vision not through programmes of direct political action but through the cultivation of individual sensibility, intellectual as well as aesthetic. This faith, strengthened by the reading of Rousseau, became the chief conviction of the German idealist tradition, of Goethe, Schiller and Hölderlin.

Lessing's last play, *Nathan der Weise* (1779) reflects his involvement in theological controversies: against the established orthodoxy, and against the progressive 'neologists' he fought the facile harmonizing of God's word and reason. His Christian faith was based upon the assumption that the exercise of reason and an historical interpretation of the modes in which revelation was (and was to be) received would lead to a form of humane morality capable of transcending confessional conflicts.

This 'dramatic poem' is written in blank verse, the Shakespearean unrhymed pentameter first used on the German stage by Wieland some

20 years earlier, a metre that was to become for most writers of the classical period the model of theatrical speech. Its central character is a Jew who has, during a pogrom, lost his wife and seven sons, and who has subsequently adopted Recha, a Christian child. Nathan has accepted his loss, like Job, as a challenge by the God of his race, has taken his misfortunes upon himself and is now sure in the knowledge that God's will and his own are one. When Recha is saved from a fire by a member of the order of the Templars who loves her (but is in fact her brother – both are the children of a lost brother of Sultan Saladin), he acts in the strength of his wisdom and moderates the Christian pride of the Templar, explaining Recha's past. Undisturbed by the Patriarch's threat that he be burned for bringing up a Christian child, Nathan suggests that miracles need not be the result of supernatural powers. He meets the challenge of Sultan Saladin that he should declare which of the three religions, Jewish, Christian or Mohammedan, is the true faith, by telling him the fable of the three rings: instead of the one beneficial ring which has for generations been left to the eldest son, a thoughtful father leaves three, one to each of his three sons, who are told by the judge, to whom they appeal for a ruling, that he cannot determine who now possesses the genuine ring. But the genuine ring, he declares, has 'miraculous' powers – each son is to determine for himself whether he is the owner.

The three religions are for Lessing three means of access to the experience of a supreme Being; each gift is authentic, its value cannot be determined by theological disputation, it must be found in an active and productive life. Truth, to put it in Lessing's terms, is beyond mere doctrine, it can only be striven for in an attitude of generous and unprejudiced love. That the play was at once banned in Austria and not performed in Germany during Lessing's lifetime is an indication of the official resistance to all public expressions of latitudinarian sentiments. Yet, *Nathan* is in substance and form the sum of Lessing's convictions and eminently characteristic of the calm, discursive manner he had achieved in his art.

Lessing remained – for Herder, Goethe and the Romantics – the distinguished representative of an age of transition that was soon to be superseded by political and intellectual changes far beyond his horizon. Herder's necrologue (1781) was the first important assessment of Lessing's work and of his method as a 'philosophical critic': despite the difference in their intellectual premises, he recognized the historical context of Lessing's convictions and was willing to justify his humanistic rather than spiritual theological position though he himself held to a concept of truth as divine reality.[15] If he misunderstood Lessing's notion

[15] J.G. Herder, *Sämtliche Werke*, ed. B. Suphan, Berlin, Weidmann, 1877–1913, XV, p. 33–5, 344. (Henceforth Herder *SW*).

of truth as a critical method, and felt that his 'striving' was merely a search for an undefined absolute, this was an error that continued for long to blur Lessing's intended meaning. Neither the Sturm und Drang writers, who postulated 'titanic' figures and whose violent and often shapeless plays Lessing viewed with the distaste of a seasoned sceptic, nor the Weimar classicists with their elaborately idealized figures, could acquiesce in his relativism; both rejected, at any rate, his conviction that the drama should represent a view of life shared widely in its moral concerns. 'There can be no question', Schiller nevertheless wrote to Goethe on 4 June, 1799, 'that among the Germans of his time, Lessing was the most clear-headed in all matters of art, that he reflected about them precisely and at the same time most liberally, and that he focused sharply on all essentials.'[16]

Lessing was the most perceptive mind of the German Enlightenment, European in his critical interests and at the same time aware of native resources as well as of the need for strengthening the role of letters in an increasingly self-confident society. In many respects a contradictory character, he was by no means without prejudice; he constantly plunged into sharp controversies in which he used his irony mercilessly; he conveyed sometimes conventional, but usually fresh and original, propositions. He judged men, theories and works of art pragmatically and without idealistic absolutes or dogmatic norms. However uneven his scholarship, he put it to lively use; he was a remarkably elegant craftsman in the theatre and a writer of incomparably lucid and effervescent German prose and verse. His intention was always to stimulate the capacity for critical thinking.

In his commitment to the pursuit of truth and to the demonstration of its specific historical and social conditions, as well as its obfuscation in ideological orthodoxy, Lessing recognized the potential of freedom that constitutes modern man. Though in his own time Lessing's standing among German critics was pre-eminent, his effect upon his contemporaries and upon subsequent generations was altogether limited. The cast of his sceptical mind, his resolute determination to examine the claims of subjective truth, to discriminate between the vagaries of faith and the promise of reasoned judgement seem to have found a more appreciative echo among English and French readers than among his own countrymen.

'What is Enlightenment?'

When Lessing left Berlin in 1767 for Hamburg and, three years later,

[16] Goethe *GA*, XX, p. 703.

Wolfenbüttel, the intellectual life of the city had seemed to him increasingly determined by a rigid rationalism in literary as well as theological matters, incompatible with the broad perspectives of his own thinking. He had grown to dislike Voltaire, detested Lamettrie and was unhappy not so much with Frederick's politics as with his sympathies for the French materialist thinkers. Yet, whatever his personal feelings, the years he had spent in Berlin were the beginnings of an ever more widely recognized pre-eminence of that community as the centre of Enlightenment sympathies. It is true that the very term 'Aufklärung' seemed elusive enough. Kant's famous answer to the question 'Was ist Aufklärung?' published in December 1784 in the *Berlinische Monatsschrift*, defined it as 'man's release from self-incurred tutelage'; he urged the courage to use reason without direction from another. While the age could not yet be called enlightened, it was an age of enlightenment: whatever the need, in religion or citizenship, for public obedience, enlightenment must mean freedom of conscience and expression.[17] It was a cautious and not quite unambiguous definition of an issue widely debated in its political and philosophical context. In the spring of the same year, 1784, Moses Mendelssohn had presented a paper to the Mittwochsgesellschaft, 'Über die Frage; Was ist aufklären?'[18] He warned against a narrow and technical use of the term and suggested that enlightenment must ultimately be a comprehensive cultural goal, the very purpose of education, of 'Bildung'. But the concept, he concluded, was as yet only vaguely familiar in Germany: 'The words Aufklärung, Kultur, Bildung are recent arrivals in our language; for the time being they are only bookish terms, and the common man barely understands what they mean.'[19] Yet, in the 25 years before Frederick's death Berlin maintained a leadership in defending the kind of progressive philosophy that seemed to many throughout Germany a basis for common action against division and injustice.

The venerable Moses Mendelssohn continued to dominate the Berlin scene. He was, as a Jew, rejected by the king for membership in the Academy but continued productive: in his discourse entitled *Phaedon oder Über die Unsterblichkeit der Seele* (1767), which earned him the sobriquet of a 'German Plato', he had stated his faith in a metaphysical universal order whose coherence and illuminating power could be perceived through aesthetic as well as rational sensibilities. The subsequent attacks on this work came from critical Kantians and religious irrationalists alike.

[17] Immanuel Kant, *Sämtliche Werke*, ed. F. Gross, Leipzig, Insel, 1920–2, I, p. 161–71.
[18] Moses Mendelssohn, *Gesammelte Schriften*, ed. G.R. Mendelssohn, Leipzig, Brockhaus, 1843–5, III, p. 399–403.
[19] Ibid., III, p. 399.

But there were others who contributed to the prestige of Berlin. J.J. Engel, a resolute and persuasive expositor of current ideas dealt for a conservative reading public in *Der Philosoph für die Welt* (1775–1803) with Bayle and Shaftesbury, Shakespeare, Goethe's *Werther* and the moral uses of poetry in an enlightened life. Lichtenberg was to call his 'Traum des Galilei' one of the finest pieces of reflective prose in the German language. Engel's plays treated domestic and patriotic themes; as director of the Berlin National Theatre from 1787 to 1794, he offered much of the dramatic literature of the day. His productions of Mozart operas were famous. His theoretical writings on poetic genres, on dramatic theory and theatrical practice, 'Über Handlung und Gespräch und Erzählung' (1774), *Anfangsgründe einer Theorie der Dichtungsarten* (1783) and *Ideen zu einer Mimik* (1785–86) anticipated themes that were to be of much interest to Goethe and Schiller.

J.G. Sulzer, the respected pedagogue, moral philosopher and defender of the arts as a means of achieving wisdom, published, in 1773, his papers delivered during the previous 20 years of membership in the Academy; in his *Allgemeine Theorie der schönen Künste* (1771), an encyclopaedic compendium widely used as a reference work, he summarized topics and concepts that had been formulated and developed by his Swiss teacher and compatriot J.J. Bodmer, by Addison, Batteux and Lord Kames. Influenced by Winckelmann, and preparing the ground for Kant and Schiller, Sulzer maintained that the aesthetic perception stirs mind and soul to a more acute capacity for judgement and reasoning. The various forms of art are the result of different psychological dispositions. The source of beauty is in the perceiving subject; the criteria for judging it are derived from taste, a faculty somewhere between feeling and thought.

There was an eminently pragmatic purpose in what even to an observer such as Frederick himself may at times have seemed harmlessly academic exercises: the debates about the origin and functioning of language in its social contexts, Lessing's examination of the public impact of tragedy or of the distinct modes of the pictorial arts as against persuasion by rhetorical or poetical devices or, indeed, Mendelssohn's translation of the *Pentateuch* (1780–83). All these served to shape a language, a stage or a canon of criticism intended to strengthen the self-consciousness of the middle class. Nor were the emancipation of 'natural' modes of thought from traditional philosophical habits, the confrontation, especially lively in Berlin, between the systems of Wolff or Thomasius and the emerging French and English attitudes, of Diderot, Voltaire, Hume and Adam Smith, merely academic matters. They were rather the result of concrete efforts at developing institutions through which the new ideas could affect the aspirations and decisions of a society that had hitherto been either inarticulate, or subservient to a monolithic political order. This historic change can be readily observed in Frederick's insistence on the choice of topics for discussion in the Academy, topics that were relevant to contemporary social issues, and in the increase in the number of German members of that body. German theatres served, increasingly, to educate the middle class, as did the opening and modernizing of half a dozen public libraries. The growing reading public was kept aware, through journals and discussion groups, of the state of European letters and scientific activity.

In this spirit an extraordinarily influential group of 24 carefully chosen learned men, the *Mittwochsgesellschaft*, sometimes known as *Freunde der Aufklärung*, was organized by Johann Erich Biester, the head of the Royal Library, a classical scholar and effective journalist: its purpose was to hear, discuss and record, every Wednesday, two papers on matters that had a bearing on human welfare. Mendelssohn's definition of 'Enlightenment' was presented to this group. No less important for the future structure of Prussian (and German) society was the intelligent if rigorous system of education, of schools in which men of unusual academic distinction – Sulzer, Gedicke, K.P. Moritz – educated a generation of well informed administrators and public figures.

To stress the importance of these multifarious efforts at creating 'emancipatory' institutions is not to forget the oppressive discrepancy in Prussia between the evident public share in liberalizing critical debate and concrete social conditions. We know from recent studies on the relative insignificance of the *philosophes* for the outbreak of the French Revolution that the immediate consequence of a body of philosophical criticism for the actual social life of a community is difficult to assess. The intellectual preoccupations which we have outlined, so important as symptoms of a critical detachment and unrest, had, in fact, little impact on Prussian life at the time. Under Frederick the Great and his successor, the nobility remained secure in all decisive administrative positions: they were paid subsidies to retain their landed property – throughout the century the most important instrument of power – while the peasantry remained subjugated. The standard of living deteriorated disastrously, in part as the result of the continuing wars: grain prices doubled between 1750 and 1800, yet wages rose during that half century by only one-third or one-half. Despite recurring economic crises – those of 1760 and 1780 were especially serious – the palpable evidence of injustice, discrimination and frustration produced, different from France, no effective challenge to privilege or attacks upon arbitrary authority.

Frederick's own philosophical range was narrow and had scarcely been affected by the presence at his court of Voltaire, Malebranche, Condorcet or Maupertuis. He revered Bayle and instructed the teachers in Prussian schools 'to follow Locke in metaphysics, and the method of

Thomasius in all historical subjects'; but his interest in literature was altogether superficial and narrowly focused upon the classicist tradition of French poetry and tragedy. Voltaire had reviewed and edited, with some three hundred verses of his own, the six books of Frederick's *L'Art de la Guerre* (1749, 1752), a didactic exercise in which the king reflected, in the style of Voltaire's *Henriade*, upon the craft of war. The poem is an indication of Frederick's natural inclination to resort to a literary stylization of his pragmatic concerns, of Voltaire's meticulous assessment of his royal student's work and of the level of literary discourse in which the two must have engaged.

Like George III, who thought Shakespeare 'sad stuff', Frederick had little sympathy for that poet;[20] he struck him as merely a purveyor of 'laughable farces worthy at best to be acted before Canadian savages.'[21] The king was in no doubt that German literature had failed to match the superior canon of French culture. He had, of course, reason enough to hold to this faith: in 1784 the Berlin Academy awarded a prize to Antoine de Rivarol's *Discours sur l'universalité de la langue française*, an essay in which, for the last time with equal cogency, the exemplary character of the French literary cosmos was proclaimed. (The royalist Rivarol soon afterwards sought refuge in Berlin.)

If we remember that Frederick read – and spoke – German only poorly, it is not surprising that his knowledge of German letters, past or contemporary, was negligible; his impulsive derogation of native talent in the famous tract *De la littérature allemande; des défauts qu'on peut lui reprocher; quelles en sont les causes; et par quels moyens on peut les corriger*, (published in French and German in 1780 but begun some 30 years earlier) showed no appreciation of the original work produced at the time, of Lessing, whose election to the Berlin Academy he refused, of Wieland, Klopstock, Herder, or Goethe. Goethe's *Goetz von Berlichingen*, published seven years earlier, he deplored as 'an abominable imitation of those wretched English plays; and yet, our public loudly applauds this disgusting drivel'.[22]

Protests against this condescending pamphlet were instantaneous: J.C. Wezel's *Über Sprache, Wissenschaften und Geschmack der Deutschen* (1781) resolutely and sharply disqualified it; the most effective counter-attack upon it came not, of course, from one of the Berlin critics, but from a Westphalian historian and essayist, Justus Möser, who in *Über die deutsche Sprache und Litteratur* (1781) eloquently put the case for a native literature, for Goethe's *Goetz* as a work of rich and colourful

[20] J.C. Long, *George III*, London, Macdonald, 1960, p. 286.

[21] Friedrich der Grosse, *De la littérature allemande*, ed. C. Gutknecht, Hamburg, Buske, 1969, p. 100.

[22] Ibid., p. 100.

nagination, and for the strength and authenticity of the German
anguage as an instrument of increasing appeal in poetry and criticism,
nd in historical and philosophical writing. In a remarkably bold essay,
Iarlekin oder Verteidigung des Grotesk-Komischen, Möser had 20 years
arlier (1761) defended the comic, even burlesque mode as no less legit-
nate and possibly more trenchant than an elevated or lofty manner;
ater he supplied political reflections for the weekly *Osnabrückische*
ntelligenzblätter, popular and appealing pieces, collected in *Patrio-*
'sche Phantasien (1774–78). As personal friend of Frederick, Duke of
'ork, who was until 1787 Bishop of Osnabrück, he was in close sympathy
ith conservative English thought. Möser was of Frederick's own genera-
on, but his voice was that of the rising counter-culture that had over
nore than a decade proclaimed its opposition to rococo, sentimental and
ationalist attitudes.

Although not living in Berlin, Möser was a prolific contributor to the
'erlinische Monatsschrift, a periodical which, even more forcefully than
Iicolai's long-lived *Allgemeine Deutsche Bibliothek* gave, from 1783
1796, expression to the critical spirit of the Berlin intelligentsia. The
ournal was edited by F. Gedicke and J.E. Biester, members of the
cademy, much interested in contemporary thought and writing, clear-
eaded and in touch with men of letters throughout Germany (both,
ncidentally, the proofreaders of Goethe's *Wilhelm Meister* for the
ublisher J.F. Unger). Of the 16 treatises written by Kant between 1784
nd 1797, all except one first appeared in this periodical, among them in
784, two of the cardinal tracts of the late German Enlightenment, his
dee zu einer allgemeinen Geschichte in weltbürgerlicher Absicht' and
ne treatise already mentioned, 'Was ist Aufklärung?' The *Monatsschrift*
eported judiciously on political events in France and America, from
788 to 1791 it regularly offered elaborate statistics on the French
conomy, printed reports by Jefferson and Franklin, published some of
.P. Moritz's letters from London and, while basically conservative,
rovided the best platform in Germany for the discussion of progressive
iews of contemporary issues. The young W. von Humboldt contributed
ree sections of his study of the limits of the power of the state ('Ideen zu
nem Versuch, die Grenzen der Wirksamkeit des Staates zu bestimmen',
792) to the *Monatsschrift*; and it was in this journal that in 1794 and
795 Friedrich Schlegel's early essays on the study of Greek poetry ('Von
en Schulen der griechischen Poesie', 'Vom ästhetischen Werte der
riechischen Komödie', 'Über die Diotima') first enunciated some of the
rinciples of what was soon afterwards to be proclaimed as the new, the
omantic' creed.

Vienna

However stirring the energy of its intellectual life and however insiste the dry, often rasping voices of its defenders of rationalism, Berlin was fa less impressive as a centre of political power and of conspicuous splendou than Vienna, the fascinating capital of an empire of considerable conse quence, even after the defeats of two wars. Maria Theresa and her so Joseph II, both firmly attached to the traditional philosophy of bene volent absolutism, were resolved to modernize the complicated govern mental and social structure of a heterogeneous political conglomera through a series of far-reaching pragmatic reforms. They sought t reduce the effective authority of the Catholic Church – respectful, course, of its dogma, religious practice and devotions – to limit th dominance of the Estates of the Realm, to secularize education, encourage participation in the political process and altogether to giv cautious scope to the humanitarian idealism of the Enlightenment.

Under Joseph II these reforms were accelerated by an impatient rul of excellent intentions but little political instinct: tight control an liberality, nationalism and cosmopolitanism, self-scrutiny and sel satisfaction alternated in hectic sequence.

When censorship was lifted in 1781 and freedom of expression assure a flood of books, pamphlets, plays and libretti, amiably or aggressive critical of political figures and institutions, was released: during the fir 18 months more than 1000 titles were published in Vienna alone, a average of 200 copies were bought of each title. The open policy prevaile until 1795 when, after the trials of Austrian and Hungarian Jacobin severe censorship was reintroduced and rigidly enforced for more than 5 years. Edicts emancipating the long-despised Jews and abolishing ser dom notwithstanding, the policies of the emperor were less concerne with insuring individual freedom than with consolidating the crown an the absolutist order. The pre-eminence of the state, which was the co summation of the divine order in a humane society, the decisive share i power of the landed aristocracy and an aura of affectionate Catholic fait remained for long the preconditions of Austrian life.

'Josephinism', like all forms of enlightened despotism, was politically failure: aristocracy and privilege emerged strengthened. Yet it ha encouraged social debate among the citizens and craftsmen of Vienn and, by its land reform, prepared the way for the elimination feudalism some 50 years later.

A society so idiosyncratic in temperament and values produced co flicts and partisan sentiments that were altogether different from tho prevailing in the Protestant north. The interest of German observe in the Viennese world was lively enough; indeed, the widely admire and envied spirit of reform and the opportunities offered by a court mpressive munificence aroused the attention, at one time or other, of nost German men of letters. Leibnitz and Gottsched had plans, never ealized, for an academy under the protection of the court; Klopstock ioped for support from Joseph for a 'German' literary institution to be ounded in Vienna; Wieland dedicated his novel *Der Goldene Spiegel* 1772) to the emperor and left no doubt of his enthusiasm for the Austrian Enlightenment; Lessing was in 1769 and 1775 received by Maria Theresa and Joseph and hoped, in vain, for an appointment as director of he projected National Theatre. Not many of them realized that the spirit n which the small German courts supported men of letters, reasonably ree to devote themselves to their own work, was profoundly different rom the subservient and still feudal framework within which the court-ppointed artist, writer or librarian functioned in Austria. Aversion not o much to foreigners as to non-Catholic candidates disqualified many of he best German applicants.

This is not to say that interest in contemporary German literature among some of the most influential Austrian authors was not lively. The o-called 'anacreontic' German poets, Hagedorn, Gleim, Hölty, Ramler, vere appreciated by readers still surrounded by rococo taste; Klopstock's *Messias* and his poetry in the manner of the Celtic bards had a pro-nounced effect on Michael Denis, the translator into German of the poems of Ossian (1768–69); J.A. Blumauer's parodistic mock-epic *Virgils Aeneis Travestiert* (1782) could hardly have been written without trong admiration not only for Pope but particularly for Wieland's *Comische Erzählungen* (1765); and J.B. von Alxinger, one of the most ultivated representatives of Josephinian urbanity, is in his poetry and in his general view of the function of literature altogether indebted to Wieland.

The strength and originality of the Austrian imagination was in its heatre, an institution for long shaped either by the tradition of the Jesuit drama or by an exuberant native stage, incomparably entertaining vhether in its provincial or its Viennese suburban practice. Rich in ngenuity, a talent for improvisation and satirical humour, the theatre vas clearly an instrument of considerable importance and effectiveness in he cultural politics of the court as well. It was a vehicle of popular criti-ism, of caustic commentary upon contemporary figures, events and oibles. Nowhere in Europe was the tie between the theatre and musical ife closer than in Vienna. Throughout the far-flung empire, on provin-ial stages and in the sumptuous estates of the nobles, French and Italian pera, ballet and pantomime flourished: in 1772 Charles Burney thought hat 'Vienna is the imperial seat of music as well as power'.[23]

[23] Charles Burney, *An Eighteenth-Century Tour in Central Europe and the Netherlands*, d. P. Scholes, London, Oxford U. P., 1959, II, p. 124.

A resolve to give dignity to the theatre, and to subordinate it to th enlightened political vision of the court and the taste of a cultivated aris tocracy motivated much of the journalistic and political work of Josep Sonnenfels, an ambitious, articulate if personally unattractive, deviou and verbose purveyor of European thought. Well into the nineteent century Sonnenfels was a figure of outstanding influence in Austria cultural and political life. He had in 1761 become president of th *Deutsche Gesellschaft*, the leading cultural organization in Vienna and as professor of political science, had since 1763 in commissioned text books on economics and finance eloquently defended such topics a modern principles of law enforcement. The young Goethe ridiculed (i 1772) Sonnenfels's pamphlet *Über die Liebe des Vaterlandes* as a piece o affectation and specious reasoning; others, Lessing among them respected his public courage, his reform spirit, especially his treatis (1775) on the abolition of torture. To many Sonnenfels seemed the mos eloquent representative of the Austrian Enlightenment: as late as 1801 Beethoven, with profound respect, dedicated his *Sonata Op. 28* to him

Sonnenfels's activities as a man of letters are, in retrospect, mor memorable than his political efforts. In his weekly publication, *De Mann ohne Vorurteil* (1765–68) and, especially, in his *Briefe über di Wienerische Schaubühne* (1767–69) – written almost simultaneousl with Lessing's *Hamburgische Dramaturgie* – Sonnenfels attacked th undisciplined (and politically uncontrollable) popular theatre and th antics of the Italian *Commedia dell'Arte* which had replaced the Jesui drama. He deplored the preponderance of French style as categorically a the irregular dramaturgy of Shakespeare. Like Lessing, he hoped t achieve a theatre of high seriousness by elevating the taste of the audienc rather than the quality of acting. His views on dramatic theory wer simple-minded and antiquated: he held to the rule of the unities of time place and action, insisted that dreams should not simply be described bu shown as stage action, and altogether rejected the artifice of Italian oper as against the touching style of Gluck. He preferred the wooden tragedie of the mediocre dramatist C.H. von Ayrenhoff – a resolute opponent o the English theatre whose *Der Postzug oder die noblen Passionen* (1770 seemed to Frederick the Great a 'true and original comedy' and the onl notable work of contemporary German literature.

Sonnenfels's dedication to the linking of Austrian intellectual life to th German rationalist establishment was not without consequence: in 177 the Emperor designated the court theatre as *The German Nationa Theatre* – today the Burgtheater – a stage, to be different from th antiquated style of the French Court Theatre and to be distinguishe from the popular farcical and improvised theater by its high standards o production and literacy. In part as a means of combatting the Slavoni cultural renaissance and the Hungarian reform claims, it was to promote the German language, German manners, taste and art. Many of its features and some of its managers, playwrights and actors were later drawn from theatres at the German courts which, in turn, looked with envy and respect to the flourishing Vienna stage. Curiously enough, however, the classical German drama of the next 25 years was to be performed not at the National Theatre but its chief competitor, the suburban *Kärntnertor* stage.

It was Sonnenfels's achievement that he encouraged interest in Lessing, Goethe, Schiller and, later, Kleist. Soon these were joined by indigenous writers: the eminent dramatist Franz Grillparzer and the exuberantly gifted playwrights Raimund and Nestroy confirmed his vision of a distinguished Austrian contribution to the European theatre.

While literature and philosophical debate had not been encouraged under Maria Theresa, the discussion of public issues became, during the latter part of Joseph's reign, lively as never before. The edict guaranteeing freedom of the press and the permission to reprint 'foreign' newspapers and books made Vienna one of the envied European centres of serious, sometimes facetious, more often savage polemical disputation. Two of the best journalists, Josef Richter and Johann Pezzl, developed the kind of ironic testing of Viennese strengths and defects that reflected their sympathy for the sharpness of judgement and style of Voltaire's *Candide*. Each produced a series of satirical novels. Richter was the editor of a most entertaining periodical, *Briefe eines Eipeldauers an seinen Herrn Vetter in Kakran* (1785–1813). Pezzl's *Faustin oder das aufgeklärte philosophische Jahrhundert* (1783) offers in the form of a 'Bildungsroman' a severely critical view of the age; it proposes to demonstrate the 'convulsive agitation of dying superstition, of fanaticism, of ecclesiastical fraud and despotism'.[24] In his *Skizze von Wien* (1786–90) he later joins the chorus of exasperated Viennese writers who represent and ridicule the comprehensive but derogatory account of the state of Austrian culture and its literary pretensions in Friedrich Nicolai's *Beschreibung einer Reise durch Deutschland und die Schweiz, im Jahre 1781* (1785–96). Nicolai's ingrained suspicion of every form of clericalism, obscurantism and superstition as well, of course, as his Protestant distaste for a mode of life too casual and genial, produced a thoroughly unsympathetic view of what he considered a spurious and, at best, sentimental sort of Enlightenment. He was pardonably sceptical of Austrian proclamations of superiority over German intellectual life. J.A. Blumauer, since 1781 the editor of the important *Wiener Musenalmanach* (1777–96) and for 12 years the chief censor, had in his

[24] J. Pezzl, *Faustin oder das aufgeklärte philosophische Jahrhundert*, (n.p.), 1783, I, p. iii–iv.

Beobachtung über Österreichs Aufklärung und Literatur (1782) maintained that Vienna was after all

> the centre around which all the smaller and larger German planets revolve. Is it not at this time the centre of attention of the whole of Europe? Does not philosophy have a far wider scope there? Is enlightenment not in full swing, and are not men leading it that many another far brighter country does not have? . . . Have not even foreign writers confessed that if German literature is to advance from its present state it can only do so from Vienna?[25]

While from a Prussian point of view, Nicolai's harsh assessment of the literary life in Vienna – he was indifferent to its musical renown – may have seemed justified, he was blind to the particular character of the Austrian Enlightenment. This developed until well into the nineteenth century within the framework of absolutism sanctioned by a devout religious faith and a disposition to acquiesce in the inevitable rather than oppose it.

End of an Era

The seven volumes of Mirabeau's letters from Berlin in 1786 and 1787 (*De la Monarchie Prussienne sous Frédéric le Grand*, 1788) give the most intelligent account of the city as it presented itself to a perceptive and civilized visitor at the time of Frederick's death in 1786. Mirabeau was not alone in his conviction that the five decades of astonishingly disciplined civil and cultural effort had in Berlin produced a style of life and of intellectual engagement that commanded respect even if it could not be universally applauded. But it was equally apparent that an age had come to its end and that the future was bound to draw the self-assured capital more and more into the restless mood of uncertainty and crisis in which the rest of Germany had lived for some time.

Extraordinary changes were indeed in prospect. Frederick's successor, his nephew Frederick William II was immediately popular but soon lost all sympathy not only by his irresolute foreign policy but by an instability of character and his curious fascination with the irrational, the eccentric and the supernatural. He left the conduct of public affairs to a most sinister figure, his Minister of Culture and Justice, J.C. Wöllner, whose interest in the alchemistic tradition and whose devoted attachment first to Freemasonic and later to Rosicrucian thought spread a militant suspicion of all rationalistic practices and institutions throughout the society of court and city. By his Edict of 1788 (which was not rescinded until 1797) he destroyed much of that tolerant climate in which for more than

[25] J.A. Blumauer, *Sämtliche Werke*, ed. A. Kistenfeger, Munich, Fleischmann, 1927, VIII, p. 83–4.

40 years the enlightened life had flourished: each religious establishment, Catholic, Protestant and Jewish, was now to shun deviation and to curb the prevailing 'moral depravity' and 'boundless liberty'. The Lutheran Church was reaffirmed as an arm of the state, and drastic censorship legislation (that remained in force until 1848) severely crippled the free flow of liberal ideas. Nicolai and Kant were for a time forbidden to publish. Travellers noted a curious interest among the cultivated society in supra-rational phenomena, in magic, sleepwalking, 'prophecy', Mesmerism or the alchemical and spiritual deceptions of the adventurer Cagliostro.

There can be no doubt that Wöllner's (and the king's) occult inclinations prepared the ground for the energies that became articulated in the 'romantic' figures and groups who were soon to emerge in Berlin. The young Ludwig Tieck, before long to be one of the most imaginative Romantic writers, was at the time deeply engaged in the study of Jacob Boehme's mystical philosophy; as though to parody his own experience, he wrote between 1790 and 1800 a series of macabre, bizarre and melodramatic short stories for Nicolai, who was shrewdly aware of the direction of public taste. Clubs, reading societies, salons and, in a measure, the theatre – after 1786 entirely devoted to performances in German, and since 1796 directed by Iffland, the best of the contemporary theatre managers – together reflected an almost hectic interest in the literature produced in Berlin and elsewhere.

One of the singularly original if quixotic talents, inexhaustible in his intellectual curiosity and output, was Karl Philipp Moritz, like half a dozen other authors a teacher in the distinguished Berlin school system. Brought up in the severest pietistic discipline, steeped in the effusive and self-deprecatory tracts of the mystical tradition, groping for an identity that should contain his paradoxical sense at once of nullity and of spiritual exuberance, he sought as educator, actor and preacher, to project the several facets of his personality. His remarkable interest in languages, ancient and modern, had much to do with this agility of mind, a number of practical as well as theoretical linguistic compilations, a handbook on letter-writing, and a series of lectures on style are symptomatic productions. Upbringing and disposition turned his interest again and again towards a meticulous analysis of the emotions: barely 24 years old, he published his first book, *Beiträge zur Philosophie des Lebens* (1781), a year later he attempted an *Experimentalseelenlehre* (1782) and from 1783 to 1793 edited *Gnothi Seauton*, the first German journal devoted to the study of psychological and parapsychological phenomena. He gave perceptive accounts of his travels to England in *Reisen eines Deutschen in England im Jahre 1782* (1783, 1785) and to Italy (where he attached himself to Goethe). These works reveal Moritz's sharp and subtle eye for social attitudes. In a short-lived periodical *Italien und Deutschland* (1789–93), he intended to mediate between the two cultures.

In two sensitive and lively prose narratives, Moritz offers at once autobiographical portraiture and religious, social and personal reflections of remarkable intensity. The first of these, *Anton Reiser*, published anonymously between 1785 and 1794 in five rich volumes, is explicitly subtitled a 'psychological novel'; the other, *Andreas Hartknopf* (1786, 1790) is designated an allegory. *Anton Reiser* is the rendering of a life, 'as true and faithful even in its smallest nuances as can possibly be imagined.'[26] What may seem disjointed incidents, broken threads and patches of darkness, become in the retrospective view of the biographer coherent and orderly. The introverted and often neurotic self-consciousness and the compulsion to self-debasement, hypocrisy and masochism are, in part, the result of Moritz's early education. Throughout the book these experiences are shown to have caused alienation and insecurity. *Andreas Hartknopf*, slight in scope yet full of topical detail, narrates episodes in the life of an intensely mystical itinerant blacksmith and preacher, trapped between orthodox rationality and religious enthusiasm.

Those writings of Moritz that are prompted by his love of the ancient world, his admiration for its manner of life and its aesthetic tenets, offer the most deeply felt documents of an experienced secular classicism free of pedantry. They balance subjective devotion to the rational as well as to the terrifying resources of the Greeks, and an objective command of the exemplary body of ancient history and art. In his *Versuch einer deutschen Prosodie* (1786), dedicated to Frederick the Great, he develops his theory of poetry: the poem, he suggests, does not, like prose, move steadily towards a conclusion but elaborates evolving patterns, reiterated as statements of delight in rhythms and sounds which, like the dance, are their own justification. Poetry is not a form of rhetorical persuasion but a system that conveys emotions and sentiments in metrical order. The elements of this poetic theory are derived from a systematic weighing of the expressive function of parts of speech within a metrical scheme. Moritz is concerned less with the efficacy of particular *classical* metres than with the specific grammatical potential of the *German* language. Goethe later recalled that it was this work of Moritz's which led him to recast *Iphigenie* from prose into iambic verse.[27]

The brief 50 pages of the essay *Über die bildende Nachahmung des Schönen* (1788) are among the most important German contributions to the classical debate: they give to Winckelmann's sensuous humanism a spiritual dimension, and argue for a total absorption of the self in the

[26] K.P. Moritz, *Anton Reiser*, ed. W. Martens, Stuttgart, Reclam, 1972, p. 122.
[27] Goethe *GA*, XI, p. 171.

ully realized and integrated aesthetic object. Here, as in his *Götterlehre* 1791), and his posthumous mythological dictionary, Moritz comes losest to the notion, to be developed by Herder and Goethe, that myth onstitutes the very language of the imagination: it focuses the formative apacity of man, translated into recurring poetic topics and metaphors. hortly before his early death, Moritz suggested the direction of his politcal ideals by translating (1792–94) Thomas Holcroft's *Anna St Ives*, a noderately accomplished English novel of egalitarian sympathies.

Moritz's work mirrors the sense of restlessness and crisis that threatened o break up the front of enlightened purpose which the older Berlin vriters continued to defend. Yet, however anxiously he tested the ncertain tensions between reason and feeling, of piety and protest, his vriting was grounded in a deep respect for the classical tradition and its thical symbolism. It was this double impulse in Moritz (who was in 1789 ppointed professor of classical studies at the Berlin Academy of Art) that nade him an impressive and appealing figure for the many younger men vho came to Berlin in the 1790s. Eager to share in the still fascinating ntellectual life of the city, they gathered in the salons of such brilliant vomen as Henriette Herz, Rahel Varnhagen von Ense or Mendelssohn's laughter Dorothea Veit, and found a stirring of revolutionary enthuiasm in the house of the musician J.F. Reichardt, Hamann's close friend nd a volatile man of affairs, who was at ease alike with noblemen and epublicans.

For all these – August Wilhelm Schlegel and his brother Friedrich, Tieck, Schleiermacher, Wilhelm von Humboldt, Friedrich von Gentz – t was not a time to look back complacently. To the reasoned optimism of heir elders, their judicious resolution of experienced discrepancies and heir capacity to compensate for political impotence by creating an aura of moral and aesthetic beauty, they now reacted with ironic detachment nd the will rather to affirm dissonance and eccentricity. It is not surprisng that those who had participated in the shaping of an enlightened ociety regarded the mood of the present with undisguised apprehension nd the conviction that the new, speculative manner could only erase the nard-won gains of empiricist thinking. Nicolai, still at work, and inflexble in his trust in the moral order of the universe, replied churlishly to Fichte's sarcastic attacks upon him ('Friedrich Nicolai's Leben und onderbare Meinungen', 1801) deploring the abstract uselessness and uperstitious fraudulence of most contemporary philosophy. To his very nd he indulged in melancholy reflections on the wrong-headed and lesolate present ('Gespräch über das jetzige verderbte Zeitalter').[28]

[28] F. Nicolai, *Philosophische Abhandlungen*, Berlin, Nicolai, 1808, I, p. 255–80.

What seemed now to many in Berlin, more than almost anywhere els in Germany, an achievement to be fervently admired was the rich work o the two formidable minds in Weimar, of Goethe and Schiller. Howeve severe and aloof, their recent pronouncements reflected an intense an incomparably challenging preoccupation with the unstable character o the age. For the new generation it was to prove compelling enough t transform the carefully nurtured rationalistic convictions of the Berli Enlightenment into a radically different critical temper, passionatel aware of its specifically modern disposition, a 'romantic' philosophy o life and art that was, within a few years, to captivate Europe.

2

Counterclaims of the Imagination

Sentimental and Sacred Poetry

Nicolai had reason enough to see in the exuberant assertions of native Viennese spirit only one more indication of those irrational impulses that threatened the concerted defences of a life of judicious reason. Together with Lessing, he had only a few years earlier raised his voice in firm condemnation of the products of those young writers who seemed determined to proclaim a sort of counter-culture, intensely preoccupied with attacking not merely the palpable defects of the prevailing social order, but altogether the efficacy of rational and enlightened judgement.

The celebration of these virtues, of the happy trust in an order that could well be called 'natural' because it appeared to reveal the graceful logic of a generously conceived universe, was the objective that nourished, especially in southern Germany and Austria, the brilliant fantasies of rococo art. The grand and heroic pathos of the Baroque is here transformed into elegant feasts of wit and ornament. Rococo taste, especially lavish in the mirrored profusion of interior decor, cultivated by secular and ecclesiastical patrons, reflects the immense charm of the divine creation in intricate designs of spirited playfulness. Castles, churches, libraries and court theatres were built and furnished so as to captivate the visitor in enchanting games of the imagination.

Literary rococo has much in common with the visual arts: for half a century, from about 1730 to 1780, it produced accomplished works of cultivated verbal craftsmanship. Brief forms such as the *Lied*, the fable, the epigram, the idyll, the pastoral or the comic or mock-heroic epic were the congenial vehicles of an essentially gregarious and 'occasional' poetic practice. The Renaissance anthology of poems in imitation of the sixth-century Greek poet Anacreon which had, in France, inspired the Pléiadegroup, and the fugitive poetry of the *petits poètes*, became, a century later the model for the German 'anacreontic' poets. In easy classical metres they gave to scenes of bucolic conviviality that quality of refined sensual optimism so characteristic of the mid-century. Gellert in his lofty didacticism, Gessner with exquisite and widely admired *Idyllen* (1756), Gleim affably moralizing, Ramler in his polished *Oden* (1767), the circles of seraphic poets at Halle and Göttingen – all testified to the pleasures of decorous thoughts and feelings. In his *Musarion* and *Oberon* Wieland offered the most accomplished German rococo epics and remained, to the end of his long life, the master of an engaging, ironic German prose.

It is not difficult to see that this brittle poetry and fiction was soon to become the target of contemptuous attacks by a generation different in aims and temperament, and less anxious to move in a courtly manner. The groundswell of opposition was growing not only to the Berlin mentality but to the rococo sensibility in the arts and in learning. Its chief moving force was an awareness of energies, imaginative as well as philosophical, private as well as collective, no longer sustained by a belief in a universe of immanent rational coherence. That such a faith in the efficacy of reason had a direct bearing on social conduct had been one of the self-evident contentions of the programme of the Enlightenment. That faith had reinforced the logic of absolute power, modified, certainly, by benevolent considerations, and had discouraged emancipatory visions of participation in a common political enterprise.

This severely hierarchical and restrictive conception of an orderly life was now challenged with increasing force and logic by counterclaims of different impulses. Although argued most dramatically in England and France, the tension between established authority and the expectations of intellectual and political liberty was felt as acutely in Germany. Since the Reformation this conflict had, especially in the Protestant states, been experienced in religious or ecclesiastical terms; its wider consequences affected public and private life and were, in turn, to determine the character of German literature throughout the eighteenth century.

The vocabulary in which the assertions of 'freedom' against 'authority' are debated in Germany is drawn in large part from English and French philosophers, Montesquieu and Locke, Hume and Diderot, and enlivened by the language of French and English fiction and poetry. What is, in all these, proclaimed as the ultimate means of heightening individual perception and communal happiness is the awareness of the 'imagination', of 'feeling', of 'sentiment', of 'expression' and of 'genius'.

These terms had been familiar for some time, carefully circumscribed and made socially acceptable by the stabilizing and harmonizing ingredient of reason and religious discipline. In English as well as French theories of conduct from Addison and Shaftesbury to Diderot and Rousseau, sentiment, judiciously controlled by reason, is the precondition of a satisfactory life.

These principles are reflected in the work of several thoughtful and popular writers whose rendering of discreet 'feeling' was to suggest the means of shaping criteria of judgement, both social and aesthetic, by which an emerging middle class could define its character and energies. C.F. Gellert's novel *Leben der schwedischen Gräfin von G**** (1747–48) is a characteristic effort, successful long after its first publication, at projecting this delicate susceptibility ('Empfindsamkeit') as the measure of an harmonious and contented mind. On a more conceptual level, Lessing's theory of tragedy, as well as his later plays, revolve around an affirmation, not only, as in *Minna von Barnhelm*, of 'feeling' as a basis of judgement more effective than abstract principles, but of the cathartic function of sympathy and compassion.

Claims of the pre-eminence of subjectivity over established social and intellectual norms were in Germany, far more than among English dissenters, traditionally an important, indeed central, conviction of the sectarian challenges to Protestant orthodoxy. And it is in the religious experience among the German 'pietistic' circles that the confrontation of authority and the defiant energies of fervent feeling becomes the means of self-justification as well as of collective action. What began late in the seventeenth century as a protest against dogmatic and institutional orthodoxy, as an effort towards a second Reformation, became in Frankfurt in P.J. Spener's 'Collegia Pietatis', in Halle in A.H. Francke's 'Foundations' and especially among a group of Württemberg theologians, a turning away from trust in salvation by established prophecies. They now looked towards the 'new life' that must, in contrition and penitence, prepare for a 'rebirth', the breakthrough of divine grace. The 'new man' whom pietistic doctrine envisaged defines his strength not within a system of theological mediation and institutional dependence but in terms of his own subjective engagement; he is part of a pantheistic universe in which every creature shares in the divine presence. In this existential commitment, the minister is no longer merely the purveyor of the divine word; he is himself a representative and witness of the spiritual life, an exemplar of that *Gottseligkeit*, that intense awareness of an omnipresent energy, that in its highest metaphorical manifestation appears in the consecrated figure of the 'genius'.

The division of the German territories into two separate regions, one Protestant, the other Catholic, had in each for long strengthened the authority of the men of the Church; in the Protestant part, this authority was effectively vested in the parochial clergy, whose social function within the community was decisive. Far more than the English vicarage, the German 'Pfarrhaus' was for most of the eighteenth and nineteenth centuries the focus of spiritual and imaginative life; its history offers an impressive record of intellectual and moral discipline; the number of German writers and artists, scholars and public figures who were the sons of Protestant pastors is astonishing.

The religious impulse, both in its individual and its collective form, as guarantor of the community of those aware of the redemptive force of feeling, is the crucial element in the strategy of protest that unites the group of Sturm und Drang writers. Precursors, sympathizers and partisans can be found throughout the Protestant lands. In Zürich, Johann Caspar Lavater, the 'divine rambler', combined a ceaseless fervour of Christian proselytizing with a sentimental interest in rudimentary physiognomy. In Münster, Düsseldorf and Hamburg groups of pietistic and mystical minds, middle class and nobility in common concern, debated and advocated the new sensibility. The Dutch philosopher F. Hemsterhuis, one of the influential modifiers of Enlightenment thought, fused Locke's sensualism, Shaftesbury's 'enthusiasm' and neo-Platonic idealism into an intellectual and ethical philosophy of the heart (*Lettre sur l'homme et ses rapports*, 1772, commented upon by Diderot), which affected Protestant and (in Münster) Catholic groups alike. It is from this sort of synthesis as well as from the many popular attempts at systematizing the varieties of psychological experience (e.g. J.G. Krüger's widely read *Versuch einer Experimentalseelenlehre*, 1756; C. Bonnet's *Essai sur les facultés de l'âme*, 1760, or J.G. Herder's *Vom Erkennen und Empfinden der menschlichen Seele*, 1778) and, no less important, from the flood of pietistic accounts of exemplary lives of believers and 're-born' Christians, that a vast literature of fictionalized self-analysis draws its justification and its materials. Friedrich Heinrich Jacobi's two disjointed novels, *Aus Eduard Allwills Papieren* (1775–76) and *Woldemar* (1779) provide, in letters and endlessly analytical reflections, portraits of 'all-willful' characters of immense spiritual arrogance whose incessantly reiterated hypertrophy of the imagination leads to the experience, coy as well as desperate, of the 'abyss of the heart'.

The metaphor of the all-feeling, all-suffering, all-creative and all-consuming heart is part of the pietistic heritage; it is given its secular range in that generation's reading of Rousseau (both *Émile* and selections from *La Nouvelle Héloise* appeared in German in 1762) and supplies the theme of a vast avalanche of sentimental fiction, often actual or pretended translations of popular English or French fare. (Within a little more than two years, between 1769 and 1771, no fewer than 275 such novels were published, among them 112 translations).

No single German writer contributed more profoundly and with more impressive originality to the imaginative shaping, to the poetic articulation of these various ingredients of a new sensibility, religious as well as secular, than F.G. Klopstock. He was the first and greatest of those eighteenth-century writers whose spiritual, intellectual and formal concerns with the resources of language and prosody create a style and a conception of the uses of poetry that were to prove exemplary for the subsequent history of German literature.

A resolution made when he was still in school (1739) to produce an epic poem on the sublimest Biblical topic suggests a belated Baroque fascination with grandeur and splendour; when he decided upon a retelling of the story of the Messiah, it was to be an achievement comparable in religious and intellectual scope to the achievements of Homer, Dante and Milton. The first three cantos were sketched in prose but, in 1746 reworked in flowing hexameters often close to rhythmic prose, with deliberate disavowal of the traditional heroic metre of French classicism.

The publication (1748) of these three cantos of astonishingly sustained power, discipline and abundant imagery, produced an enormous effect upon German readers, especially the poets: the topic – Christ's mediation between an adjudicating God and sinful, defective mankind – is developed within a theological scheme palpably opposed to the prevailing orthodoxy. Through the penitent satanic figure of Abbadona, who is eventually redeemed in Christ, it shares in Leibnitz's notion of a cosmos of pre-stabilized harmony with its rejection of radical evil. In his attempt to represent the divine presence as a system of benevolent and intelligible acts, Klopstock avoids, in Milton's manner, any quasi-realistic rendering of the supernatural world, and evokes in language and imagery of highly charged emotional abstraction a sense of the divinity beyond reason and all familiar habits of the imagination. It is in the subjective processes of the poet-seer's 'thinking' that the truth of creation, 'God's thought', the structure of a universe not conceived entirely in Copernican terms, is transmitted to the reader, whose receptivity is at every moment galvanized and drawn into an intense communal experience. Far from the detached composure of the traditional epic narrator, Klopstock's poetic voice and gestures are at every moment grandly charged and compelling to the point of prophetic fervour. If since early in the century it had become the writer's chief task to 'touch the heart', Klopstock now attempts with his 'sacred poetry' to move the whole soul.

Like most of his contemporaries, Klopstock is profoundly preoccupied with the efficacy of language, not in its mimetic capacity but its expressive force: expressive less of the personal character of the self – this was to be the secularized Sturm und Drang modification of Klopstock's intention – than of the poet's character as an inspired transmitter of the divine, as an entranced and eloquent witness to the presence of the creative spirit. What makes Klopstock such an eminent poet is precisely the fact that the testimonial voice is not conveyed in the sort of ecstatic and uncontrolled language of either the religious sectarian fanatics or the Sturm und Drang playwrights, but with a most sophisticated command of metrical and rhythmic devices and a superb feeling for the possibilities of extending and transfiguring the German language.

Long before the complete *Messias* appeared in 20 cantos (1780), 10 dealing with the Passion, the rest with Christ after Resurrection, Klopstock's miscellaneous poetry, his odes, elegies, hymns, were circulated among his admirers, copied and given an almost fetishistic value. They were tokens of shared sensibility, signs of a community of men and women held in a common faith in intense but highly self-conscious sympathy. They seemed capable of suspending momentarily the overriding distinctions of class and privilege. Beyond their apostrophe of love and friendship, of sublime sentiments and solemn assertions of an all-embracing Being, their blend of humane and patriotic themes, these poems were the products of a uniquely form-conscious writer who infused traditional classical models, such as the Horatian ode, with a modern expressive resilience.

The language of the *Messias* and of Klopstock's poetry altogether is syntactically far from simple; he compels his readers by intricately designed turns of phrase, by the use of paradox and an involuted order of boldly compounded words, to meet a spiritual challenge. Poetic language, he insisted, has its own mode of functioning and differs from that of prose. He is in this respect an acknowledged precursor not only of Hölderlin and Novalis but of the German symbolists, of Stefan George and Rilke. Indeed, his effect on the formal devices as well as the imagery of German classical and romantic poetry was profound. Instead of conventional topics, he offered moving projections of the moment of poetic dedication and inspiration; he justified the severest obedience to the demands of prosody, to pitch and metre, to tone and mood, by his insistence on the highest possible cognitive function of the poet and his craft. If he sought in his *Oden* (1771) and his curiously contrived patriotic plays to replace the familiar classical myths by what he considered 'Nordic' or 'Germanic' topics, he contributed through the evocation of shared national emotions to the blurring of provincial and class distinctions.

The customary assessment of Klopstock's achievement has tended to isolate and overemphasize either the sentimental or the powerfully irrational elements of his work. Yet, his central concern was not with the ecstatic assertion of the self or, as in Goethe's *Werther*, with the inevitable isolation and alienation of the feeling soul but with the means of giving to the work of the poet something like institutional sanction. This is the ever more urgent preoccupation of all significant German writing during the latter half of the eighteenth century.

Though since 1751 supported by an annuity from the Danish king,

and Scottish collections such as Bishop Percy's *Reliques of Ancient English Poetry* (1765), and confirm the high value which Herder placed upon the supernatural, national and lyrical features of this kind of poetry. Shakespeare was for Bürger the 'natural' arch-poet; yet his own prose version of *Macbeth* (1782) turns the heroic tragedy into a crude melodrama, an indication of his predilection for the stereotypes of fear, horror and mystery and for the sensational visions of the popular imagination. It was Bürger, incidentally, who translated and amplified *Baron Munchhausen's Narrative of his Marvelous Travels and Campaigns in Russia* (1785), tales of the outrageous exploits of a country nobleman near Göttingen, written originally in English by R.E. Raspe.

What had brought these young men together was the distinction of Göttingen as a modern, secular and 'critical' university. Founded in 1734 by George II, the Hanoverian on the British throne, it was, with Edinburgh, Leyden and the Geneva Academy, one of the most enlightened in Europe. On its faculty were scholars such as the constitutional lawyer Stephan Pütter, the staunch defender of the historical imperial law against the notion of 'natural law', and the historian A.L. von Schlözer, the best-informed investigator of European political institutions and the author of an uncommonly substantial *Briefwechsel meist historischen Inhalts* (1777–82). The inspiring C.G. Heyne, the founder of the systematic study of classical philology, art-history, archaeology and mythology, had an extraordinary influence on the German poets and essayists of the last quarter of the century. The mathematician and, since 1769, professor of experimental physics, Georg Christoph Lichtenberg was among the Göttingen luminaries an unwavering mocker of irrationalism. Inexhaustible in his wit, yet humane and generous, he published scientific and popular essays on a multitude of subjects in the *Göttinger Taschen-Calender* (1776ff) and the *Göttingische Magazin der Wissenschaften und Litteratur* (1780–85). Eager to record the absurdities and vanities of the age, he might have become a novelist in the manner of Sterne if his temperament had not inclined towards the monologue. A vast number of aphorisms, which he was in the habit of almost daily jotting down, has assured his place in German eighteenth-century literature as a truly enlightened mind, free of solemnity, prejudice or partisan sentimentality, who viewed the contemporary scene before and after the Revolution with pointed detachment. Since 1773 he had planned sustained satirical attacks upon the sentimentality, clumsiness and provinciality of German writers; he was unambiguous in his scorn for the fashions of the day – mysticism, religious enthusiasm, or Sturm und Drang proclamations of eccentric energy – and a superb observer of men and women and the oblique evidence of their psychological make-up. In his diaries and letters from England (1774–75) he reported shrewdly on life in a capital that became of ever greater interest to German readers eager to see beyond their narrow horizon. At Kew he was an esteemed guest of George III, his king, and was introduced to Garrick of whose dazzling genius he writes with admiration. In elaborate commentaries on Hogarth's engravings (*Ausführliche Erklärung der Hogarthischen Kupferstiche*, 1794–99) Lichtenberg interprets the range of Hogarth's characters in the meticulously rendered setting of English life, the greed, the dubious morality. Published at the end of his life, this much admired work is supreme evidence of the passionate intelligence of one of the most imaginative and vivacious critics of his time.

Magi of the North: Hamann and Herder

Klopstock was the immensely admired model of the writer as citizen, as the voice of a community of feeling and as a craftsman in command of the European heritage of poetic invention. His reflections on the nature of poetry, on language, on metrics and rhyme (*Über Sprache und Dichtkunst. Fragmente*, 1779–80) remained current well into the romantic era. He was on the other hand, far surpassed in originality, depth and scope by two theologians, in turn most respectful of Klopstock, whose views of God, of man and of history gave not only direction to the Sturm und Drang fellowship, but a new vocabulary and self-confidence altogether to the generation that dominated the last third of the century. J.G. Hamann and J.G. Herder were East Prussians, steeped in pietistic belief, unceasingly enquiring into the nature of those spiritual energies which constitute the creative character of man, his capacity to produce a record of his attempts at comprehending a world of inexhaustible variety. Critical and discursive by temperament, they were in emphatic disagreement with the fundamental proposition of the Enlightenment, that conclusive insights can be derived only from irrefutable rational truths.

Hamann's earliest writings were the result of a religious crisis which compelled him to face the relationship between reason and faith. In *Sokratische Denkwürdigkeiten* (1759) an anonymous piece of some 60 pages written in his characteristically opaque and metaphysical style, he calls for 'Socratic' doubt in the efficacy of reason – much like Hume, whose radical scepticism he admired. He insists, defending himself against the views of his friend Kant, on the impotence of rationalism in the face of existential experiences. Socrates' confession of 'ignorance', he argues, was a form of belief in a 'daimon', the 'genius' to which the great poets, Homer or Shakespeare, testify.[3] That concept, which was earlier and later in the eighteenth century employed in a wholly secularized sense, is here used with decided religious emphasis. Without religious

[3] J.G. Hamann, *Sämtliche Werke*, ed. J. Nadler, Vienna, Th. Morus Presse, 1950, II, p. 73–5.

faith and the recognition of the temporal character of reality, of the concrete historical constellations which defy all efforts at abstract systematizing, all claims to philosophical certainty are for Hamann mere pretentious delusions. His best known work, *Kreuzzüge des Philologen* (1762) suggests in its ironic title a conception of 'philology' not merely as offering learned information but as creating a state of mind – a suggestion of the double role of the 'philologist' as lover of the word and lover of that comprehensive spirit of reason which, in the sense of the Gospel of St John, the Greek term 'logos' implies. This collection of loosely argued essays contains an attack on Mendelssohn's negative review of Rousseau's *La Nouvelle Héloise*, and in 'Aesthetica in Nuce', emphatically states Hamann's own aesthetic theory, especially his theory of language, a 'rhapsody in cabalistic prose' in 50 brief pages that were to become a manifesto of the Sturm und Drang movement.[4]

Hamann here begins with a passionate attack upon the rationalist manner of orthodox Bible exegesis: God, he argues, has at the beginning of creation, in an act of self-abasement, spoken to man as arch-poet in the language of the imagination and of feeling. The fundamental structure of the universe Hamann defines as altogether 'verbal'. All creation – nature, history, the Scriptures – is intelligible in the hieroglyphs of God's language, a poetic medium which, in turn, has remained the only valid speech through which men can communicate their deepest concerns. (Hamann, and later Herder in a similar context, seem to think in the terms of the contemporary philosopher G. Vico.) Language is for Hamann a metaphorical system that points to the symbolic character of the world, of a universe which cannot be exhausted, or relieved of its inherent ambiguity, by any of the available philosophical syntheses – materialism, deism or Platonic idealism.

Hamann recognizes that language, however inspired, is bound to remain an unreliable instrument: it illuminates and seduces at once, it may give access to ultimate meanings but it may also confuse and mislead. In Goethe's *Faust*, in Faust's and Mephistopheles' contrasting views of speech, this ambiguous functioning of language becomes a central theme. Nature is for Hamann the 'text' of creation which has been obscured by the abstract exegesis of secular rationalism and which must be freshly translated by the poet from an originally 'angelic' idiom into human speech. Only Klopstock, 'the great restorer of lyrical song',[5] had acknowledged the powerful imagery of the Psalms and the prophetic books as the true source of all poetry, modern as well as ancient.

Hamann's own style corresponds to this view of language: it seeks to compel participation in the act of 'translating'; where Klopstock employs

[4] Ibid., II, p. 195–217.
[5] Ibid., II, p. 215.

intricate syntactical patterns, Hamann engrosses the reader (much like his beloved Sterne in *Tristram Shandy*) with a profusion of notes, quotations and allusions. Against the deceptive clarity of the rationalist philosopher he urges what he calls 'symphasiology', a manner of passionately engaging the reader who, by bringing his senses and feelings into play, must find the unspoken point of comparison between two metaphors. Hamann remains a puzzling but grand counter-figure to men like Lessing and Kant, whose concerns he shared but whose recourse to secular reason he rejected. Goethe spoke with admiration of the 'sybilline leaves' of the Magus of the North as F.K von Moser, the author of *Herr und Diener*, had first called him. 'Whenever you turn to them, you feel that you have made a discovery; the meaning that each passage conveys, touches and stirs us in so many ways.'[6]

It was inevitable that Hamann's rejection of the autonomy of rational man should put him in conflict with Kant who maintained that reason, pure and independent of experience, must be the premise of all philosophical discourse. Hamann, on the contrary, asserted that reason and experience are inseparably related in the symbolic signs of necessarily ambiguous language. But with his strong belief in the 'rebirth' of man as the precondition of an authentic life, Hamann was equally in disagreement with Herder, whose philosophy advances, with each of his provocative works, more firmly towards a belief in the natural evolution of human capacities and, therefore, in an historical structure and progression of existence.

Johann Gottfried Herder, 14 years younger than Hamann, is the most impressive German representative of philosophical convictions that have, in various ways and in different areas of experience, shaped essential features of the modern imagination. If a central concern is to be extracted from his enormously varied, fragmentary and yet vigorously argued work, it is the insistence on modes of understanding appropriate to the vast complex of human creativity, self-articulation and vision. For previous thinkers, these achievements had been warranted by rational and normative criteria derived from a universe of immanent logic. Herder's view of the abundance and circumstantial nature of life in all its manifestations, of its historical concreteness, led him to seek a critical theory and a system of value judgements that prepared the ground for most of the philosophical positions which the two subsequent centuries evolved. Throughout his life he remained a theologian, even if he held a view of God, of revelation and of faith that differed not only from orthodox Protestant belief, but equally from Hamann's spiritualism, Hume's empiricism or Kant's assumption of religion as an *a priori* function of the

[6] Goethe *GA*, X, p. 449, 564.

human mind. God is for Herder not a metaphysical concept, an abstraction of the absolute, but the central energy that sustains life. This is reflected in the consciousness of man and in his capacity, differentiated by his particular historical situation, to comprehend the divine presence and to relate, in feeling and thought, the countless phenomena that testify to its creative force. Nature is therefore not so much the object of scientific enquiry as a system of experienced relationships through which the divine power reveals itself. Such a theology was and is, of course, open to severe criticism: it tends to secularize the meaning of revelation and has, indeed, led to a questionable faith in history as the instrumentality of God's purpose to advance man's humanity.

Herder's early essays deal during the 1760s with 'aesthetic' issues in the sense that they define the character of human perception as the capacity of encompassing all resources of being. Instead of distinguishing perception and reason, the 'aesthetic' function from the 'poetic', will from reflection, Herder postulates a single and total energy which in turn reflects a power (*Kraft*) that creates and permeates the universe. (Sulzer had elaborated on this same concept in a lecture, 1765, to the Berlin Academy, entitled 'Von der Kraft (Energie) in den Werken der Schönen Künste'.) Even though this force may not be rationally definable, it must be presupposed in all forms of significant behaviour. The universe is intelligible only if we think of it as accessible in acts of experience. It is this assumption, translated into the particular context of understanding intellectual (or perceptual) challenges, which gives to works of art their central importance. Herder's essay 'Über die neuere deutsche Literatur' (1767) as well as his 'Kritische Wälder' (1769) – 'sylvae' is the classical title of works of miscellaneous content – move beyond Lessing's distinctions made a few years earlier in his *Laokoon* between the spatial and the temporal conditions of art and poetry and maintain that it is the 'power' of the work of art which interacts with a similar receptivity in the viewer or listener to produce an effect upon the sensibility. The assessment of a work of art should not, as previous aesthetic theories had postulated, depend upon any static principle of 'taste', but upon an intricate variety of presuppositions, historical, local, social and personal. A comparison between Lessing's and Winckelmann's views of beauty and taste leads Herder to argue that no normative theory of art is acceptable, that each genre has its specific mode of impact upon the imagination and that only a recognition of the 'thrust' that enlivens a work of art, differentiated by the particular conditions of its origins, can be the criterion of its effectiveness.

All arts derive their value and efficacy from the mediation of the senses: seeing, hearing and touch must be brought into play as we reflect upon a painting, a piece of music or sculpture. Poetry is the most complex and the most telling of these: it operates through the medium of language which offers not merely signs for concepts, but significant challenges to all our powers of experience. Thinking is 'inward speech'. It is not surprising that Herder returns again and again to the issue of language, its nature, its efficacy, its history – at that time topics of intense discussion.

In his prize essay *Abhandlung über den Ursprung der Sprache* (1772) written for the Berlin Academy, he rejects two of the widely shared theories of the origins, that is, of the first principles, of language. One of these assumes a divine act as the primary impulse giving rise to speech, the other understands the emergence of languages as the result of a 'social contract'. Both views, the first not far from that held by his friend Hamann, Herder dismissed. A third, propounded by Condillac to the effect that language evolved from the instinctual cry of animals, he was at pains to refute, but only insofar as he thought it important to stress the gradual articulation of this primary instinct in acts of consciousness. Languages may thus be thought to have an affective character which Herder, with his fondness for historical terms, conceived of as 'primitive' and as the expression of emotions or passion, joy or sorrow, close to the immediate, all-present 'energy'. This is the material of poetry. As language becomes the tool of reflection, it turns into an instrument of civilized abstraction and detachment (a palpable premise of French classicist literature); indeed, language, far from being a universal system of rational signs, is the particular product of the collective social and historical consciousness of its speakers. 'The genius of a nation's language is . . . the genius of its literature'.[7]

Herder's insistence on a genetic and specific differentiation of cultures, ways of life, types of thinking and speech produced a conception of literature which led him on the one hand to place a high value on primary poetic productions of a distinct cultural (or 'national') cast, and on the other, to the recognition of specific excellences in the various phases and settings of literary history. Instead of a rigid belief in absolute standards of judgement – such as Winckelmann seemed to postulate *vis-à-vis* Greek art – Herder argued the importance of relating a native character and a native tradition to achievements made legitimate and telling by their historical context. Not single-minded imitation, therefore, but a constant testing of indigenous qualities against comparable achievements of other cultures, other experiences, other myths is the gist of Herder's theory of criticism.

It was part of the critical attitude towards his own age and its problematical forms of social life (a conviction that determined the character of literature throughout Europe, but particularly in the disjointed and politically unsatisfactory world of Germany), that led him to point to

[7] Herder *SW*, I, p. 147.

models of regeneration in what he considered the productions of primary 'genius'. That concept was common enough in eighteenth-century critical discourse. The very term had been rejected as un-German by Gottsched but given currency through Johann Adolf Schlegel's translation of J. Batteux's *Traité sur les beaux-arts réduits à un même principe* and his successively modified commentary (1751, 1759, 1770). It became part of the vocabulary of sensibility where genius meant the capacity to create, as Addison had formulated it 'by the mere strength of natural parts, and without any assistance of art or learning'. There is 'something nobly wild and extravagant in these great natural Genius's that is infinitely more beautiful than all the turn and polishing of what the French call a Bel Esprit.'[8] Shaftesbury had compared the imaginative strength of the genius to the bold creative act of Prometheus; for Lavater (*Physiognomische Fragmente. Zur Beförderung der Menschenkenntnis und Menschenliebe*, 1775–78) the genius was *proprior deus*. Sulzer, the Berlin theoretician, had summed up the prevailing understanding of the term in an essay 'Entwicklung des Begriffs von Genie' (1757).

Herder's use of the word, stimulated by Shaftesbury's theory of an 'original genius' whose 'enthusiasm' becomes the source of perceptive and cognitive art, as well as by Edward Young's *Conjectures on Original Composition* (1759) – 'an original may be said to be of a vegetable nature; it rises spontaneously from the vital root of Genius; it grows, it is not made'[9] – is in keeping with his vitalist philosophy: it designates that striking imaginative freshness and originality which, he thought, gave greatness to the Bible, Homer, Chaucer and Shakespeare. These he regarded with other critics (e.g. Robert Wood's *Essay on the Original Genius of Homer*, 1769) as close to the 'folk' imagination, not essentially different from those poems, songs and ballads which English and Scottish collections such as Bishop Percy's *Reliques of Ancient English Poetry* had recently brought to the attention of European readers. He himself discussed extensively, collected, and at times rewrote poetry from many nations (*Volkslieder*, 1778–79; later as *Stimmen der Völker in Liedern*, 1808) whose distinguishing feature was not so much their popular origin as 'truth, faithful accounting of passion, of the age and its customs'.[10] He saw no reason why he should not include poems of his own, Goethe's 'Lied vom Fischer' or the delightful 'Abendlied' by his friend, the gentle 'folk-poet' Matthias Claudius. Others had written sentimentally about the charms of the simple life reflected in folk poetry (G.A. Bürger: 'Herzensausguss über Volkspoesie', 1776); for Herder it was a more complex

[8] Addison and Steele, *The Spectator*, ed. Gregory Smith, London, Dent, 1967, I, p. 482.

[9] Edward Young, *Conjectures on Original Composition*, ed. Edith J. Morley, Manchester, Manchester U. P., 1918, p. 7.

[10] Herder *SW*, XXV, p. 308.

matter. Folk literature seemed to him splendid evidence of that variety of cultural attitudes and products of the imagination which testified to the truth of his differentiating view of history. Through the calculated advocacy of folk-materials he hoped in the cultivated poets and readers to recover a long-lost sense of naiveté. The 'Ossianic' poems (which James Macpherson claimed to have translated into rhythmic English prose from the Highland Gaelic of a Scottish national poet of the third century), struck him as rich in precisely the kind of devices that made the tradition of European balladry so impressive. They were, he thought, great literature, oral, not written documents, intense, musical and rhetorical in their gestures.

The publication in which he wrote so eloquently about Ossian and Shakespeare ('Auszug aus einem Briefwechsel über Ossian und die Lieder alter Völker'. 'Shakespeare') suggested in its very title, *Von deutscher Art und Kunst*, 1773, something of the native direction which Herder hoped to give to German literature. This volume, which includes Goethe's eulogy of the medieval architect of the Strasbourg minster ('Von deutscher Baukunst'), became for the emerging Sturm und Drang writers a most influential programmatical collection. A generation earlier the Swiss critic J.J. Bodmer had cautiously drawn attention to German poetry of the Middle Ages and praised Shakespeare; Wieland had produced German prose versions of 17 of Shakespeare's plays; and the playwright had recently been the object of Lessing's profound admiration.

For Herder, Shakespeare represented a radically modern form of the poetic imagination, the very prototype of an 'original genius', whose instinct for a captivating kind of theatre had achieved great art despite an obvious indifference to the traditional categories of dramatic theory. Here Herder followed English – as against French – criticism which had held similar views ever since Addison's question in the *Spectator*: 'Who would not rather read one of his Plays, where there is not a single rule of the stage observed, than any production of a modern Critick, where there is not one of them violated?'[11] But Shakespeare was for Herder as well a master of realistic portraiture not only of 'characters' but of that universe of interests, class distinctions and beliefs that provides the topics and moods, the imagery and, above all, the language unmistakably of his place and age. All of Shakespeare's figures 'are complete, yet individual beings, each participating, cooperating, acting as a character and in his way in the historical events . . . . Each pursues his purpose, works and creates and lo: unwittingly becomes the blind instrument of a higher design, of a totality created by an invisible poet.'[12] Another reason for Herder's interest in Shakespeare was his conviction that Shakespeare

[11] Addison and Steele, op. cit., IV, p. 356.
[12] Herder *SW*, V, p. 238.

had used elements of folk-tradition in order to overcome the disparity between 'learned' and 'popular' literature – a distinction that had, in his opinion, confined the works of French classicism to a limited class of readers.

Herder's aesthetic notions, his theories of language and poetry, give concreteness to his anthropological conception of history and his central preoccupation with the problem of understanding it. His *Ideen zur Philosophie der Geschichte der Menschheit* (1784–91) was to be the most ambitious synthesis of his philosophy of historical judgement. It was written at a time when the revolutionary events were about to open new perspectives for a mind unambiguously committed to a progressive humanitarian idealism, yet deeply disturbed by what he felt to be a disastrous fascination among his contemporaries with speculative transcendentalism. If, like most Enlightenment writers, he believed in the freedom of conscience and decision by which men make their choice within an historical scheme, he rejected any suggestion that the standards by which historical change, by which the vitality of individual actions or social organizations can be judged, should be universal. History, he was convinced, was the sum of the creative use made by civilizations of the inestimable opportunities which temporal and local conditions provided. In the face of the immeasurable variety of cultural projections no single criterion for their interpretation can be adequate. Every age has its own character; its forms of life, its political and artistic style. What Herder insisted upon was the plurality of cultures achieved by groups, nations or classes who articulate their aspirations in social or artistic performances of a characteristic sort. Culture can be emulated, but not imitated.

Herder's terminology for the evolution, mutation and mortality of the chain of shaped experience had biological implications which were suggested to him by C. Bonnet's *La Palingénésie philosophique* (1769). It allowed him to see each phenomenon as unique and at the same time as an instance in a process of growth in humanity: each stage of history, as he formulated it in the characteristic vocabulary of the late Enlightenment, 'has the centre of its happiness within itself'.[13] The metaphorical term for this potential of development in the individual as well as the society is the German word *Bildung*. The concept was used cautiously in earlier German and French works on natural evolution (Buffon, von Haller); Herder was the first to use it to indicate a pattern of historical and political progression. In its most comprehensive sense *Bildung* henceforth becomes one of the postulates by which the German middle class is encouraged to define its educational vision and its opportunities for excellence.

[13] Herder *SW*, V, p. 509.

Sturm und Drang

It was a propitious occasion which, in the winter of 1770, brought about the meeting between Herder, not yet 30 years old, and Goethe, nine years his junior, much different in temperament and background, yet each instantly and intensely attracted to the other. Herder had journeyed from Riga to France and Germany in search of an opportunity to develop ideas formed in his years as preacher, as an avid reader and an alert observer of the intellectual currents of the age. From 1762 to 1764 he had in Königsberg listened to Kant's lectures on logic, metaphysics, mathematics, geography and ethics and had, through him, become familiar with the works of Rousseau and Hume. His 'Journal meiner Reise im Jahre 1769' (1846) contains disjointed but telling reflections of a mind in essential respects attached to the basic rational optimism of the Enlightenment, but sceptical of the sterility he felt in the formalized culture of the French, whose great contemporary figures, d'Alembert or Voltaire, he was inclined to regard as witnesses to the decadence of the age, and whose notions of taste and politeness struck him as indications of debility. His counter-vision rested upon the living thought and the acute experience of the present, and drew on the Ossianic poems as a fresh source of sublime feeling transcending in spiritual power the ideal of equanimity offered by his elders.

We have an account in Goethe's *Dichtung und Wahrheit* of the extraordinary impact of Herder's personality upon the student of law and political science at the University of Strasbourg; Herder, already remarkably learned, single-minded and peremptory, yet inclined towards brooding melancholy and self-doubt, produced an indelible impression upon the young Goethe, himself a striking and exceptionally gifted figure of tireless intellectual curiosity and an uncommon talent for friendship. Whatever literary and philosophical interests Goethe had developed, they were acquired during not quite two years of desultory studies at the fashionable and conservative University of Leipzig in the bookish world of one of the centres of enlightened rationalism, and again, at home in Frankfurt, in passing contacts with friends close to the pietistic faith and the alchemical and cabalistic mysteries. Strasbourg was a different place altogether: enchanting in the beauty of the surrounding countryside, dominated by its superb minster, more relaxed as a city of southwestern Alsatian charm and far less ceremonious than Leipzig. He was drawn by Herder into an orbit of powerful new masters: Homer, Pindar, Shakespeare, Ossian, Hamann, the English novelists, Sterne and Goldsmith. Folk poetry, hymnic sublimity, powerful dramatic portraiture, 'nature', 'motion', 'space' – these were dimensions of a new-felt life which Herder opened for him. His letters testify to a glorious sense of growth in perception; his admiration for Herder is unhesitating, however nstinctive the resistance to his often crotchety manner.

The works which were directly or indirectly to result and of which we hall speak later – poetry, essays, dramatic sketches, even, two years ence, that *tour-de-force* of an entirely original novel, *Die Leiden des ungen Werthers* – could not have been written without Herder's alvanizing zeal for ways of seeing and understanding that released eligious and secular impulses, and sharpened eyes and ears for realities vhich moral and intellectual conventions had concealed. Herder loquently demonstrated the powerful presence of these realities in some f the great poets who could now be read not as specimens of a becalmed ort of perfection but as instances of a creative drive that moved the total ensibility precisely by its centrifugal force.

In 1771, clearly still under the spell of Herder's magic personality, oethe rapidly sketched a loosely constructed quasi-Shakespearean ramatic portrait of a 'great German', the Renaissance knight Goetz von erlichingen. Goetz is the model of a rebel in an age of transition, the efender of 'natural law' against the power of church and state that is ased on petrified, formal authority; he holds to his faith in integrity and obility as a free servant of the empire, an heroic but doomed fighter gainst legalistic and dishonorable institutionalized power. Goetz's first nd last thought is 'liberty', he is the representative of an 'ancient order' vhich has inescapably been superseded, and of which he is the pathetic vitness. Friendship, loyalty and freedom of conscience are defeated by unning, treason and plotting. Herder's favourite themes re-emerge: the ascination with a moment of historical transition embodied in a figure of ncorruptible defiance, the struggle between the devious establishment nd a group of fallible but sharply specified figures outside the centres of ower – a colourful world seen with a compassionate eye and rendered n firm and expressive speech. In a revised form (1773) *Goetz* was erformed with enormous success in Berlin in the spring of 1774 and soon ecame the object of intense partisanship. Klopstock and Wieland raised it; to Herder it seemed somewhat self-conscious, 'gedacht'; essing deplored its lack of dramatic structure: 'He fills guts with sand nd sells them as rope. Who does that? Is it possibly the poet who gives us biography in dialogue form and touts it as drama?'[14] Nicolai ridiculed t; for Frederick the Great it was disgusting drivel, and an instance of that oorish lack of taste that made German literature so unpalatable.

The play nevertheless became at once part of the repertoire of most German theatres. It offered, certainly, a dangerously seductive model: ts loose (and essentially epic) structure seemed to give legitimacy to xuberant and often melodramatic sketches of felt greatness and barely

[14] Lessing *Werke*, V, p. 788.

articulated social protest but with little dramatic logic. Goethe himsel subsequently thought of it as reflecting a passing phase of his life, anc would not have it performed in Weimar until 30 years later.

At the time, the topic of the creative and exceptional individual con tinued to preoccupy him: he planned a drama dealing with Caesar, anc wrote a few powerful and moving scenes of a 'Prometheus' play (1773) Even in those early years he was haunted by the figure of Faust, the seeke of an elusive truth at a turning point in the history of thought, no longe content with the presumed certainties of the medieval world, groping fo means of access to wisdom and craving a state of bliss in knowledge beyond orthodoxy. No doubt Hamann and Herder, for Goethe the proto types of radical questioners, provided the models from which in the course of the next few years a tentative dramatic biography of Faust, ar *Urfaust*, was to emerge (1775), his first attempt to deal with a poetic complex that occupied him in one way or another for the rest of his life

Strident Voices: Sturm und Drang Drama

For the time being, *Goetz* seemed to draw together the mood of restless ness among those who found in it the imagery, the language and the daring that enabled them to translate an instinctive sense of the new inte poetic form. The dramatic writing which appeared in Germany in the 10 years after 1770 is more remarkable for its documentary fury than for any lasting effect upon the subsequent history of German intellectual, socia or literary life. In so far as it offers the sort of consonance which is com monly thought of as the Sturm und Drang sensibility, this is the result of a challenge as passionate as its programmatic focus was indistinct, throwr defiantly at the political realities of the age. On the other hand, the radicalism of its gestures and the flamboyance of its protests all too fre quently conceal a profound melancholy as to the prospects of a more humane life. It shares, of course, Rousseau's conviction, set forth in his eloquent (and immensely popular) psychological novel *Émile* (1762), of the alienation of man from his authentic self, and the conclusion that al is fundamentally good as it comes from the hand of the Creator and that all degenerates under the hand of man.

But it would be difficult to point to a single philosophical model to which the Sturm und Drang poets subscribed. They thought to an impor tant degree in the terms of contemporary materialist and sensualist theories and were inclined to see merit in d'Holbach's conclusion that the all-compelling laws of nature could only lead to a fatalistic acquiescence in the inevitable; they were, at the same time, parodoxically, persuaded by Helvetius' doctrine that the objective unreason of the existing socia order could be modified by the demonstrative assertion of spontaneous subjectivity. The essentially empirical character of this central Sturm

und Drang proposition distinguishes it from the specu
of the later romantic faith.

Many of those who were most deeply affected by He
of accepted modes of judgement were, during the n
produce plays, prose, even poetry of a defiant, rough-ca
style. Their common impulse, later designated as the 'Sturm und Drang' mentality, was defined in confessional essays and letters – none attempted anything like a critical statement of systematic coherence. They were far from thinking of their work, published or merely circulated in manuscript, as representing a clearly focused literary doctrine. What links the diffuse and multi-faceted efforts by men of varying intellectual disposition and talent is the resolution to declare, in blunt and deliberately offensive terms, their deep distrust in the contemporary practice of reason, and a determination to question prevailing forms of thought and conduct. The Sturm und Drang rebellion is, in fact, the first in that succession of European (and American) anti-cultural protests that have challenged the social and intellectual assumptions of an establishment whose inherent contradictions and whose obsolescent conventions can be attacked most forcibly by asserting the superior power of incoherence, formlessness and eccentricity.

The violent tone of many of the Sturm und Drang plays and their extravagant topics may seem nihilistic; they are, however, even at their most aggressive, with few exceptions, built upon a fundamentally rational view of life. They presume the stability of 'nature' and 'man' which needs now to be reasserted in their deep estrangement from the prevailing cultural conventions. The belief in the rationality of existence remains, but the proclamation of 'reason' as the justification of the existing political and aesthetic systems henceforth becomes suspect.

What gives an unmistakable tone and texture to the most interesting work of these artists, poetry, critical reflection, painting and even music, is not merely the discovery of 'feeling' – this had earlier been an ingredient in the religious pathos of the pietists and in the demonstrative sentimentality of rococo manners and art. It was a new sense of place and time through which the claims of inspiration and spontaneity were now asserted within distinctly secularized notions of greatness and genius against the traditional (aristocratic) assumptions of civilizing decorum. The benevolent function and the conciliatory effect of feeling upon social conduct is now bluntly denied. Radicalized and freshly explored, it is now sanctioned not by its social efficacy but by the integrity of its sheer and sublimely 'natural' force. In its fullest awareness, it is the as yet unfathomed and undefined resource of a life whose primary feature is not balance and equanimity but indeterminacy and openness. 'Sentiment' now takes on a spurious and trivial connotation: as 'sentimentality' it comes the despised instrument of convention.

The recurrent topics of the Sturm und Drang writers are, in Herder's sense, 'nature' as a creative resource, history as a projection of local and collective experiences, man and his total perception, the poet as the supreme example of 'genius' – all these dramatized in figures (like Goetz) of powerful energy and defiant authenticity. In so far as these ideas are cohesively stated and not merely as brief critical asides or scattered in the creative works themselves, they are, above all, polemical and tend, like Goethe's address commemorating Shakespeare's birthday (1771), to take the form of ironic advice to the bemused elders who, with their polite and impotent philosophy, are about to be driven from the Elysian shelter, critics whose aridity has made them blind to the overwhelming life-force that is Shakespeare.

Shakespeare was, henceforth, to be the touchstone of greatness. Lessing had briefly referred to his original genius; Herder was to sum up the shared admiration in a measured essay (1774); Lenz, Goethe's friend, concludes his *Anmerkungen übers Theater* (1774) with an emphatic paean to the great innovator; H.W. von Gerstenberg's *Briefe* had praised his superiority over French classicist dramaturgy. For the Sturm und Drang dramatists, Shakespeare and his contemporaries supplied the justification for a radical dissolution of the dramatic form. In 1765 Gerstenberg translated Beaumont and Fletcher's *The Maide's Tragedy* (*Die Braut*) and, in his own play, *Ugolino* (1769) makes use of Dante's episode of the incarceration of the rebel Ugolino and his three sons, and their death by starvation. Before Gerstenberg later modified the hero's end, the play offered an almost expressionist scenario without any dramatic motivation of the issue of guilt: existential anguish is constantly asserted by the four characters during the stormy night in the oppressive confinement of a tower; it is a gauche but powerful piece of ecstatic lyricism, affecting by its sustained projection of suffering in the face of death.

The most impressive talent among the Sturm und Drang dramatists was undoubtedly J.M.R. Lenz. Like Hamann and Herder, he was born in the northeast; while a student of theology and a tutor in an aristocratic family, he met Goethe and his circle in Strasbourg. An extraordinarily restless mind, he later became insane and died miserably in Moscow. The intricacy and complexity of Lenz's character and the curiously 'literary' nature of his life were later sharply recorded by Goethe: in *Dichtung und Wahrheit* he recognizes his profound and inexhaustibly productive talent; but tenderness, restlessness and sophistry seemed in him to be in constant conflict, and his sublime gifts were touched with sickness:

> his imagination was that of a rogue, his love as well as his hatred were unreal, he was wilful in his ideas and feelings so as to be constantly occupied. He tried to

aristocratic and middle-class ways of life, here generalized by a critique of fashionable sentimentality and of pretentious notions of social privilege. The violent confrontations and deaths that make up the plot are awkwardly resolved by the withdrawal of the survivors from life at court to the bucolic peace of a Rousseauean retreat. The powerful, ejaculatory prose and attempts at distinguishing individual and social attitudes give a measure of interest to a Sturm und Drang document which is more impressive in its theatrical energy than in any coherent social philosophy.

Whatever Klinger's merits or shortcomings as a singularly prolific playwright, his career after 1780 as an official in Russia is more notable – especially from 1803 to 1817 as Curator of the University of Dorpat. The artistic and intellectual scope of his life is not as yet fully appreciated: detached from the German scene and closer to French ways, he was to recover his faith in a rational culture which the Sturm und Drang experience had attacked or by-passed. He returned to the masters of the Enlightenment: Kant, Voltaire, Diderot and Rousseau whom he now recognized as the progressive precursors of the French Revolution. In his later plays, his philosophical novels, and his exceptionally rewarding *Betrachtungen und Gedanken über verschiedene Gegenstände der Welt und der Literatur* (1803–05) he represents a critical modern humanism, not always relished by the society he judged, but enlivened by the memory of his participation in the impetuous protest movement of the Sturm und Drang.

The titanic rebel and his instinctual revulsion against convention is one of the central themes of the decade: it supplies the plot of J. A. Leisewitz's *Julius von Tarent* (1776), a tragedy of fratricide, much admired by Lessing and Schiller. Sophisticated in its structure and disciplined in its prose language, it is the work of a man of wide intellectual and social interests, a member of the *Hainbund* in Göttingen, a close acquaintance of Lessing and Nicolai and later a distinguished lawyer and public servant.

The Duke of Tarent rejects, because of her inferior rank, the girl loved by both his sons. The two brothers, each in his own way pursuing an enlightened political career, are by temperament incompatible. Guido is the proud soldier, Julius the dilatory philosophical mind who longs for a life in distant parts of the world, dedicated to the serene 'reasons of love'. In an attempt to free the girl from the convent to which she has been banished, Julius is killed by his brother, who is in turn murdered by the Duke. Rousseau's social criticism is here sharply confirmed: 'Must the human race, in order to be happy, be imprisoned in a state in which everyone is the slave of the other and none is free? Is everyone welded to the chain by which he holds his slave?'[18] Leisewitz tells the story in the hope that justice

[18] Ibid., I, p. 580.

and equity, illuminated by that love for which Julius dies, may modify the despotism that is mirrored in the harsh conflicts of the play.

The year 1776, in Germany so rich in dramatic statements of protest and defiance, produced one work of distinct historical interest: Heinrich Leopold Wagner's 'tragedy in six acts', *Die Kindermörderin* (1776), is concerned with the topical case of a mother's killing her illegitimate infant. The play proved successful precisely because of its strands of Richardsonian class morality, bourgeois sentimentality such as Diderot and Lessing had made appealing, and sudden flashes of that private despair which crystalized in so many incidents in Sturm und Drang writing. Goethe's later suggestion that Wagner plagiarized the 'Gretchen' episode in his *Faust* which he had read to him at the time has little weight: instead of the touching seduction and despair of a loving girl, the entanglement of Wagner's 'little Eve' is part of a facile mechanism by which the morality of the lower middle class and the transparent game of an irresponsible officer are brought into a conflict made pathetic more by the rhetoric of anger and denunciation than by an inescapable demonstration of true passion.

The stylistic and thematic mixture, here and elsewhere, of the trivial and the esctatic, of a momentary assertion of defiance and a relapse into the accepted social clichés is thoroughly characteristic of Sturm und Drang writing. Their aesthetic horizon was, at best, delineated in Louis-Sebastian Mercier's *Du Théâtre ou Nouvel Essai sur l'Art Dramatique* (1773), which attacked Boileau's neo-classicist poetics and called for a theatre close to contemporary life and providing moral and, by implication, political education. On Goethe's urging, Wagner translated it (in 1776). The Sturm und Drang playwrights turned away, particularly from Diderot, the master of Lessing and of popular critics such as J.J. Engel and J.J. Eschenburg, and rejected Diderot's concept of a 'domestic' drama as tepid sentimentality.

In his *Geschichte der romantischen Literatur* (1803–04), A.W. Schlegel roundly scores the misguided manner of the Sturm und Drang fraternity.[19] Theirs was, indeed, a disputation between strident voices, often more intent on shouting than on being considered. These gifted writers, impatient with the prevailing social and aesthetic order, who proclaimed in life as well as literature the cleansing power of irregularity, tended to discredit sustained thought and discourse, and preferred the man of violent action to the scholar, the aphoristic declamation on the stage to the book or the study.

[19] August Wilhelm Schlegel, *Kritische Schriften und Briefe*, ed. E. Lohner, Stuttgart: Kohlhammer, 1965, IV, 138.

Apotheosis of Feeling: Goethe's *Werther*

Goethe had eagerly seized upon Herder's manifold intellectual impulses and, during his few months as adjunct lawyer in Wetzlar, produced a number of poetic and essayistic pieces that were circulated among his friends. The most sustained work of that time was, of course, his lyrical novel, *Die Leiden des jungen Werthers*. But even the poetry of the three years before the composition of that story shows the degree to which the hectic spirit of the Sturm und Drang could be brought into focus and become productive in a mind uncommonly gifted and thoughtful. The several exuberant poems written in Strasbourg and soon after ('Willkommen und Abschied', 'Mailied') produce a tone and idiom altogether new in German poetry. An excited sensibility, free of all preconceived religious or social restraints, here defines itself in a natural setting that evokes, and responds to, the poet's abundant sense of life. Yet even these secular poems could scarcely have been written – or appreciated by their readers – without Klopstock's innovations in language, imagery and rhythm. Goethe is entirely aware of the poetic tradition and far from discarding available forms treats them with full recognition of their efficiency and resonance.

His immediate indebtedness in subject and attitude is to Herder; his commitment is to a kind of poetry which fashions the gift and power of the word into an instrument that testifies to an all-sustaining energy, to the presence not of any divine architect or of an inscrutable Godhead, but of a sense of being by which the community of feeling and speech is illuminated and strengthened. When Goethe translates the Ossianic 'Songs of Selma', he is fascinated by a poetic manner he thought truly inspired; in the dithyrambic 'Wanderers Sturmlied' (1772), he conveys the intermingling of physical self-awareness during a rain storm and a state of spiritual exaltation, speaking in the manner of Pindar, which Herder and Hamann had recognized as the epitome of ancient genius. Here, the very language of nature, non-syntactical and imperative, is heard by the attuned mind. 'Strange hymns and dithyrambs' he later called these verses, 'half nonsense', passionately chanted in free rhythms, the medium Klopstock had urged for the stirring expression of powerful feeling.[20] Such impulsive evocations were soon to be subjected to the scrutiny, not of trivializing reason, but of reflections that relate them to the chain of poetic experience and link the present to its antecedents in the 'sacred past'. 'Der Wanderer', also written in 1772, places the 'genius' in a classicist landscape, idyllic as well as heroic; Theocritus and his German imitator Gessner provide formal models, Goldsmith's 'The Traveller' (1764) the exemplary mood, Rousseau the nostalgic invocation of nature.

[20] Goethe *GA*, X, p. 570.

Goethe's preoccupation with matters of poetic design and structure was in these early days no less alert than 15 years later when the efficacy of form and its derivation from a concretely defined system of natural order became a paramount ingredient in his classicist theory of art. In one of the pieces that in 1776 introduce Wagner's translation of Mercier's *Du Théâtre*, he speaks of form in terms that are still somewhat imprecise but cautions against the then fashionable summary attacks on 'French' rules.

> There is a form, [he asserts] that is distinct from that [French] order, much as external perceptions are distinct from our inner sense; form cannot be grasped by hand but must be felt. Our heads must be able to survey what another head can comprehend, our hearts must feel what may fill that of another.[21]

The character of such an 'inner form' – reminiscent, of course, of Shaftesbury's concept – is not easy to define, because 'there is something false in every form, even that most sincerely felt, but it is once and for all the prism in which we gather the sacred rays of nature as a fiery vision in the heart of man', that prism is 'like the secret stone of alchemists, vessel and matter, fire and cooling furnace'.[22]

Whatever passion we may discern in Goethe's poetry before 1775, it is never uncontrolled or mere rhythmic effusion. The erotic give and take between the poet and nature lends to the poems of these years an almost ecstatic force, free from conventional religious formulae, yet profoundly religious in their recognition of a 'nexus' of all creation. In 'Mahomets Gesang' the river-image, as its connotations expand, embraces a whole cosmos of feeling and culture, life as movement, beginning and ending in the acknowledged power of a supreme being whose majesty is confirmed in the celebration of its splendour. In 'Ganymed', the poet himself is part of that ever-flowing, ever-stirring reality of an elemental nature; indeed, he exists only as he responds to the evidence of the creative genius. This is poetry that transcends its contemporary or historical models. The novelty is not difficult to recognize: the compelling tone of torrential sequences of exclamations and evocations, a blending of familiar images and brilliantly fresh contexts. Where Goethe uses classical mythology he means to illuminate anew an available canon; he is neither now nor later an allegorical poet. Classical images remain part of his effort at giving legitimacy to the intense fathoming of the present by analogies and metaphors drawn from antiquity. A powerful ode such as 'Prometheus' employs a persona who is of the class of superior beings not despite, but because of, his challenge to Zeus, that embodiment of established authority. The claims of this distant god are as legitimate as the assertion of self in

[21] Goethe *GA*, XIII, p. 48–9.
[22] Goethe *GA*, XIII, p. 48.

Prometheus's own 'burning heart', both are subject to the fateful compulsions of time.

What makes these outbursts of genius so remarkable and what distinguishes Goethe's early work from that of his Sturm und Drang contemporaries is the ever more articulate recognition that the assertion of powerful feeling as the chief vehicle of a sense of being carries within itself the problematical consequences of its own radicalism. The work of art must, after all, be received by an audience attuned to the tenor of the work; and the relationship of the artist to his often obtuse audience is the theme of a number of poems in which, more specifically than in the enthusiastic and impulsive essay on Shakespeare and that on the Strasbourg architect, the purpose and goal of the artist becomes the urgent topic. Here the genius, confronted by pedantic critics and their narrow-minded objections, defends his fresh vision and sensibility either proudly or with a touch of resignation ('Kenner und Künstler', 'Künstlers Morgenlied', 'Künstlers Abendlied', or 'Adler und Taube'). Three brief dramatic sketches, 'Künstlers Erdewallen', 'Des Künstlers Vergötterung' and later, 'Künstlers Apotheose' are further evidence of his weighing the claims of inspiration against those of artistic discipline.

Goethe's Strasbourg essay, 'Von deutscher Baukunst', written in the spirit of Herder, praises the great craftsman whose 'gothic' genius had produced an impressive example of truly 'characteristic art';[23] in July 1775 he undertakes a 'Third Pilgrimage to Erwin's Grave' and, as he views and meditates upon details of the magnificient structure of the minister, he reflects once again upon the difficulty of conveying the inexpressible, of stirring the imagination of those for whom the world is merely a shadow box in which images tumble past and disappear.

The problem of speaking intelligibly of the ineffable is a theological issue; for Goethe it had its aesthetic urgency. Many of his contemporaries seemed at that time to prefer the inarticulate testimonial outcry to shaped and unambiguous speech. He was not so much troubled by the noisy imprecision of the litanies of protest in Sturm und Drang dramaturgy as by the prevalent spiritualism that struck him as pretentious in the writings of some of his friends. F. von Stolberg, J.C. Lavater, Klopstock, even Herder, seemed to him at times dubious mystagogues, seducers of the spirit, false prophets.

By temperament self-critical and inclined to find relief in parody and persiflage, he now takes advantage of every pretext to exercise his skill in writing broad satire; where his friends sputter their social protest in blasts of inflated language, Goethe, always intent on expanding his literary equipment, attacks in several grotesque sketches the sham of much

[23] Goethe *GA*, XIII, p. 23–4.

current lofty discourse ('Satyros oder der vergötterte Waldteufel', 1773; 'Ein Fastnachtsspiel vom Pater Brey', 1774) by using strong and colourful speech, dialect, Biblical or pseudo-classical allusions and jingling verses in the manner of the mastersinger Hans Sachs.

All these more ephemeral pieces indicate Goethe's desire to speak effectively. But it is in a larger and more demanding formal design that his resolution to give a comprehensible account of the elusive substance of feeling is most magnificently realized. Within three months, from February to April, 1774, he writes *Die Leiden des jungen Werthers*, the description of the glory and the failure of a love so all-absorbing and all-demanding, so radical in its scope that it cannot be integrated satisfactorily in any social community. This is, of course, in the most general definition, the theme of Rousseau's *La Nouvelle Héloise*, and Rousseau's close identification of nature and sentiment is part of Goethe's vision. But the idyllic and serene beginning of *Werther* is deceptive: it is intended to draw the reader into hearing a confession which soon transcends the limit of understanding. The letters and diary-like accounts which convey Werther's growing terror of the inescapable consequences of his belief in total feeling and love become in the course of the narrative more and more oblique and desperate; they have little of that dramatic logic which made Richardson's epistolary novels such exciting documents of voyeurism.

Unlike Clarissa's seduction and pious atonement, Werther's love for Charlotte is not a public affair; his early record of happiness, inspired by his childlike faith in the nourishing presence of nature, the flame of love which suddenly envelops him and Charlotte – a charming but almost wholly neutral creature – the craving for companionship, all these soon turn into despair as Werther's love is rejected and shown to be beyond fulfilment. Homer as an invoked and remembered voice gives way to Ossian, creative and blissful nature to an overpowering cosmos in which Werther finds not rest but only the solace of surrender. His suicide is the inevitable consequence of a noble but unreflected insistence upon the authentic act, of the total consecration of self to an apotheosis of feeling.

To read *Werther* as a sentimental love story or to interpret it as primarily a document of social protest is to miss Goethe's intention. That Werther's temperament is in conflict with the attitudes, conventions, even the language of the aristocracy is, of course, significant enough; yet society is only the incidental determinant of his condition. His problems are not caused so much as put in relief by social disparities. The book was to make palpable and intelligible more, possibly, by its form than its melancholy plot, a state of mind of hitherto unrecorded complexity, of emotions ranging from delicate lyricism to the agonies of doubt, frustration and despair. At once precise in the sharply observed actuality of its

·tting and the carefully interlocked data of the pathological case history, *'erther* is, above all, a cry for understanding and sympathy in readers ho found themselves challenged and overwhelmed by an altogether new nd of serious narrative. For many of its details the novel draws on oethe's own exuberant love for another Charlotte. But beyond these ıtobiographical ingredients, the book conveys the first attempt on the art of a deeply perceptive but equally self-critical poet to show the roblematic, even tragic, implications of the discovery of feeling that had iven his generation a new sense of strength.

At the time of its publication, *Werther* seemed in an astonishing ıanner to formulate and explicate an experience that was, in one form r another, indistinctly shared by many – the experience of a clash etween the emerging self-confidence of subjective judgement on the one and, of the cognitive and sympathetic power of the emotions and, on the ther, of the established and stubbornly practiced forms of life, both ·udal and middle-class. The moving force of *Werther* lies not so much in ıe meticulous unfolding of Werther's love as in the lyrical radiance with hich his exalted state of mind illuminates the world about him. essner's *Idyllen* (1756, 1772), as well as his *Briefe über die Landschafts-ıalerei* (1772), so much admired by Diderot and Rousseau for their vocation of bucolic happiness and their suggestion of passing serenity, re here echoed, but free of any precious pastoral affectation.

When Goethe later spoke of the 'somnambulist' condition in which *Verther* was composed, he had long outgrown the state of mind that had roduced the novel; in fact, the work reveals a degree of artistic control ıat few could at the time have expecred of the young poet. The narrative ructure is carefully integrated, metaphors and motifs are skillfully ›ined and a range of moods from radiant happiness to utter despair is rchestrated in a score of exceptional coherence. At the same time, in resenting the agony of passion as well as its glory, the book contains ithin itself a critique of that total feeling which the generation so fur-›usly asserted against convention and decorum; it uncovers the inherent ontradictions of single-minded protest, indeed, it suggests its ultimate npotence. The narrator of Werther's 'Passion' transmits the self-pitying tterances of the lover with unmistakable irony; if the memorable phrase Vhat is the heart, what is the destiny of man?' insistently recurs through-ut the book, this is an admission not merely of the force but of the ambi-uity of that defiant faith in the subjective creativity which gave to the turm und Drang generation its ardour.

Even if we assume in the contemporary readers some familiarity with he great English and French models, with Richardson, Goldsmith and terne, *Manon Lescaut* and *La Nouvelle Héloise*, the novel must have truck them with the force of revelation: it proved to be a catalyst of

widely shared emotions as well as frustrations. Countless imitation
varied its most obvious features and it was not difficult for Nicolai, th
inveterate defender of rational demeanour, to compose a jejune persi
flage under the counter-title *Freuden des jungen Werthers* (1775). Ther
was, at any rate, in theme and form nothing of equal freshness in con
temporary fiction: no other novel, German or foreign, had rendered th
tragic progression of love imbued with religious fervour, but not sanc
tioned by institutions of church or society. If it was Goethe's hope tha
through this account of a mind in search of community he would crystal
lize the indefinite substance of Sturm und Drang passion, he contribute
indeed to a clearer notion of what fiction might achieve.

Fiction and Autobiography

Several factors, not least economic and technological, were at the time i
Germany about to produce an enormous increase in the printing an
consumption of books. The varied subject matter – didactic treatises o
conduct, travel sketches, sermons, casual poetry, moral and aestheti
effusions – which the obsolescent popular journals, following the mode
of the *Spectator* and familiar in Germany as 'Moralische Wochen
schriften' had for long offered to a middle-class public, was after 177
absorbed, often critically, in the substance of fiction. In the 30 year
between 1770 and 1800, more than 6500 novels were published, one
third of these actual or pretended translations from the French o
English. Neither the size nor the composition of the reading public of tha
time can be reliably assessed: it was largely anonymous, with an indis
criminate taste, eager to buy (or read in the increasingly popular lendin
libraries and reading societies) what legitimate publishers (P.E. Reich
the 'first publisher of the nation', Nicolai, Breitkopf, Cotta, Goeschen
Unger) and unauthorized reprinters of German and foreign works such a
C.G. Schmieder in Karlsruhe and I.G. Fleischhauer in Reutlingen had t
offer. The most enterprising purveyor of such reprints was J.T. vo
Trattner in Vienna, who, with offices in every German-speaking tow
from Cracow to Strasbourg, employed 200 editors and printers, and ha
some 40 presses constantly in use. During the 15 years of freedom fro
Austrian censorship he published no fewer than 1500 titles. It was unde
Trattner's imprint, specifically protected by an imperial patent, tha
most of the contemporary German authors were made available t
Austrian readers.

Merck's brief essay 'Über den Mangel des epischen Geistes in unsern
lieben Vaterland' (1778) is the shrewdest assessment of the shortcoming
and promises of the contemporary German novel. He deplores, as other
before and after him, the lack of native subject matter and a failure t
draw convincing characters; generous and faithful rendering – withou

political bias – of every-day social life seems to him preferable to the fashionable Sternean technique of endless reflections by an obtrusive narrator. Merck was familiar enough with the prevailing taste. An ever growing number of translations of French and English fiction reflected the appetite of German readers for glimpses of the fascinating world beyond their horizon and, in turn, made their own provinciality all the more apparent. Reports of travels in exotic lands, often leaving readers in some doubt as to the borderlines between fact and fiction, but satisfying a curiosity for other ways of life, assumed an important share in the developing book trade. Popular collections of 'remarkable accounts' of travel suggested that 'happiness' might be found in distant and unspoiled societies.

Friedrich Nicolai's previously mentioned 12 volumes of a *Beschreibung einer Reise durch Deutschland und die Schweiz, im Jahre 1781. Nebst Bemerkungen über Gelehrsamkeit, Industrie, Religion und Sitten* (1785–96) surveyed the cultural topography of the south, not without prejudice but with a huge array of statistical information. It was meant, in part, to counter the flood of subjective travel fiction which Sterne's *Sentimental Journey* (1768 in J.J. Bode's German translation) had occasioned. Novels such as J.G. Schummel's *Empfindsame Reise durch Deutschland* (1770–72) or Musäus's *Physiognomische Reisen* (1778–79) drew with measured irony on the native scene; of J.T. Hermes, the author of one of the most delightful of these, *Sophiens Reise von Memel nach Sachsen* (1769–73), Wieland was to say that 'among all our novelists [he] is supreme in his knowledge of the world and his treatment of German manners.'[24]

Another work of wide appeal, miscellaneous in its ingredients and rich in local colour, is T.G. von Hippel's *Lebensläufe nach Aufsteigender Linie* (1778 – 81). It interweaves several biographical strands with theological, psychological and social reflections, and permits the ever-present Sternean author-narrator to comment in a spirit of cheerful moralizing on provincial charms or absurdities, on the discrepancies between thought and action, feeling and prejudice. Products such as J.M. Miller's sanctimonious *Siegwart. Eine Klostergeschichte* (1776) or J.G. Müller's laboured 'comic tale', *Siegfried von Lindenberg* (1779), did not for long survive their inflated popularity; the liveliest in realistically drawn figures and well developed attacks upon fashionable educational theories is another novel by J.G. Schummel, *Spitzbart. Eine komi-tragische Geschichte für unser pädagogisches Jahrhundert* (1779). Striking in its acid tone and its pointedly grotesque encounters is the *Lebensgeschichte Tobias Knauts, des Weisen* (1773–76) by J.C. Wezel, an uncommonly

[24] *Der Teutsche Merkur*, 1773, April, p. 76–86.

perceptive observer, which exposes the inanity, pretentiousness and rudeness of German society.

Much of this literature was produced, translated or reviewed by writers whose life was, compared to England or France, remarkably insecure and unrewarding. The majority came from the agrarian population of the smaller towns and cities; many were the sons of artisans or were raised in the frugal severity of the Protestant vicarage, who chose the relatively easy study of theology in hopes of a modest appointment by patronage, or a life of poverty among the poor. Most depended upon a meagre income as tutor, librarian, translator or travelling companion; few could count on the sort of noble generosity that supported Klopstock for much of his life.

Despite the large number of popular or learned journals with their jealous coteries of contributors, all felt the lack of a cohesive literary establishment. It is true that Berlin and Vienna, Hamburg and Leipzig maintained their reputation as crossroads of literary traffic, but smaller communities depended upon the ambition and resources of the local ruler, secular or ecclesiastical, Protestant in the north, Catholic in Westphalia and throughout most of the south. To choose the profession of artist or writer in order to speak on matters of public concern meant either to acquiesce prudently in the existing social and cultural conventions – invoking perhaps a vision of universal humanism – or to assert the dignity of inwardness, of philosophical speculation, of poetry or of the illusionary world of the theatre.

Autobiographical accounts of the difficulties faced by those struggling to escape the restraints of their early life, poverty, bigotry or familial intolerance, towards some form of self-realization became increasingly fascinating. The author of one of these, Johann Heinrich Jung-Stilling, was a schoolmaster at 14, read Homer, Paracelsus and Jacob Boehme, studied medicine in Strasbourg and there met Herder and Goethe. He became a distinguished ophthalmologist and eventually professor of economics and political science at Marburg. The account of his *Jugend* (1777) Goethe helped to edit; it was followed by *Jünglingsjahre* (1778) and *Wanderschaft* (1778), testimonials to the quiet Christian fervour that sustained so much of German provincial life, and a touching picture of a characteristic middle-class existence, in which the hypochondriac, the servant of God, and the man of action are barely kept in balance. In several later novels, (*Theobald oder die Schwärmer*, 1784, and especially *Das Heimweh*, 1794–96), Jung-Stilling evokes once again the world of those secure in their quietistic faith, happy in a muted life, yet preparing for the richer prospects beyond.

A second autobiography that gained wide popularity has been touched on in an earlier context: it is Karl Philipp Moritz's *Anton Reiser*, written etween 1785 and 1794 but conveying the mood of the 1770s, the 'inner istory' of a young man whose oppressive childhood in poverty, quarrel-ome family life and sectarian harshness lead him to religious studies. Iumiliated by his dependence on the generosity of the wealthy, he scapes into the landscapes of poetry, of Young's *Night Thoughts*, of hakespeare, *Werther* and Bürger's 'Lenore'. At moments of elation he ranscends his depression; he attaches himself to A.W. Iffland, one of his ellow students (later the celebrated actor), and resolves to realize his reams on the stage – that refuge of the imagination from misfortune nd oppression. The work concludes with the bankruptcy of the company f actors whom Reiser has joined – an open ending that suggests his etermination to disavow all harmonizing prospects. Moritz's self-ortrait is an analytical study of singular intelligence, specific in its escription of social and psychological conflicts and aware of its symp-omatic character. No other work of the time renders with greater under-tanding the agonizing discrepancy between an obtuse but powerful eality and its defiance, not so much in shrill protest as in imaginative rojections. It is at once a realistic document of life in poverty and the onfession of private and intimate anguish; as such it is a link between the turm und Drang mentality and the young Romantic writers whom Ioritz was to encounter in Berlin.

The third of these remarkable narratives of self-scrutiny, Ulrich räker's *Lebensgeschichte und natürliche Ebentheuer des Armen Iannes im Tockenburg* (1789) offers, without claiming to be 'elevated' iterature, an engaging picture, uncoloured by false idealism, of a lebeian' life. Patched together from some 4,000 pages of diary, Bräker ells of his youth and manhood as a shepherd and labourer who is pressed nto service in the Prussian army, deserts, and returns to his native witzerland to live miserably as a peasant. Later he joined one of the Swiss Moral Societies' for popular enlightenment, wrote a study of the cotton rade and, in 1780, put together his thoughts on the 36 Shakespeare plays vhich J.J. Eschenburg had translated: 'Etwas über William Shakespeares chauspiele von einem armen ungelehrten Weltbürger, der das Glück enoß, ihn zu lesen'. The world of the poor and disadvantaged is nowhere escribed so concretely as in Bräker's *Lebensgeschichte*, free of the athos of self-pity, and clear-headed in its rejection of the condescending latitudes of social benevolence.

Disaffection with an unrewarding life is the common denominator of nuch German writing in the 1770s. In the novels of W. Heinse the tedious resent is transcended by the radical assertion of sensuous passion. An dmirer of Winckelmann, and attracted by Wieland's charmed Greeks, Ieinse places his classical (or Renaissance) figures in settings of intoxi-ating light and colour. His first work, *Laidion, oder die Eleusinischen*

Geheimnisse (written 1771, published 1774) exemplifies the fundamental resolve of the Sturm und Drang generation to discredit the power of the petty courts, to challenge in violent gestures the established conventions social as well as artistic, and in fantasies to seek relief from the tedium of the commonplace. *Laidion* is the description, sent posthumously by a 'divine hetaera' to her lover, of the enchantments of Elysium, where Orpheus, Solon and Aspasia have judged her, and where she now recalls her life on earth as an incomparable beauty and the friend of brilliant men. Far from suggesting a pallid admiration for Greek serenity, Heinse projects that 'dionysian' view of Greece which Nietzsche was to formulate more coherently in his *Geburt der Tragödie* (1871).

Heinse's most impressive work, though written some years later, reiterates the Sturm und Drang faith in a life of exceptional dimensions. *Ardinghello und die glückseeligen Inseln* (1787) is the first major German novel in which the career of an artist is related in a hectic but brilliant sequence of encounters between over-charged, amoral and utterly splendid men and women. A driving spirit, passionate artistry, philosophical subtlety and immense energy are combined in the young painter and singer, Ardinghello Frescobaldi, a sixteenth-century Florentine nobleman, whose friends (especially the liberated Fiordimona) form a company of demonstrative flamboyance: love, the revenge of past crimes, piracy and the utopian dream of an ideal republic on Naxos and Paros provide the incidents of a plot which is itself less important than Heinse's descriptions of Venice, Florence, Lake Garda, Genoa, Naples and Rome, or the lengthy discussions of works of art and of philosophical issues. In a celebrated passage, a conversation on the roof of the Pantheon, Heinse expounds his pantheistic views of the universe and his desire to merge with the cosmos in total abandonment to sensuous beauty.

If *Ardinghello* is an encomium to art, it is specifically the enchantment of music (on which he had written earlier, 1771, in *Musikalische Dialogen*, published 1805), that gives some thematic coherence to the indifferent plot of *Hildegard von Hohenthal* (1795–96). Hildegard, a paragon of beauty, and a magnificent musical (and linguistic) talent, meets at the court of her uncle the conductor Lockmann, from whose exorbitant love she escapes to Italy. There she sings, disguised as a castrato, and stirs Rome by a performance of one of Lockmann's compositions. Eventually she succumbs to the charms of an English nobleman while Lockmann, now famous, marries a lovely Italian girl. What the novel lacks in narrative skill, it amply provides in discourses on music and art. Written more than 20 years after his first novel *Laidion*, this late work is a deliberate mêlée of styles and levels of appeal: it juxtaposes moments of great delicacy and scenes of pointed tawdriness, the display of noble and bourgeois manners, the disguises and secret meetings of the sentimental novel and encounters of uninhibited physical joy. Whatever the risks of offering such a disjointed composition, Heinse hoped above all to avoid the vacuous preciousness of trivial fiction. In his work as well as in letters written from Rome, a temperament initially close to that of the Sturm und Drang finds an idiom, more impressive and original than that of most of his contemporaries: he was an artist of considerable seriousness whose total commitment to an aesthetic creed assures him a rank of exceptional importance. 'I never saw', Hölderlin was to say, 'such limitless intellectual culture and so much childlike simplicity.'[25]

The Whirlwind Spirit: J.H. Füssli

The illumination of an unsatisfactory present by the demonstration of greatness powerfully felt, whether Homeric or Ossianic, Biblical or historical, which the men of letters hoped to achieve in their dramatic or poetic overstatements, is most radically demonstrated in the work of the Swiss painter and writer, Johann Heinrich Füssli. The theologian J.C. Lavater in Zürich, that genius in cultivating intense personal relationships with every contemporary in whom he recognized the spark of spiritual affinity, first drew attention to this exceptional talent.

The son of a well-known engraver, Füssli received his early education in theology and the classics, and his introduction to literature, to Homer, Horace and the Nibelungen saga, to Dante, Milton and Shakespeare from the revered critic Johann Jakob Bodmer. He left his native Zürich in 1763, worked in Berlin for a short time with J.G. Sulzer on his *Allgemeine Theorie der schönen Künste* and as an aspiring writer met several of the men of letters. His poetry, some 40 pieces produced to that time, chiefly odes in the spiritual manner of Klopstock, remain within the diction of the late rococo and have little of the confessional directness of the Sturm und Drang. His visions went into his painting: 'Since coming to England', he wrote in 1765 to a friend, 'German literature is dead for me.'[26]

He moved to London in 1764, where he became known as 'the wild Swiss', living precariously on the fringe of the world of art and the theatre. He translated Winckelmann's *Gedanken über die Nachahmung der Griechischen Werke* as *Reflections on the Painting and Sculpture of the Greeks* (1765), omitting the cardinal word 'imitation'. Stirred by the break between Rousseau and Hume, he read Rousseau (whom he later met in Paris), and concluded that the individual and society seemed forever in conflict with one another and that art and morality were fundamentally incompatible. Füssli's *Remarks on the Writings and*

[25] Friedrich Hölderlin, *Sämtliche Werke und Briefe*, ed. G. Mieth, Munich, Hanser, 1970, II, p. 724.

[26] H. Füssli, *Briefe*, ed. W. Muschg, Basel, Schwabe, 1942, p. 111.

Conduct of J.J. Rousseau (1767) maintains that the arts are a divine gift which elevate by terrifying and overwhelming; here is the key to his later obsessive and violent work.

Reynolds encouraged him to become a serious painter and from 1770 to 1778 he was in Rome together with the Swedish sculptor Johan Tobias Sergel and a group of English and Scottish artists, John and Alexander Runciman, John Brown, George Romney, James Northcote and the sculptor Thomas Banks. Here he developed the bold stylistic features that make his work so singularly fascinating. Focusing upon the human figure, upon nudes of excruciating intensity, vehicles of dark and tortured passion in a vaguely defined but ominous space, he produced extraordinary drawings, dream projections and confessions of an agonized mind. Michelangelo, the creator of figures and groups as incarnations of energy, soon replaced Winckelmann as his ideal.

In 1779 he returned to London and henceforth moved, awkwardly but defiantly, among the academicians, becoming himself a member (and Keeper) of the Royal Academy and professor of painting. Blake was captivated by Füssli's eccentric designs and in a famous ditty acknowledged his affection:

> The only Man that I e'er knew
> Who did not make me almost spew
> Was Fuseli: he was both Turk and Jew – –
> And so, dear Christian Friends, how do you do.[27]

While undoubtedly in turn sympathetic to Blake's vision, and of considerable influence upon his art, Füssli was indifferent to its mystical and prophetic impulses. In 1792 he published, as a gesture of continuing friendship, a translation of Lavater's *Essays on Physiognomy*, adding some of his own studies of expressive heads and figures and including four engravings by Blake. Blake's name was, as yet, known only to a circle of friends; Füssli enjoyed wide admiration. 'Fuseli is a man of genius' George III remarked to Benjamin West in 1804. 'He is not only an able man', West replied, 'but is distinguished as a literary character and known to all of Europe'.[28]

His fame was to rest on one of the most characteristic of his paintings, the celebrated 'Nightmare' (1781): a sleeping girl, head and arms dropping over the edge of her bed, is haunted by a dwarfish monster sitting on her stomach while a fantastic beast, the nightmare, stares through the bed curtains. The sense of horror and mystery in that memorable work reflects the pathological tensions in Füssli which give even to his more

[27] *The Complete Writings of William Blake*, ed. Geoffrey Keynes, London, Nonesuch Press, 1957, p. 551.

[28] R.C. Alberts, *Benjamin West*, Boston, Houghton Mifflin, 1978, p. 313.

ademic work its feverish, whirling aura. In his formidable dramatic sions, he focused upon widely shared poetic themes and motifs that rved and galvanized an imagination obsessed by fantasies of demonic ality. Füssli's much admired illustrations of the great poets, of akespeare and Milton, are more than mere pictorial translations of erary scenes and characters; they explore symbolic situations, reconler familiar incidents and are evidence of a mind who rebels against a ceptive faith in equanimity, fragile order and reason.

Füssli's contemporaries in Germany recognized the force of his talent; avater had been the first to speak of him to Klopstock, to Herder and oethe. 'He is the most original genius I know', he wrote to Herder in '74, 'sheer force, abundance and calm! A warrior's fury, yet feelings of e highest sublimity . . . . His spirits are whirlwinds, his servants flames fire! He walks on the wings of the wind. His laughter is mockery of Hell id his love – murderous lightning.'[29] Goethe was deeply moved by his rly work ('What fire and fury there is in that man!')[30]; some of Füssli's etches inspired the 'Witches' Kitchen' scene in *Faust*. When, some years later, Goethe speaks more critically of that divided and selfstructive character, and the dream distortions of the 'phantomist', he uld no longer accept the effusive energy of his illustrations: 'Poetry and inting are in Füssli constantly at war . . . one respects him as a poet, it as a painter he makes the viewer impatient.'[31]

Goethe's distinction points by implication to Füssli's historical contriition: unlike Lessing (and the mature 'classicist' Goethe) he intended to eak down the borders between the genres. He denied that it was the nction of painting to lead, through the pure line and historical subject atter, to a detached contemplation of beauty, while poetry was to stir e imagination to a sense of life. In making painting the instrument of ission and powerful emotions, Füssli transcends an aesthetic principle which eighteenth-century theory had strictly adhered. What made his t so striking for his early friends, and so suspect for later critics such as e German traveller and essayist, Georg Forster (who reported in 1789 Füssli's role among the London artists)[32], was precisely his deliberate ixing of 'poetic' or literary, and painterly intentions.

Füssli did not explicitly relate his work to the political issues of the time; turned his furious agonies inward and produced monstrous dreams of xual violence, haunting images of a deeply troubled self. In his illustraons of accepted literary masterpieces, he sought social conformity, but

29 H. Füssli, *Briefe*, op. cit., p. 168.
30 Goethe *GA*, XVIII, p. 263.
31 Goethe *GA*, XIII, p. 119.
32 Georg Forster, *Werke*, ed. G. Steiner, Frankfurt, Insel, 1970, III, p. 158–9.

even these illustrations, like Blake's, pull the reader beyond the pa
into a mood of puzzling and bizarre designs. His strength as well as h
defects were characteristic of a perplexed generation whose vehement b
unreflected rebellion against established modes of life and agair
traditional canons of art resulted in a groping for expressive forms th
remained largely idiosyncratic until they were absorbed in the Romant
experience.

Attacks on Feudal Abuses

The militant tenor of much Sturm und Drang writing is, of course,
reflection of dissatisfaction with certain aspects of contemporary politic
practice. Yet, the aggressive protests against abuses by the nobilit
against harsh and lawless behaviour, against the ruthless exploitation
the lower-class citizenry – from tenant farmers to clergy and writers
all these are by no means indications of an articulated progressive poli
ical philosophy; they are part of a 'climate of opinion' created by enligh
ened advocates of humane social relationships. A popular journalist suc
as W.L. Wekhrlin, for instance, devoted his life to ever-renewed attac
on injustice, on the terror of the arbitrary death penalty, on corruption
high places. Impressed by the popular reforms of the Austrian court
he lived in Vienna from 1767 to 1776 – and determined to make use
the available measure of freedom of speech, he published a journal
travel sketches (*Anselmus Rabiosus' Reise durch Ober-Deutschlan*
1778) and a number of short-lived magazines and almanacs (*Felleise*
1778; *Chronologen*, 1779–81; *Das Graue Ungeheuer*, 1784–87; *Hype*
boreische Briefe, 1788–90). Wekhrlin's fearless views, although fund
mentally inspired by monarchical sympathies and by regrets at th
decline of patrician values, led several times to his arrest. His social co
victions were those of Montesquieu, Voltaire and the Encyclopedist
rational, utopian and libertarian and, during the last years of his life,
sympathy with the Revolution. What gives to Wekhrlin's writings hi
torical significance is their wide circulation, especially in the Cathol
southern states where obscurantism and intolerance were far mo
evident than elsewhere.

A talent in some respects as restless as Füssli, though more direct
intent on public effectiveness, was the Swabian poet, musician and poli
ical pamphleteer, C.F.D. Schubart. A theologian by training, he wa
from 1769 organist and director of music at the Stuttgart court of Duk
Karl Eugen. Dismissed, and in 1773 expelled from Württemberg becau
of his sharp criticism of court and clergy, he edited in Augsburg and late
in Ulm a literary and political journal, *Deutsche Chronik* (1774–77
Because of his ridicule of one of the Duke's mistresses, he was in 177
kidnapped by order of Karl Eugen and held without trial for 10 year

Released in 1787 upon the intercession of the Prussian court, he was once again installed as music director of the Stuttgart theatre and as court poet.

While the immediate targets of Schubart's *Deutsche Chronik* were the iniquities of Karl Eugen's court, his energy and courage rallied widespread anti-aristocratic sentiments and sympathy for national and humanitarian causes. He was intensely stirred by the work of the Sturm und Drang playwrights and applied social as well as artistic criteria in his reviews of current literature, of *Goetz* and *Werther*, of Lenz's *Hofmeister*, Klinger's plays or of J.C. Wezel's novels.

Schubart's poetry was among the most popular of the age: influenced by Klopstock, it has a lightness of touch and an eloquence which quicken, particularly, the thrust of his political poems ('Die Fürstengruft', 'Kaplied', 'Der Gefangene' in *Gedichte aus dem Kerker*, 1785). His attacks on wilful government and despotism made him a widely admired spokesman of decency in the face of feudal corruption: Schiller's *Die Räuber* contains much of the spirit of Schubart's 'Zur Geschichte des menschlichen Herzens' (1775).

In his posthumously published *Ideen zu einer Ästhetik der Tonkunst* (1806) he provides brief essays on such topics as 'Musical Colouring', 'Musical Genius', 'Musical Expression' and miscellaneous reflections by a writer and musician who urges vivid feeling as the source of a special sort of insight and who seeks to relate this impulse to the requirements of craftsmanship and of the musical practice of the time. He is aware of the shift from the *style galante* to the more rousing musical forms of the 1760s and 1770s, and above all of the increasing musical receptivity of middle-class audiences that were now admitted to the performances of court orchestras. The infusion of sentimental or 'expressive' moods in the music of Bach's sons, and the touching and delicate sensibility in the compositions of J.J. Quantz, G. Benda or J.F. Reichardt are indications of that extension and liberalization of the imagination which Schubart eagerly shared. Like Füssli, he remained throughout his life the restless genius so characteristic of the unquiet temper of the Sturm und Drang.

The Young Schiller: Ambivalence of Greatness

There can be no doubt that Schubart's personality and ideas had a strong influence upon Friedrich Schiller, the most talented of the young Swabian writers. Schiller's philosophical, theological and political beliefs were formed in the atmosphere of Württemberg life, enlightened yet deeply committed to pietism.

The social convictions of that community had been significantly shaped by Friedrich Karl von Moser, a political scientist of firm religious beliefs, who was the most vigorous Swabian critic of feudal despotism.

He defended the Württemberg citizens in their recurring conflicts with Duke Karl Eugen and, as a result, was for several years imprisoned without trial. His famous tract, *Der Herr und der Diener geschildert mit Patriotischer Freyheit* (1759) projects an equitable society and pleads for a benign ruler within a framework of 'progressive' absolutism. In Moser's spirit, Schubart addressed himself eloquently to the relationship between religious and political duties, between the claims of a Christian morality and the limited obedience due a government whose secular power tends to become absolute and autocratic.

Schiller's education was at the *Karlsschule*, that training ground for the Swabian court bureaucracy, for the military, architects and physicians – an altogether modern institution over which Duke Karl Eugen exercised the severest control. It left in him throughout his life the tension between a belief in an absolute, divinely sanctioned order and the fallible human being, free to choose between redemption and damnation. The issue which remained for long the centre of Schiller's thought is the possibility of reconciling divine and secular law, the duties of the faithful and those of the citizen. Nowhere else in Germany were these problems felt and argued so seriously as in Württemberg, where a tradition of activist piety and the rule by a secular power of extraordinary absolutism coincided.

From beginning to end Schiller's thinking is dramatic, his poetry and his plays explicate his intellectual preoccupations. Not only his earliest play, *Die Räuber*, but his thesis for a medical degree and his first poems, all revolve around the conflict between a presumably perfect universal order and the ambiguous role which man – part animal, part angel – at once determined and potentially free, is condemned to play within the divine creation. If the artist, Schiller argues in the language of the early Enlightenment, is to share in the divinity by recreating that universe in his work, he is performing, with total dedication, a task which all men are called upon to attempt.

Like Lessing, Schiller regarded the drama as the most telling mirror of the psychological make-up of man, in which the disparate impulses of the heart, the proudest and the basest of his capacities, should become visible to even the dullest eye. The theatre, he was convinced, is the 'school of practical wisdom', the most efficacious instrument for the education of man. On the stage, moral values and alternatives of social action may be clarified, and the most puzzling motives and dispositions, 'the secret clockwork of the soul' can be made intelligible.

In Schiller's first play, *Die Räuber* (1781, 1782) the conflict between 'nature' and 'mind' produces a dialectic movement of powerful dramatic effect. Two contrasting forms of thought are pushed to their logical culmination: the brothers Karl and Franz Moor represent principles and ideas that are, as always in Schiller's work, given not only unambiguous psychological concreteness but the flourish of rhetorical eloquence. Franz, sceptical and materialistic, denies the coherence and truth of any transcending order. Creation seems to him the result of a senseless, perverse act: it is, he maintains, by no natural law that as the second-born son, mis-shapen and unattractive, he should be excluded from his father's inheritance. He is resolved to assert his dominance over a capricious system and intends, rationally and in the manner of an enlightened despot, to deny Karl his rights. Instead of the letter in which Karl begs his father's forgiveness for his wild escapades as a student, Franz produces false evidence to show Karl's reckless conduct, and is authorized to act as he sees fit: he rejects Karl's plea.

Karl himself is a superbly drawn Sturm und Drang figure, passionately determined to bring about a Rousseauean, 'naturally' ordered society, and a rebel against depraved absolutist morality. Having received Franz's letter, he turns in violent defiance against a society that has arbitrarily excluded him, and resolves, with the help of a band of outcasts, to realize his vision of divine justice. As he furtively returns once more to see his native castle, he is recognized by Franz – who plans to kill him but is paralysed in a sudden frantic awareness of his moral bankruptcy. Overwhelmed by the anguish of his satanic estrangement from God, he kills himself. Karl, having caused his father's death by admitting to be the leader of the band of outlaws, gives himself up.

This melodramatic plot proved on the stage tremendously effective. At the first performance, 'the theatre was like a madhouse, eyes rolling, clenched fists, hoarse cries in the audience. Weeping, strangers fell into one another's arms, women close to fainting tottered towards the exit. It was a state of total dissolution, as though from the mists of chaos a new creation had broken forth.'[33] Flamboyant, almost Baroque, in its language, the play contains the essence of Schiller's early moral philosophy. Virtue and evil, rebelliousness and resignation, are here not clearly separate spheres of judgement but the interlaced ingredients in a complicated psychological mechanism. There is a certain sublime genius, Schiller insists, in both brothers; greatness of idealism in Karl and greatness of devilish depravity in Franz. Both are 'extraordinary men' and it is this projection of a superhuman dimension, as well as the explicit confrontation between utopian protest and corruption, that gave to the play its immense appeal among the Sturm und Drang generation. Its provocative message was readily understood: Duke Karl Eugen banned it at once. He threatened to incarcerate Schiller, who thereupon fled (1782)

[33] A. Pichler, *Chronik des Grossherzogl. Hof- und Nationaltheaters in Mannheim*, Mannheim, 1879, p. 67–8.

from Stuttgart to Mannheim, whose theatre seemed likely to support his dramatic plans.

Nobility of intention overwhelmed by the scheming of a depraved establishment is the recurring theme of Schiller's early work. Much of his youthful poetry, contained in his *Anthologie auf das Jahr 1782*, with its grandly evocative odes or gloomy nocturnal pieces, is indicative of this conflict. He experiments, as yet, with received forms; ballads alternate with occasional pieces, echoes of Klopstock are neutralized by the convivial tone of the poets of the *Hainbund*, fiery odes stand next to amorous effusions. The spiritual dualism between affirmation and impotence, life and death, ideal and actuality is barely reconciled in insistent if florid rhetoric. Where he suggests a Faustian groping for the unknown, he advances merely to the threshold of nothingness. Resentment of the inhumanity of despotism is countered by a Rousseauean proclamation of universal sympathy and the assertion of a divine presence felt in even the most disparate phenomena. These pieces, however tentative and deficient, and later characterized by Schiller himself as 'wild products of youthful dilettantism'[34] are nevertheless highly self-conscious exercises towards the later philosophical poetry in which reflection and imagination are more coherently fused.

In *Die Verschwörung des Fiesco* (1783), his second play, he portrays a political figure whose involvement in matters of state and in the intrigues that produce success or failure is here shown in its specific and human context. The ambivalence of greatness and power is dramatically unfolded in an historical setting. Liberty or despotism, morality or force are the alternatives that create the action: in the struggle for Genoa, Andreas Doria, the venerable Doge of Venice, and his nephew hope to win the contest which Fiesco, a fiercely patriotic Genoese, secretly opposes. Fiesco himself plans to rule Genoa; but, however noble his concern for the freedom of his native city, his friends fear that he will rule dictatorially. As he is about to announce the rejection of the Dorias, his plan is betrayed and although mercy is promised, Fiesco now proclaims his own rule and refuses all pleas to remain loyal to the Doge. Verrina, his closest friend who knows of Fiesco's ambition, fails to move him to reason and eventually kills him. The legitimate rule of the Dorias continues.

The play was not a success: its intention was not immediately clear. What Schiller wanted to show was the nature of 'republican freedom': it is Fiesco's tragic flaw that he hopes to win freedom for Genoa only to sacrifice it to his own craving for power. Verrina, who loves him, yet fears for the liberty of the republic after Fiesco's victory, is his antagonist. The

[34] F. Schiller, *Sämtliche Werke*, ed. G. Fricke and H. Göpfert, Munich, Hanser, 1965–7, I, p. 862. (Henceforth: Schiller *SW*).

dramatic action is largely the means of explicating Fiesco's contradictory personality, the chief object of Schiller's curiosity. The noble and the base, the impulsive and the calculating, public spirit realized at the price even of crime and deception – these were motifs already touched upon in *Die Räuber*; here they are contained in a single personality. Even though the setting is now elaborately historical and the propelling concerns political, it is the complicated character that seems to suggest a Shakespearean sort of tragedy.

Schiller's first plays were written at remarkable speed. The third of these, barely a year later, *Kabale und Liebe* (1784), is a 'bourgeois tragedy', a genre which Lessing's *Miss Sara Sampson* and *Emilia Galotti* had established on the German stage and which Schiller now charged with a severe and entirely unsentimental current of social and political criticism. The theme of the play is the clash between middle-class values – honour, love, independence, honesty – and the exploitation and repression of men and women by prejudice, arbitrariness and political scheming. Bourgeois pride determines the action; in speech and gestures as well as in the assertion of social self-confidence, it is an eminently convincing document of contemporary issues and feelings.

Once again the ingredients of a complicated plot are assembled and exploited with the technical skill of a consummate logician. Ferdinand, the son of a nobleman, and Luise, the daughter of a bourgeois court musician, cannot be permitted to marry – the code of both classes would not tolerate it. Moreover, Ferdinand's father, who has obtained his high office of President through corruption and murder, is determined to marry his son to his duke's discarded mistress. Luise's reluctance to elope is misinterpreted by Ferdinand. By a devious intrigue, the President has arrested the musician and his wife and now suggests that Luise can save her parents from the death penalty for insubordination only if she will write a spurious love letter to a high official at court and swear that she acted of her own free will. Ferdinand learns of the letter, but Luise, bound by her oath, cannot clear herself. She hopes to die with Ferdinand, and in that way annul her oath and restore her innocence. Her father's protest that suicide wilfully breaks the bond of family paralyses her action: she can neither die nor live honestly. In the end, the lovers take poison together, Luise tells Ferdinand the truth about the letter and forgives him for doubting her. He, in turn, moved by her example, forgives his father.

Religious convictions, the sanctity of the oath, the unquestioned respect for the father, the deep sense of dependence upon the laws of God are crossed and challenged by the realities of the secular, the feudal system. The conscience of the middle class is, in fact, made itself an instrument of oppression by the representatives of absolutist power.

Two weeks after the triumphant first performance of *Kabale und Liebe*, Schiller saw on the same stage a performance of *Emilia Galotti*. Lessing had died only three years earlier, yet the difference between these two 'bourgeois tragedies' must have struck the spectators as symptomatic of a changing political climate. *Emilia Galotti* ends with a moral compromise: Galotti saves the honour of his daughter by her death; in *Kabale und Liebe*, Schiller denies, by Ferdinand's and Luise's deaths, that the assertion of honour can compensate for the loss of life. The Prince's guilt in Emilia's death is not punished, but Ferdinand's father surrenders to justice and thus confirms the moral judgement of the audience. By attacking the decrepitude of the feudal system, by pitting its arrogant power against the desperate pride of the middle class and its own weapon of humane values, *Kabale und Liebe* is closest in spirit to the expectations of the Sturm und Drang.

It was another 'portrait of family life' such as the Sturm und Drang, with Diderot in mind, found so appealing, which Schiller now planned to write as one of the texts contracted for by the Mannheim stage. *Don Carlos*, begun in 1783 was some three years in the writing. He was, during that time, much involved in sporadic theatrical matters, read the French classicists and Shakespeare, wrote reviews, and projected a 'Mannheim Dramaturgy' of which only an important affirmation of the civilizing effect of the stage ('Die Schaubühne als moralische Anstalt betrachtet') actually appeared. Like many intelligent young men with literary ambitions, he published a journal (*Rheinische Thalia*, 1785), which, apart from providing a vehicle for his own work, he hoped might help to overcome the isolation and frustration of German writers.

For his new play he wavered between lofty and demanding iambic pentameters and the easier (and more bluntly effective) prose speech of which he had shown himself such a master. When the play appeared in 1787 – Schiller was not yet 28 – its design had gradually undergone substantial modifications, the result as much of his astonishing growth in artistic skill as of a change in his outlook on life. The conflict emotionally reflected in his previous writing, and in that of many of his contemporaries, between an optimistic affirmation of a wise and generous (divine) order and the grim realization of palpable defects in men and institutions is now developed more objectively and with a clearer awareness of the legitimacy of power.

He had at first planned to repeat the pattern of antagonism, familiar from *Kabale und Liebe*, between a tyrannical father, King Philipp of Spain, and his idealistic son, Don Carlos. Love, Schiller wanted to show, the love particularly of Don Carlos for the Queen Elizabeth, who was originally to be his own wife, is here denied by the arbitrary exercise of political power and its ruthless instrument, the Inquisition. But this issue oon struck him as unrewarding. In the figure of Marquis Posa, he added a new dimension. Posa, Don Carlos's close friend, has just returned from he Netherlands and now appears as the advocate not only of the uppressed but of a faith in republican generosity, of a universal humane rder and of freedom of conscience that will turn fearful obedience into oy and happiness. (Schiller's celebrated ode 'An die Freude' was written n 1785, though not set to music by Beethoven until some 35 years later.) The collision between idealistic fervour and the stern institutional realties of absolutist and clerical power is the chief theme of the play. Don Carlos is involved in a series of intrigues; he and Marquis Posa, by their lemands for freedom and humanity, challenge a ruler whose commitnent to the omnipotence of the state is inexorable but whose personal greatness gives credibility to a struggle between two legitimate philosphies. Posa must pay for his convictions with his life; Carlos, resolved o carry on the fight for liberty, is arrested and handed over to the Inquisition.

As a piece of craftsmanship, *Don Carlos* is not without flaws – Schiller himself sought (1788) to explain his intentions in 'Briefe über *Don Carlos*' – but it is a brilliant testimony to the deepening of Schiller's understanding of the capacity of the dramatic form to illuminate the ramifications of an intellectual issue. The proclamation in *Don Carlos* of freedom of hought and expression, the clash of power and conscience, the achievenent through the tragic action of the play not merely of compassion but of judgement and resolution – all these indicate the widening range of Schiller's intellectual resources.

Don Carlos marks the end of that show of blunt protest and rebellion in which the Sturm und Drang generation, often more violent than coherent, had declared its dissatisfaction with the prevailing forms of life, with political practices and religious attitudes as well as with notions of aesthetic effectiveness. In Schiller's youthful work all these are powerful mpulses; yet, the four plays show the gradual shift from anarchical lespair towards a vision of a new community dedicated to universal idealsm and the free play of untried energies of mind and heart. What had hitherto been vaguely felt in Rousseauean metaphors became, in *Don Carlos* and through the pathos of the living and dying Marquis Posa, the proclaimed articles of the French Revolution. It was entirely appropriate that a few years later, in August 1792, the Paris Assembly should have awarded to 'Le Sieur Gille, publiciste allemand' the title of honorary French citizen. It is true that when the document reached Schiller in March 1798, the notification seemed to come 'from the realm of the lead': those who had signed it had long since been executed.[35]

[35] Goethe, *GA*, XX, p. 545.

The success of a novel-fragment, *Der Geisterseher* (1787, 1789) was due primarily to its subject matter, drawn from contemporary sources, in which political scheming, crime, and fascination with the supernatural form the ingredients (Aus den Memoires des Grafen von O**). It is one of the best examples of a 'Gothic' novel in which supra-human machinery triumphs over the capacities of the individual. For Schiller it was an exercise of a formal sort: in terse prose he organizes an intricate plot, creates suspense through a chain of mysterious events and holds the reader's attention by involving strange characters in puzzling relationships. It was to be his only major narrative work; had he continued as a novelist he might well have written superior fiction, accomplished in design, rich in philosophical reflection and a sense of the magic of storytelling.

Increasingly Schiller now sought to move from the rendering of individual conflict and alienation towards a comprehension of the historical circumstances in which these problems could be shown to have general validity. The study of history, of that great spectacle of human aspirations and failures, seemed to him the indispensable premise for an understanding of the existential tension between freedom and compulsion. That was to be the theme of his plays to come, as well as of the essays in which he elaborated his philosophy of culture.

His interest in historical scholarship took on paramount importance: in 1786 he was ready to turn from specifically literary enterprises to a more systematic investigation of historical and philosophical problems. Two years later he had completed *Geschichte des Abfalls der Vereinigten Niederlande* and planned the publication of a series of historical memoirs. His studies were, of course, far from mere antiquarian research: he instinctively focused upon the dramatic collision of individual effort and the fateful coercion of events. The perception of a tragic force in history, forever challenged by an indefatigable human will, remained the mainspring not merely of his belief in the prospects of freedom but of his resolve to speak urgently to German readers whose role in the coming revolutionary struggles and whose willingness to accept a new spiritual and social order, he was determined to direct and strengthen.

Economic as well as strategic considerations made it imperative for him to seek an attachment in whatever form to one of the more liberal and lively courts. He had found the Duke of Weimar interested in him as man of letters and historian, and in 1789 he was appointed lecturer in history at the University of Jena. There and in nearby Weimar he could count on the stimulating presence of incisive and productive minds. He was soon to meet Wieland and Herder and, before long, Goethe, who had just returned from his two years' stay in Italy and with whom, after an initial period of polite but cool exchanges, he was to form a close friendship.

3

New Horizons

Goethe in Weimar

In 1775 Johann Wolfgang Goethe accepted an invitation by the Duchess Anna Amalia of Weimar to join the court, at first as companion to her son, the young Duke Karl August, but soon as an active member of the duke's administration. He was aware of entering into a commitment that would impose upon his exuberant and independent personality not only the demands of an aristocratic society but the obligations inherent in a position of increasing public responsibility. Weimar, the residence of the duchy of Saxe-Weimar-Eisenach, was a town of some 6000 inhabitants, the 'capital' of one of the most modest German states, far from charming, altogether rural, without industry and quite poor, off the travelled roads and now to be governed by the 18-year-old duke, eight years Goethe's junior.

However limited in its financial resources, the court was soon to offer Goethe exceptional scope. Weimar was one of the few small feudal communities which, unlike the powerful, French-oriented Berlin establishment of Frederick the Great, was ready to draw young German men of letters and of administrative ability into its midst, and through them to develop an enlightened élite capable of assimilation into the aristocratic society. At the same time, the court was by no means convinced of the wisdom or desirability of encouraging any rapid emancipation of the middle class, and later firmly resisted such revolutionary notions. Goethe had been warned by his father that he might find himself reduced to a decorative figure at a petty court; he was, indeed, at first, with very few exceptions, to find that society unrewarding. But the duke, intemperate and impulsive, became an unfailing and clear-sighted friend who drew Goethe almost at once into the circle of his closest advisers and administrators.

Thus, unlike other German writers of the time, Goethe found himself in a strategic position that allowed him to translate the fresh sensibility of his generation, ready to challenge received ideas, into feasible modes of persuasion and action. The record of his instantaneous involvement in the business of government is impressive. He learned to deal with pressing matters, with the financial conditions of the duchy, with the improvement of roads, the modest revival of mining, with education or unemployment. But beyond these immediate tasks, he thought of himself with increasing conviction as a public servant. He was then and in the decades to come determined to strengthen or create institutions, whether literary or scientific, that were to make the substance of modern thinking available for public use, for study or research and, through journals or the theatre, for reflection and growth in political maturity.

In 1775 he was at once consicous of the change in the conditions of his life, of a new framework of values within which his talent, his intensely spontaneous receptivity, his aspirations as a poet had to be contained without being immobilized. If among the sputtering rebels of the Sturm und Drang he had the reputation of being a 'genius', he was now testing the usefulness of his remarkable gifts and his past affirmations of authenticity, enthusiasm and freedom, within a life of pragmatic, concrete and socially determined requirements.

With many of his former friends he maintained a lively correspondence, some he attempted to draw to Weimar, from others he gradually detached himself. Towards one of his earlier acquaintances, Johann Heinrich Merck, he continued to feel respect and affection. Merck, whose critical observations on contemporary fiction we have noted earlier, was a brilliant, widely read and profoundly pessimistic man of letters whose creative works (especially his two anti-aristocratic tales, 'Geschichte des Herrn Oheims', 1778, and 'Lindor, eine bürgerlich-deutsche Geschichte', 1781) are less original than his mordant criticism. He had translated Hutcheson's *Enquiry into Beauty and Virtue*, Addison's *Cato* and Hawkesworth's *Voyages*, may have had a hand in editing the first collection of Klopstock's *Oden und Lieder* (1771) and, at his own expense, had published Goethe's *Goetz von Berlichingen* (1773). Contemptuous of all forms of grandiloquence or sentimentality, his sarcastic intelligence possibly suggested features of Goethe's Mephistopheles.

Something of the Sturm und Drang eagerness to experience and feel in a community of congenial minds, and a determination to reject a life of unexamined conventions, remained in the decade to come the often demonstrated premises of Goethe's life. At the same time his literary production was inevitably determined – in its subject matter as well as its form – by the pressures and restrictions of the courtly society. He had completed two plays, *Clavigo* (1774) and *Stella* (1776), spontaneously sketched, and finger-exercises rather than confessions, before he arrived in Weimar. Both revolve around a central figure with an uncommon capacity for love and a need for affection, yet swayed by expediency or sudden infatuation into betrayal and disloyalty. Here, as so often in Goethe's early work, the power of passion is shown in its ambiguity: a fascinating character, challenged by moral imperatives, is made destructive by his very capriciousness.

A strong instinct for the immediacy, the abundance and fertility of the phenomenal world was in Goethe's production during his years before Weimar magnificently rendered in a number of poems of almost explosive immediacy ('An Schwager Kronos', 'Prometheus', 'Auf dem See', 'Herbstgefühl'.) Yet such assertions of vitality now alternate with moments of melancholy awareness of the constraints on his spontaneous perception. This equivocal state of mind is one of the impulses that produced the first draft of a Faust-play, more colourful and balladlike in its plot and its language than the subsequent, elaborated version of the career of this Renaissance magus. Faust is eager for knowledge beyond scholarship, and finds the promise of it in the love for a girl of enchanting simplicity. He is determined, like Werther, to experience in that love a power of being that tragically defies the norms and assurances of convention. The essential elements of the Sturm und Drang disposition – a conjunction of pantheism, of Shakespeare and Rousseau – are in this sketch articulated: the titanic assertion of will, the craving for the certainty of the heart, the transcending of a social order that has lost its compelling authority. Yet, when in 1775 he read some of these vivid scenes to his new acquaintances at the Weimar court, he must have recognized that the play represented convictions which, even for himself, had become increasingly problematical. He chose, wisely, not to publish this one-dimensional text, no longer adequate, and not yet sufficiently complex to suggest legitimate counter-positions. (It was discovered more than a century later in a manuscript copy by the hand of Luise von Goechhausen, one of the ladies of the Weimar court, and published in 1887 as *Urfaust*.)

For Herder, who was on his urging appointed Superintendant-general in Weimar, he felt the closest affection, an attachment which Herder himself later brought to an end. But the extravagant manner of several of his Sturm und Drang friends seemed more and more intolerable, and the sentimental and sanctimonious spiritualism of Lavater now struck him as ridiculous. With the 'dramatic whim' *Der Triumph der Empfindsamkeit* he parodied in 1778 (publ. 1787) the infatuation with sham feelings and precious manners. This is one of several occasional but pointed pieces with which he amused the court society and at the same time detached himself from the fashion of tearful and ethereal affectation which in many circles the reading of *Werther* had created.

Wieland

One of those who had earlier contributed to the distinction of the Weimar court, Christoph Martin Wieland, the editor of the most influential German literary and cultural journal (*Der Teutsche Merkur*), was a man of letters of remarkable intellectual and professional stature. Swabian by origin and brought up in the spirit of pietism, he soon developed more sceptical tendencies which he tested in discursive poems and moral tales. During six formative years in Switzerland, invited by the critic and poet J.J. Bodmer, he developed his talents as a versatile writer of touching odes and hymns, of epic poetry in accomplished hexameters and of prose dialogues on philosophical and sentimental topics. He avidly read the Greek and Latin classics, *Don Quixote* and Shakespeare, and adapted Nicolas Rowe's tragedy *Lady Johanna Gray* (1758), the first drama in German to use blank verse. A frequent guest in the elegant Warthausen establishment of Count Stadion, a high German political dignitary, he found there after 1760, an enviable society, witty, graceful, cosmopolitan and altogether shaped by French literary and artistic taste. This was the intellectual and social climate which Klopstock and Lessing had specifically rejected. But Wieland had absorbed something of the 'progressive' spirit of the patrician circles in Zurich and now the style of Warthausen appeared to him a synthesis between as yet amorphous and scattered energies of 'bourgeois' self-confidence and an open-minded aristocracy.

As though to assert his share in the 'English' mood of many of his contemporaries, he engaged in what he himself called a 'literary adventure', and produced (1762–66) German prose versions of 22 of Shakespeare's plays. Considering the fact that he used Warburton's poor text, that he knew little Elizabethan English and that he meticulously left out all puns, the result could only be an unsatisfactory approximation; yet this first extensive translation was an extraordinary achievement which largely determined the character of the German Shakespeare reception for some time to come.

Several of Wieland's novels, decisive for the development of German fiction, and in their subject matter indicative of a tension in himself between 'natural reason' and 'imaginative enthusiasm', were published in quick succession. The first, *Der Sieg der Natur über die Schwärmerey, oder Die Abentheuer des Don Sylvio von Rosalva. Eine Geschichte worinn alles Wunderbare natürlich zugeht* (1764), in the mode of Cervantes, is indebted for its technique as well to Fielding and Sterne and draws many of its motifs from the *Contes des Fées* of Mme d'Aulnoy. The double emphasis in the title itself upon the victory of reasoned conduct over the seductions of wilful spiritualism and miraculous mirages suggests a theme that was to occupy Wieland throughout his career. The narrative recounts the maturing of a young man from sentimental dreams and delusions to an acceptance of the reality of an intelligently perceived 'natural order'. The movement from enchantment to distinct judgement, from excited fanciful visions to an achievement of happiness is developed in a sophisticated strategy in which narrator and reader are closely joined. Absurd and sublime moods constantly challenge the balance between physical and spiritual satisfaction in scenes and on levels of discourse that mix delicate and grotesque description, lyrical prose and satire. By the lucid musicality of its prose and the brilliance of its intellectual encounters, *Don Sylvio* represents one of the finest achievements of German eighteenth-century fiction.

It is surpassed, not in its wealth of delicious fantasy but in the seriousness of its critical assessment of Enlightenment positions, by Wieland's most widely-read novel, *Geschichte des Agathon* (1766–67, 1773, 1794). Platonic spirituality and 'enthusiasm' are here resolutely discredited and any easy notion of the innate goodness and dignity of man is dispelled; experience rather than obedience to rigid norms is now the source of virtuous capabilities. Agathon, a young Greek of the pre-classical fourth century, educated in Delphi by priests of dubious morality, is subject and object at once of an elaborate plot of adventures, of love affairs and philosophical and religious encounters, of political aspirations and failures, of idealistic expectations and disappointments. These unceasing intellectual and emotional challenges, the conflicts between sentiment and reason, the prospects of comprehending the ambivalences in goodness, beauty and truth, are only in the third version of the novel brought into a relationship of meaning. The long-suspended resolution is made plausible by a civilized and ironic narrator, whose psychological and political worldliness gives to an elaborate game of learned story-telling an abundance of incident and rhetorical brilliance which no previous German novel had achieved.

Agathon attempts to present a coherent picture of a life shaped by that reciprocity of immediacy and reflection, that 'aesthetic education' which was a few years later to be the tenor of one of Schiller's major essays and of Goethe's *Wilhelm Meister*. Lessing admired the work as 'undeniably among the most excellent of our century' and was distressed by the 'profound silence which our critics have observed about it or the cold and indifferent tone in which they have spoken of it. It is the first and only novel of classical taste for a thoughtful mind. A novel? Let us give the book that designation, it might bring it a few more readers.'[1] If he

[1] Lessing *Werke*, IV, p. 554–5.

thought that *Agathon* had perhaps been written 'too soon' for an unprepared German public,[2] it nevertheless provided the occasion and the material for the first German theory of fiction. C.F. von Blanckenburg's *Versuch über den Roman* (1774) is an enlightened and well-informed survey of contemporary English and French aesthetic views, of Shaftesbury, Lord Kames, Burke and Diderot, with distinct sympathy for Fielding's colourful and engaging story-telling and sceptical of Richardson's didactic pathos. It suggested that *Agathon* supplied a pattern of concrete situations through which, beyond a mere succession of episodes, the development of a credible character could be demonstrated. 'Unless the poet has the merit of elucidating the "inner" man and can teach him to know himself, he will have . . . none.' This 'inner man' is, after all, 'the most important concern of our existence.' Thus, 'the development and shaping of a character by means of several encounters, or to put it still more precisely, his "inner history" is the essential and specific feature of a novel.'[3]

Blanckenburg urged intelligent men and women to take the novel seriously: far from providing an escape into worlds of magic and illusion, it should serve as an effective instrument of social education.

In 1772 Wieland published a 'political' novel, *Der Goldene Spiegel*, in which he elaborated, unsystematically and with deference to the establishment, his views of the best possible state. Far from venturing serious criticism of the feudal order, he regarded enlightened despotism as the ideal form of government, most likely to assure the well-being of the citizens, opportunities for religious freedom and the development of cultural institutions. The book echoes Rousseauean ideas on the conflict between nature and culture; it is narrated obliquely in a fanciful Chinese setting, and was clearly intended as an apotheosis, not of Frederick the Great, but of Joseph II and his benevolent autocracy. Yet it was not Vienna but the court at Weimar that responded: Wieland was invited by the Duchess, a singularly intelligent woman, to be tutor to the two princes. He retired from this function shortly before Goethe's arrival, to pursue an incomparably productive and influential career as editor and novelist.

In a spectacular fashion his journal, *Der Teutsche Merkur*, shaped for over 35 years (1773–1810) an emerging German cultural consciousness – with varying degrees of sympathy for prevailing currents of taste, at first devoted more to literary, later to social and political matters. Within a year of its first appearance, Wieland could speak to some 2000 subscribers; 10 years later 1500 had remained loyal. Throughout the 1770s

[2] Ibid., IV, p. 554.

[3] F. von Blanckenburg, *Versuch über den Roman*, Facsimile reprint, ed. E. Lämmert, Stuttgart, Metzler, 1965, p. 355–6, 392.

nd 1780s the *Merkur* was one of the most widely read periodicals in urope. Wieland himself set the tone and maintained a high and consisnt level of informative and stimulating writing; he proved a much ought-after, if feared and often arbitrary editor who claimed the disrming privilege of commenting in footnotes on the opinions of his conibutors. J.H. Merck helped him to edit early issues, and after 1786 he as for 10 years assisted by his son-in-law the philosopher K.L. Reinhold, ne of the most effective interpreters of Kant, and as professor at Jena, of reat importance for the evolving interest in transcendental idealism.

In the remarkable number of essays which, until 1801, Wieland ddressed to the large and varied group of his readers he reflected and ommented, in a style both personal and exemplary, on books, ideas and vents that stirred or divided the age. His determination to develop a erman equivalent of the *Mercure de France*, or of current English urnals such as the *Gentleman's Magazine*, was sustained by an astonishg command of contemporary literature and a readiness to turn intelgently to every public issue that seemed worth articulating: the role of e writer in Germany, patriotism, the Jesuits, Freemasonry, the French evolution, early German literature, mythology, etc.

What Wieland offered to his readers was not least a prose of unparalled ease and clarity, a style of casual but compelling and lively speech, a nse of dialogue and of the well told tale. That he was the master of light nd lucid poetry he had demonstrated in an exquisitely chiselled comic oem in limpid Alexandrine verse, *Musarion, oder die Philosophie der razien* (1768), Wieland's *fête galante*, a glittering tableau of witty isputations and conviviality set in an arcadian landscape. Another plendid piece of rococo charm was the spirited verse narrative, *Oberon* 1780), an account of the adventures of one of Charlemagne's knights in he Orient, fused with the fairytale magic of Oberon and Titania. It was he work that gave him the greatest and most lasting reputation in ermany and abroad: in 1800 John Quincy Adams translated it into nglish.

By his tireless example as man of letters, by his tolerance and his hisorical judgement, Wieland demonstrated that literature was a means of iving cohesion to a public made up of aristocratic as well as middle-class eaders. His manner and voice were invariably restrained and conliatory and it is not surprising that the radical proponents of genius and riginality among the Sturm und Drang dramatists and, later, the omantic poets and philosophers, ridiculed his entirely civilized and ragmatic cast of mind. His 'Singspiel' *Alceste* (1773), written with great acility in Winckelmann's spirit, had seemed to the young Goethe to isplay a pathetically inadequate understanding of those 'Greek' features hich for the Strasbourg circle were not so much harmonious and serene

as powerful, splendid and awesome. Goethe countered with an impe
tinent little satire, *Götter, Helden und Wieland* which Wieland regarde
as 'unspeakably malicious and odious behaviour' towards him[4] but, wit
self-denying urbanity, he recommended this small work 'to all lovers c
the Pasquinian manner as a masterpiece of persiflage and sophisticate
wit'.[5]

As soon as Goethe had settled in Weimar the two men met and were a
once reconciled. Goethe was bound to be amused by Wieland's comi
novel, *Die Abderiten* (1774, 1781), with its ironic reflections on the follie
and absurdities of life in a small town, and soon established a close rela
tionship based on mutual respect for their very different temperaments
Wieland's philosophical and political judgement was far more circum
spect than Goethe's; unencumbered by governmental responsibilities, h
could afford to be detached, even in his later anti-revolutionary sent
ments. He was by instinct a mediator between individuals, points of vie
and ways of life: it was largely through his journal that Austria becam
acquainted with contemporary German letters. Goethe later spoke wit
warmth and conviction when he eulogized Wieland as one of the grea
men of the century.[6]

Goethe: Man of Letters

Goethe's appointment to Weimar must be seen as an event of uncommo
significance. He was clearly far more than a talented young man with
moderate legal training whose services were enlisted as part of the norma
social usage of the noble or well-to-do; he was an exceptionally promisin
and (unlike many of his friends) civilized young writer. Whatever th
quality of the work he produced during the next decade, it reflects hi
growing sense of the public function of the man of letters. A firm convic
tion distinguished Goethe from nearly all his contemporaries: if the pre
occupation with matters of the heart, with philosophical or poetic issues
with the alternatives of social conduct, was to have lasting consequences
it must be effectively related to the conditions, needs and resources of a
society in transition.

This issue had been clearly recognized by Herder, who eagerly sought a
response to his theories from those in power: 'If my voice', he wrote in
1774 in *Auch eine Philosophie der Geschichte*, 'had any power and coul
be heard far afield, how fervently would I urge all those who contribut
to the civilizing of mankind: Do not offer us mere platitudes abou

[4] T.C. Starnes, 'Verschiedenes zur Korrespondenz C.M. Wielands', *Jahrbuch des freie deutschen Hochstifts 1980*, Tübingen, Niemeyer, 1980, p. 8.
[5] *Der Teutsche Merkur*, 1774, II, p. 351–2.
[6] Goethe *GA*, XII, p. 693–716.

'improvement"! That is mere paper culture! If possible, act and create institutions.'[7]

Goethe's letters in those first years in Weimar reveal the conflict he felt between resolute dedication to his offices and an awareness of the subordinate role his literary work must play. In the poetry which he managed to write, he seems to sublimate his imaginative restlessness and his lyrical talent to the point where they become almost furtive, turning upon themselves in a spirit of constant introspective questioning, and seeking reassurance in transcendent solitude. His love for Charlotte von Stein, seven years older than he and the wife of a court official, an intimacy deeply private, sustaining and strengthening the rich resources of his perception and judgement, inspired some of his most splendid and moving poetry ('Warum gabst du uns die tiefen Blicke', 'An den Mond', 'Wanderers Nachtlied'). Charlotte von Stein, not perhaps an extraordinary personality, was a cultivated and sensitive woman with whom he could read the Greeks, Quintilian, Spinoza, Ossian and Shakespeare and to whom he could speak of his scientific interests. But more than any effusive affinity of spirits, their association provided a space of reflection and self-scrutiny within the strenuous demands of the day.

He delighted and animated the society of the court by occasional readings from his work in progress and by appearances in amateur theatricals: it was in such a well-disposed circle that he read from his *Faust* and from a piece of fiction that has something of an autobiographical core and must be taken as an essay towards an accounting of his own potential. *Wilhelm Meisters Theatralische Sendung* (not published until 1911, from a copy by another hand) is a novel of somewhat conventional design but rich in vivid figures and incidents. In it, a young man, Wilhelm Meister, is drawn away from the distasteful paternal world of business towards the fascinating prospects and delusions of art. His hopes of giving to his aspirations as an artist a measure of seriousness and responsibility lead him to the theatre as an instrument of cultural progress.

This fragment of a novel, later to be reorganized and enlarged, is a significant document of personal, and implicitly social, transition: it formulates the challenge by a vivacious personality to a world carefully keeping apart its pragmatic and aesthetic ideals. Wilhelm is the victim of this discrepancy. He seeks satisfaction and reconciliation in the theatre, but remains uncertain of the range of his own capabilities and sceptical of the adequacy of the chosen institution. The novel reminds us that in Germany the theatre was about to assume an important role: Hamburg, Mannheim, Stuttgart, Gotha and Vienna had all recently established

[7] Herder *SW*, V, p. 544–5.

stages and assembled companies that, although uneven in their standards of performance, yet offered varied fare and attracted audiences of increasing size and broad social provenance.

The colourful rendering of Wilhelm's experiences in a social setting more richly explored than that in *Werther* is controlled by the detachment and irony of the narrator – Wilhelm's 'mission' remains a dubious pursuit. The context of personal encounters in which his art must prove its value was only gradually to unfold in intricate relationships. At the end of 1785, Goethe put the manuscript of six parts aside and did not resume serious work on it until eight years later. By then the perspectives of his life had widened and his political judgement grown more discerning; a radical reassessment of the institutional framework could now give direction to Wilhelm's 'apprenticeship' towards self-confidence and community.

Still more characteristic of Goethe's state of mind was a play which he began in 1780 and which, like other major projects, he found himself unable to complete. The two acts of *Torquato Tasso* which he read to the duchess in the summer of 1781 developed only one aspect of a plot that was later to be elaborated: the love of the Italian poet Tasso for the princess Leonore, the offering, that is to say, of an intensely felt devotion of exalted feeling, to a person constrained in her responses by ritual and convention. This is, if we sufficiently abstract, clearly an explication of the dichotomy, evident in his earlier work, of impulse and restraint, the demonstration – as in *Werther* – of an inspired self, faced by an order frustrating in its recognized legitimacy.

A tendency to spiritualize the lyrical impulse, to encode the cultivated tenderness of Charlotte von Stein in a figure of serene nobility, is evident in the first (prose) version of *Iphigenie auf Tauris*, a play which Goethe finished in only two months in 1779. (In the Weimar performance in April of that year he himself acted the part of Orestes, the superb actress Corona Schröter played Iphigenie). Even before its transformation into the balanced and measured blank-verse of the final version (1786), it represents an impressive (if somewhat schematic) attempt to come to terms with the question of the usefulness and validity of traditional concepts, both aesthetic and religious, within modern assumptions of individual judgement and responsibility. Against a background of two modes of divine authority, one 'barbarian' and the other Greek, the meaning of an inescapable bondage to 'fate' in the minds of its victims and agents is meticulously explored. The experience of a ritualistic compulsion is here entirely internalized, modifying the familiar impulses of the classical model, and resolved through the gradual recognition of moral and psychological counter-resources. These are drawn from the quality, freely and intelligently accepted, of a life subordinated to the scrutiny of conscience, generosity and compassion. This formidable argument is in the play made explicit by four characters, each contending in a different key, but all seeking to deal with what seems inexorable, in a growing awareness of their critical, their 'humane' capacities. Thoas, the king of Tauris, moves from archaic ritualism to a tentative understanding of alternative attitudes, Orestes from being agonized by the horror of the Furies to a comprehension of the nature of his obsession: he is relieved of the awesome burden of the curse not so much, as has often been thought, by Iphigenie's 'humanity' as by his own efforts at articulating his condition. His friend Pylades, a cunning pragmatist, learns to respect moral obligations. While Iphigenie herself at first acquiesces in her fateful assignment as the exiled priestess of Diana, she gradually transcends her absolute submission by discerning the 'mythical' nature of the power of the gods.

It is clear that Goethe here deals with an issue of far more than classicist' implications, an issue that was at the very centre of eighteenth-century theology: the autonomous modern consciousness faces a divinity which, in the sense of ancient belief as well as contemporary Protestant orthodoxy is an implacable and arbitrary power. How can the 'enlightened' mind cope with such a fatalistic prospect? He sought, in any case, to offer a more differentiated sort of access to myths and images that had hitherto, in Wieland's *Alceste*, for example, remained merely formulaic. He drew the conceptual conclusions of the play in large measure from his own preoccupation with the balance to be achieved between the claims of subjective integrity and objective forms of order. Both facets are in this first version of *Iphigenie* delineated in highly generalized metaphors and their reconciliation is largely sentimental.

The growth in human, philosophical and literary capacity that separates Goethe from the mood of the two or three hectic years before Weimar is in *Iphigenie* obvious enough. Yet memories and projects of that earlier time remain alive and surface in his plans, his work and his letters: *Faust* and *Werther* are reappraised, the fragment of a play dealing with Egmont, the popular leader of Flemish opposition to the Spanish Catholic policies of Philipp II, which he sketched as early as 1774, is occasionally taken up but put aside to evolve later as one of the major projects of his Italian years. Not until 1783 when he assesses his condition in the splendid poem 'Ilmenau' can he draw the sum of the Weimar experiences and define the elements that had carried him to an awareness of new purposes and new capacities.

His love for Charlotte von Stein may have contributed less to this emerging self-consciousness than the growing satisfaction and clarity which he derived from interests of an entirely different and intellectually rewarding sort. After 1780 he found himself more and more drawn into scientific fields, mineralogy, osteology and botany, into studies which were to occupy much of his time in the years to come. Beginning by classifying the geological features and plants of his immediate neighbourhood, he examined and collected, at first in a desultory fashion but soon systematically, objects that struck him as suggestive of certain evolutionary patterns. In 1784 he found, independent of the same discovery four years earlier by the French anatomist Vicq d'Azyr, that the intermaxillary bone is, in a barely identifiable form, present in man as well as, more plainly, in animals – evidence, as he suspected, of typological analogies. Close attention to the functional relationships of bones strengthened his aversion to speculative and moralizing schemes such as Lavater's *Physiognomische Fragmente* (1775–78).

In an essay 'Über den Granit' he speaks of this primeval stone as 'the very foundation of our earth', 'the first firmest beginnings of our being'.[8] He is led to reflections on origins, on development and differentiation; like Montesquieu and Herder, he sees the determinant importance for man of an adequate understanding of his physical setting, of climate and soil. Here (and in the solemn verses 'Die Geheimnisse', 1784–85) his voice, worldly and without sentimentality, takes on the elevated tone of a Renaissance poet. It is no contradiction, he insists, that his interest in the human heart, 'the youngest, most varied, mobile, changeable part of creation' should now have led him to examine the 'oldest, firmest, deepest, most unshakable' phenomenon in nature.[9]

The conviction that certainty of knowledge and an understanding of first principles can be derived from the objective world, that they need not be superimposed upon it by speculation or inductive reasoning becomes henceforth the mainspring of his work, whether in science, in poetry or in his social philosophy. Discussions with Herder and one or two other Weimar friends, his correspondence with scientists, among them the Göttingen physicist G.C. Lichtenberg – all these are indications of a growing resolution that the pursuit of science should be the cardinal concern of his life. 'Forgive me', he writes to F.H. Jacobi on 9 June 1785, 'if I keep silent when there is talk about a Divine Being which I for one can recognize only *in rebus singularibus* . . . I seek the Divine *in herbis et lapidibus*.'[10] A year later he admits the richness of his friend's life, 'yet, God has punished you with metaphysics and has driven an arrow into your flesh; He has blessed me with physics so that I may be happy in the contemplation of His works.'[11]

Whatever intellectual stimulus this new persuasion may have given

[8] Goethe *GA*, XVII, p. 479, 481.
[9] Goethe *GA*, XVII, p. 480.
[10] Goethe *GA*, XVIII, p. 851.
[11] Goethe *GA*, XVIII, p. 924.

him, it could only contribute to his restlessness under the constant pressure of administrative chores that were too often in the pursuit of policies he could not accept. His resolve to break out of the Weimar world led him, in September 1786, to depart surreptitiously and to travel incognito, via Munich, Verona, Venice and Florence, to Rome. He had just completed a revision of *Werther* and had concluded an agreement that would result in the first publication of his collected works. To his mother in Frankfurt he wrote from Rome on 4 November: 'So many dreams and wishes of my life are now resolved . . . I shall come back a new human being.'[12]

Rome: Winckelmann

It is well to recognize that Goethe's Italian journey from 1786 to 1788 is far more than an enriching interlude in a remarkable life. It deeply affected his being, and led in subsequent years and decades to insights and conclusions of extraordinary consequence for himself and the history of German literature.

What he saw in Rome had for long stirred the enthusiasm and the curiosity of European travellers; it was amply described in the guidebook he carried with him, Johann Jacob Volkmann's *Historisch-Kritische Nachrichten von Italien* (1770–71). His eye and sensibility had, in some measure, been preconditioned by the climate of opinion and the criteria of reverence which the great art historian J.J. Winckelmann had established some 30 years earlier. In the abundance of classical treasures or in the work of Raphael, that acknowledged successor to the Greeks, he now found (at least in the first flush of excitement), Winckelmann's tenet confirmed that 'the general and predominant mark of Greek masterpieces is noble simplicity and tranquil greatness both in posture and expression.'[13]

Winckelmann had taken this key phrase of his most influential work *Gedanken über die Nachahmung der griechischen Werke in der Malerei und Bildhauerkunst* (1755) from the writings of his teacher Adam Friedrich Oeser, and had polemically directed it against the passionate distortions in the Baroque statues and pictures he had seen in Dresden, where until 1754 he was librarian. He had come to admire ancient art as evidence of a state of mind of exemplary coherence, of an attitude reflected in works whose richness could be fully appreciated only in an act of intense relationship from viewer to object.

The 'great and grave soul'[14] that illuminates the Greek statutes speaks

[12] *Goethes Briefe*. Hamburger Ausgabe, ed. K.R. Mandelkow, Hamburg, Christian Wegner Verlag, 1964, II, p. 18.

[13] J.J. Winckelmann, *Kleine Schriften und Briefe*, ed. W. Senff, Weimar, Böhlau, 1960, p. 44.

[14] Ibid.

to the critic and connoisseur with compelling force, an involvement neither purely subjective nor merely sensuous but balanced by a moral, indeed, puritanical discipline. The contemplation of a work of art should lead to a sense of community among congenial seekers of truth, an 'aesthetic truth', comprehensive and powerful enough to offer something of a religious experience. It was this notion of beauty as a means of access to truth, Platonic in its origin but here given the radical force of a secularized faith, that was to sustain in the decades to come the theory and practice of German – and European – classical and romantic art.

In 1755 Winckelmann's mentor in Rome, Raphael Mengs, was not only the outstanding German artist, but was considered the greatest living European painter, more highly esteemed than Tiepolo. He alone was permitted to sit rather than humbly kneel as he painted the Pope's portrait. He was the extravagantly praised 'pittore filosofo' of the Parnassus-fresco in the Villa Albani (1761), that veritable manifesto of neo-classicism. In his eclectic *Gedanken über die Schönheit und den Geschmack in der Malerei* (1762) Mengs rejected Baroque illusionism and maintained that any concept of beauty must be derived from the wisdom of the ancients and from close attention to 'natural' proportions. The masters of the Renaissance, he thought, had rediscovered and restated certain elements of that classical formula of 'wisdom in beauty'. For his own paintings he generated forms and colours from careful historical study, and aimed at a synthesis of the principles of ancient sculpture and those derived from Raphael's canvasses.

Together with Mengs, Winckelmann had written interpretations of several pieces of Greek statuary: the best of these, a description of the celebrated Apollo Belvedere (1750), was in attitude and language a model for later romantic writings on art; the peerless character of this statue – in fact a Roman marble copy of a Greek work – was re-emphasized in his *Geschichte der Kunst des Altertums* (1764). Winckelmann here sought not so much to list stylistic characteristics as to convey in a heightened emotional language appropriate to the new kind of critical discourse, the impact of a masterpiece upon a viewer willing and eager to be drawn into its aura and to be affected by its ethos: 'In the presence of this miracle of art,' he writes of the Apollo, 'I forget all else, and I myself assume, so to speak, an exalted position so that I may look upon it in a worthy manner.'[15]

In his *Gedanken über die Nachahmung der Griechischen Werke . . .* (1755), (an essay of just 40 pages, of which only 50 copies were printed), the most influential of his publications, indeed, his credo, Winckelmann

[15] J.J. Winckelmann *Geschichte der Kunst des Altertums*, ed. J. Lessing, Berlin, Heimann, 1870, p. 255–6.

developed these ideas most insistently. Subsequent writings (*Anmerkungen über die Baukunst der Alten*, 1762; *Versuch einer Allegorie, besonders für die Kunst*, 1766; *Monumenti antichi*, 1767–68), however academic their topics, reinforce the conviction that a work of art demands of the viewer a full personal commitment – as much to the ubstance of nobility in the ancients as to the rich resources of perception and understanding in the modern consciousness. 'There is but one way for us moderns to become great, perhaps even unequalled; it is by imitating the ancients.'[16] This is one of the opening sentences of the *Gedanken*, he work of a man in whom historical scholarship, anthropological and aesthetic interests and a deep pedagogical instinct coincided; it is the key locument of the emerging European neo-classicist movement.

The avowed purpose of Winckelmann's *Geschichte der Kunst des Altertums* is to give a survey of classical artists, illustrated by examples to be found in Roman collections, and an account of the geographical and thnological conditions that produced the variety of ancient art from the Egyptians and Phoenicians to the Greeks and the Romans. But it is, entrally, an analytical enquiry into the 'style' of Greek sculpture from its primitive origins to the sublime achievements of Phidias and the perfecion of Praxiteles. Earlier historians such as Vasari had been primarily nterested in the artist's manner of representing or 'imitating' nature. Like Bernini who 'discovered nature' by contemplating the Venus di Medici, Winckelmann now concluded that the work of art should teach us to see and comprehend nature more clearly.[17] In that sense to 'imitate' he Greeks was to recover in a contemporary sensibility the spiritual and ormal values represented by classical art – a thesis that had its origins n the attacks of Montesquieu, Fénélon and Dubos on aesthetic ogmatism and in their evocation of the 'natural' virtues of the Greeks. Winckelmann was anxious to offer that ideal precisely as an antidote to hat he considered 'French' taste and preciosity – a prejudice which he ever abandoned, and which became, in large measure through him, the xed and unexamined target of Sturm und Drang criticism.

Winckelmann's approach to art, like that of Edmund Burke's *Enquiry nto the Origins of our Ideas of the Sublime and Beautiful* (1757), is phyological in the sense that beauty is for him consummate health perfectly endered. The formal perfection of ancient works of art is thus a direct eflection of the fully developed Greek personality. Winckelmann here nd elsewhere echoes Shaftesbury's belief in the identity of moral oodness and achieved beauty.

The *Geschichte* is the synthesis of Winckelmann's admiration for

16 J.J. Winckelmann, *Kleine Schriften und Briefe*, op. cit., p. 30.
17 Ibid., p. 37–8.

ancient art and civilization. By no means easy reading, it is extraordinarily rich in critical and historical insight. Indeed, it belongs in that series of incomparable philosophical interpretations of history that appeared within a few years at the mid-century: Montesquieu's *Esprit des Lois* (1748), Turgot's lecture on the progress of the human spirit (1750), Voltaire's *Siècle de Louis XIV* (1751), Rousseau's second *Discours* (1755) or Hume's *History of England* (1754–62). All of these reflect a profoundly optimistic view of a world that had achieved political and social stability, an enviable degree of well-being and, above all, the conviction that scientific and moral forces held the universe in a moderately reassuring equilibrium.

Anxious to make the encounter with works of art a matter of serious study and reflection, and warning against considering it a mere 'amusement of the eye', Winckelmann recognized the importance of directing the taste and judgement of a new class of lovers and buyers of art towards moral precepts enhanced rather than dissipated by the aesthetic experience. As a close adviser on matters of art to Cardinal Alessandro Albani, the President of the Papal archives, and as cicerone to the German nobility, he became a central figure in that exhilarating spectacle of archaeology, taste and power that for half a century, from the excavations at Herculaneum (1738) and Pompeii (1748) to the French Revolution, drew artists and collectors from all over Europe to Rome. There were influential and erudite antiquarians, dealers and collectors such as Thomas Jenkins and James Byres; but few travellers failed to turn to the Abbé Winckelmann for an introduction to the treasures of the city. Diderot called him 'ce charmant enthousiaste' and in his *Salon* of 1765 praised Winckelmann's 'excellent ouvrage . . . rempli de chaleur, d'enthousiasme, de goût, de vues grandes et profondes'; he ranked him with Rousseau: as Rousseau had attacked modern culture by invoking the integrity of nature, so Winckelmann disparaged much of the art of his time by evoking the formative energies of ancient sculpture.[18]

Winckelmann's death in 1763 by the hand of an assassin was a shock felt throughout Europe. It cut short a life in which the sentimental rococo features gradually gave way, as Friedrich Schlegel put it, to a haunting awareness of 'the antinomy between the ancients and the moderns.'[19] The influence of Winckelmann's intuitive theory of understanding was incalculable: Lessing, Herder, Hamann and many others, not the least Walter Pater, were profoundly indebted to him. 'It was Winckelmann,' Goethe was to say in his Italienische Reise,

> 'who first urged upon us the need to distinguish between different epochs and to

[18] Diderot, *Salons*, ed. J. Seznec and J. Adhemar, Oxford, Clarendon Press, 1960, II, p. 207–8.

[19] Friedrich Schlegel, *Literary Notebooks*, op. cit., p. 40.

recognize the different styles in their slow growth and eventual decay. Any real lover of art will readily accept the importance of this demand . . . . But how can we achieve this insight? . . . A steady training of the eye over many years is necessary, and we must first learn in order to be able to ask questions.'[20]

Vinckelmann, Hegel thought, 'was one of those who created in the field f art a new organ of the spirit and altogether a new way of seeing.'[21]

The relationship between an assessment of the historical conditions of rt and an alert and sympathetic openness on the part of the interpreter ecame one of the premises of nineteenth-century historicism. Classical cholarship and the historians of art defined their goals first in Vinckelmann's terms. Many of the younger writers recognized the force f Winckelmann's devotion to the classics in the lectures on archaeology nd mythology with which, after 1763, for almost half a century the enerable C.G. Heyne made the University of Göttingen the European entre of classical studies. Beyond textual and conjectural criticism, he d his students through the reading of Greek and Latin authors to the iscovery of a rewarding cosmos of life.

Goethe in Italy

he Rome to which Goethe came in October 1786 – under the assumed ame of Philipp Moeller – was an essentially modern city, with an bundance of monuments of Renaissance and Baroque art, crowded ith evidence of past greatness. He was at once captivated by the energy f its daily life, the vitality of the imagination among its people, the ever-stonishing interweaving of past and present. Different from Paris, the olitical and cultural capital of feudal Europe, or London, the hub of a ew world power, Rome had become the centre of artistic life. It offered o European painters and writers inexhaustible materials for the study of ncient, medieval and Renaissance culture. Countless English gentlemen nd German aristocrats formed their taste in Rome and commissioned rtists (like P. Batoni or Gavin Hamilton) to paint their portraits urrounded by the admired relics of ancient glory.

Goethe was, on the whole, indifferent to this elegant tourist industry. He was and remained an amateur who sought stimulus and exchange of deas among a group of gifted German or Swiss writers and artists: H.W. Tischbein, Angelica Kauffmann, J.G. Schütz, the sculptor Alexander Trippel and J.H. Lips, from whom he learned the technique f engraving. During his stay in Italy he produced more than 1000 ccomplished drawings; much of his time was devoted to watercolour

[20] Goethe *GA*, XI, p. 182.
[21] G.W.F. Hegel, *Asthetik*, ed. F. Bassenge, Berlin, Aufbau Verlag, 1965, I, p. 71.

painting. The distribution of the features of a landscape within a tellin
design, the elucidating effects of colour seemed to him a means of unde
standing the proportions and rhythms to be discovered in the organi
world itself. In one of the few poems written in Italy, 'Amor a
Landschaftsmaler', the act of seeing in the manner of Claude Lorrair
the emergence of a work of art from an intense, even erotic, contem
plation of the ingredients of landscape, is metaphorically rendered.
Angelica Kauffmann knew few among her Roman friends who, i
matters of art, 'saw' better than Goethe. Indeed, the growth in Goethe
comprehension of natural and aesthetic structures was in large measur
the result of the development of his tactile and visual perception.

His sense of colour and space, his admiration for the rich evidence c
creativity in the monuments of the past, his delight in the exuberan
present, unclouded by speculation or abstract norms of perfection – a
these were fresh impulses that were later, in Weimar, to be explored an
organized in scientific and literary studies, in ceaseless exchanges wit
congenial friends and above all, in a growing body of poetry. Now, he dis
cussed historical and theoretical topics with artists and critics such a
A.L. Hirt, Heinrich Meyer and, particularly, with K.P. Moritz, whos
treatise *Über die bildende Nachahmung des Schönen* (1788) was t
summarize the aesthetic principles they debated at the time.

He was less interested in medieval art or religious pomp than in th
evidence of shared public life that had found shape in ancient temple
or theatres, in palaces and parks, in the Coliseum or the Via Appia,
concern that seemed to him continued, and grandly reasserted i
Michelangelo, and in the strength and wisdom of Raphael. Withou
pedantry but paying careful attention to the historical and topographica
importance of each object, he collected coins, inscriptions and cameos
read Livy and altogether sought to define the ingredients of his new self
confidence.

Soon Goethe was eager to move south: in Naples he met J. Philip
Hackert who taught him perspective and modelling – and of whom
Goethe was some 25 years later to write a generous and historicall
penetrating memorial. He was introduced to Sir William Hamilton, th
British envoy and collector, with his fascinating 'geheimes Kunst- un
Gerümpelgewölbe'.[23] Miss Emma Hart, not yet Lady Hamilton, seeme
to him to grace an establishment of almost magic charm.[24] He went on t
Sicily and there the lush Mediterranean setting stimulated his interest i
plants, stones and curious creatures such as sea-urchins. In the Palerm
botanical gardens he was struck by an idea which became a key metapho

[22] Goethe *GA*, I, p. 387–9.
[23] Goethe *GA*, XI, p. 360.
[24] Goethe *GA*, XI, p. 228–9.

of his subsequent thinking: the coherence in the organization of all parts of a plant – seed, stalk, leaf, calyx, petal, stamen, pistil – however modified, suggested a botanical model, a primary *Urpflanze*, that points to a distinct morphological order, to the principles of metamorphosis.

This concept he was to define in his *Versuch, die Metamorphose der Pflanzen zu erklären* (1790) as the effect of ceaseless mutation of a constant whose character is maintained even as it is transformed. The particular botanical specimen seemed to Goethe the symbolic instance of a universal morphological law which, translated into the vocabulary of art, led him to the projection of 'archetypal' forms, infinitely capable of modification. The term he uses for this totality that has its own inherent potential of metamorphosis and growth is *Gestalt*, for him by no means a Platonic abstraction but a principle drawn from experienced evidence. 'For the whole complex of the existence of an actual being', he was later to say, 'the German language has the word "Gestalt" '.[25] He was certain that nature and art equally require the specification and ordering of variety in one overriding category and this, for Goethe, was the concept of form. Form, organically (or structurally) differentiated, he now sought and found in stones, leaves, clouds, and in an analogous sense, in poems and paintings, in literary genres and in musical compositions.

The impact of the Greek temples at Paestum, south of Naples, of the amphitheatre of Taormina and of the serenity of the Sicilian landscape suggested to him a tragedy revolving around the encounter between Nausicaa, the daughter of Alcinous, and the great wanderer Ulysses; only a few scenes in verses of exquisite delicacy were completed. Work on the suspended *Tasso*-fragment was resumed. Art and the natural world are for him henceforth interdependent realms mirroring not so much sentimental experiences as homologous instances of order. In certain scenes of *Faust* which were written in 1788, such as the episode 'Forest and Cavern' or 'The Witches' Kitchen', the abundance of the Italian experience of nature, the comprehension of its dynamic coherence is given dithyrambic expression.

Literary work occupied him constantly: in December 1786 he had finished in Rome the poetic version of *Iphigenie* and in September 1787 he concluded work on *Egmont*. The autobiographical ingredients in these plays are not, of course, of a factual sort, but concern Goethe's state of mind. He was delighted by a characteristic, a classical equilibrium in the Italian landscape, the altogether astonishing identity of exuberance and form, the balance, as he saw it, of freedom and order. *Iphigenie's* 'classical' features are now more sharply delineated and the attitudes of

[25] Goethe *GA*, XVII, p. 13.

each of the play's figures derive from his own experience and reflection. 'I am myself a troubled stranger', he wrote to Herder in January 1787, 'who is overwhelmed by visions, not by the Furies but by the Muses and Graces and the whole powerful presence of the blessed gods.'[26]

In *Egmont*, too, we recognize a process of maturing: it was the affirmation in the central character of a sense of being, of self-assurance without arrogance or guile, a personality with an awareness of its inadequacy and fallibility. Here it is not, as in *Goetz*, an historical constellation that defeats a hero, but his charismatic essence, his 'demon', that makes him vulnerable. Egmont's opponent, Alba, only now introduced into the plot, is in his total commitment to political realities an equally powerful counteragent. Egmont, historically the hero of the Dutch struggle for independence, is in the play transformed into a youthful idealist, radical in his contempt for devious action and for the cautious strategy of success, unwilling to match the tactical intelligence of those in authority. He is at the end arrested, accused of treason and condemned to die. In a final scene, a dream vision of great, almost operatic lyricism, he recognizes his beloved Klärchen. Although she has failed to stir the citizens to act against religious fanaticism and absolutist power, and in despair has poisoned herself, she is now the embodiment of liberty for which he too will accept his death.

It is an ending which later critics of the play, especially Schiller, considered inconclusive and evasive; for Goethe it suggested at once the affirmation of Egmont's strength of being, his unchanging faith in his 'demon' and the acceptance of its inevitable inadequacy. It is the 'tragedy' of the central character as well as a reminder of the failure, equally tragic, of the people to achieve liberty.

Whatever its ambiguity, *Egmont* is perhaps the most telling document of Goethe's growth in perception, his readiness to accept life without any superimposed abstract idealism and to shape in a tight web of language and imagery a play in which all elements – the 'demonic' as the source of inner power and as the cause of blindness, the issue of freedom, the realities of political power, even the range of poetic speech – are carefully differentiated with a remarkable instinct for the strength and the limitations of man, for the interlocking of the social and the private.

Torquato Tasso, too, he continued to rework: early in 1787 he read a recently published biography of the poet and immediately recognized in the courtier Antonio the antagonist through whom the dramatic conflict of the play could be sharpened. The play, which he completed in 1788 a few weeks after his return to Weimar, is now an account, grandly unfolded in exquisite verse, of the artist who finds himself compelled to

26 Goethe *GA*, XIX, p. 54.

subordinate his genius to the convictions and manners of a courtly society. It is unmistakably a document with political implications: the genius, more refined and subtle than its personifications by any of the Sturm und Drang dramatists, claims a place of distinction, even of authority near or above that of the court. By comparing himself to the heroes of the past he challenges the pre-eminence of the feudal and monarchical system. Equally important are the formal features of the play: here for the first time we recognize the lively, solid, even colourful 'classicism' which – different from Winckelmann's static manner, and without recourse to any of the discredited normative theories of beauty or perfection – was to give shape and energy to all of his major works.

Goethe was aware of the ineradicable impact upon his future of what he had seen and learned to feel and to record in Italy. 'The chief purpose of my journey was to cure myself of a physical and moral uneasiness that troubled me and in the end made me useless in Germany, and to quench the feverish thirst for an authentic sort of art; the first I have nearly achieved, the other completely.'[27] It was an experience of profound renewal, summarized, as he travelled north, in all its complexity in moving passages of *Tasso* and, later, in the superb series of the 'Roman' elegies. His diary and the carefully gathered letters of these years formed the substance of *Die Italienische Reise* (1816, 1817, 1829), the most beautiful and richly figured of his autobiographical works.

Goethe: Art and Nature

Goethe's decision to go to Italy had in some measure been prompted by his disappointment at the slow progress of those economic and political reforms which he considered essential for the duchy. On his return to Weimar in June 1788, he was, at his request, for the time being relieved of all administrative obligations. When he was again drawn into public responsibilities, he knew that he must relate his convictions to the social and political changes which the Revolution foreshadowed. Like most of his German contemporaries, he was anxiously aware of the pressures which directly or indirectly were to affect life throughout Europe. He shared, after 1790, the widespread uneasiness at the radical turn of events in Paris but recognized the irrevocable collapse of the existing feudal order; while convinced of the need to maintain an effective, responsible government, he was too pragmatic merely to hold to the traditional assumptions of benevolent paternalism.

[27] *Goethes Briefe*, op. cit., II, p. 78.

By its family ties to Prussia, the Weimar court was compelled to take sides in the strategic manoeuvres that preceded and followed the Revolution; Goethe himself, sceptical of Frederick's absolutist politics, had, in 1785, resisted his Duke's pro-Prussian partisanship in favour of the anti-Austrian 'League' of the German princes. As he witnessed, in September 1792, the defeat of the Prussian-led forces at Valmy, he realized that the hour of reckoning had come for the German states. What was now needed was to take stock of the existing social structure and to mobilize, in new institutions, the cultural resources of the nobility as well as of the middle class.

This conviction henceforth determined Goethe's private and public life. Indeed, his role in the cultural and literary history of the subsequent decades can be properly assessed only if it is understood as, far from withdrawal into esoteric pursuits, an unremitting effort at defining and creating the instruments by which his vision of a reinvigorated German society could be made concrete and persuasive. The cultivation of the imagination, of the arts, literature, philosophy, science had hitherto been the concern of privileged individuals. He was certain that the stirring of religious, political and philosophical unrest that had asserted itself in the passionate declarations of the Sturm und Drang should now become productive in shaping the more open society of the coming century.

Goethe's private life seemed, after his return from Italy, in many respects frustrated and disappointing: his personal relations in Weimar were not entirely unstrained (Charlotte von Stein had been deeply offended by his sudden and secret departure) and the German public at large showed little interest in the recent publication of his collected works. Two sets of poems, one elegiac, the other epigrammatical, reflect the tensions of a mind whose joy in the concreteness of experienced life encountered only indifference and hostility.

A series of elegies, in letters to Schiller entitled 'Erotica Romana' and later (1795) simply 'Elegien', composed in recollection of his life in Italy, is perhaps the finest sequence of sustained love poetry in German literature. The growth in perception and the exploration of a world of immense variety, splendid as evidence of past greatness and compelling as a challenge to the present; are rendered in superbly disciplined language and a brilliant use of allusive metaphors. The tone of these poems draws together memory and immediacy, it links passion and reflection, the actuality of myth and the continuity of felt time; an instinctual, even epicurean, delight in the telling power of forms come alive is the unmistakable signature of Goethe's classicism.

As he wrote the elegies, he thought of Ovid and Propertius. He had Martial, the master of the epigram, in mind for the collection of miscellaneous brief poems which he composed during and after a short stay

Venice, a place far less attractive or stimulating for him than classical
ome. These *Epigramme. Venedig 1790* (1796) are evidence of a sharply
ritical mood, an awareness of the confining social and political circum-
ances of his own life. What makes them remarkable is the skill with
hich entirely occasional material is here cast in a genre that proves its
ecific usefulness for polemical and argumentative, yet civilized,
iscourse.

The moderately appealing dramatic fragments, 'Die Aufgeregten'
1791–92) and *Der Bürgergeneral* (1793) offer evidence of Goethe's
eaction to the French Revolution: comic figures represent radical senti-
ients – in the one the agitator seeks to persuade the villagers to make
ng-overdue demands on their lord; in the other, a silly fellow pretends
be a Jacobin general and hopes to create revolutionary sympathies
mong the peasants. Intervention by sensible members of the nobility
esolve the conflicts in both plays. The farcical setting seemed to Goethe
ppropriate enough. He used it again in another production, *Der Gross-
ophta* (1792), originally planned as a libretto for a comic opera dealing
ith that mysterious 'affair of the diamond necklace' at the court of Louis
VI, in which the celebrated swindler Cagliostro was implicated. The
lay gave Goethe an opportunity to express, at least obliquely, his convic-
ion that the Revolution was the predictable popular reaction to an
responsible and corrupt ruling class. Intelligent understanding of
gitimate grievances and generosity might be a means of social change
iore effective than the potential holocaust of a revolution. To take these
asual pieces as entirely conclusive evidence of Goethe's attitude towards
he events across the Rhine overestimates their documentary value; they
re, certainly, indicative of double strands in his thinking. On the one
and he was sceptical of easy optimism or vague enthusiasm for simple-
iinded goodness, and on the other, determined to join all efforts at
eveloping new forms of social responsibility.

He now had the supervision of the growing scientific collections at
ena, and was of decisive importance in developing that university into a
trong and modern place of teaching and research. He was at the same
ime in charge of the new Weimar court theatre, for him a most promis-
ng vehicle for advancing the political maturity of the middle class. That
hese involvements were not based on an exaggerated faith in the human
otential is apparent in a polished work of caustic assumptions, the epic
oem 'Reineke Fuchs', published 1794 in his *Neue Schriften*. Here, in
lowing hexameters, Goethe retells the medieval prose tale of Reynard
he cunning fox, whose adventures among his peers in the kingdom of the
ion, his skill in maintaining himself against the establishment and his
ltimate appointment as Chancellor of the realm is the most Voltairean
f Goethe's narrative works, another instance of his formal mobility and

of his increasing skill in relating a given subject matter to an appropria
form.

An essay, 'Einfache Nachahmung der Natur, Manier, Stil', conceive
in the wake of Italian reflections and written in 1788 for Wieland
Teutsche Merkur, is an attempt at deriving the several modes of art fro
anthropological premises. The first of these artistic approaches is th
imitative, which is confined to a restatement of the external features of a
object, unreflected and wholly respectful of its particular character. I
the second, a particular *manner* is achieved, an arrangement of par
directed by a selective intelligence, and suggesting something of th
personal character of the artist. *Style*, the third mode, is the most admi
able – it combines the previous approaches but, having comprehende
the total organic structure of the object, renders it as a representative
the type that informs the individual variant; it depends upon an adequat
understanding of the object's function and must be 'truly grounded i
knowledge'.[28] It is in this mode that art can claim to be among the highe
of human endeavours.

Goethe here defines more distinctly than before the relationshi
between art and nature. Art, he insists, cannot be mere 'imitation'
nature, it is a system *sui generis* that must rest upon a close comprehen
sion of the conditions of the observed world. At its most satisfying, art
the result of articulating our comprehension of order, empirically to b
found in nature and translated into aesthetic structures of an interna
logic which, while not identical with that of the natural object, are never
theless analogous to it. With its emphasis upon explicating a form c
knowledge that is both empirical and conceptually satisfying, Goeth
offers in this essay a first concise outline of his classicist theory.

The literary output of these years is modest in scope and largely
matter of revising, completing or projecting. For the new collection of hi
works he pulled together what he had written in Frankfurt and in Italy c
Faust and thus made these, as yet fragmentary, scenes for the first tim
available to a wider audience. In 1791 he resumed work on *Wilhelm*
Meister, now taking that impressionable character beyond the dubiou
world of the theatre towards a wider social experience and a mor
cautious assessment of the available opportunities for self-realization
The novel was not completed until several years later when Schiller'
criticism produced an acceptable conclusion.

In his scientific work, an ever more central concern, he extends hi
interest in botany and mineralogy to the study of optics and to tha
complex of empirical and philosophical questions which later converg
in his theory of colour. He shares more and more in the contemporar

[28] Goethe *GA*, XIII, p. 68.

iscussion of scientific issues and specifically encourages the court to upport various kinds of research. In the course of these scientific activi- ies he clarifies his view of the fundamental relationship between observa- ion and theory, between the particular phenomenon and the framework f judgement through which it assumes greater significance. Science had een an area of fascination ever since his youthful, more instinctive, nterest in alchemy and Renaissance cosmology. But his empiricist bent ad gradually led to more concrete scientific pursuits, to investigations hat were of interest to him not merely for their immediate results, but as he premises of a theory of culture based on biological and anthropolog- cal data. Within such a comprehensive horizon of purpose, he regarded is poetic work and his interests in art as altogether dependent upon an dequate and modern understanding of the physical universe. Science nd art thus offered interlocking means of access to knowledge.

In Italy he had come to the conclusion, set forth in *Versuch, die Meta- norphose der Pflanzen zu erklären*, that the instrumental features of atural growth – metamorphosis, polarity and intensification – may vell offer something like a 'pattern' of every kind of creativity. His *Beyträge zur Optik* (1791–92) is an attempt at outlining the characteris- ics of colour, based on a physiological theory. He insists on deriving these lmost entirely from sensory observations and, in pointed opposition to Newton, in non-mathematical terms. By basing his conclusions on the mportance of the eye's response to colour, he thought he could prove the ndivisibility of white light – light, he argued, must be mixed with dark- ess to produce colour. This is achieved by the light's passing through an paque medium: it appears yellow if it passes through vaporous air, the lue of the sky is produced by light's refraction through the atmosphere gainst the 'darkness of infinite space'. In the later *Farbenlehre* this dubious contention is elaborated and defended with incredible stubborn- ess, not only against Newton but against nearly all serious students of hysics. But Goethe's primary error does not invalidate his host of exact nd original observations concerning the dependence of colour upon the hemical composition of objects and, most important, his interest in the sychological effects of colour.

If in these experiments Goethe drew conclusions from carefully con- idered but inadequate data, this was in part the result of his postulate hat the testing of natural phenomena should be free of all speculative nterference. At the same time, he had reached a point in his intellectual levelopment at which a resolute faith in the significance of a particular henomenon was so longer sufficient. His philosophical creed had itherto rested on an acceptance of Spinoza's pantheistic formula: *deus ive natura*, on the assumption of an immanent structure of meaning, a rinciple of harmony or truth to be recognized *in herbis et lapidibus*. The

collecting and comparing of objects had seemed a wholly rewardin
exercise. He was soon to doubt that this empirical manner of enquiry wa
adequate, or even entirely free of subjective judgement. The relationshi
between the observing mind and the object was bound to become an issu
of overriding, and by no means merely scientific, consequence.

An essay entitled 'Der Versuch als Vermittler von Objekt und Subjekt
(1793) is the first document of Goethe's growing dissatisfaction with thi
naive sort of empiricism and of his tentative recognition of the role o
conceptual hypotheses and propositions in the ordering of evidence an
in the strategy of scientific research. He had previously resisted th
subjectivity of his Sturm und Drang friends, whether offered in religious
aesthetic or social terms; what now concerned him most was the danger o
permitting arbitrary speculation to misdirect observation and t
jeopardize the validity of his experiments.

He could, at any rate, not remain unaffected by the discussion among
the Jena philosophers of the Kantian categories in which the relationshi
between subject and object should be defined: useful theoretical conclusions, he now learned, can be drawn from even the most exacting
experiments only if a conceptualizing capacity is presupposed, a capacity
which, Kant maintained, exists in our consciousness *a priori*, independent of experience.

The academic community at the University of Jena, scientists as well as
philosophers, was deeply engaged in an assessment of the two cardina
intellectual achievements of those years – Kant's three *Critiques* and
Herder's *Ideen zur Philosophie der Geschichte der Menschheit*. Herde
built his theory of cultural evolution on the assumption of an instinctua
power in every individual and every society to develop rational, sensua
and emotional resources towards full participation in a universal,
humane society. It was a concept that appeared to advocate an idealism
based on sweeping interpretations of anthropological evidence. Kant's
theory of consciousness was far more exacting and closely argued: i
amounted to the most radical modern proclamation of the constituent
role of ideas – precisely and logically defined – in the processes of
experience and cognition.

The discussion of Kant's theories had, since 1787, been stimulated by
the philosopher K.L. Reinhold, who lectured on Kant's system to most
of the University's 900 students and made Jena the centre of 'critical'
studies. His *Briefe über die Kantische Philosophie* (1790–92) is a popular introduction to that revolutionary system. The relationship between
the efficacy of the senses and their control by some sort of intellectual
discipline had been discussed throughout the eighteenth century by
philosophers and writers of the most divergent persuasions. In Germany
it had provided the topic of much discursive fiction: Wieland, as we have

een, warned indefatigably against a faith in the spurious satisfaction brought about by excessive sensuality and the delusions of speculative enthusiasm'.

Goethe's own first reaction to Kant's theories was cautious. They rested on what he thought was a dogmatic and therefore somewhat uncongenial subjectivism. He admitted in retrospect that Kant's *Kritik der reinen Vernunft* (1781), which he read in September 1793, was

> altogether outside my realm of interest. Nevertheless I took part in many a conversation about it and, with some attention, I could observe that the old central question was here resumed: how much does our own self, and how much does the external world contribute to our intellectual life? I had never separated the two, and when I speculated in my own manner about the objective world I did so with unconscious naiveté and, indeed, believed that I could see my own opinions before my eyes.[29]

Although our life begins with experience, he was willing to concede that it is not true to say that the whole of our knowledge can be derived from experience. Knowledge of the objective world is impossible without granting a decisive role to reflection; it is the capacity to bring conceptualizing judgement into the epistemological act, the availability of *Geist*, as the disciples of Fichte would soon put it, that constitutes the privileged role of man within the world.

The character of Goethe's own poetry as well as the direction in which the novel *Wilhelm Meister* was to be continued, depended upon a clear grasp of the impact of specific concepts on the process of understanding, upon the comprehension of the relationship between 'ideas' and 'reality', between 'mind' and 'nature' – a dichotomy which, ever since his Strasbourg days, he had found easy to dismiss as a dualism incompatible with his pantheistic beliefs.

He was now prepared to consider it a legitimate, even disturbing, challenge. Indeed, he was soon to discover that it had, in an intellectual context different from his own, preoccupied the thinking of Schiller, in the years ahead to become his closest critic and friend.

[29] Goethe *GA*, XVI, p. 874.

4

The Whole Man

Schiller: Art and Social Action

Schiller's visit to Jena in August 1787, almost a year before Goethe's return from Italy, was for him the beginning of nearly two decades of the most sustained literary productivity, of an intellectual engagement, of a creative and critical effervescence that is without parallel in the history of German letters. He came to terms with the radical work of Kant and Fichte, and the canon of ancient literature and philosophy; and soon, in close exchanges with Goethe, integrated this cosmos of tradition and contemporary thought in a theory of culture, of the role of a highly reflective sort of art and of social action that determined the articulation of the European experience of modernism for generations to come.

For the *Teutsche Merkur* he produced his first extended philosophical poem, 'Die Götter Griechenlands' (1788): in keeping with Wieland and the Weimar circle's admiration for Winckelmann, he contrasts the Christian yearning for a distant Beyond with the immediacy and presence of the Greek gods.[1] This was an idealistic view of classical life, never quite abandoned, which Jacob Burckhardt firmly rejected in his *Griechische Kulturgeschichte* as 'one of the grossest falsifications of the historical judgement that has ever occurred, all the more irresistible the more innocently and convincingly it is presented'.[2] Wieland encouraged the writing of yet another characteristic poem, 'Die Künstler' (1789), a long and involved but revealing exposition of the historical scheme to which

[1] A second part of the poem appeared in Schiller's *Gedichte I*, 1800; the first part was much revised in *Gedichte II*, 1803.

[2] Jacob Burckhardt, *Griechische Kulturgeschichte*, Stuttgart, Kröner, 1952, II, p. 30–1.

Schiller remained committed – the path to freedom leads from a state of happy unconsciousness to a condition in which the awareness of a conflict between sensuality and truth produces a divided consciousness and, ultimately, a reconciliation of these opposites through learning and the arts.

Schiller's access to meaning was altogether through history. His large-scale accounts of the liberation of the Netherlands (1788) and of the Thirty Years' War (1792) were no mere by-products of the lectures he gave at Jena: the one topic was related to work on *Don Carlos*, the other suggested the material of his later *Wallenstein* plays. His inaugural address (1789) dealt with the question, 'What is universal history, and to what purpose do we study it?' It was a plea for a 'philosophical' understanding of the dynamic progression of history towards a state of rationality. The models for his scheme he found in A.L von Schlözer's *Universalhistorie* (1772) and in Gibbon's *Decline and Fall* (1776ff.), in Livy, in Herder's *Ideen* and, particularly, in Kant's essay 'Idee zu einer allgemeinen Geschichte in weltbürgerlicher Absicht' (1784). All these recognized the teleological thrust of history in a movement beyond incidents and accidents towards a society dedicated to the pursuit of moral law.

When Schiller ceased lecturing in 1794, his concerns had become more specific: he was now anxious to focus on an issue to which all his subsequent thinking and writing was to return. It was the problem of defining the task which an historical understanding of the revolutionary present put to his generation, the task, that is, of analysing the character of an age in disarray and of examining the resources that might offer prospects of individual and collective recovery and 'freedom'. The overwhelming course of events during the last half century had been a dominant preoccupation of men of letters everywhere: the shift of power in America from colonial rule to independence seemed modest and almost benign compared to the radical passing of sovereignty in the French Revolution from one class to another. Social life in Germany was bound to be affected by these events and no writer, whatever his allegiance or persuasion, could afford to remain indifferent. The extraordinarily vivacious and argumentative group of men in Jena and Weimar was immediately drawn into partisan declarations: while Wieland's *Teutsche Merkur* remained impartial and ambiguous, the informative *Allgemeine Literaturzeitung* contained ample material for discussion. Founded by F.J. Bertuch and edited by C.G. Schütz and G. Hufeland, this daily publication appeared from 1785 to 1803 in Jena, from then until 1849 in Halle. It offered anonymous reviews of nearly every book published in Germany and of much foreign literature, and with its distinguished contributors – Kant, Schiller, the Schlegel brothers, Humboldt, Fichte and others – was the leading critical journal of the period.

With many others, Schiller recognized the enormous consequences of the Revolution; they were critical of Jacobin politics, critical, that is to say, of the notion that the feudal order, which appeared at the time generally prepared to modify its claims to absolute power based on landed property, should at once give way to the untried authority of the middle class. That class, Schiller and Goethe were certain, was in Germany wholly unprepared for wide-ranging responsibilities; it was their hope that by a process of evolution the traditional qualities of the aristocracy might sustain and enhance the progressive thrust of the 'bourgeoisie' and that the intellectual and cultural energies of the middle class should in turn modify the established monolithic exercise of feudal power. An education of broadly cultural scope must precede the enunciation of specific political goals.

While Schiller's historical studies occupied him intensely, he translated Euripides' *Iphigenie* and Aeschylus' *Agamemnon*, studied K.P. Moritz's *Über die bildende Nachahmung des Schönen*, reflected systematically on aesthetic topics and reviewed Goethe's recent plays, *Egmont* and *Iphigenie*. In an important assessment of the poetry of G.A. Bürger, he deplored the excessively personal element in the work of what he considered a flawed character, and defined the resources that seemed to him indispensible in a poet. It is, Schiller maintains, not merely the choice of material suitable for a symbolic treatment of broad philosophical significance, or the capacity to project an 'ideal of perfection' that distinguishes the major writer, but the ability to transcend his subjectivity, to distance himself from an immediate occasion and impulse, and to act not only as a human being but as artist. Schiller here insists categorically on detachment in the poetric act, on a form of 'alienation' such as Diderot had thought essential for the actor: 'Let the poet beware of writing of pain while he is still in pain . . . he must begin by becoming a stranger to himself, to separate the object of his enthusiasm from his individuality, to contemplate his passion from an assuaging distance.'[3] For the first time Schiller defines the central purpose of poetry as the achievement in critical self-consciousness of a relationship between instinct and intellect; only the mediation of the private under the discipline of the ideal can produce art of compelling moral force. The turn towards a classical theory of art is unmistakable in this important review. It is reiterated even more sharply in another, equally critical, piece, 'Über Matthissons Gedichte' (1794): the individuality of the poet, Schiller asserts once

[3] Schiller *SW*, V, p. 982.

gain, must be made universally effective, all accidental features of his elf as well as of the object to be illuminated, must be extinguished in avour of what is 'necessary' and illustrative of general principles of truth nd beauty. More and more resolutely Schiller moves towards a view of oetry as severe in its premises as it is demanding in its consequences for he function of literature. He rationalizes his own poetic manner, which ncreasingly subordinates every spontaneous impulse to the rigid control f ideas and formal categories. If art is to serve a purpose beyond personal ndulgence, if its effect is to be 'political' rather than merely scintillating, f at a time of scattered and unfocused purpose it is to recover the 'whole nan' and an enlightened, harmonious citizen, an unambiguous distinction must be maintained between the partial truth of actuality and the verriding truth of art. Reality provides the miscellaneous materials for he poet. Truth is made manifest in a fictive construct, in the appearance, ('Schein') of virtual coherence.

With this idealistic theory, Schiller shifts almost completely away from is youthful pietistic belief in 'virtue' as the achieved coincidence of sensuality and duty, and in the ability of the virtuous 'heart' to feel the ssential harmony inherent in the apparently disjointed and contradictory universe. It was his systematic study of Kant that had transformed his religious scheme. In the poem 'Die Künstler' and the essay 'Über die ragische Kunst' (1792) he suggests – not far from the spirit of Lessing – that the aesthetic experience amounts to the resolution (by the reader) f the tension between the sensual and the moral nature of man. In *Über Anmut und Würde* (1793) he reflects Kant's influence again; in 'Über die isthetische Erziehung des Menschen in einer Reihe von Briefen' (1794) nd in the essay 'Über naive und sentimentalische Dichtung' (1795–96) e is entirely committed to the new philosophy and ready to enunciate it vithin the purposes of his cultural vision.

Schiller's argument in these essays is tightly structured and cannot be asily summarized. He proceeds from Kant's conviction that obedience to he 'categorical imperative', a sense of morality beyond all immediate mpulses, achieves the state of potential 'freedom' that constitutes man; e accepts the Kantian thesis that 'beauty', as well as truth and goodness, nust rest on judgements derived from a conceptualizing faculty that is no ess universal than logic or morality, 'Reason' and 'sensuality', 'duty' and inclination', 'spirit' and 'nature' are in Kant's scheme in fundamental conflict with one another; for Schiller the highest form of human reality is chieved when that conflict is resolved in the 'unity of the moral personality'. This condition is the state of 'grace' (*Anmut*) that is characteristic f the 'beautiful soul'. Where that state is jeopardized by the pressure of nstincts and compulsions, the peremptory demonstration of 'dignity' *Würde*) is necessary.

From this general framework, prefigured in Shaftesbury's postulate o 'moral grace and dignity', Schiller derives his aesthetic theory. 'Beauty' he argues not far from Winckelmann, is that mode in which the mind (o the 'soul') has so thoroughly 'transformed' matter that material realit has lost its accidental character and has become the vehicle of an intel lectual or spiritual intention. In this state of 'beauty', the sensual is not s much destroyed, as rather completely unfolded, its structure is revealed its range explored. This exercise of 'freedom', the functioning of th mind within a high moral purpose towards a total absorption of matter permits Schiller to say that beauty is the achievement of freedom, o 'freedom in appearance' (*Freiheit in der Erscheinung*).[4]

But just as *Würde* must be brought into play where a radical conflic between inclination or instinct and duty arises, the resolution of matte and mind in 'beauty' may prove impossible or illusory. The ineluctabl compulsions and the 'irrational' implications of such concepts as 'fate' o 'death' cannot be neutralized in the serenity and harmony of beauty: th appropriate manner in which these must be experienced and representec is the 'sublime' state of mind achieved in the form of tragedy ('Über da Erhabene', *ca.* 1793).

Schiller's emphatic belief in the efficacy of art relates the moral anc the aesthetic sphere metaphorically rather than in sharply definec categories; it rests on his determination to project and delineate a visior of culture in which emotional; critical and creative decisions can, by a majestic act of will, produce a community of common human excellence To enunciate this vision seemed to him urgent at a time of evident political and social transformation, at a moment when the clear-cu philosophical and anthropological dualism of subject and object which the preceding decades had asserted, was no longer credible, when the ancient dichotomies of religious orthodoxy or the traditional justifica- tions of the distinction between 'masters and servants' had become profoundly questionable. In the face of revolutionary challenges, these antinomies require fresh and universally applicable resolutions. Art and politics – an understanding of art and of its public functioning – are clearly interdependent.

It is in this sense that 'Über die ästhetische Erziehung des Menschen in einer Reihe von Briefen' can be said to offer an almost heroic theory of beauty, a theory which he gradually developed and which he now under- takes to test within the context of modern culture. 'Beauty' of a certain kind is the category from which far-reaching political conclusions may be drawn. 'The spirit of philosophical enquiry is being expressly challenged by present circumstances to concern itself with the most perfect of all

[4] Schiller *SW*, V, p. 400.

works of art, with the construction of true political freedom.'[5] For 'Art is one of the daughters of freedom, and takes her orders from the necessity inherent in minds, not from the exigencies of matter.'[6] Schiller admits to having chosen an approach which may appear inappropriate and alien to the age. But his defence is bold and unequivocal: 'If man is ever to solve the problem of politics in practice [i.e. of power *vs* reason], he will have to approach it through the problem of the aesthetic, because it is only through Beauty that man makes his way to Freedom.'[7] This is the proposition upon which Schiller hinges his radical faith.

Here and elsewhere Schiller makes the sort of assumption that Rousseau's model had provided: the 'natural' organization of men, the social framework that derives its legitimacy from force rather than from laws, is being superseded by the 'moral' justification of a state in which ideals of conduct, however tentative and untried, can create a free society. This society, Schiller concludes in the fourth letter, must have the character of 'wholeness'.[8] 'Wholeness' is a condition – lost in the present state – in which individual aspirations and those of a given social reality coincide.[9] Whatever consolation the often invoked image of an idealized Greece may offer to the present, the progressive sophistication since that golden age and the consequent cultural disorientation is irreversible.[10] 'The cultivation of the individual', that inevitable corollary of modern life, has brought about the 'sacrifice of wholeness'. It is the premise of Schiller's vision of a new society 'that it must be possible for us to restore by means of a higher art the totality of our being which the arts themselves have destroyed.'[11]

The two fundamental resources of man's character, sensuousness and rationality, enable him to develop two related capacities: by the first man turns everything which is 'mere form' into reality; by his own power to create form he can transform within himself everything which is 'mere world'. Such antithetical concepts are the mark of Schiller's discursive method. Two 'drives' – the term used by Fichte in his much-discussed Jena lectures on epistemology (*Grundlage der gesamten Wissenschaftslehre*, 1794–95) – accomplish this transformation: the one Schiller now calls the 'sensuous drive' (*Stofftrieb*), the other the 'form drive' (*Formtrieb*). These categories are not so much descriptive of psychological impulses as indications of the (aesthetic) principles by which the

5 Schiller *SW*, V, p. 572.
6 Schiller *SW*, V, p. 572.
7 Schiller *SW*, V, p. 573.
8 Schiller *SW*, V, p. 578–9.
9 Schiller *SW*, V, p. 579.
10 Schiller *SW*, V, p. 582.
11 Schiller *SW*, V, p. 588.

sensuous and the rational conditions of man can be given shape and direction. The sensuous drive proceeds from the physical existence of man; 'form' from his 'absolute' or 'rational' existence. 'Form' is the summary indication of the activity by which rational man can give order and coherence (*Gestalt*) to the amorphous material of perception.

If the 'sensuous drive' demands that there should be change and that time shall have a content, and if the 'form drive' implies that time shall be annulled and that there shall be no change, a third principle, the 'play drive' (*Spieltrieb*) is directed towards 'annulling time within time, reconciling becoming with absolute being and change with identity'.

In the fifteenth letter, Schiller draws his conclusion: the object of the sensuous drive is 'life', the play drive has as its object the creation of 'living form'. Here Schiller reaches the core of his argument: it is that 'man "plays" only when he is in the fullest sense of the word a human being, and he is fully a human being only when he "plays" '.[12]

The juxtaposition of these two potentialities suggests 'play' as the 'aesthetic' state of mind in which man can experience his highest capacity, his wholeness: in contemplating 'living form' or 'beauty' he recognizes his humanity. The 'aesthetic condition' is the achievement of an equilibrium in self-awareness. 'Freedom' constitutes the specifically human being who has the power to create in 'play' a virtual universe, a world of semblance (*Schein*). As though to circumvent the Platonic warnings against the subversive effect of art, he asks in the twenty-sixth letter:

> How far can 'semblance' legitimately exist in the moral (actual) world? The answer is briefly and simply this: to the extent that it is aesthetic semblance; that is to say, semblance which neither seeks to represent reality nor needs to be justified by it, aesthetic semblance can never be a threat to the truth of morals.[13]

Schiller's thesis was to be of enormous consequence for the role of art as it emerged in the generation to come.

> In the midst of the fearful kingdom of power and in the midst of the sacred kingdom of (rational) laws, the aesthetic impulse-to-form is at work, barely noticed, on the building of a third joyous kingdom of play and semblance, in which man is relieved of the shackles of circumstance, and released from all that might be called constraint, alike in the physical and moral sphere![14]

Beauty alone and its comprehension in the exercise of 'taste' can bring harmony into society:

> all other forms of perception divide man, because they are founded exclusively

[12] Schiller *SW*, V, p. 618.
[13] Schiller *SW*, V, p. 660.
[14] Schiller *SW*, V, p. 667.

either upon the sensuous or upon the spiritual part of his being; only the aesthetic mode of perception makes him whole; only the aesthetic mode of communication unites society, because it relates to what is common to all.[15]

Because the aesthetic realm seemed to Schiller no less in need of a 'constitution' than the political, he hoped to elaborate these principles more fully in a later essay.[16] As it is now concluded, 'Über die ästhetische Erziehung' is a document of the highest historical importance. Its formal argument, modifying Kant's *Kritik der Urteilskraft* towards the moral efficacy of art, constitutes the programmatic outline of a German theory of 'classicism'; it is continually preoccupied with the definition of a personality whose 'wholeness', logically argued as a *Gestalt* of complex 'aesthetic' balance precariously achieved, and of normally discrepant energies, is the condition of 'freedom' within a society as yet defined only by its negatives. However disparate German social life and thought during the subsequent 20 years may have been, Schiller's analysis offered the challenging terms in which the prevalent sense of disjointedness could be discussed. Together with him, the remarkable group of scholars who were at work in Weimar and Jena, some sympathetic to Kantian idealism, others, like Herder, increasingly distrustful of its esoteric and, as he felt, a-historical doctrine, formed a community of purpose from which incalculable impulses extended into German and European intellectual life.

Meeting of Minds: Goethe and Schiller

It was by no means predictable that Goethe and Schiller should find themselves drawn to one another and that they should before long join in a common strategy. For some time Goethe had felt a strong antipathy to a personality that seemed to him in essential respects unattractive: Schiller's manner – severe, brilliant, analytical, incessantly reflective and at almost every moment ready to subject ideas to the stern categories of a radicalized Kantian philosophy – was uncongenial. He had little sympathy for the undercurrent in Schiller's thinking of Protestant rigour; he was by temperament averse to Schiller's rhetorical pathos and his articulation of convictions and ideals in dramatic designs of insistent intellectual stringency. Different from his own empirical bent, Schiller seemed inclined to subordinate experience to conceptual logic; any antithetical distinction between nature and mind struck Goethe as a simplification that merely by-passed the task he had set for himself, the task of searching for coherent patterns of order in the world. In October, 1790, he had visited Schiller in Jena and on that occasion touched cautiously

[15] Schiller *SW*, V, p. 667.
[16] Schiller *SW*, V, p. 1148.

on Kant's early essays. Later he suspected, rightly or wrongly, that certain passages in Schiller's *Über Anmut und Würde* had been critically directed at himself. He had not hesitated to support and confirm Schiller's appointment as professor of history at Jena, but maintained towards the younger man a pointed reserve.

It was a mutual interest in aesthetic issues that brought the two together in June and July 1794. In a retrospective account 'Glückliches Ereignis', Goethe later dramatized the moment after a meeting of the Jena Research Society (that had been established a year earlier, on 14 July 1793), when they agreed on their disapproval of the atomistic manner in which the paper they had just heard had dealt with a scientific issue. Schiller deplored the 'fragmented' approach, Goethe in turn suggested a more coherent, dynamic and deductive method. He outlined his empirical 'morphological' procedure and sketched his model of an *Urpflanze*, the prototype of a plant, from which a necessary interplay of unity and variety could be deduced. Schiller countered that no such conclusion could be drawn directly from experience; surely Goethe must rather presuppose an idea. 'I was surprised,' Goethe admitted later, 'and a little miffed, because the point that separated us was plainly clarified by his statement. I recalled Schiller's remarks in *Über Anmut und Würde*, and the old annoyance [at Schiller's way of reasoning] was about to come over me again. But I pulled myself together and said, "I can only be pleased to have ideas without knowing it, even ideas that I can see with my own eyes." '[17]

The difference in their ways of thought was at that moment defined: Schiller – while by training non-speculative and hostile to the transcendental idealism soon to be developed by Fichte and Schelling – had learned from Kant to distinguish precisely between object and subject; Goethe's concrete thinking distrusted philosophical constructions and deductive reasoning. He moved towards a kind of generalization he preferred to call 'symbolic'. Schiller's skill in extrapolating led him to outline in a celebrated letter to Goethe (23 August 1794) the positions that had emerged from that conversation. Soon he developed what seemed at first merely a contrasting of personal ways of thought into a systematic distinction between two types of modern poetic perception; a year and a half later, the resulting essay, 'Über naive und sentimentalische Dichtung' (1795) was to be of momentous significance not only for the relationship of the two men, but for subsequent theories of criticism. It was, moreover, at an historical juncture of inestimable consequence, evidence of a grander purpose: ostensibly aesthetic arguments were more and more urgently to reveal their political implications.

[17] Goethe *GA*, XVI, p. 869.

'The Most Important Event in Europe . . .'

In that catastrophically hot and dry summer of 1794, the turmoil of the Revolution appeared to have reached a critical stage: the defeat of the Girondists had diminished the cautious sympathies of the German landed gentry, months of terror, the execution of the King and of the radical Jacobin leaders Danton and Robespierre produced sharp divisions among German conservatives and liberals. Accounts by German travellers of the early phase of the Revolution (J.H. Campe's *Briefe aus Paris*, 1790, J.F. Reichardt's *Vertraute Briefe über Frankreich*, 1792–93, in which he describes his visits to the National Assembly and to the Jacobin Club), or by actual participants in the revolutionary wars (*F.C. Lauckhardts Leben und Schicksale von ihm selbst beschrieben*, 1792–1802) were eagerly read.

The debate for and against the prospect of radical changes in Germany inspired by the Revolution had for some time been heatedly carried on in publications of limited circulation. The German aristocratic refugees who left their estates in the territories occupied by the French army were not universally welcomed elsewhere, and enthusiasm for the Revolution was noisily demonstrated in some parts of the country. Unrest appeared to be spreading: since 1792 an uneasy coalition of Silesian weavers, peasants and landowners had openly rebelled against oppressive taxes. In Strasbourg, Mainz, Kiel and Altona, 'Jacobin' clubs, opposed to all forms of feudal sovereignty, attempted to mobilize artisans and peasants, and hoped for republican administrations. Mainz, occupied in October 1792 by General Custine's French troops was, by a vote of less than 10 per cent of its citizens, for four days declared a republic. In Jacobin circles the intellectual impulses of the European Enlightenment continued strong. English deism, the moral philosophies of Locke, Hume and Shaftesbury, French materialist thought and, of course, the events in America, provided the background of their discourse.

Firmly counter-revolutionary publications such as L.A.C. von Grolmann's *Eudaemonia* (1795–98) or H.A.O. Reichard's *Revolutionsalmanach* (1793–1803) were probably more widely read than Jacobin pamphlets and journals such as Karl Clauer's *Der Kreuzzug gegen die Franken* (1791), but the scope of revolutionary literature must not be underrated. The most uncompromising among the partisans of the Revolution was A.G.F. Rebmann, a man of uncorruptible idealism, the founder, in Aachen, of a 'radical' reading society and the author of numerous pamphlets in which he defended himself against the suspicion of being an agent in the pay of the Revolution, *Kosmopolitische Wanderungen durch einen Teil Deutschlands* (1793–95), or *Wahrheit oder Schminke* (1794), *Vollständige Geschichte meiner Leiden* (1796) and, from 1798 to 1801, of a more and more resigned *Obscuranten-Almanach*.

The majority of German intellectuals remained essentially respectful of existing authority. They preferred to put their trust in a more or less enlightened feudal government and tended to fear that any form of popular sovereignty would lead to political and social disorder. The universities, Protestant as well as Catholic, were more receptive to notions of change: at Kiel and Jena, as well as Bonn, Cologne and Münster, the philosophical and theological faculties defended the Revolution as an attempt to justify government by reason and law. As late as 1798 Kant asserted that the Revolution 'can have as its cause no other but a moral disposition in man'.[18] Fichte welcome in 1793 the Revolution in a pamphlet with the blunt title 'Zurückforderung der Denkfreiheit von den Fürsten Europens, die sie bisher unterdrückten' that nearly jeopardized his appointment at Jena; though anti-monarchist, he hoped for reform by the princes and insisted that the dubious claims of organized society should, in any case, be challenged by assertions in one form or another of radical subjectivity. The critical self, alienated from society, can postulate a 'humane' order only as a process of 'permanent revolution'. What he envisaged in his passionately moralizing writings was a rational society beyond the interests and constraints of the state.

In two eloquent lectures Fichte reminded his listeners in 1799 (publ. 1802), of the unique opportunity to develop through the Freemasonic lodges a modern social philosophy rejecting discredited utilitarian pragmatism; men of all ranks and persuasions could there bring their particular qualifications and insights to the common purpose of developing a cosmopolitan culture of 'the whole man'. Lessing, as we have seen, was a strong, if critical, advocate of masonic ideals; in 1791 Mozart offered his *Zauberflöte* as a testimonial to that masonic faith in universal brotherhood.

The order of the *Illuminati*, founded in 1776 by Adam Weishaupt, pursued a strictly anti-Jesuit policy and offered a graduated scheme of secular education that progressed from a novitiate state to the more advanced conditions of *Illuminati minores* and *majores*. Each phase required the command of certain areas of knowledge, scientific as well as literary, and a familiarity with deistic and materialistic theories. Dedicated to egalitarian notions of secular progress, natural law, tolerance and political activism, the order was strongly opposed to the *ancien régime*. Suspicions of republican sympathies and presumed attempts to influence the politics of the court led to its interdiction in Bavaria in 1784. It was this ban that seemed to have intensified the active

[18] Kant, *Sämtliche Werke*, op. cit., I, p. 638.

interest of its members elsewhere in the events and prospects of the French Revolution and, inevitably, their designation as German Jacobins. Distinguished men such as Goethe, Wieland, Nicolai, Herder, Pestalozzi and the young Beethoven were among its six or seven hundred members. By their social composition and their reasoned humanism, the *Illuminati* were of remarkable influence and shared significantly in the discussion of controversial political issues.

Groups with similar concerns such as the *Rosicrucians*, though more specifically mystical in their beliefs, contributed in turn to the effectiveness of secret societies. Saint-Martin, Swedenborg, Lavater and Mesmer were quietly their instrumental agents; at many of the smaller German courts, meetings of a curiously occult cast brought together men of diverse standing but strong utopian motives. Frederick William II, the insignificant successor to his great uncle, was surrounded by Rosicrucian advisers. For many freemasonry was a suspicious form of deceitful, even conspiratorial *Schwärmerei*, especially since the infamous adventurer Giuseppe Balsamo, Count Cagliostro had been exposed: Cagliostro, constantly on the move between the courts of Paris, London, St Petersburg, Warsaw or Strasbourg, had promised miracle cures through his carefully guarded elixirs, had, in 1786 been imprisoned in the Bastille and expelled from France only to have him found in Rome an independent lodge of the 'Egyptian Rite'.

The progressive role of these associations and the appeal of their supranational political vision cannot be overrated. It was their avowed hope that a world-wide community would create a society free of the crippling distinctions of class, of arbitrary political authority or of ecclesiastical doctrine.

There was little doubt among men of letters that, whatever the outcome of the revolutionary movement, a turning point had been reached in contemporary German life. When Herder, always strongly anti-monarchical, spoke of the Revolution as nearly the 'most important event'[19] in Europe since the introduction of Christianity and the Reformation, he only echoed a consensus that the Revolution represented the epoch-making emancipation of efficacious reason. It is not surprising, under the circumstances, that intelligent and well-informed writers who expressed even guarded sympathy with the Revolution, or favoured republican forms of government were at the time – and in the view of subsequent literary historians – summarily discredited. Georg Forster and A. von Knigge are characteristic examples.

As a passionate advocate of the revolutionary cause, Forster became

[19] J.G. Herder, *Briefe zur Beförderung der Humanität*, ed. H.-J. Kruse, Berlin, Aufbau Verlag, 1970, II, p. 334.

president of the Mainz Jacobin Club and urged a union with France of the territories west of the Rhine. At the time of his early death in Paris he was defamed by his countrymen as a renegade and a fanatic. He was, in fact, one of the ablest and most perceptive men of his time. His career was astonishingly varied and restless: born near Danzig, he had, as a young man visited Russia, lived in London, accompanied his father on Captain Cook's second voyage (1772–75) and written an admirable account of it (in English 1777, in German 1778–80) – a document which so impressed the poet J.H. Voss and his friends that they planned to establish a community of poets on Tahiti where, they had been assured, they would find men much like Homer's Greeks.

Forster travelled widely, taught natural history in Kassel and Wilna, was in 1788 librarian in Mainz. In 1790 he joined Alexander von Humboldt on a trip through Belgium, Holland, England and France (*Ansichten vom Niederrhein*, 1791–94). A writer of clear and firm prose, an observer and recorder of the social and cultural life abroad as well as in Germany, he was committed to the cosmopolitan ideals of the Enlightenment, yet close to Herder (and the later romantics) in his appreciation of national features and customs, landscape, art and architecture.

When Friedrich Schlegel published his essay on Forster (1797), he praised him as a liberal and progressive mind who 'combined French elegance and popular style, English public spiritedness and German depth of feeling and thought.'[20] By no means self-evident in Germany at that time, Forster was a writer profoundly dedicated to broad social effectiveness:

> What he considered the specific advantages of our age [Schlegel concludes,] and the most satisfying result of commerce, was to recognize the interrelationship of the most diverse fields of knowledge and their diffusion through society. . . . The joining together of all knowledge that is essentially related yet at present dissociated and fragmented, into one indivisible whole seemed to him the sublime goal of the scholar's work.[21]

Of the popular men of letters with outspoken masonic sympathies, Adolf von Knigge was one of the most energetic and engaging. Familiar as the author of an influential social conduct manual for the rising middle class, *Über den Umgang mit Menschen* (1788), he was in his convictions and his publications less single-minded than Forster but, as a member of the landed gentry and an official in several responsible positions, remarkably eloquent in defence of the Revolution and in his

[20] Schlegel *KA*, I, 2, p. 93.
[21] Schlegel *KA*, I, 2, p. 99.

advocacy of parliamentary government. His satirical and pedagogical writings – autobiographical sketches, plays, sermons, novels – reflect an enlightened, at times rather pedestrian, pragmatism; his translation of Rousseau's *Confessions* (1786–90) indicates the source of his dedication to the scrutiny of traditional social assumptions. In his *Geschichte des armen Herrn von Mildenburg* (1789–97), the most readable of his novels, the ingrained prejudices of his class frustrate a nobleman's hopes of a humane life. But it was Knigge's more explicitly political fiction (*Benjamin Noldmanns Geschichte der Aufklärung in Abyssinien*, 1791; *Des seligen Herrn Etatsraths Samuel Konrad von Schaafskopf hinterlassene Papiere*, 1792) with its anti-absolutist, anti-Prussian sentiments, its fervent appeal for help from the more progressive rulers, and in *Das Zauberschloss* (1790) with its projection of a republican government by the middle class, that caused him to be attacked as echoing the propagandists of the Enlightenment. In *Josephs von Wurmbrand . . . politisches Glaubensbekenntnis* (1792) Knigge urges the direct social responsibility of the writer, insists on his capacity to reflect the state of mind of the community, and encourages the active exercise of enlightened political judgement. It was not surprising that the royal censors in Hanover heavily fined the publisher of this work and reprimanded the author for attacking the civil and religious authority, and for defending and openly advocating rebellion. All of Knigge's subsequent writings had to be submitted to the censors before publication.

Unlike more radical Jacobins, Knigge hoped for the gradual emancipation of that middle-class element in German society which was not in a revolutionary mood. In France a complex power structure had in 1789 been successfully challenged by the uprising of a heterogeneous bourgeoisie who commanded a measure of landed property and an effective role in the established bureaucracy. In the German states this class was not strong enough to marshall revolutionary sentiments; its economic condition was almost fatally weakened by the prevailing system of customs barriers between hundreds of sovereign territories that prevented the development of an internal German market. The German middle class depended for its welfare almost totally on the landed aristocracy and eagerly cultivated the advantages of belonging to a princely bureaucracy. Indeed, its relative impotence made it susceptible, through decades of ideological and military conflict, to strong counter-revolutionary forces that were helped by widespread sympathies with English conservative sentiments. Göttingen, the Hanoverian university accountable to King George III, became understandably a centre for the spreading of Burke's ideas: his *Reflections on the Revolution in France* was in 1793 translated by F. von Gentz. A.W. Rehberg's *Untersuchungen über die Französische Revolution* (1793), a characteristic conservative tract, argues that 'the laws of reason are by no means adequate to derive from them a bourgeois society'; the 'so-called dignity of the citizen' is a fiction without practical political significance.[22]

The clashing aspirations of the two political philosophies, activism and the more detached reflections of philosophical idealism, are compellingly portrayed in two novels by Maximilian Klinger, *Geschichte eines Teutschen der neusten Zeit* (1798) and its sequel, *Der Weltmann und der Dichter* (1798). With *Fausts Leben, Thaten und Höllenfahrt* Klinger had, in 1791, distanced himself critically – and satirically – from the Sturm und Drang movement which 15 years earlier he had himself helped to inaugurate. The surprising theme of the two later novels is the paralysing effect of the Revolution upon thought and art. The conflict between the hero's rejection of a continuing feudal rule and his fear of radicalism is not so much reconciled as by-passed in a concluding invocation of Rousseau.

There could be no doubt, whatever the intellectual or sentimental sympathies, that any future German society was bound to recognize the self-confidence of the middle class. Yet even if that society was to be shaped by the rational impulses which the French Revolution had so spectacularly set free, it was nevertheless the heir to a tradition of culture to which the aristocracy had in their best representatives contributed a responsible ethos and a long experience in public administration. Class distinctions had in Germany for long been drawn more sharply than elsewhere. The court, the attached nobility, landed proprietors, army officers, and the leading families of a few independent cities were the social core. They were supported and served by a large body of minor officials, by an agrarian class – four-fifths of the total German population was engaged in agriculture – that was restricted by various forms of dependency. There existed a growing mass of legally unprotected holders of small property and another of artisans and merchants, rigidly organized and delimited in their appropriate guilds. To an increasing extent the landed nobility was in debt to the urban middle class.

Education in the broadest sense, towards the creation of a solidly articulated middle class, was obviously an overriding revolutionary task. As it was defined by nearly all contemporary men of letters, by Kant, Herder, Schiller, Goethe or Fichte, this project required broadly 'philosophical' premises and their integration in an intellectual system, an 'anthropology', of the exemplary though not unchallenged consistency of Kant's three *Critiques*. To emancipate the middle class it was necessary first of all to define those intellectual and emotional resources

[22] A.W. Rehberg, *Untersuchungen über die Französische Revolution*, Hannover, Ritscher, 1793, p. I, 12, 49f.

hat were not predetermined by historical, social or religious constraints. These, many contended, must be derived wholly from that primary and emancipatory capacity of reason which constitutes the dignity of the individual and provides the justification of the new society, not class-bound but 'humane' and thus universal.

No doubt, in retrospect, the resolve of many of the best minds to post-pone concrete political action and to concentrate on a systematic exploration of available forms of modern philosophical discourse seemed merely a dilatory and evasive manoeuvre. In a bitter passage, Heinrich Heine voiced the passionate regret of the next generation at the inability or unwillingness of the German intellectuals to recognize the opportuni-ties for change which the Revolution had offered them: it was, he wrote in 1830, 'as though the French who had so much pressing work to do for which they needed to be wide awake, had asked us Germans in the mean-while to sleep for them and to dream; it was as though our German philo-sophy were but the dream of the French Revolution.'[23]

Cultural Visions and Social Change

The need of a philosophical or anthropological scheme within which the potential of liberated reason could be made an instrument of social change appeared inescapable and pressing to the most serious analysts of the age. In ringing terms Schiller stated the political concerns that had led him to the composition of his 'Über die ästhetische Erziehung':

> The gaze of the philosopher and of the man of the world alike is fixed expectantly on the political scene where now the very fate of mankind is pre-sumably being debated. Is it not culpable indifference towards the well-being of society if we fail to share in this general debate? . . . A question which has hitherto always been decided by the blind right of might is now, so it seems, being brought before the tribunal of Pure Reason itself; and anyone who is capable of putting himself in the centre of things, and of raising himself from an individual into a representative of the species, may consider himself at once a member of this tribunal, and at the same time, in his capacity as human being and citizen of the world, an interested party who finds himself more or less closely involved in the outcome of the case.[24]

Goethe was convinced that the prospects of a new and cosmopolitan community had in France been corrupted by the immature elements of the Revolution and envisaged a strategy of action that was conservative, yet clearly political in its fundamental aims. He could conclude that, while in seventeenth-century France, social and political maturity had

[23] Heinrich Heine, *Sämtliche Werke*, ed. O. Walzel, Leipzig, Insel, 1914, V, p. 390–1.
[24] Schiller *SW*, V, p. 573.

been concomitant with the efflorescence of a superb literature, in the far less sophisticated German society of the eighteenth century, political intelligence and progressive social action could only be the result of a preparatory education pre-eminently in philosophical and aesthetic terms. The convergence of experience, reason and creativity outlined in Kant's *Kritik der Urteilskraft* provided the valid model of the sort of intellectual and moral discipline, of historical understanding and contemporary insight that might shape the post-Revolutionary German society.

It is true that for the present Goethe put his faith in the best among the German aristocracy and the established upper-class merchants; he never ceased to believe in the unequivocal obligations, moral as well as economic, of the governing to the governed. Averse to radicalism in any form, he feared the impact of the Revolution, certainly in its intransigent phases, upon an ill-prepared German society. But what concerned him most was the threat he saw coming from France to the existing system of small states, a system that seemed to him not only to offer resistance to Prussian and Austrian dominance but to provide more adequate scope for the gradual release of middle-class energies. He recognized that unlike France and England, where a high literary culture had been achieved within a national framework of political and economic power, any contribution to world literature was in Germany bound to be made by the small and politically interdependent 'Kleinstaaten'. In Weimar, well staffed public institutions would ensure the involvement and training of a broad group of citizens, through the kind of education designed to create not merely technical competence but an understanding of the contemporary world and its ever more scientific and technological character.

It was with such considerations in mind that Goethe advocated the disentanglement of the duchy from the struggles of the major powers. He welcomed the Treaty of Basel by which, in April 1795, Weimar joined Prussia in withdrawing from all hostilities in order to become part of the neutral German territory that was now separated from the southern states still in the throes of war. The years of relative quiet which this important treaty ensured – at the price of agreeing to the cession of the west bank of the Rhine to France – are the decade during which in Weimar and among a small group of men of letters elsewhere, the project of a modern, 'bourgeois' German culture was to be advanced.

Between Goethe and Schiller the exchange of ideas on historical and aesthetic matters soon focused on a theme that had for long been a topic of European literary criticism – the difference in mentality and artistic practice between the ancients and the moderns. To specify this issue neither in melancholy nor in hortative terms and to move beyond Winckelmann's emotional enthusiasm seemed to Schiller essential if the classical heritage was to be made relevant for a cultural vision upon which

ocial change in Germany could be predicated. He developed this pro-
osition in the celebrated essay, 'Über naive und sentimentalische
ichtung'.

The difference he had recognized between Goethe's and his own intel-
ectual cast of mind he now generalized in a system of contrasting types of
erception. 'naive', and 'sentimental' or 'reflective', are terms describing
ot merely psychological attitudes but modes of seeing the world and of
roducing images of it. If a state of pre-cultural and 'naive' simplicity and
appiness was the foil for Rousseau's critique of modern debilitated life,
chiller identifies the 'modern' state of mind as altogether divided within
tself, as haunted by a sense of conflict between experience and reflection,
magination and reason, nature and culture. This alienated conscious-
ess cannot be healed by an invocation of natural innocence; we cannot
eturn to a state of simplicity or harmony, we must attempt to create it
vith a full awareness of modern intellectual and moral tensions. The
ntinomy between nature and mind, this is to say, can be resolved only in
cultural setting that provides for the free play of perception, of the
aesthetic' capacity of man.

Schiller defines this aesthetic experience in a theory of literary per-
ormance and receptivity: 'naive' poetry is the result of an unbroken,
nimetic relationship to actuality; 'reflective' art is sensible of an ideal
eyond the experienced reality. The naive poet 'is' instinctively in unison
vith nature; the sentimental poet 'seeks' nature in a world that has
ecome sceptical of its own cultural framework. The sentimental poet is
he modern artist par excellence:

> His observation is blurred by fancy, his power of reflection by feeling; he closes his eyes and ears so that he may become wholly absorbed in his own thoughts. His mind can receive no impression without at once turning to contemplate its own play. . . . Thus we never receive the object itself, only what the reflective mind of the poet makes of the object; and even when the poet himself is that object, when he wants to represent his own feelings, we do not apprehend his feelings directly at first hand, but only their reflection in his mind, what, as spectator of himself, he thought about them.[25]

atirical poetry stresses in the reflective mode the poet's dissatisfaction
vith actuality as an ugly and degraded state; if he mourns the loss of an
deal world that cannot be recovered, his manner is elegiac; to deal with
he world as though the ideal were still present produces idyllic poetry.

'Über naive und sentimentalische Dichtung', though sketchy in detail,
s a masterpiece of rhetorical skill. Thomas Mann repeatedly called it an
mmortal essay.[26] It is, certainly, evidence of Schiller's forensic talent. A

[25] Schiller *SW*, V, p. 731–2.

[26] Thomas Mann, *Gesammelte Werke*, Frankfurt, Fischer, 1974, IX, p. 177, 378, 626.

fascinating conversationalist, he was extraordinarily effective in captivat ing the listener's – or reader's – attention in a net of brilliantly calcu lated, tightly argued sentences. His philosophical discourse is neve private or meditative, but has a passionate public ring. He was an orato *manqué* who articulated the force of his ideas not before a vaguel imagined audience, the indolent readers of tepid fictions, but before a assembly of minds, like the young men at Jena who avidly listened to him to Fichte and Schelling, committed to the pursuit of truths that woul give them direction and faith. Unlike Lessing's more histrionic debatin style, Schiller's was that of the agitator of the spirit, whose unyieldin intensity of conviction made him, throughout the nineteenth century, th patron of every revolutionary movement.

While Schiller focused upon the French Revolution as the paramoun event of the time and as the chief impulse of those historical and aestheti reflections that led him to a theory of modern culture, Goethe, les inclined to embrace prospects that struck him as utopian, sought th premises of a 'new order' in his scientific studies. Far more systemati than many cultivated contemporaries with a polite interest in the curiosi ties of natural history, he assembled extensive collections of objects fron every field of knowledge, art as well as science. He was aware that th incomparable substance of the classical heritage to which he remainec deeply attached, could be given validity in the present only by relating i to the essentially scientific direction of modern thought.

His first response to Schiller's thesis was a set of notes paraphrasing ir his own terms the key positions of Schiller's aesthetic argument. Schiller' question, 'In what sense might the idea that beauty is perfection ir freedom be applied to organic phenomena?', he answers by asserting tha the concept of beauty which Schiller had deduced speculatively can b derived more satisfactorily from the structure of a fully realizec organism: 'We may call a perfectly structured organism beautiful if w can imagine, as we observe it, that it has the capacity at will to make fre and generous use of all its organs.'[27] He formulates this proposition, at th same time, more concisely in two aphorisms: 'Perfection is achieved whe all necessary functions are achieved, beauty when the necessary i performed without its being obvious', and 'perfection may be achievec with disproportionate elements, beauty demands proportion.'[28]

In the scientific procedure as Goethe understood it, a complicatec interaction of observation, description, experience and judgement i performed in an exemplary manner. The configuration of a concrete

[27] J.W. Goethe, *Werke*, Hamburger Ausgabe, ed. E. Trunz. Munich, Beck, 1972, XIII pp. 21, 23.

[28] Goethe *GA*, IX, p. 639.

›ject, its *Gestalt*, is a model of organization, function and coherence, to : explored and made intelligible by the artist no less than the scientist. ny theory of art must therefore be based upon adequate scientific sight. The relationship of the single, observed instance to its more neral class, the dependence of a specific feature upon the typical is the ue to which scientists and artists alike must constantly return. He ntinued to think that the larger concept from which a particular stance can be derived was not abstract, Platonic or Kantian: it was the rimary phenomenon', the 'Urphänomen', to which observation and periment had led him.

Schiller's recourse to an 'idea' he countered by insisting that his own npirical procedure and terminology did full justice to the concrete ngularity of an object as well as to the general 'type' under which it must : subsumed. His 'morphological' and 'typological' thinking, he lieved, clearly offered the key to the entire compass of scientific quiry. He had noted in his journal in 1790:

> I was absolutely convinced that one universal type, articulating itself by metamorphosis, is common to the whole of organic life; every feature of it should be observable without too great difficulty in intermediate stages, and be recognizable even in mankind where it reaches its greatest complexity.[29]

This sentence, with its faith in a unified theory of all organic life, ggests one of the reasons why Goethe's scientific work seemed unacceptle to most contemporary – and later – scientists, who tended to olate specialized areas of research and to develop a wide range of approiate methodologies. Yet, it was precisely from the interplay of observaon and reflection, from the contention of an evolutionary relationship etween the particular and the general that Goethe's and Schiller's sthetic and political postulates seemed capable of deriving common inciples.

[29] Goethe *GA*, XI, p. 626.

5

The Flag of Truth and Beauty

Die Horen

Schiller, resolute and anxious to translate conceptual conclusions in strategies for winning assent, had for some time planned a journal uncompromising intellectual distinction: it was to be called *Die Horen* the name invoking the daughters of Zeus, Eunomia, the goddess of ord and good government, Dike, the goddess of justice, and Irene, th goddess of peace. Here the new 'critical' ideas were to be articulated. H was aware that, given the state of German literacy, such a journal coul address itself to only a minority, but a minority that consisted of the be in the nation. It was to be an 'epoch-making' undertaking – the list those whom Schiller persuaded to contribute was formidable, an array literary and philosophical eminence never before assembled in a Germa publication. Goethe was ready to join Klopstock, Matthisson, A.W Schlegel, W. von Humboldt, Fichte and Herder, rationalists such Garve and J.J. Engel, the political journalist F. von Gentz, the actor playwright Iffland and C.F. von Blanckenburg, the writer on litera theory. They were asked to form a 'society' which would produce, anon mously, a canon of reflection and creative work that was to contribute t the 'quiet articulation of better concepts, clearer principles and mor attitudes on which ultimately any improvement in our social conditio depends.'[1]

What seemed to Schiller to distinguish the planned publication fro others was his determination to 'exclude above all and unconditional everything that has to do with matters of official religion and politic constitution.'[2] But beyond this, the prospectus of *Die Horen* formulat

[1] Schiller *SW*, V, p. 871.
[2] Schiller *SW*, V, p. 867.

ıe demanding ideals of its editor in stern prose:

> At a time when the sounds of war trouble the nation, when the struggle of political opinions and interests carries this war into almost every circle, and only too often drives away the Muses and Graces . . . it must seem risky, yet, perhaps, meritorious, to invite readers who are so thoroughly distracted, to a diversion of an altogether different sort. . . . The more the narrow interests of the present excite, confine and subjugate our minds, the more urgent is the need, through a universal and more elevated interest in what transcends all present conflicts, to reunite the politically divided world under the flag of truth and beauty.[3]

A lofty programme indeed. The 77 essays in the issues of the first year 795) represent an effort of incomparable idealism. Goethe's contribuons bear the imprint of his characteristically concrete thought. In a ries of tales, 'Unterhaltungen deutscher Ausgewanderten', told in the ıanner of Boccaccio by a group of expropriated refugees, he argues – ith what seemed to some remarkable detachment – the civilizing ffect of convivial story-telling among understandably distraught and reoccupied men and women. Tolerance and sociability were for him learly important values now threatened by the Revolution. A strangely ridescent 'Märchen' concludes the collection, weaving ideas and events, ıntastical and allegorical elements, into a superb canvas of the imaginaon that suggests multiple meanings and resists unequivocal interpretaon. The parable ends in praise of the mythical confluence of all living ıings and, by implication, in the hope that the drift towards chaos may e resolved in an acceptable 'natural' order.

When he agreed to contribute his 'Roman' elegies, Goethe did so to nd, in Schiller's spirit, modern legitimacy to a classical genre, to luminate and enhance the disciplined fusion of 'naive' and 'reflective' oetic impulses. The exuberant and sensuous poems were not readily nderstood: Herder, at first an active contributor but soon disaffected, marked that the journal *Die Horen* might more appropriately be called *ie Huren*.

In a short essay entitled 'Litterarischer Sansculottismus' Goethe comıents on the poverty of German literary life; as yet, he says, nothing like a anon of German 'classics' exists, no works that could claim to mirror a oherent cultural life. He was at pains, nevertheless, to point to the attered evidence of an emerging national literature.

Die Horen was a courageous venture, in view of the extraordinary umber of periodicals that were then current throughout Germany and vailable in reading societies everywhere. Something like 250 journals,

[3] Schiller *SW*, V, p. 870.

among them Bertuch's *Journal der Moden und des Luxus* (1786–182
for cultivated women readers, competed for a limited and exceeding
heterogeneous audience. Not only indifference but opposition to th
severe tone of *Die Horen* was soon apparent. While some contributor
among them Wilhelm von Humboldt and A.W. Schlegel, continued
supply manuscripts, others – Fichte, for one – soon withdrew. Half
the contents of the second year were translations. At the end of 1797 it wa
clear that, determined to by-pass the political anxieties of a deep
troubled society, it could not count on sufficient support, and cease
publication. 'I have just,' Schiller wrote to Goethe on 26 January, 179
'formally signed the death warrant of the three goddesses Eunomia, Dik
and Irene. Shed a pious Christian tear upon these noble dead but send n
condolences.'[4]

Nicolai, one of the most uncompromising critics of the Weimar proje
(and in turn angrily denigrated), saw in Schiller's project only the obtru
sive reflection of a modish speculative philosophy which, in his opinior
could not possibly lead to effective reform. J.F. Reichardt, the editor
the Francophile periodicals *Deutschland* and *Frankreich*, shocked by th
chilling aloofness of the enterprise, voiced the disappointment of man
others. In his 'Unterhaltungen deutscher Ausgewanderten', he wrot
Goethe had used an ostensibly non-political journal for partisa
purposes; he had spoken for the aristocracy and their conceit and ha
drawn a biased picture of the events in France. Had he not trivialized th
problems that confronted Germany? Was his opinion of the Germa
public so low that he could seriously think of entertaining them wit
trifling stories at a time of profound national anxiety?[5] Goethe an
Schiller hit back at the large, and by no means dishonorable, band c
their critics with a curious collection of anonymous 'Xenien'. Thes
cutting epigrams in classical distichs, suggested by Martial's *Xenia*, c
gifts to departing guests, appeared in Schiller's *Musen-Almanach für da
Jahr 1797*; they were a witty and brilliantly devastating 'declaration c
war' against reviewers and journalists, pitiless in their disdain of th
ignorance, platitudinousness and narrow-minded pedantry of contem
porary German letters.

Wilhelm Meister

One of the pieces which Goethe contributed to *Die Horen*, an adaptatio
of Mme de Staël's *Essai sur les fictions* (1795), offered critical categorie
for an assessment of fiction at a time when an overwhelming flood c
popular novels, German, English and French, had devalued rather tha

[4] Goethe *GA*, XX, p. 505.
[5] *Deutschland*, I, 1. Stück, Berlin, January, 1796.

enhanced the prospects of that genre. She distinguishes the novel from historiography and memoirs, or the mere excitement of the imagination from a differentiated treatment of emotions within a broad social context: a novel 'is one of the finest products of the mind. It affects with quiet force the thinking of those (private) individuals who will sooner or later contribute to the shaping of public morals'.[6] This essay and conversations with Wieland, whose *Agathon* (1794) had just appeared in a final version, undoubtedly had their bearing on Goethe's decision to reorganize for the forthcoming collection of his *Neue Schriften* (1792–1800) the manuscript of *Wilhelm Meister* he had begun some 20 years earlier. The novel was to be called *Wilhelm Meisters Lehrjahre* (1795–6).

Wilhelm's enthusiasm for the theatre was now to be merely a passing phase of his growth in consciousness, pointedly illuminated by the narrator's irony. Certain autobiographical elements in the first version were subordinated to a more calculated fictional design. Wilhelm's energies, haphazard but, as he discovers, mysteriously directed by others, are gradually gathered in self-awareness within an envisaged social order that integrates the values of his bourgeois youth and those of a responsible modern aristocracy. Related spheres of interest – religious, artistic, political – intersect. Several women have a significant effect on him: Philine, with her wholly instinctual love, the active Theresa, the calm and devoted Natalie, the hysterical Aurelia and especially Mignon. Mignon, a child of incest, androgynous, puzzling and eccentric, in every respect a romantic figure of pure inwardness, becomes strangely attached to Wilhelm, yet is the antithesis of the very ideals which are to guide him. She is the embodiment of myth and mystery: together with her father, the harpist, she symbolizes an irrational force against which reasoned projects such as the masonic 'Society of the Tower' cannot offer adequate security. A variety of lives is thus slowly unfolded before Wilhelm.

Lothario is an altogether exemplary personality: like Natalie, that pure, almost abstractly balanced character whom Wilhelm ultimately marries, he represents the responsible potential of the nobility. Through the 'Confessions' of Natalie's aunt – the 'belle âme' of Richardson and Rousseau, and of Shaftesbury's 'morality in beauty' – in whom, as Schiller puts it, the subjective and the objective, 'inclination' and 'duty' creatively coincide, Goethe tells how a fulfilled life has come about.

Wilhelm Meister has no clearly delineated pattern of purpose or development. It is the account of an open and receptive mind, slowly shaped by that principle of organic 'Bildung', the gradual intellectual and moral maturing of the individual towards insight and responsibility. Close in meaning to Shaftesbury's 'inner form', the idea of Bildung was given

[6] Goethe *GA*, XV, p. 350.

scientific sanction in the work of the biologist J.F. Blumenbach ('Über den Bildungstrieb', 1780) as a 'form drive', a *nisus formativus*. Goethe – and W. von Humboldt, who had lent to the concept its specific pedagogical connotation ('Theorie der Bildung', 1793) – modified the deterministic character of the term and suggested its 'political' implications: not merely the achievement of a fully developed self seemed to him the central aim of 'Bildung', but the integration of subjective capacities within a given social order.

The lively, even exuberant, pace of the original version of *Wilhelm Meister* with its essentially provincial setting was now transformed into a reflective narrative that demonstrated a tentative progression with a cosmopolitan goal. 'It may well give posterity', said A.W. Schlegel, 'far too favourable a notion of our present state of culture.'[7] If we read the novel with Goethe's political convictions in mind, and deduce its meaning from the classical ethos that he hoped at that time to defend, we can conclude that by its 'ennoblement', bourgeois life is here sublimated in the sphere of the cultivated aristocracy and purged of its economic preoccupations. Some of its readers, the poet Novalis among them, though captivated by the book as a whole, found this motivation unacceptable; yet, for the younger romantics, the novel represented the very prototype of a modern, wide-ranging, self-reflective work of the imagination. Friedrich Schlegel devoted one of his first critical essays to an analysis of the book which he considered, like the French Revolution and Fichte's deeply admired *Wissenschaftslehre*, a cardinal event of the age.[8]

Epic Poetry: Theory and Practice

It was characteristic of Schiller's altogether more systematic manner that, despite his emphatic praise, he should in his correspondence with Goethe have deplored in *Wilhelm Meister* a certain vacillation between realistic and speculative tendencies and, especially, a merely 'half-hearted' attempt to confront Wilhelm with the idealistic philosophy in which Schiller himself had found the means of transcending the present.[9]

The letters between the two are extraordinarily rich documents of literary criticism: they touch upon matters of poetics in the context of contemporary attitudes, they reappraise the classical concepts of tragedy and, with special emphasis, the validity of genres within a modern theory of literature. The desire, in particular, to reassess the uses of genres was, of course, not merely taxonomic; it reflected the conviction that formal

[7] August Wilhelm von Schlegel, *Sämtliche Werke*, ed. E. Böcking, Leipzig, Weidmann, 1847, XI, p. 206.

[8] Schlegel *KA*, II, p. 198.

[9] Goethe *GA*, XX, p. 213–15.

categories, fully and intelligently defined, do not impede but stimulate and release poetic speech. Within a larger cultural context they ensure the continuity of tradition, coalesce as codes or ritualistic signs, and altogether give to literature that institutional stability which seemed to Goethe and Schiller an important strategic means of shaping the thoughts and actions of the German middle class. They were interested less in stylistic definitions than in the relationship of certain forms of literature to the social realities. To maintain formal requirements meant to concentrate and specify the impact upon the reader of a given intellectual or emotional substance, and to enhance the effect of a literary work beyond the obvious appeal of its subject matter.

Epic poetry, they were convinced, represented poetry at its most effective. Its restrained manner, the mertical and prosodic discipline which is imposed upon the storyteller, and its calculated mixture of lyrical and dramatic effects had assured the ancient poet an audience interested in the subject matter as such and its archetypal resonance. Could the contemporary public with its private preoccupations, its appalling ignorance of history and its indifference to the implications of form, respond adequately to the modern, reflective poet? As the circle of understanding readers was so dismayingly small, the creation of a receptive audience was for Goethe and Schiller, as it was for Wieland and Herder, the most pressing task.

Schiller's temperament inclined to the dramatic, Goethe's remained committed to the epic mode; in a brief essay, 'Über epische und dramatische Dichtung', Goethe summarizes their views, echoing the discussion of the same topic in the fifth book of *Wilhelm Meister*. In both instances, the two genres are defined by reference to authorial attitudes rather than historical principles: the epic mode is that of the ancient 'rhapsodist' who speaks in the past tense, quietly composed, invisible behind a curtain and uninvolved; the dramatic impulse is that of an actor who is altogether present, an individual who impatiently demands attention, compels sympathy and wholly enthralls the listener. While the epic poet constructs a broad canvas of 'public' action, the dramatist is concerned with internalized conflicts that can be projected in a relatively narrow span of space and time.

The assumption that the epic mode with its lyrical as well as dramatic overtones was – historically and typologically – a 'primary' form had led both Goethe and Schiller in 1797 to the composition of a series of ballads. But that proposition clearly warranted an experiment of a more demanding scope. The classical scholar F.A. Wolf had in his edition of the Homeric poems denied a single authorship and maintained that the relative coherence of the poems was the work of later writers. Encouraged by the implications of a theory that justified a whole series of successive

'Homeric' poems, Goethe now planned a specifically modern epic. Where the Homeric poets achieved objectivity by speaking of events that had occurred in the distant past, Goethe sought to accomplish the same end by eliminating all ephemeral features of contemporary life and by giving a high degree of typicality to events and figures drawn from the living present. *Herrmann und Dorothea* (1798) was the result; in an elegy written to introduce the poem, he justified the project: 'To be an Homeric poet, albeit the last, is splendid.'[10]

Goethe had admired the rendering of middle-class life in J.H. Voss's *Luise* (1795), an idyllic poem that seems to us insipid and philistine rather than inspired. In *Herrmann und Dorothea* the idyllic element is threatened: its central action concerns the fate of the Protestant families who were driven from Salzburg in 1730. Their life in deprivation and insecurity appeared to anticipate that of the victims of the French Revolution. The enthusiasm which France's neighbours had initially shown for the ideals of the Revolution had soon turned into animosity and resistance towards the refugees.

The poem relates the world of the German middle class to the larger issues of European politics. While the traditional epic poem offers a picture of social order, firm in its beliefs and norms, the theme of *Herrmann und Dorothea* is the challenge to that order by disruptive historical forces. It employs the familiar props of the idyll: a country setting, coherent patterns of family and community, and the temporal unity of a festive Sunday. Yet, these ingredients are here deprived of their peaceable and benevolent character. The harmony of the family is jeopardized, the neighbourhood is divided, that particular Sunday is a day of misfortune. It is in the controlled rendering of conflict that the poem achieves its purpose. Intention and material, art and historical fact seem perfectly integrated, every feature and every figure of the small world is illuminated in its potential of self-scrutiny against the background of revolutionary turmoil, every detail gives colour and reality to it. Each impulse and relationship within the family and the village community contributes to Goethe's intention of confirming the concrete and experienced faith in the energies of the German middle-class life.

The epic structure of the poem – for each of the nine cantos one of the Muses is in turn invoked – its language and its imagery are made splendidly transparent; the 'prosaic' character of bourgeois life is given 'poetic' presence; the classical postulates of an interdependence of the general and the particular is impressively fulfilled. Wilhelm von Humboldt's review essay on the poem (in his *Ästhetische Versuche*, 1799) is one of the first extensive analyses of any of Goethe's works, and a

[10] Goethe *GA*, I, p. 207.

summary – somewhat too esoteric for Goethe himself – of a classical theory of poetry. For Schiller the poem represented 'the peak of our entire modern art'.[11]

The spacious and solid epic form remained for Goethe the medium that offered to author and audience the most compelling challenge and satisfaction: he was tempted to deal with the historical figure of William Tell, and considered a poem of eight cantos on the death of Achilles. A projected epic entitled 'Die Jagd' was (1828) cast in prose under the title *Novelle*, one of several such exemplary tales and perhaps the finest product of Goethe's classical projects; it was the model for the genre in which the Germans produced their most impressive narrative work throughout the nineteenth century.

It may seem surprising that Goethe and Schiller addressed themselves specifically to the lyrical mode only insofar as it could be circumscribed in terms of prosody and not in the 'attitudinal' categories from which epic and dramatic forms were deduced. With few exceptions such as 'Meeresstille', 'Glückliche Fahrt', 'Dauer im Wechsel' or the poems contained in *Wilhelm Meister*, Goethe's lyrical production of the years around 1800 is of a supremely formal sort: several elegies ('Alexis und Dora', 'Euphrosyne', 'Amyntas') and his contribution to the collection of ballads in Schiller's *Musen-Almanach für das Jahr 1798* ('Die Braut von Korinth', 'Der Zauberlehrling', 'Der Gott und die Bajadere') suggest his interest in balancing subjective and generic considerations. Perhaps the most accomplished German didactic poem, integrating scientific subject matter in an elegiac form is Goethe's 'Die Metamorphose der Pflanzen' (1798). To convey his scientific ideas more engagingly he projected (but did not execute) a still more comprehensive poem in the manner of Lucretius's *De rerum naturae* or of Erasmus Darwin's *Zoonomia, or the Laws of Organic Life* (1794).

For Schiller the transformation of philosophical concepts into poetry of cogency and lofty pathos was an entirely congenial exercise. Yet his historical and aesthetic writings had so preoccupied him that he did not resume writing poetry until the summer of 1795 ('Poesie des Lebens'), a pause of nearly seven years. The five successive volumes of an annual anthology of poetry, *Musen-Almanach* (1796–1800), which he edited contain some of his most impressive work. He is there concerned as intensely as in his critical essays and plays with addressing the reader in a voice of persuasion and pleading. More plausibly than the ill-fated *Die Horen*, the new publication suggests the tenets of a classical creed: its programmatic poetry is addressed directly, as though it actually existed, to a receptive bourgeois society. Apart from accomplished ballads such as

[11] Schiller, *Werke*, Nationalausgabe, Weimar, Böhlau, 1977, XXIX, p.105.

'Der Ring des Polycrates', 'Der Taucher', and especially 'Die Glocke', these poems echo the utopian theme of his essays; 'Das Ideal und das Leben' illuminates the chief concepts of the 'Ästhetische Briefe'. 'Das Eleusinische Fest' and 'Der Spaziergang' deal with the evolution of a humane culture. Antiquity and the modern experience are constantly contrasted and lead from an awareness of a disjointed present towards a prospect of individual and collective creativity.

The assessment of ancient literature and art, Greek epic and dramatic poetry as well as the distinguished work of contemporary classical philologists was throughout Europe a most lively concern; it produced an unmatched level of critical exegesis not only among Goethe, Schiller or Wilhelm von Humboldt ('Über das Studium des Altertums', 1793), but among the generation of younger critics, especially August Wilhelm and Friedrich Schlegel. Works such as Wood's *Essay on the Original Genius of Homer* (1769), C.G. Heyne's reviews of philological scholarship in the *Göttingische Gelehrte Anzeigen* or F.A. Wolf's *Prolegomena ad Homerum* (1795) were eagerly read and interpreted, Pindar and Aeschylus were translated. J.H. Voss's version of Homer (1793), Virgil and Ovid, K.P. Moritz's *Über die bildende Nachahmung des Schönen* (1788), his *Götterlehre* (1791) and his brief but important *Versuch einer deutschen Prosodie* (1786) are texts that contribute decisively to a 'classical' vision.

The insistent testing in all of these works of the resources of antiquity must not be misunderstood. It was not, as for Winckelmann or Hölderlin, nostalgic in character but sought, rather, to apply the formal conclusions of Greek poetic theory to modern topics and states of mind. If Greek culture was to be made useful and alive, its achievements must not be mechanically – or sentimentally – imitated and reasserted; they should lead to a clear recognition of the radically different conditions under which classical and modern art came about. With its critical energy and its wealth of mythological symbols, the Greek tradition seemed to yield to an intelligent modern poet remarkably effective topics and formal devices. If such a theory of an exemplary Greek culture seemed to some peremptory to the point of disregarding its historical context, Goethe countered by suggesting that a genetic model was preferable to any obedience to presumed historical continuity. For Schiller the power of the arts amounted, at any rate, to a triumphant assertion of will and of the idea over the accidental substance of nature or of history.

In 1797, the year of the demise of *Die Horen*, plans were made for a new publication, *Propyläen*, which, Goethe wrote to the publisher Cotta, was to contain

> the reflections of a few congenial friends on nature and art. The subject matter

of natural history and science is to be dealt with in a manner that should be useful for the practicing artist and serve his purposes. Art is here to mean particularly painting and sculpture, their theory, practice and history.[12]

In his programmatical introduction, Goethe justifies the new periodical (1798–1800) as a forum for those willing to go counter to a prevailing subjective and spiritualist taste, who are prepared to reject the instant satisfaction provided by the entertainment market in favour of a more rewarding but also more demanding experience.

His close collaborator on this new venture was the Swiss painter and critic, Heinrich Meyer, whom he had known in Rome, a scholar with an extensive knowledge of ancient and Renaissance art, pedantic in manner and thoroughly disliked by younger artists whose work he subjected to scathing and derogatory criticism. The topics in *Propyläen* ranged, somewhat awkwardly, from Greek sculpture to Etruscan art, from Renaissance painting to the contemporary taste of the Paris directoire. Meyer's enquiry 'Über die Gegenstände der bildenden Kunst', outlined by Goethe himself, which appeared in the first issue, put the case for the decisive role of appropriate subject matter in any classical design; W. von Humboldt and his wife supplied an account of the painters Gérard and David, whom they had met in the company of Napoleon.

Goethe wrote the most substantial pieces. What now urgently concerned him was a clear differentiation between 'art' and 'nature', and the justification of the work of art, its production as well as its critical reception, by criteria at once intellectual and moral. The ancients, Goethe concluded in Italy, had, 'like nature', created works of striking coherence. He was now more cautious in his use of metaphor: art achieves its most compelling effects when it illuminates the principles of order and organization that can be observed in natural phenomena. Nature and art function differently; but art cannot claim to offer significant knowledge if it does not ultimately convey, through the intelligence and passion of the artist, something of the structure and purpose, the *Gestalt*, of the rendered world. Perfection in a work of art is the signature of an artist who has observed and recognized the patterns available in reality and has, in turn, reflected upon the nature of his own intellectual presuppositions. It is clear that art and science are seen as interdependent, yet each is bound by its special requirements: 'When an artist seizes upon a natural object, that object no longer belongs to nature. Indeed, we might say that the artist at that moment creates an object by extracting its significant, characteristic, interesting features or, rather, by endowing it with significance.' Quite appropriately, Goethe undertakes a reconsideration

[12] Goethe *GA*, XIX, p. 338.

of the Laocoon group (1798),[13] through which Winckelmann had clarified his understanding of the character of Greek art, and which Lessing had employed towards a distinction between painting, or art, and poetry. Against Lessing, Goethe now insists that the aesthetic effect of that group is due to the artist's success in eliminating all non-essential features. Laocoon is but a name that should not be taken to suggest a particular historical figure or event; the group represents the archetype of a father and his sons mortally threatened by danger. 'If I knew no other interpretation of the group I would call it a tragic idyll.'[14]

'Characteristic' and 'interesting' – terms upon which the young romantics seized as key concepts of their own theory – refer in Goethe's scheme not to the fascinating particular, but to the satisfaction gained from a recognition of coherence and relationships. To achieve an adequate and intelligent performance, the artist must seek 'to develop at least a command of certain theoretical presuppositions of his work, if not a complete theory.'[15] It is for him self-evident that such a theoretical testing of poetic practice must not be confused with the stringent sort of theoretical procedure which philosophical – or scientific – analysis requires; yet, close reflection upon aesthetic propositions as the necessary ingredient in the making and judging of art, so important in all modern aesthetic considerations, is a chief premise of the classical programme. Again and again the target of Goethe's polemical pieces is the naturalistic fallacy which confuses the truth of nature and the truth of art. He translates, and comments upon, sections of Diderot's 'Essai sur la peinture' (1798–99) and, with respect for the great critic, puts his views of the relationship between 'nature' and 'art' into question.

In a treatise of exceptional lucidity, 'Über Wahrheit und Wahrscheinlichkeit der Kunstwerke' (1798), he distinguishes the two modes: 'A perfect work of art is the product of the human mind and as such also a work of nature. But by relating and unifying the disparate elements of a phenomenon and by recognizing the significance and dignity of even the most ordinary objects, the work of art is above nature.'[16] The inexperienced may deal with the work of art merely as a commodity; but the lover of art

> will see not only the truth of what has been represented, but the happy choice of subject matter, the spirited composition, the transcending appeal of the small cosmos of the work of art. He will understand that he must elevate himself to become an artist in order to enjoy the work; he is bound to feel that he must pull

[13] Goethe *GA*, XIII, p. 145.
[14] Goethe *GA*, XIII, p. 165–6.
[15] Goethe *GA*, XIII, p. 153–4.
[16] Goethe *GA*, XIII, p. 180.

> his diffuse life together, must live with the work of art, contemplate it repeatedly and thereby raise himself to a higher form of existence.[17]

The most elaborate and the most elegant of the reflections in the six ssues of the *Propyläen* is 'Der Sammler und die Seinigen', a set of letters oined in a delightful narrative in which six characters defend their lifferent views of art. The 'collector' and his guests weigh the conceivable ustification and use of art: it must, they conclude, address itself to the whole man', that 'rich entity of unified variety'.[18] Whatever satisfaction nay be derived from religion or philosophy, however captivating a articular experience or idea, man truly constitutes himself only in the ecognition of the totality of thought and feeling that is gathered in the vork of art, in the resolution through beauty of the discrepancies and ensions which are inherent in modern life.

'Der Sammler' represents Goethe's most urbane contribution to a eriodical which asserts the theoretical postulates of an austere Greco-Roman classicism nowhere actually rendered in his work. It insists on onvictions which he knew were far from those held by most contemporary artists. A cursory survey, 'Flüchtige Übersicht über die Kunst n Deutschland' (1799), indicates his categorical disapproval of the naturalistic' tendencies that appeared to dominate the important centres of art. 'Naturalism' was for him meritricious, the offering of mere nimicry as art, the mindless copying of an actuality that gratified without challenging, reproduction devoid of the critical power of art to eighten perception and to clarify judgement.

He deplores that this fallacious view seemed to be at home particularly n Berlin, where the 'prosaic' spirit of the age was most unhappily lisplayed.

> Poetry has been displaced by history, character and the ideal by plain portraiture, symbolic treatment by allegory, landscape painting by mere 'vistas', the universally human by the patriotic. Perhaps they will soon realize that there is no such thing as 'patriotic' art or science. Art and science belong, like everything noble, to the world as a whole; they can be promoted only by the free and universal traffic among all the living, always aware of what we have inherited and what we know of the past.[19]

Viennese artists, Goethe concludes, are also on the wrong path:

> historical subject matter seems preferred over the poetic, allegory over the symbolic . . . too much is capricious, too little attention is paid to the strict

[17] Goethe *GA*, XIII, p. 181.
[18] Goethe *GA*, XIII, p. 294.
[19] Goethe *GA*, XIII, p. 329.

> observance of principles, science is neglected; they are more intent on pleasin the eye than on satisfying the mind.[20]

In a respectful reply, the most accomplished Berlin artist, the sculpto G. Schadow, himself dedicated to classicist art in the manner of David reminded the revered Goethe of the energies – concrete, contemporary national and by no means merely fashionable – that could in fact b found among artists in Berlin and elsewhere.

Goethe: Perception of Colour

Since it was Goethe's conviction that an intelligent and discriminatin public could be created only by developing resources of judgement seemingly aesthetic but in fact involving capacities far more comprehensive he continued to pursue his scientific studies with undiminished seriousness. The classical postulate as it evolved during that decade was for hin plausible only if it could be sustained by conclusions drawn from th experimental and descriptive work he devoted to mineralogy, anatomy entomology, and above all else, to optics and the perception of colour Science and art required analogous procedures: in his theory of art h insists upon the role of a certain conceptual awareness in clarifying an integrating the observed reality, upon a critical procedure that move from intuition to comprehension to the demonstration of structura coherence. Early in 1798 he spoke to Schiller of 'rational empiricism' a the premise of all knowledge, beyond arbitrariness and open to the probability of constant modification.[21] The exact and discriminating classification of entomological materials, or the anatomical study of fish, bird and frogs were as important to him as intricate poetic compositions suc as *Herrmann und Dorothea*.

With his characteristic fondness for discovering models and pattern he recognized at the very end of *Farbenlehre* that the course of hi creative life was determined in large measure by the interaction of hi interests in science and art:

> moving from poetry to art and from art to the study of nature, more and mor regarding as a central objective what was originally intended only as an aid i my work. But having spent enough time in those strange regions I happil found my way back to art through the study of physiological colours and thei moral as well as aesthetic effect.[22]

The most persistent topic of his scientific thinking remained the challenge of colour and its perception. He knew that he was in fundamenta

[20] Goethe *GA*, XIII, p. 330.
[21] Goethe *GA*, XX, p. 499.
[22] Goethe *GA*, XVI, p. 717.

›nflict with Newtonian principles if he refused to approach functions
nd relationships of light in mathematical formulae. But his interest in
›lour was wholly different from Newton's: he was intent on understand-
ıg the world of colour as a system by which, through the paramount and
ıpremely sensitive instrument of the eye, the structure of the visible
›smos in its barely comprehensible range could be experienced.

As a 'primary phenomenon', colour is a pre-eminent feature in the
›tality of an intelligible natural order.[23] We can adequately assess it only
s we experience it; used and articulated in art, it produces a special kind
f intellectual, even 'moral' challenge. Unlike Schiller who, with Kant,
nd in the wake of the long-standing quarrel between the partisans of
›*lore* and *disegno* distrusted the factor of colour as a seductive and dis-
ırbing feature in the aesthetic process, Goethe maintains its positive
alue throughout even the 'classicist' essays in *Propyläen*. While in the
inear' aesthetic theories of the eighteenth century colour had an
ssentially decorative function, Goethe's emphasis upon its perceptual
haracter makes it a crucial element in the creative process. Colour is the
ıeans of enhancing that 'appearance' (*Schein*) which the work of art
ıust achieve and which can be realized only as the result of a total artistic
ommitment, scientific as well as aesthetic. He speaks of that commit-
ıent eloquently in a passage of his *Farbenlehre*, the work in which he
:peatedly emphasizes the closest possible relationship between science
nd art:

> Unfathomable intuition, a firm grasp of the present, mathematical depth, physical precision, height of reason, sharp intelligence, alert, wistful phantasy, a loving delight in the sensuous – nothing can be spared for that lively, fruitful seizing of the moment which alone can bring about a work of art no matter what its content.[24]

'he German romantic painters, P.O. Runge (*Farben-Kugel*, 1810) and
:.D. Friedrich, as well as English artists such as Turner and Constable
nd, in our time, Kandinsky and Klee, found Goethe's theory of colour
erception entirely acceptable and stimulating.

The progress of Goethe's scientific work was for the next 20 years
eported in a series of publications addressed not only to scholars but to
ıformed laymen whose social and political role, he felt, was bound to be
ıcreasingly influential. Neither learning nor religious faith nor, indeed,
he matter of politics seemed to him equally promising: the interdepen-
.ence of scientific research offered and demanded new and modern
›rms of cooperation. He was determined to explore ways of giving insti-
utional scope as much to scientific enquiry as to the work of men of

[23] Goethe *GA*, XVI, p. 69.
[24] Goethe *GA*, XVI, p. 333.

letters. He had for some time devoted himself energetically to creatir research institutes at the University of Jena. With his active support di tinguished chairs were established in the natural sciences: anatom botany, chemistry, mineralogy, astronomy, pharmacology were taug by men whose publications were as important for the subsequent histo of ideas as those of the remarkable philosophers, historians and phil logists at Jena – the orientalist H.E. Paulus, Fichte, Schelling, A.W Schlegel, Hegel and H. Luden, the editor of *Nemesis. Zeitschrift f Politik und Geschichte*. Goethe himself supervised not merely the a school, the libraries and, later, the galleries and museums, but th botanical institute, the observatory and the veterinary academy. For a these he remained responsible to the end of his life.

The Weimar Theatre

No institution engaged his attention and care so intensely as the theatr Members of the court as well as citizens of the town had for some tim taken part in more or less improvised performances of French an German plays such as Voltaire's *Mahomet* or Lessing's *Minna vo Barnhelm*; Goethe's enthusiasm for the theatre and his willingness t write for it, to act, dance and direct, soon gave to these events a more tha local reputation. Works by Goldoni, Molière, Gozzi, Cumberland an others were offered in fresh translations and with musical interlud composed by Weimar musicians such as J.F. Kranz, F.S. Destouches an after 1819, the brilliant pianist and composer, Nepomuk Humme Mozart's pupil and the friend of Beethoven.

In 1780 a separate theatre was opened for costume and masked balls t which all citizens ('except livery-men and maids') were admitted and a which simple pantomimes were soon replaced by allegorical masque Goethe wrote several of these; it was a form to which he returned later i the second part of *Faust*. From 1784 to 1791 the court engaged Josep Bellomo's company, a troupe of some 20 professional actors who pe formed plays of wide appeal, Italian and German *Singspiele*, and ever fortnight a new opera. Many of the actors were Austrian, and Viennes comedy and musicals dominated. When in 1791 Goethe took over th direction of the court-sponsored theatre, he knew he would have to b tolerant in the choice of dramatic material: during the 26 years of hi management, there were 87 productions of plays by the enormousl popular August von Kotzebue and 31 by A.W. Iffland. Mozart's opera were almost constantly in the repertoire, *Die Zauberflöte* was performe 82 times, *Don Giovanni* 68 and *Die Entführung aus dem Serail* 49 During the single season of 1791–92, Goethe produced Shakespeare *King John, Hamlet* and *Henry IV*.

His own experience as an amateur actor and the importance h

attached to an adequate reading of the text suggested to him an ever more severe discipline of speech, gesture and movement on the part of the performers. J.J. Engel had compiled a comprehensive manual for actors, *Ideen zu einer Mimik* (1785–86), that set forth – with delightful illustrations by the popular engraver J.W. Meil – a detailed system of postures and gestures. When in 1796 Iffland, the greatest German actor of the time, appeared on the Weimar stage as a much admired guest, his completely controlled technique convinced Goethe that the 'naturalistic' manner, even in the graceful and refined form Diderot and Lessing had urged and that had been practiced by such master-actors as K. Ekhof and F.L. Schröder, should be replaced by a more sophisticated style. Iffland seemed to meet the classicist requirements admirably by performances that minimized all individual features.

From W. von Humboldt (1799) Goethe had received an account of the French stage and was resolved to create in Weimar a tradition of equally controlled performances. F.H. von Einsiedel's *Grundlinien zu einer Theorie der Schauspielkunst* (1797) had shown the way; Goethe's own 'Regeln für Schauspieler' (1803) laid down the precise rules for reciting poetry or prose, for overcoming the prevalent 'rhythmophobia',[25] the resistance to speaking blank verse, which even Iffland was in the habit of breaking up by interjecting a redundant 'Ach Gott!' There must be absolute obedience to the text; and 'let the actor remember that he is not so much to imitate nature as to render its ideal substance and that he must therefore in his performance combine the true with the beautiful.'[26]

The 'Weimar style' was intended to produce a theatrical event in which lighting, costumes, scenery and music were carefully coordinated with the restrained movements of the actors. Seminars on the craft of acting were organized; extensive rehearsals aided the understanding of the dramatic and poetic intentions of the play. Considering the lively attendance of the whole range of Weimar society, the theatre could well serve as a vehicle, perhaps the most important element, of the 'aesthetic' culture. Here, the work of art and its interpreters, director, performers and craftsmen, stage scenery painters, lighting masters and costume designers, the audience and the voice of the critic could be brought together in an enterprise that was bound, Goethe felt, to have its social consequence.

The only German stage that could rival Weimar in seriousness and purpose was the Berlin National Theatre which Iffland directed after 1796. His chief playwright was August von Kotzebue, prolific and successful beyond compare, the author of at least 230 plays, a supreme

[25] Goethe *GA*, XIV, p. 18.
[26] Goethe *GA*, XIV, p. 81.

theatrical talent quite indifferent to any academic theory. He was altogether platitudinous and opportunistic, but by instinct close to popular taste, to gossip and fashionable talk, and clever in satirizing literary pretentiousness, whether classical or romantic. The list of his plays seems endless; such titles as *Menschenhaß und Reue* (1789), *Die Indianer in England* (1790), *Der weibliche Jacobiner-Clubb* (1791) and *Die deutschen Kleinstädter* (1803) suggest the characteristic mixture of moralizing, sentimentality, exotic vistas and simple-minded humour. It is a measure of Kotzebue's energy that in addition to his work for Iffland (and other stages) he wrote numerous novels, travel books, volumes of essays and reviews. His journal, *Der Freimüthige oder Berlinische Zeitung für gebildete und unbefangene Leser* (1803–07) was one of the publications directed explicitly against the taste and spirit of Weimar.

The distinction of the Weimar theatre after 1797 was in no small measure due to Schiller's share in the repertoire. Since the completion of his major essays he had turned with an almost fanatical sense of purpose to the writing of plays and 'dramatic poems': *Wallenstein, Maria Stuart, Die Braut von Messina* and *Wilhelm Tell* were all first performed in Weimar. Beyond these, he adapted such masterpieces as *Macbeth*, Lessing's *Nathan*, Racine's *Phèdre*, Gozzi's *Turandot*. Goethe acquiesced only slowly in having his own works performed on the local stage: it was Schiller who provided a stage version of *Iphigenie* (1802), Goethe himself rewrote *Goetz von Berlichingen* for a performance in 1804 and again in 1809, now in a classical five-act division. *Tasso* was first acted in 1807, *Faust I* – published in 1808 – not until 1829. Schiller's intense dedication to the theatre, to its effectiveness as a cultural and political instrument, cannot be overrated.

Schiller: Tragedies of Greatness

Although the exchange of ideas and the collaboration between Goethe and Schiller continued beyond the turn of the century, Schiller tended to pursue his own intellectual concerns. What absorbed him increasingly was the element of fateful compulsion in the lives of eminent historical figures and, on the other hand, the exercise of freedom not merely as an ideal transcending the hazards and contingencies of life, but now, in all its precariousness and jeopardy, as the very condition of man.

As early as 1791 he had reflected on the character of Wallenstein, that spectacular soldier and statesman, a representative of humane and enlightened values, who achieved greatness during the Thirty Years' War only to be destroyed more by his ambition and his blind faith in the stars than by vested interests and religious partisanship. As a dramatic figure he was the tragic hero caught in a fateful constellation of overwhelming circumstances.

The difficulties of subjecting the historical material to a dramaturgical pattern had seemed insurmountable. Wallenstein was not a 'noble character' like Marquis Posa in *Don Carlos*, that document of pre-revolutionary idealism; he is the victim not of 'fate' but of the defects in his own personality and the machinations that enmeshed him. By 1797 Schiller appears to have found the adequate form: changing from prose to iambic pentameter, he gave to the material a certain epic rhythm and to the historical figures a sufficiently general cast. By weaving several incidental plots into the account of Wallenstein's career, he creates counterfigures and strands of interest beside the dominant political conflict between Wallenstein and the imperial and ecclesiastical authority. The love between Wallenstein's daughter Thekla and the son of General Piccolomini, his committed opponent, offers an almost idyllic sphere of integrity and devotion in contrast to the sombre background of intrigue and plotting, of duplicity, treason and superstition.

The pacing of the action is the key to the effectiveness of the 'dramatic poem' in three parts: as Wallenstein, the admired hero, turns hesitantly from legitimate greatness to ambition and the usurpation of power, it is his indecision that deprives him of options and inescapably defeats him. The grand but profoundly ambivalent character is caught in a net of actions both planned and involuntary. In the colourful first part he is at once the dominant figure and the cause of conflicts that are later to be elaborately developed. The pressures of incompatible political aspirations, of church and state, of Germany and Spain, of princes and generals, soldiers and peasants, create the dramatic tension. Figures, events, ideas, motifs and symbols are carefully balanced, mirrored and confronted – they illuminate the entanglement of a self-deluded Wallenstein in circumstances which he is unable to master; tragic irony assures his downfall at the moment when he imagines himself triumphant.

A play of such intellectual and formal complexity, of such tightly riveted elements in which the fragility of greatness, ambiguity, falsehood and delusions are shown in their ominous logic, necessarily provoked a multitude of interpretations. Goethe read it as the representation of a remarkable and eccentric human being; Hegel saw in it the frightful destruction of potential greatness by an inexorable fate: 'When the play ends, all is over; the realm of nothingness, of death has been victorious . . . this is not tragic but horrifying.'[27] Such a critical view has been countered by the suggestion that the 'demonic realist' Wallenstein is constrained and mastered by the majestic forces of history, that the play is an affirmation of history disavowing its agents. But no analysis that suggests

[27] G.W.F. Hegel, *Werke*, Berlin, Duncker & Humblot, 1835, XVII, p. 411, 413.

a clear-cut distinction between character and the force of circumstances between freedom and compulsion, can do justice to Schiller's design: i was precisely the interlocking of motifs that offered a supreme challeng to his artistry. Without recourse to a classical concept of fate or to th postulates of modern idealism, without, indeed, resolving the awesom discrepancies in a rational or utopian scheme, he wished to produce a work of absolute formal coherence and balance. He was committed to th Sophoclean dramaturgy in which the resources of character are unfolde in the ineluctable consequences of actions and events.

At the same time, to regard *Wallenstein* as an exercise in formalism i to misjudge the seriousness of Schiller's intention: he had recognized th public indifference to his philosophical discourse and was unwilling t offer, in whatever form, moral or political prescriptions. More uncom promising than ever, he now held all the more nobly to his ideal of a 'aesthetic culture' in which art – the artist, his work and the critica reflection on the work – was to form a magnetic field of experienc capable of articulating judgement and resolve, and of creating for a obtuse and disoriented society at least a sense of alternatives.

It was, once again, an historical topic that in 1800 produced *Mari Stuart* (publ. 1801). In the analytical manner of Euripides he coul unfold Maria Stuart's conflict with Elizabeth, the Catholic refugee i Elizabeth's hands, and dramatize not so much psychological issues as th inner logic of a situation whose conclusion is determined before the pla begins. It was to be a 'poetic drama', enhancing the historical matte which he had found in Hume's *History of England* and other sources. Th clash of personalities, of political and religious differences, of frustrate love and ambition among the supporting figures, and of divided loyaltie leads, after a magnificently orchestrated confrontation of the queens, t Mary's execution.

A sequence of five almost mathematically balanced acts relates Mary' humiliation, Elizabeth's grandeur as she is wooed by the King of France the meeting of the queens, Elizabeth triumphant over Mary as she sign the death warrant and, in the final act, Mary's moral victory ove Elizabeth. Unlike *Wallenstein*, it is here not the assertion of power but th condition of the victim that is the compelling motif. While a 'Trauerspiel in the German designation, it is not, in Schiller's own definition of th genre, a 'tragedy': moral integrity and not, as in *Wallenstein*, th question of right or wrong, is the central issue. Self-confidence an despair are the alternately shared moods, the victory of one moment is th cause of defeat in another; the execution of Mary seems to confirm he innocence, Elizabeth's success amounts to her moral failure, guilt an virtue are paradoxically held in abeyance. With its tight yet rapidl developing action, the splendid sequence of theatrical scenes, th loquent thrust of its verse, *Maria Stuart* is an elegant work, but also the nost artificial of Schiller's plays. Its logic, once again, demonstrated chiller's insistence on the primacy of form, the elucidation of conceptual ensions in an intricate texture of symmetries and correspondences.

In *Die Jungfrau von Orleans* (1802) history is no longer the compelling pace that confines alternatives of action; it serves here more as the icturesque setting for the legendary events of Joan's life. The divine njunction to be superhuman, to spare no enemy and to disavow all arthly love is observed until she falls in love with the English commander ionel, whom she cannot bring herself to destroy. Now no longer secure n her religious charge, she must become martyr and prophet. Captured y the English, she escapes, returns to battle, is victorious but wounded nd dies in angelic glory as 'Heaven opens its Golden Gates'[28] to receive er.

The play is a 'romantic tragedy'; it does not conform to any historically letermined genre concept. Sophoclean tragedy was, after all, appro- riate for an age that cannot return; to impose the living product of a articular time as measure and model for an entirely heterogeneous age vould destroy art rather than recognize its dynamic character. 'If we had modern form of tragedy it would have to wrestle with the impotence, he indolence, the lack of character of our age, and with the ordinariness f our thinking; it must therefore show strength and character and seek to tir the soul and to elevate but not dissolve it.'[29] The play seems to reflect ympathy with the suggestion of romantic critics such as F. Schlegel – vhom, as a person, Schiller violently disliked – that the classical drama- ic structure must in a modern work necessarily be blurred by pictures- que, colourful or even miraculous features. It is a work, stirring as much y its theatrical – even operatic – effects, its tableaux, the alternation f lyrical and reflective speech, the effective use of imagery and symbols, s by its central archetypal theme: Joan's progression from an idyllic eginning, the loss of innocence in her involvement in history and love, nd her achievement of a state of perfection.

Schiller's recurring intention in these plays is the testing of Greek atterns of tragedy under the pressure of modern subject matter; his pre- ccupation with dramaturgical challenges produces in quick succession lans, sketches and theatrical reflections. He wonders if 'as a contem- orary of Sophocles, I too might have won a prize'.[30] In 1802 and 1803

[28] Schiller *SW*, II, p. 812.
[29] Schiller, *Werke*, Nationalausgabe, op. cit., XXX, p. 177.
[30] *Der Briefwechsel zwischen Friedrich Schiller und Wilhelm von Humbold*, ed. S. Seidel, erlin, Aufbau, 1962, II, p. 229.

he completes a strangely artificial play, *Die Braut von Messina*, a impressive though not entirely convincing exercise in formal craftsman ship, an experiment with, so to speak, masks and puppets, made espe cially abstract by the introduction of a chorus. The plot is whol invented: two hostile brothers, reconciled by their mother, are to mee their sister Beatrice – who was to have been killed as a child but wa saved secretly by her mother. Both, ignorant of her identity, have earlie fallen in love with her. Don Manuel is about to marry her when he learn the truth; Don Cesar kills his brother in whose arms he finds Beatrice, an commits suicide. So melodramatic a series of actions can be made plausi ble only by the most oblique devices: the movement of the action itself i not shown but narrated in reports by the characters and, especially, b the separate sections of the chorus, partisans of the two brothers and a the same time the representatives of the spectator's judgement.

Whatever classical features the play may convey, they are given modern, secularized turn: circumstance and coincidence rather than an transcendent fate bring about the dramatic conflicts. If there is a curse a work, it is to be found within the character of the individual members o the family; no truly tragic figure emerges. The play appears to have bee written for the sake of exploring the possible functions of a chorus. Th published version is prefaced by an elaborate justification of this device It was to be the means of 'openly and honestly declaring war on natural ism';[31] by separating reflection and action, it would allow the event to unfold unencumbered and lend to the drama a genuinely poeti dimension. While no longer the 'natural organ' of an ancient tragedy, th chorus is in the modern context a medium of a specific 'aesthetic' sort, a such to transform the 'common modern life into the ancient poeti world.'[32]

Die Braut von Messina is pre-eminently a domestic tragedy; Schiller' next play, *Wilhelm Tell* (1804), again with considerable theoretica weighing of the technical problems, links the private sphere to the public. Tell's assassination of the tyrannical Gessler is, in one sense, an act o personal revenge and rehabilitation, but its justification and its conse quences have obvious political implications. The bucolic simplicity of the Swiss setting is disturbed by the arbitrary exercise of power in the hands of the occupying Austrian authority and its representative Gessler. Tell, the central figure, for some time resists the urging of his fellow citizens that he should join in the conspiratorial bond. But Gessler's capricious command that he shoot an apple from his child's head compels Tell to reconsider his passive confidence in a 'natural' social order; he decides

[31] Schiller *SW*, II, p. 819.
[32] Schiller *SW*, II, p. 819–20.

› do away with the tyrant. His deed becomes an exemplary action and ·stores faith in a collective order, now no longer a condition instinctively .ken for granted, but an achievement made significant by a moral ecision.

The force of history as a negative as well as positive impulse produces ıat interplay of individual responsibility and collective action, of .atural' energies and moral principles to which Schiller, after his ısthetische Erziehung', returns again and again as the central precon- ition of freedom. Yet, *Wilhelm Tell*, the last play he completed, is not › much a theatrical rendering of philosophical – or political – ositions as a particularly captivating instance of Schiller's artistry; he ıses most skilfully a well-reasoned and gripping dramatic action with icturesque, lyrical and musical features. While by no means the potheosis of a national hero – neither he nor Goethe considered the ıerely patriotic a sufficiently substantial aesthetic motif – *Wilhelm 'ell* is, as it was meant to be, a 'popular' play. A superlative success when was first performed in March 1804, it has remained Schiller's most ppealing work.

Of the numerous plans that occupied Schiller during the two or three ears before his death, only one, a 'Demetrius'-fragment, is sufficiently eveloped to permit the conclusion that he would here again have eturned to the problem of the compulsion of history which, as in *Vallenstein*, entangles and contributes to the destruction of the prob- :matical hero.

It was in Berlin that Schiller's work was most enthusiastically received: ıere Iffland's productions of *Wallenstein* (in 1799), *Maria Stuart* (1801), *ie Braut von Messina* (1803) and *Wilhelm Tell* (1804) effectively estab- shed the Weimar classicism. For two weeks in May, 1804, Schiller was ffland's guest in Berlin, royally received and proud to find himself ımultuously admired by an audience of cosmopolitan taste – a ıoment of unaccustomed public sympathy for the spirit and artistry of Veimar. The theatre had quite obviously proved its galvanizing power: e was reassured that the project of an 'aesthetic' education could best be dvanced through it. In the theatre the artist, his work, its interpreters nd those to whom it is addressed are drawn into one single, interrelated ursuit. In that chief 'institution of morality' he could make use of his best esources, the critical and the creative, the analytical and the poetic, and xplore the issue of freedom, the chance of a triumph of the mind, of leas and purpose in a fundamentally destructive and dangerous world. lis late works had shown man as the object of fateful constellations, ersonal, social, religious or historical; it was only in extremes, he knew, hat the human energies of resistance and of comprehension could be ested.

Schiller's plays were conceived not as moral tracts but as demonstr
tions – at times radicalized to the point of austerity – of the kind
detachment that would make the tragic sense of life intelligible ar
tolerable. Against the arid state of mind of the contemporary Germa
society, against the dull immersion in naturalism, he would, with eve
available device of the stage, with an utmost of poetic power, wit
insistent reminders of beauty, of nobility and passion, reassert the visic
of the new man, the whole man, of which the revolutionary minds of th
century had never ceased to dream.

To the end – he died in May, 1805 – he remained dedicated to th
ideals which sustained his faith in the intellectual capacities of a socie
that could be charged with political responsibilities. A month before h
death he wrote to Wilhelm von Humboldt,

> I cannot tell you much about the literary life in which I no longer much shar
> Speculative philosophy, if it ever held any interest, has scared me off by i
> hollow formulae; in that barren field I found no living spring for me and r
> nourishment. But the profound basic ideas of the philosophy of idealis
> remain an eternal treasure, and if only for its sake we must consider ourselv
> happy to have lived in this age.[33]

[33] *Der Briefwechsel zwischen Friedrich Schiller und Wilhelm von Humboldt*, op. cit., I
p. 269.

6

Classical and Romantic

The Modern Temper: New Voices

Schiller's death in 1805 meant for Goethe the loss of a friend of exceptional intellectual energy, uncompromisingly dedicated to the life of the mind, the first personality since he had encountered Herder in Strasbourg, of strong and compelling convictions, the first who had challenged and stimulated him, and who had pressed him to assess his own eminently self-centred ways. It had been Schiller's faith in the ultimate public effectiveness of literature, of art and the theatre that had persuaded Goethe, at times against the grain of his more conciliatory temperament, to join in a militantly sustained campaign of cultural criticism and reform. In this common purpose they were united; in the particular premises of their thinking they differed fundamentally. However willingly Goethe accepted Schiller's encouragement, he remained – even in the works that owed their completion to Schiller's unrelenting pressure – attached to his own concrete and unspeculative manner. Alike in their faith in the classical heritage and its efficacy as an instrument of political education, they differed in their interpretation of its essential qualities.

In keeping with his pessimistic view of history, Schiller rejected the present as wholly unsatisfactory and postulated in often passionate and dithyrambic terms, a utopian vision of the 'whole man' in a harmonized society. For Goethe the course of history could not be schematically abstracted: its challenges were occasional, its failures and triumphs contingent not upon any immanent logic but upon human effort in a given place and time. Art was for Schiller an ever-repeated attempt at invoking that vision of a total equilibrium of sensual and intellectual capacities considered by the Greeks as the central goal of a civilized life. His 'classical' postulate depended therefore upon a fanatical affirmation of art as immutable, achieved in a singular fashion by the great poets of antiquity and now, at a moment of deep conflicts, to be reasserted not so much like the Greeks as in their spirit. Although Goethe shared in Schiller's negative judgement of the present, his judgement of the prospects of art and of any recourse to classical models rested, however pragmatically defined, upon historical considerations. Nothing could be further from Schiller's ideal of timeless art than Goethe's statement, written in 1804,

> We cannot for long deal attentively with works of art without realizing that they are products not only of different artists but of different ages, and that we must consider their place of origin and their place in time as well as the merits of the individual artist.[1]

Goethe had in Italy formed the conviction that Winckelmann's sentimental 'neo-classicism' could not offer an adequate basis for the sort of dynamic defence of classical values, anti-normative as well as anti-metaphysical, which had during the years with Schiller distinguished his own contributions, his theory of art and its effectiveness in the joint project of intellectual and social cultivation. Even if that project had now lost its most resolute advocate, its central faith remained alive in Goethe's work throughout the next decade: he would not cease to counter spiritualist alternatives with concepts derived from his scientific studies and, above all, his broadly based admiration for the canon of great art that included the masters of the Renaissance.

What Goethe had lost in Schiller was to have been intimated in a solemn choral requiem, but this remained a project. His poetic homage is contained in an epilogue to a dramatized rendering (1805) of Schiller's poem 'Die Glocke': a superb summary of the creative and philosophical character of his friend, of his dedication to a life of the mind, and his power in impassioned speech and created figures and images to make the whole man the fiduciary of the future.

Admiration for Winckelmann's 'modern' life of inner tension and self-consciousness ennobled by a vision of Greece had persuaded Goethe to preface, with a splendidly discursive biographical essay, a collection of 27 letters by Winckelmann to his friend Berendis, that were in the possession of the Duchess Anna Amalia. In *Winkelmann und sein Jahrhundert* (1805) Winckelmann's views as a critic are subordinated to features of his life and character which Goethe in turn relates with extraordinary insight to the historical background. (Heinrich Meyer's 'Entwurf einer Geschichte der Kunst des 18. Jahrhunderts' is an important complementary contribution to this volume.)

Winckelmann, born a 'pagan', maintains the enviable balance of

[1] Goethe *GA*, XIII, p. 429.

ancient poets, historians, philosophers and scientists between an instinctual affirmation of the concrete experience and a willingness to reflect coherently upon it. His talent for friendship, his love of beauty, his reverence for the radiant works of Greek art, his sensitive interpretations of their redemptive power – all these appear here held together by a mind and character of remarkable unity. As a eulogy of Winckelmann, the essay is at the same time a major statement of what might be called Goethe's own classicist anthropology, his theory of the relativity of history, its errors to be faced and resolutely countered in new tentative positions, the acceptance of the evanescence of greatness and of beauty. Openly or by implication, he dissociates himself here, too, from contemporary attitudes he had come to reject as unproductive or altogether destructive: the romantic turn towards Christian subject matter and sentimental piety and the danger of philosophical fashions that seemed to him to leap into speculation without due reference to the empirical world.

We must not forget that the emergence of a sensibility that gradually found its articulation in a 'romantic' theory of culture, of art and literature, coincided precisely with the efforts of Goethe and Schiller to define and proclaim a 'classical' doctrine. The centrality of the ancient world as a foil of the present, the efficacy of the classical canons of thought and taste for the contemporary experience, either of the Greek philosophical and aesthetic tradition, or the Roman symbolism that shaped the imagination of the two great political revolutions, had throughout the eighteenth century been axiomatic. Within the brief period of a few years in the late 1790s, it produced in Germany the catalysis of two distinct philosophical and artistic attitudes.

Two young men of letters, the brothers August Wilhelm and Friedrich Schlegel, had both for some time been preoccupied with the issues central to Schiller and Goethe. Indeed, they began as their ardent admirers: Wieland described them as their 'shield bearers'. The early writing of both Schlegels revolved around the relationship of the classical heritage to contemporary culture and, as a significant corollary, the contribution made to this issue by the poets and philosophers in Weimar and Jena. August Wilhelm Schlegel, the more systematic and agile of the two, only eight years younger than Schiller, had been fascinated by his poetry and become a contributor to *Die Horen*. The example of Schiller, of Goethe and, especially, of Herder, sharpened his interest in a kind of literary criticism that reflected as much upon its own critical procedures as upon a given work; in reviewing *Wilhelm Meister* and *Herrmann und Dorothea*, Schlegel was the first to draw attention to the major shift in Goethe's poetic style after his stay in Italy. With a passion kindled by his Göttingen teacher G.A. Bürger, he wrote about Shakespeare and by 1810

had produced German translations of 17 of his plays, versions that have t
this day remained unsurpassed.

His brother, Friedrich Schlegel, brilliant, imaginative and ambitious
came to Jena in August 1796. Disaffected by Schiller's moralizing pathos
understandably offended by 19 biting *Xenien* which Schiller ha
directed against him, and, in any case, more readily attracted to Goethe
he was nevertheless anxious to be accepted by both. He had earlier bee
inclined to dismiss Goethe's work as the product of a self-centred min
but, after reading *Iphigenie*, he admitted that its 'music' seemed to hin
'close to the winged abundance and the firm tenderness of the ancients'.
He now confessed to admiring no poet more than Goethe, that singularl
'Greek' writer among the Germans. In several eloquent essays he began t
shape his own conception of a classical culture and hoped to become th
Winckelmann of Greek poetry. One of these essays, 'Über die Diotima
(1795), had examined the identity of the Diotima figure in Plato'
Symposium and proceeded to a discussion of the (long underrated) role o
women in Greek culture and, especially, of the achievements of wome
poets.

In his comprehensive study, *Die Griechen und Römer* (1797), a
important section is entitled 'Über das Studium der griechischen Poesie'
Here he distinguishes the modern poetic temper from its antecedents
ancient literature culminates in the 'objective' manner of Sophocles
'modern' literature begins at the end of the Middle Ages and achieves it
most telling model in the radically 'individualistic' or 'mannerist' Shake
spearean drama. 'Shakespeare among all artists represents the spirit o
modern poetry most completely and strikingly';[3] *Hamlet*, that supremel
philosophical tragedy, exemplifies in theme and style the modern moo
of disharmony and despair.[4] In Shakespeare Schlegel recognizes th
'great preponderance of the individual, the characteristic and the philosophical'.[5] A still more telling feature of the 'whole modern aesthetic
culture' is its 'interesting' impulse – interesting here suggesting a strong
subjective involvement of the mind: 'interesting is every origina
individual who possesses a striking intellectual substance or aesthetic
energy'.[6] All these categories are in this early essay employed with obvious
emphasis and echo criteria Goethe employed in his *Propyläen*, in the
hope that a new poetry, aware of its historical heritage as well as its

[2] *Friedrich Schlegels Briefe an seinen Bruder August Wilhelm*, ed. O. Walzel, Berlin
Speyer & Peters, 1890, p. 171–2.

[3] Schlegel *KA*, I, ed. E. Behler, p. 249.

[4] Schlegel *KA*, I, p. 248.

[5] Schlegel *KA*, I, p. 241.

[6] Schlegel *KA*, I, p. 252–3.

contemporary function might achieve 'beauty' and 'objectivity' and lend dignity to the inescapable dissonance of modern man.

Schlegel's passionate analysis may well have been arrived at independent of Schiller's distinction between naive and reflective poetry; it is clearly intended to pay homage to Goethe in whom he saw at that time (and in his studies during the subsequent years) the reassuring force, 'the dawn of authentic art and pure beauty',[7] that would free German literature of its chaotic and shapeless limitations, and liberate it from what, at the time, he considered the dubious preponderance of the disorderly and mannered. The centre of gravity of Goethe's work lies 'midway between the interesting and the beautiful, between mannerism and objectivity'.[8]

Schlegel was to reassess and soon to qualify these convictions in slowly evolving 'romantic' postulates. His absorption in Fichte's speculative and subject-centred philosophy was bound to alienate him more and more from Schiller and Goethe. Schiller had in 1795 curtly rejected a contribution of Fichte's for *Die Horen*; philosophical and political differences continued to separate them. He considered the young Friedrich Schlegel increasingly distasteful as a person, obsessed by 'Graecomania' and altogether too mercurial. In a series of 127 aphorisms published in J.F. Reichardt's *Lyceum*, Friedrich, now in Berlin, formulates convictions which are respectful of Goethe but umistakably close to Fichtean ideas. These spirited, if at times cryptic, pieces are the first articles of the 'romantic' doctrine. He directly attacks Schiller's *Horen* and its classicist position; when that journal ceased publication (1797), the two brothers at once produced their own, *Athenäum* (1798–1800), by which, as Friedrich wrote to August Wilhelm, they hoped 'within five to ten years to be the critical dictators of Germany'.[9] It was to become the most important instrument of early romantic thought.

Athenäum contains not merely specific literary criticism but enquiries into the problematic character of contemporary culture; with a few exceptions it was written by the Schlegels themselves. One of the contributors with a singularly original and captivating voice was Novalis (Friedrich von Hardenberg), whose work – abruptly terminated by his early death in 1801 – lends characteristic features to the romantic sensibility. It is a synthesis of the main currents of late German eighteenth-century thought: pietistic in its emotional premises, fascinated by occult phenomena, politically committed to a hierarchical social order, to the

[7] Schlegel *KA*, I, p. 260.
[8] Schlegel *KA*, I, p. 261.
[9] *Friedrich Schlegels Briefe an seinen Bruder August Wilhelm*, op. cit., p. 301.

absolute authority of the state, and a staunch faith in the German pas
and in the cultural mission of German philosophy and art. His lyrica
poetry, particularly his six 'Hymnen an die Nacht' with their celebratio
of the enveloping aura of the night, and their serene acceptance of deat
had a strong influence upon the later French symbolists.

In *Athenäum* the key maxims of the romantic position are categoric
ally formulated in loosely joined aphorisms; 116 is the most celebrated

> Romantic poetry is a progressive universal poetry. Its task is not merely t
> reunite the separate genres of poetry and to link poetry to philosophy an
> rhetoric. It is intended, and compelled, to mingle and fuse poetry and prose
> genius and criticism, artistic poetry and nature poetry and should make poetr
> lively and sociable and life and society poetic, make wit poetic and fill an
> saturate the forms of art with solid subject matter; it must animate all this wit
> resonant humour. It embraces all that is poetic, from the most stupendousl
> complex aesthetic systems down to the sigh and the kiss uttered in artless son
> by the child creating its own poetry; . . . Other kinds of poetry are fixed an
> can be fully analysed. Romantic poetry is poetry in process: indeed, that is it
> specific character that it must be thought of as perennially in flux and never a
> complete. It cannot be adequately defined in any theory; only a divinatory sor
> of criticism could dare to characterize its ideal . . .[10]

Friedrich Schlegel soon elaborated the last sentence by contending tha
an intense preoccupation with theoretical implications must accompan
the poetic act – a conviction that was to become an axiom of all sub
sequent European criticism. Any theoretical reflection must contain th
history and sum of previous critical opinion. Throughout that history
myths have crystallized the imagination, and mythology must therefor
again offer the modern poet the materials of his art. To myths, now
Christian as well as classical, Schlegel attaches a radiance of spiritua
meaning that was far from Goethe's understanding of them as archetypa
concentrates of natural or historical phenomena. The most radical of th
451 aphorisms explicates the notion of 'romantic irony', clearly inspire
by Fichte's subjectivism, which postulates total intellectual and imaginative mobility *vis-à-vis* an infinitely elusive objective world and its metaphysical challenges.

In the three volumes of the *Athenäum*, Kotzebue and Iffland, thos
popular dramatists of a more and more discredited rationalism as well as
Schiller and Herder, were sharply attacked; at the same time a number o
essays express admiration for Goethe's work. Friedrich's brilliant and
inspired analysis in poetic prose (1798) of *Wilhelm Meisters Lehrjahre*

[10] Schlegel *KA*, II, p. 182–3, LIX–LXIV.

praises the novel as an 'absolutely new and singular book';[11] his reservation – that it is not sufficiently 'mystical' – he recorded in his literary notebook. Another survey of Goethe's development as an artist, of his movement towards an objective manner, points to *Wilhelm Meister* as the prototype of modern, reflective fiction, indeed, as the model of that expansive, mobile and ironic rendering of the world – and of the mind – which only the form of the novel can achieve. The German term for the novel, *Roman*, suggested the concept 'romantisch': the novel is the comprehensive vehicle of the poetic spirit, the 'universal' form in which not only the totality of the modern experience can be rendered, but in which all formal possibilities are subsumed. Friedrich's novel, *Lucinde* (1799), was to exemplify this all-embracing theory of radically open fiction in which 'an artificial chaos'[12] replaces a consecutive plot with consistent characters, and in which the process of writing becomes itself the topic of the narrative procedure.

These early indications of a 'romantic' conception of literature were general enough and could not seriously offend Goethe, who had often insisted on the creative role of the imagination – though always clearly sustained by a respect for the concrete natural object. Novalis considered Goethe (in 1798) 'the true representative on earth of the poetic spirit.'[13]

Yet the gulf between the younger men of letters and Goethe was rapidly widening. As early as 1797 Friedrich Schlegel had noted: 'The perfect novel will have to be a much more romantic work of art than *Wilhelm Meister*; more modern and more classical, more philosophical and more ethical, more poetic, more political, liberal, universal, social.'[14] And *Don Quixote*, not *Wilhelm Meister*, was soon to represent for him the model of romantic fiction. Novalis's later opinions of the novel were equally critical. Nevertheless, Goethe remains for them the outstanding figure of modern literature and culture. When in 1809 Schlegel reviews the first volume of Goethe's recently collected works (1806–10), he admires the lyric poet and restates his respect for *Wilhelm Meister* but leaves little doubt of his own differing critical assumptions. He is sceptical of Goethe's genre concept and reiterates his contention that the novel and not epic poetry is the form truly adequate to the modern sensibility. Indeed, while *Don Quixote* is the supremely 'romantic' work, exuberant in its imaginative inventiveness and colour, *Wilhelm Meister* is the characteristic product of that 'modern' temper which Schlegel now distinguishes from the 'romantic' by its 'exact awareness of criticism and theory and the decisive impact of the latter'.[15]

[11] Schlegel *KA*, II, p. 133.
[12] Friedrich Schlegel, *Literary Notebooks*, op. cit., p. 142.
[13] Novalis, *Schriften*, ed. R. Samuel, Stuttgart, Kohlhammer, 1960, II, p. 459.
[14] Friedrich Schlegel, *Literary Notebooks*, op. cit., p. 44–5.
[15] Schlegel *KA*, II, p. 138.

Other strikingly 'modern' publications reinforce Schlegel's positior in 1797 Ludwig Tieck and W.H. Wackenroder, both Protestants, ha published anonymously a work for which J.F. Reichardt, Hamann's Eas Prussian compatriot and friend, had supplied the title, *Herzensergies sungen eines kunstliebenden Klosterbruders* – a touching and delibe ately inconclusive series of anecdotes and incidents from the lives c divinely inspired painters, among them Albrecht Dürer, 'our venerabl ancestor', artists of great creative power of feeling and vision, inspire rather than analytical, pious and susceptible to the revelation of beauty Wackenroder, close to Blake in his theory of grace as the condition of art was far from dogmatically advocating the superiority of medieval or earl Renaissance art: all art, whatever its style, expresses God's presence. I 1798 August Wilhelm Schlegel reviewed this work of stylized simplicit with enthusiasm. Only a year later he stated in the form of an imaginar conversation among friends ('Die Gemählde'), his own reactions an those of his brother, of Caroline Schlegel, Fichte, Novalis and Schelling to paintings they had recently seen in the celebrated Dresden Gallery. Ar is here taken as the supreme 'text' of nature, with its religious and mytho logical substance conveyed in poetry and painting, and to be interprete in a continuing critical discourse. The greatest painters such as Leonard or Raphael defy conceptual analysis and are accessible only in a state o devout contemplation.

More and more the original 'classical' interest of the Schlegels becam diffused and transformed into a 'spiritual' theory of art and life for whicl Goethe and Schiller could feel only distaste: it seemed barren in its funda mental lack of a central commitment to the interdependence of realit and its conceptual articulation. Publication of the *Athenäum* ceased i 1800; in 1801–04 August Wilhelm Schlegel's Berlin lectures 'Übe schöne Literatur und Kunst' offered the first large-scale survey of th evolution of a European spirit in literature and the role of Germa medieval poetry, of the newly rediscovered *Nibelungenlied*, whicl ranked close to Homer. Schlegel stressed the importance which the art o the Middle Ages and its spiritual power had recently assumed in his ow thinking and in that of his friends. Mme de Staël was among his audience

From 1802 to 1804 Friedrich Schlegel lived in Paris, learning Sanskri from the orientalist Alexander Hamilton; it was there that he began t think of converting to the Catholic faith – which he realized in Cologn in 1808 – and to proclaim his specifically Christian theory of art. At th Louvre he saw the works of early Italian, Flemish and German master which Napoleon's looting had assembled and which were then far from generally admired. Van Eyck, Memling, Dürer, Mantegna, Bellini an Perugino convinced him of the overriding importance for modern art of Christian and national subject matter. In letters to his brother and i their latest journalistic venture *Europa* (1803–05), the break with any sort of classical thinking, indeed, with the ideas of the Enlightenment altogether, becomes unmistakably apparent.

Schlegel's spontaneous, even impressionistic descriptions of paintings and works of art challenged the aesthetic creed of the Weimar *Propyläen* and profoundly affected the style of German painters until well into the nineteenth century. Religious sentiment, whether in painting or poetry, is from now on the weapon offered to young artists in their struggle against the spirit of the time: 'Greek poetry will only mislead them into strangeness or pedantry . . . it is romantic poetry they ought to read'. A few years later he adds to this text: 'What matters most is that the artist be in earnest about his deep religious feelings, in true piety and a living faith'.[16]

These convictions sustained the 16 lectures which Friedrich Schlegel delivered (1812) in Vienna under the title *Geschichte der alten und neuen Litteratur*. He there offers a strong plea for literature and art as the comprehensive embodiment of the history of human endeavour and, in its present potential, as the great reconciler of the religious and spiritual traditions of a politically and culturally divided Europe. Dedicated to Metternich, these lectures reminded a distinguished audience of the capacity of literature to mirror the intellectual substance of a nation, and of its power to unite reason and 'Christian philosophy' towards a new flowering of the poetry of truth. The romantic positions are now fully and self-confidently developed.

The fundamental tenets of a 'romantic' system, now claiming to be the comprehensive form of a 'modern' consciousness, had, in 1808 been formulated coherently in 37 lectures *Über dramatische Kunst und Litteratur* which August Wilhelm gave in Vienna. These rich reflections have remained the chief locus of the romantic theory. They were at the time widely discussed; Goethe read them with interest as they were published between 1809 and 1811. They confirmed his respect for A.W. Schlegel's intellectual stature and contributed to his cautious sympathy for some aspects of the romantic point of view. Unlike Schiller, he had from the beginning sought to maintain an attitude of tolerant urbanity towards both brothers. Through August Wilhelm he had become acquainted with the works of Calderon, whose *Il Principe Constante* in Schlegel's translation struck him as the model of a 'modern' tragedy. In January 1802, the Weimar Theatre performed August Wilhelm's *Ion*; it was not a success. A few months later the production of Friedrich's play *Alarcos* caused a mild scandal: that stilted tragedy in rhymed verse, classicist in style but romantic in matter and costume, roused the

[16] Schlegel *KA*, IV, ed. H. Eichmer, p. 149.

audience to roaring laughter, which was silenced only by Goethe's imperious shout, 'Man lache nicht!'

It was the romantic assertion of an infinite spiritual abundance, aimed at diffusing rather than differentiating consciousness, that seemed to Goethe an intolerable threat to the dignity of art and thought. If for the romantic poets the rendering of the totality of being permitted, or even demanded, a measure of eccentricity, of irony and distortion, Goethe held to his faith in the telling power of the concrete phenomenon and the morphological coherence of its *Gestalt*. In a famous piece published in July 1805, in the *Jenaische Allgemeine Literatur-Zeitung*, rejecting F. Schlegel's notion that a regeneration of art could only come from a close study of late-medieval painting, he broke angrily with the romantic writers by attacking their 'shapeless view' of art, the 'neo-Catholic sentimentality', the humbug, the *Unwesen*, of books such as *Herzensergiessungen* or Tieck's novel *Franz Sternbalds Wanderungen* (1798) which seemed to him 'a more serious threat to art than all those Calibans who demand reality'.[17] Goethe's animosity towards what he considered spurious critical attitudes continued undiminished for more than a decade. By no means uninterested in medieval art, Goethe rejected nevertheless the vapid and, as he felt, reactionary infatuation with spirituality and its unexamined fervour. At his urging his collaborator H. Meyer directed in 1817 a violent and summary attack against 'Neudeutsche religiös-patriotische Kunst'.

Coherence and Harmony: Schelling and Hölderlin

It was not so much the poets as the philosophers and scientists of the 'romantic' generation towards whom Goethe felt a certain sympathy: he had considerable respect for the work of the young physicist, Johann Wilhelm Ritter, who was interested in metallic and animal electricity and in 1802 discovered ultraviolet rays. He was much admired by Novalis; from 1803–04 he lectured at Jena on galvanism, his most important writings are contained in the posthumously published *Fragmente aus dem Nachlass eines jungen Physikers* (1810). Closest to Goethe's own philosophy of nature appeared F.W. Schelling, who had studied with Hegel and Hölderlin and had, in 1795, published a work of major impact upon the young romantics, *Vom Ich als Prinzip der Philosophie*, an eloquent though not uncritical discussion of Fichte's thought. Goethe urged his appointment – at the age of 23 – to the Jena faculty, reassured that, unlike Fichte, he was free of 'Sansculottist tournure'.[18] His

[17] Goethe *GA*, XIII, p. 451.

[18] F.W.J. Schelling, *Briefe und Dokumente*, ed. H. Fuhrmann, Bonn, Bouvier, 1973, II, p. 132.

Ideen zur Philosophie der Natur (1797), *Von der Weltseele* (1798) and *Erster Entwurf eines Systems der Naturphilosophie* (1799) he read with the liveliest attention.

For five years from 1798 to 1803 Schelling was in Jena the most compelling and brilliant exponent of 'transcendental idealism', a philosophical system that captivated the brightest minds. It was derived in part from Kant and Fichte, in part from the tradition of German mysticism. Yet, Schelling soon moved beyond the total subjectivism of Fichte, the absolute primacy of the self as the sole force constructing, or 'positing', the world outside itself. What appealed to Goethe was Schelling's approach to the organic world, not in the empirical manner of Boyle or Newton, but 'from within' and in its totality. This totality constitutes the very essence of life and determines the character of all natural phenomena. An 'identical' spirit is evident in the physical world and in human consciousness, in matter and mind; the creative functioning of nature is therefore analogous to the creative capacity of man. The 'blind and mute' spirit of the objective world is made palpable and telling in the accretions of human activity, most impressively in the pursuit of art.

In art, conscious and unconscious mental processes combine to produce artifacts, forms and constructs which, like natural phenomena, reveal the creative energy and meaning inherent in a pantheistically conceived universe. Schelling's *System des transcendentalen Idealismus* (1800) is his most comprehensive theory of knowledge; there he follows the movement of consciousness from sensation to perception, from perception to reflection, from reflection to will. The objective and the subjective, Being and Reflection, must in man be in constant interplay: his cognitive powers produce scientific systems, his 'will' permits alternatives of morality, his feeling and perception create the cosmos of art.

Goethe's interest in Schelling's thought was due to the congenial emphasis on the primacy of the concrete natural phenomenon and, especially, to his theory of the 'symbolic' character of the work of art: in finite terms art conveys the creative possibilities of nature. He felt equally in agreement with Schelling's pantheistic faith and the importance of the aesthetic sensibility as a mode of access to meaning. But when he planned (but never executed) a long poem in collaboration with Schelling on the operations of nature, he recognized clearly enough a difference in their ultimate concerns: Schelling's more speculative, his own more immediate and poetic. In *Von der Weltseele*, Schelling referred with admiration to Goethe's elegy 'Die Metamorphose der Pflanzen' and, particularly, to his concept of polarity as a universal generative principle. Goethe's grateful if somewhat ironic reply was, four years later, a spirited poem (1802), also entitled 'Weltseele'.

In February 1802 he praised Schelling's clarity and remarkable profundity. 'I would see him more often,' he continued, 'if I did not have hopes for moments of poetic productivity; philosophy always destroys the poetic impulse in me – probably because it drives me towards the objective world. I can never for long maintain a purely speculative state of mind without feeling compelled to find, for every proposition, a concrete equivalent, and I therefore at once escape into nature.'[19] In a programmatical lecture *Über das Verhältnis der bildenden Künste zur Natur* (1807) Schelling relates the aesthetic propositions offered in Lessing's *Laokoon*, in Winckelmann's theory of art and in Goethe's *Propyläen* to his own system of transcendental idealism. Whatever the effect of Schelling's philosophy on later romantics – it became a major ingredient in Coleridge's thought – for Goethe it meant a further differentiation and diffusion of the 'classicist' dogma.

It was obvious that the enthusiasm for the ancient world with which the Schlegel brothers had begun had gradually given way to a mystical sort of idealism. In April 1805, in one of his last letters, Schiller reminds Wilhelm von Humboldt that 'the harm which [the Schlegels and their friends] have caused in young and feeble heads will be felt for long, and the sad sterility and wrong-headedness that is now characteristic of our literature is but the consequence of this vicious influence.'[20]

In a final skirmish, the most intractable classicist principles were rallied to urge upon artists precisely those percepts that were challenged and attacked by the romantic rebels. Between 1799 and 1805 Goethe and a few of his close collaborators, designating themselves 'Weimarische Kunstfreunde', offered annual prizes for the best drawing illustrating certain prescribed classical topics. The judges, apart from Goethe and Schiller, were the philologist F.A. Wolf, the art historian H. Meyer, and K.L. Fernow, the ablest critic in the Weimar establishment, who had in 1796 lectured in Rome on Kant's aesthetics, and whose theories of a modern classicist art, (*Canova*, 1806; *Römische Studien*, 1806–08), systematically formulate the guiding principles of the group.

Invitations to competitors and assessments were first published in *Propyläen*, later in *Allgemeine Zeitung*. Once more the exemplary nature of Greek life was stressed: in the Homeric universe, 'the art of the ancients created a world in which every genuine modern artist willingly immerses, to find his models and his highest goals'.[21] The primacy of a suitable topic, that cornerstone of the classicist creed, the importance altogether of subject matter for the achievement of formal coherence, is

[19] Goethe *GA*, XX, p. 881.
[20] *Der Briefwechsel zwischen Friedrich Schiller und Wilhelm von Humboldt*, op. cit., II, p. 269.
[21] Goethe *GA*, XIII, p. 254.

insistently stressed. It was a noble if crippling requirement, bound to provoke strong protest from the most gifted of those who submitted their work to Weimar, only to be judged on narrowly academic and technical grounds. 'We are no longer Greeks,' was the proud rejoiner of P.O. Runge, one of the best of the young painters. 'Those Weimar people chase after "subjects" as though the whole of art were contained in them.'[22]

It is not surprising that a lack of participants and the disappointing quality of submissions led in 1805, with an award to C.D. Friedrich for two sepia landscapes, to a termination of the enterprise. The conclusion seemed to Goethe inevitable that the impact upon contemporary artists of fashionable religious sentiments had produced doubtful results: 'We can neither take pleasure in their divinatory, shapeless view of ancient art, nor consider it the true, useful and productive manner.'[23] His efforts at a disciplined theory of art had obviously been in vain: 'Soul is now placed above the spirit, nature above art, and thus the able as well as the incompetent are attracted. Everyone has a soul, many have a natural talent; but the spirit is rare and art is a difficult matter'.[24]

Goethe was prepared to admire medieval culture and art as such; in 1814 he was in Cologne and there saw with considerable interest the collection of German and Flemish paintings which Melchior and Sulpice Boisserée had been able to assemble. But antiquity and classical humanism remained the creative ingredients of Goethe's own Protestant tradition, sustained by that emancipatory impulse that had gone out from the Reformation and the Enlightenment. To these he owed his most fundamental convictions. The Catholic and the medieval, much as he respected and even admired the splendid monuments of their art and literature, lay outside his experience and interest.

The notion of Greece as the paradigm of a coherent life he had evolved in Italy; it was never fundamentally to change. For him the ancient world was a living presence, Greece, its life and its art, the crystallization of a potential that needed only to be seized and comprehended to offer abundance of satisfaction. Schiller's pellucid poem 'Das Glück' had rendered this state of supreme happiness in unforgettable stanzas. Goethe fully shared the spirit of that implacable sentence with which Schiller had closed the ninth letter of his 'Über die ästhetische Erziehung': 'The modern poet must mature under Greek skies; when he has grown to manhood let him return to his century a stranger, not to delight but to cleanse it, terrifying like Agamemnon's son.'[25]

[22] *Hinterlassene Schriften von Philipp Otto Runge*, Hamburg, Perthes, 1840, I, p. 6.
[23] Goethe *GA*, XIII, p. 451.
[24] Goethe *GA*, XIII, p. 456.
[25] Schiller *SW*, V, p. 593.

It was this attachment to the immutable evidence of the glory as well as the sublime terror of classical culture that distinguishes Goethe's view of Greece from that of the romantics. For him, the characteristic features of the classical life were naturalness, objectivity, an alert sense of the marvelous universe around us, and its rendering in a telling and measured form. His 'hellenism' was free of melancholy: antiquity was for him concretely available in literary documents and works of art; the romantic notion of Greece and the classical heritage presupposed, on the other hand, that this cosmos had to be recreated, indeed, 'created', in a modern intellectual framework. Both Schlegels and their friends had on several occasions spoken of ancient art and literature as a canon that could be made alive only by being drawn into the questioning and testing fire of modern consciousness. 'It is a great mistake,' Novalis had written in 1798, 'to think that classical objects exist once and for all. It is, in fact, only now that the true "classical state of mind" is beginning to emerge. It comes about under the eyes and in the mind of the artist. The ancient remains are merely specific stimuli for *creating* classical antiquity.'[26] This was a radically subjectivist assertion with which Goethe could not agree; it was a view that he found, for instance, fatally flawing the poems of the young Friedrich Hölderlin, a writer for whom Schiller had considerable respect but who seemed to Goethe preoccupied with an emotional, even pathological, longing for a realm of harmony beyond the reach of the debilitated present, with precisely that nostalgic view of Greek culture with which he himself had little sympathy.

Hölderlin, like Schiller, Schelling and Hegel, was profoundly determined by his Swabian background and his pietistic and classical education. He had rejected a theological career and was resolved to speak as a poet to an age and a society whose disjointedness and impiety he recognized as sharply and passionately as Schiller. Having published only a few miscellaneous poems, he was not widely known when he first came to Jena in 1794. Schiller, whose idealistic pathos and whose lofty odes on love, friendship, freedom, immortality and harmony had influenced Hölderlin's early poetic ambitions, thought highly of the shy, outwardly diffident young man. Goethe suggested that writing poetry in the idyllic mode might temper his apparent subjectivity; he had, after all, read Klopstock, Edward Young, Winckelmann and Rousseau.

In Weimar he met Herder, but he was most deeply stirred by the person and the philosophical fire of Fichte – 'the soul of Jena . . . I know of no other man of such depth and energy of the mind'[27] – and by a central contention of his system. The traditional foundation of his piety, the

[26] Novalis, *Schriften*, op. cit., II, p. 640.
[27] Hölderlin, *Sämtliche Werke*, op. cit., II, p. 622.

concept of personal identity embedded securely in a divinely sanctioned order was here shaken by Fichte's notion of an autonomous spirit creating reality, a supremely defiant consciousness 'willing' its counter-presence into actuality. However grand and demanding such a philosophical construct, it put in severe question the unity of mind and nature, of self and the sustaining world, in which Hölderlin firmly wished to believe. A document known as 'Ältestes Systemprogramm des deutschen Idealismus' containing ideas formulated by Schelling and written down in 1795 or 1796 by Hegel in the presence of Hölderlin and Schelling, reveals the intensity and direction of their philosophical preoccupations, and suggests Hölderlin's effort, beyond the impact of Fichte, to recover and articulate a new assurance of unity and community. In the abundantly significant world of natural life and in the awesome spectacle of the spirit unfolding its potential of greatness, he found his longing for harmony and coherence movingly asserted.

Greece was for Hölderlin – as it was for nearly every poet of the time – the metaphorical model of a fervently envisaged life of meaning, offered and received in the act of reciprocal taking and giving. His love for Suzette Gontard, the wife of a Frankfurt banker, lent immediacy to this vision of the spirit realized in awareness and community. A passionate but faltering and fragmentary fictional account of the experiences of Hyperion in Greece, related in letters to his friend Bellarmin and to his beloved Diotima, elaborates Hölderlin's great elegiac theme of the mutability and frailty of a civilization whose religious passion and whose incomparable achievement of exemplary and near-immortal art could not save it from destruction.

Yet, *Hyperion* (1797–99), echoing the neo-hellenic ardour which Hölderlin found prefigured in his friend Heinse's novel *Ardinghello*, is no mere sentimental apostrophe of lost harmonies. Despite the concluding melancholy doubts in the readiness of the Germans to receive this testimony to a sublime faith, it is a first indication of Hölderlin's poetic undertaking to maintain, and proclaim as prophet, the memory, the recovery and the continuing reality of greatness. In Hyperion's letters we follow the unfolding of consciousness from a state of innocence to one of intense perception; here and later Hölderlin describes in a series of poetic encounters the 'eccentric path'[28] of man, his defection from a state of unqualified being to the recovery of equanimity and a sense of unity, the resolution of existential dissonances through the experience of a natural order and of love. As poet among philosophers, Hölderlin projects the glory of the Kingdom of God on earth, at moments of festive exaltation, of that illuminated sense of the all-presence of the Divine, which his

[28] Ibid., II, p. 483.

earlier pietism had anticipated and which, in the few years before hi mental breakdown, he proclaimed in poetry of unequalled splendou and formal intensity. Stirred, like so many of his contemporaries, by th promise of the French Revolution, he fuses in vivid metaphors th hellenic heroes, the epiphany of Christ and the historic protagonists of hi own time, Rousseau and Napoleon. Goethe's sharp distinction betwee the Greek and Christian traditions is in Hölderlin's work resolved. Hi miraculous vision unfolds in a landscape of beauty and wildness, castin the arch of history from Asia and Greece to the Danube, the Rhine an the forests, meadows and towns of his native Swabia. This is great poetry singularly inspired, yet perfectly controlled, consummate evidence of th spirit in life become speech and image.

In the magnificent intensely resonant images of hymns and elegies suc as 'Brot und Wein', 'Der Rhein', 'Friedensfeier' and 'Patmos', increas ingly sparse and precise in their design, he celebrates his native land as modern poet evoking the fateful but almost forgotten memories of th race. Poetry, as he creates it, and as he reflects upon it in his letters and i miscellaneous brief but terse essays ('Über die Verfahrungsweise de poetischen Geistes', 1798–99) is for him – different from Hegel – form of cognition superior to philosophy, that renders in metaphorica language the totality as well as the specificity of the spirit and reveals th structured order of the natural and the historical ground of being.

Between 1798 and 1800 he produced three poetic fragments, tenta tively entitled 'Der Tod des Empedokles' in which he attempted to reviv the formal concentration of Greek tragedy. These are a record of extrem and desperate introspection. At the end of a political upheaval Empedokles, the Sicilian seer, rejects (in the first draft) a call by th citizens of his native Agrigentum to become king: his rule cannot create new order, but his sacrificial suicide may symbolically lead to a revolu tionary renewal of his society. In the later versions the political motiva tion of Empedokles's suicide is altogether eliminated: it is now the conflic within Empedokles between nature and consciousness that become instrumental. By blurring the distinction between self and nature, b considering the unity which only the gods can assure as his own achieve ment, he has betrayed the mystery of the divine. Only his voluntary deat can reassert the power of the gods to bestow harmony. The restoration o the golden age, the celebration of universal unison and peace is here once more Hölderlin's obliquely elaborated theme.

His translations, or adaptations, of Sophocles's *Oedipus* and *Antigon* (1804) as well as of Pindar's Olympic hymns, which he regarded as 'the sum of poetry' (1800), are the result of careful[29] metrical and stylisti

[29] Ibid., I, p. 823.

studies and of his determination to bring the Greek world to life not in measured Apollonian speech but in a poetic language of passionate commitment.

The heroically accepted distance between the radiant world of Greece and a spiritually and politically fragmented present, the coherence of his vision, his recognition of the historical contingency of all existence and his unremitting search for an adequate poetic form give to Hölderlin's classicism a compelling immediacy greater than that expressed by any of his contemporaries.

7

Enlightened Humanism

Herder: Truth and Justice

Goethe had little doubt that the classical project, which may have seemed chilly and detached to those who failed to understand its underlying concerns, was based on a correct analysis of the prevailing social and political conditions. In the German states the middle class, for long uneasy about abuses by its masters, was yet convinced of the propriety of a reasonably benevolent government from above, and recognized that its economic security depended upon the feudal order. Strong religious loyalties – Protestant and Catholic – shaped and divided its life. Yet, in all classes, the events beyond the Rhine compelled a reconsideration of their future prospects.

To Goethe the impact of the Revolution upon an underdeveloped society seemed fraught with possibly catastrophic consequences; ready to warn against an upheaval of inestimable outcome, his voice was directed less against a change in present political realities than against the seduction by momentary excitement. For the German aristocracy as he had come to know it, he felt little admiration: in some of his later works, notably *Die natürliche Tochter* (1804) and *Die Wahlverwandschaften* (1809), he was to record their inadequacy. It is true that, unlike Lessing, he never assumed the role of defender of bourgeois values; his aim was to relate to a reformed nobility a middle class made more and more self-confident and competent in political judgement.

Though correct in his analysis, Goethe may well have been mistaken in the strategy and tactics which, sustained by Schiller's intransigent utopian idealism, he pursued for more than a decade, towards creating a mature and intellectually discriminating middle class. His purpose could not become readily intelligible as long as its terms seemed abstract, its 'aesthetic' goals remote from the realities of the day and, above all, its derivation as well as its justification resolutely divorced from effective historical convictions. The peremptory Weimar programme was based upon a distrust of the radicalized consequences of the Enlightenment, manifested, he thought, in the fury of the Revolution. None of the eminent theorists of the English or French eighteenth century, except for a time, Diderot, can be said to have had a decisive influence on his thinking; he was prepared to accept, to admire and to invoke the English and French poets, literary critics and scientists – with the single exception of Newton. But towards the philosophical and political thinkers in France, England and America he remained entirely indifferent. His interpretation of events was always pragmatic and directed at concrete issues. He had little interest in weighing the possible implications of the constitutional problems that preoccupied the English Parliament; the American Revolution, the Declaration of Independence and the evolving Constitution offered him no viable model for a European society already beyond feudal absolutism. His questions to later American visitors concerned geological rather than, except casually, political matters.

The historical thrust of cultures rising and declining, refining and consolidating their spiritual, political and cultural energies, multifarious, yet sharing in the grand progression of a common purpose – these were the features in the design of civilization which the Enlightenment had articulated in systems of secular rationalism or religious humanism. It was the vision of a *novus ordo seculorum* which the revolutions in America and France had sought to translate into new societies.

In the spirit of these convictions some of the best minds in Germany more and more openly turned away from the Weimar project. What those anti-revolutionary sentiments and classicist pronouncements seemed above all to lack was a belief in the creative energies of history, in an organic movement of reason: their idealism of extreme severity limited rather than engaged the rich capacities of feeling.

These, certainly, were reservations which Herder gravely, even desperately, reiterated in opposition to Goethe's and Schiller's utopian classicism. He recognized that their thinking did not altogether lack historical perspectives; yet by postulating the paramount validity of Greek attitudes and insights, their views were not easily compatible with the sort of historical pluralism which Herder continued to assert. Among those who dissociated themselves from the doctrines of an objective or subjective Kantian or Fichtean idealism, whether classical or romantic, Herder was the most deeply troubled. For more than 10 years, from 1785 to 1797, he had published miscellaneous pronouncements, *Zerstreute Blätter* – excerpts from oriental poetry and thought, translations from Latin, or appreciations of older German literature – and, in *Gott:*

Einige Gespräche (1787), reflections on theological subjects in the spirit of Spinoza.

The political events were disturbing enough and delayed the completion of the fourth volume of his *Ideen zur Philosophie der Geschichte der Menschheit* (1791). Despite the Jacobin turn in France, he remained republican in his convictions: the Revolution was for him an event of inestimable importance from which he expected a fundamental change in the German feudal system. *Briefe zu Beförderung der Humanität* (1793–97) now contain his political creed. Although disorganized and unsystematic, this collection of essays, aphorisms, quotations and translations is characteristic of Herder's stubborn, yet incorruptible faith in the energies of inspiration and the fulfillment of the human potential in a succession of great historical exertions. The creative individual, the social organism, religious sentiments embodied in Christianity, all these are now judged and evaluated within the framework of a humane advance, of *Humanität* – a term which occurs barely a dozen times in Goethe's writings or letters, but which is the *leitmotif* of Herder's mature philosophy. It is a concept for which Herder is less indebted to classical models – though he argues its derivation from Cicero – than to Diderot's definition (*Humanité*) in the *Encyclopédie*, with its overtones of benevolence and generosity, and to the rhetoric of the French Revolution.

The *Briefe* were at first to have testified to the progression of 'humaneness', its spectacular assertion is the two central experiences of modern European history, the Protestant Reformation and the French Revolution. The work was designed as a fictitious correspondence between two friends of different points of view, and was clearly intended to put Herder's liberal opinions in an ostensibly impartial frame. The defence of the Revolution against its conservative detractors and of a republican form of government against those who held to a continuing monarchical structure was one of its main intentions; that the experiences of the Revolution offered a model for the German future, and that the political capacities of the German middle class should not be underrated were convictions radically different from those insistently pronounced by Schiller and Goethe, and were a clear disavowal of those who welcomed and protected the aristocratic refugees. A particularly incautious draft of the first set of letters is preserved only in manuscript form; if published it would have seriously offended Herder's patron, Duke Karl August. The revised version touches upon a variety of topics in which the political matter is only discreetly interwoven.

Herder begins the (published) series with a discussion of Benjamin Franklin's admirably sober pursuit of rational idealism, after brief references to Frederick the Great and Voltaire, now as never before admired as the defenders of the ideals of a humane culture. He moves on to a disquisition on 'the spirit of the times' – the term *Zeitgeist* had, in 1769, been his own coinage. Enough examples of this dynamic spirit, Herder argues, can be given in the totality of human effort: art and poetry, as well as the sciences and political history, provide the topics and means of a humanizing progression. As Schiller and Goethe began their campaign of an aesthetic culture, Herder adduces in parts 5 to 8 of the *Briefe* a wealth of historical evidence testifying to the long and splendid tradition of an enlightened and reasoned humanism. Challenging their low opinion of the contemporary German audience, he returns to the title of an essay he had written 30 years earlier, 'Haben wir noch das Publikum and Vaterland der Alten?' While there he had been pessimistic ('*quis leget? aut duo, aut nemo!*') he is now more hopeful. It may well be true that the present taste is not as mature as that of the ancients (among whom Herder includes the Hebrews), yet there now exists a public that has the advantage of an extensive religious experience and at least some awareness of national capacities, a community bound by history and language.

In a comparison of the successive cultural achievements of the European nations, the Germans – late, to be sure, and in a defensible sense imitative – are shown as mediators and interpreters of the emergent humane life. As if to offer an example of greatness of mind and talent, not ancient but baroque, and of writing made effective by its cultural context, he had compiled and published elsewhere (*Terpsichore*, 1796) a 'Cenotaph' for the poet Jakob Balde, one of the most accomplished writers of the German Renaissance. Herder translates his Latin poems that reflect the will to confront an age as disturbed as the present. They encompass deeply religious, patriotic and humanistic sentiments, products of an original mind, of political perspicacity and of dedication to the living tradition of learning.

A collection of essays on the 'Gallicomania' of the German courts, excerpts from Lessing's anti-feudal writings, and a good deal of poetry, some against slavery and the European colonial policies, some in praise of the exotic primitivism and the noble savage, conclude the *Briefe*. It is a strange, awkwardly organized but telling document of Herder's anguished position between near-despair in the present, and a passionate faith in the progress of enlightened humanism, a community of free citizens 'in that large City of God on Earth, ruled, ordered and directed by *one* law only, *one* daimon, the spirit of universal reason and humaneness.'[1]

[1] Herder, *SW*, XVII, p. 143.

Despite a brief and polite reference to Goethe's formal discipline Herder's *Briefe* could not have been more pointedly in conflict wit Goethe's and Schiller's aims. The line, he felt, between his old friend an himself must now be sharply drawn. As a defender of the Enlightenmen he had resented the *Xenien* and the attacks upon worthy rationalist such as Nicolai and his close friend, the aged poet J.W. Gleim. He was moreover, convinced of the popular function of poetry and therefor disliked the palpably élitist and exclusive attitudes of Goethe an Schiller; and he was categorically opposed to the Kantian philosoph which was the foundation of Schiller's aesthetic essays and of his concep tion of art as a supreme form of play and beauty beyond time and place It is not surprising that Herder, the resolute administrator of the Weima school system and for over 40 years an effective teacher and contributo to a modern theory of pedagogy, found the goals of his two classicis polemicists abstract, whimsical and out of step with the realities of th age.

He had, in any case, for some time thought his friend Goethe wantin in generosity and warmth. During his journey to Italy a few years earlie (1788–89) he had come to realize the difference in their encounters wit the classical world: he must be careful, he writes to Goethe, not to follow in his footsteps and 'to bring home an indifference towards human being which would for me be far less appropriate than for you, since I could not like you, put a world of art in the place of what is extinct.'[2] He dislike *Wilhelm Meister* as a book without clear moral direction, as but anothe instance of Goethe's aloofness for the sake of aesthetic effect.

He felt distaste not only for the tone and manner of some of th Weimar products; he was inclined to attribute the sickness of the con temporary mind to the horrendous and paralysing consequences o Kant's wrong-headed idealism. 'The century or the decade has drowne in Kantian word brooding,' he wrote in December 1797, 'a new man wil arise, and the flood will subside.'[3] Two years later he rejects Kant eve more categorically:

> That man has corrupted our language and has despoiled all the temples an places of worship of the Muses; he has dispersed the whole human capacity fo knowledge in a spiritualist realm and makes the efficacy of our acts of wil dependent upon a supra-sensory 'Thou shalt'; he does this with a forbiddin and presumptuous arrogance towards all other ways of thinking or seeing, an

[2] J.G. Herder, *Briefe*, ed. W. Dobbek and G. Arnold, Weimar, Böhlau, 1981, VI p. 101.

[3] *Herders Briefe*, ed. W. Dobbek, Weimar, Volksverlag, 1959, p. 382.

drags along young and old on his disgusting road of transcendental egotism and, and, and. . . .[4]

e was resolved to challenge Kant, his old teacher in Königsberg, and in 799 did so in *Verstand und Erfahrung; Vernunft und Sprache. Eine etakritik zur Kritik der reinen Vernunft*, directed obliquely at the antian elements in Fichte, who was dismissed in that year from his Jena niversity position because of injudicious pronouncements on religious sues. Herder's book, written in the spirit of Hamann, whose incomplete anuscript of the same title he had before him, was an attack on Kant's hilosophical elaboration of a tension between consciousness and the bjective world and, especially his delimiting of the creative act to a single uman capacity which Kant called 'understanding'. Knowledge, or con- iousness, Herder counters, recognizes and accepts the whole pheno- enal world; it must not be subordinated to Kantian terms. That same pacity serves to understand the historical world as well. Indeed, it can omprehend nature precisely because nature and mind share in a univer- l energy. The faculty of judgement is a complex of human energies: 'it is e same mind that thinks and wills, understands and perceives, exercises ason and has desire.'[5]

Like Klopstock, another resolute foe of the Weimar aesthetic idealism, erder regarded the whole of Kant's work, dependent as it seemed on at carefully circumscribed capacity, 'der Verstand', as a huge piece of rbal obfuscation. In the first paragraph of his *Metakritik* Herder aintains that it is absurd to 'criticize' reason, one can only demonstrate s uses or abuses.[6] The linguistic foundation of all conceptual under- anding Herder accepts in the terms that Locke had indicated. Using arts of Leibnitz's philosophy, he refutes the Kantian distinction between nthetic judgements *a priori* and analytical judgements; he rejects ant's notion that there is such a thing as 'naive' or 'pure' perception hich receives the data of the empirical world, and once again he eclares the dynamic character of understanding and the affective power f the object or phenomenon to be received. Space and time are for erder no mere formal categories; each must be existentially experi- nced. He argues from a position which stresses the total resources of xperience, feeling, sight, as well as reason for the conceptualizing of ality.[7] 'Idealism' is the very opposite of his realism; it separates and dis- riminates at the expense of the vital resources of man, the unity of intel- ctual and imaginative capacities confronting a world of 'matter' which not neutral or formless but itself energetic, informed and challenging.

[4] Herder, ibid. p. 400.
[5] Herder, *SW*, XXI, p. 18.
[6] Ibid., XXI, p. 2.
[7] Ibid., XXI, p. 64–6.

For *Kalligone* (1800), a further comprehensive effort at defining h position (now directed at Kant's *Kritik der Urteilskraft*), Herder choos the field of his own strong predilection, the theory of aesthetics, or of ar He was bound, of course, by his philosophical disposition to reject t Kantian derivation of the 'beautiful' from an act of disinterested ple sure; on the contrary, interest is the very precondition of perceiving wi all our organs the astonishing unity in the multifarious phenomena life, and by no means a pure form of knowledge as Kant defined i beyond associations of a personal or social sort.

Goethe's and Schiller's aesthetic theories were verbal and conceptua Herder insisted on the superior power of the senses, of sight, hearing an touch. It is true that the eye had throughout the eighteenth century bee regarded as the central instrument of perception: 'Sight,' Goethe ha said, 'is man's noblest sense.'[8] Yet, art was for the classical imaginatio pre-eminently a matter of design. Colour, however essential to Goethe a vehicle of differentiating sensitivity, must in any classicist theory of a be subordinated to the controlling order of linear forms. Herder no reminds his readers of the importance of a more dynamic sort of seeing, kinetic encircling of the object. As early as 1778 he had evolved a theo of sculpture (*Plastik*), in which touch perception was a central pr requisite of interpretation. In *Kalligone* he reiterates his belief that th ear is no less a part of the total apparatus of discrimination. Once again he maintains the creative interaction of the human totality with th totality of nature: experience, reflection and imagination, the senses well as the mind, the organism as a whole must be mobilized.

Granting its Herderian terms, *Kalligone* was a more appealing piece criticism than his earlier attack on Kant's first *Kritik*. Yet it was n widely noticed and did not seriously displease either Goethe or Schille But differences of opinion and purpose could not be bridged. Herder anti-aristocratic thinking, his rejection of Goethe's praise of classic perfection, his own historical relativism and, to some extent, person irritations contributed to an increasing hostility. While he continued t admire Goethe's poetry, towards Schiller he felt a strong dislike, an deplored the use of the Weimar stage as an instrument for the promotio of Schiller's 'Kantian' plays.

In 1801, two years before his death, Herder founded the journa *Adrastea*, in which he unmistakably defined his anti-classicist position The breach was now irrevocable. Taking as his title the name of th goddess of truth and justice, he surveys the 'enlightened' resources o philosophy and poetry that could be marshalled in opposition to th classicist theory. Convinced that the majestic movement of histor

[8] Goethe *GA*, IX, p. 600.

offered his compatriots rich opportunities to remember and to project images of greatness, he looks to the past century as well as to the future. 'We ourselves create the new century, for it is the age that shapes men and men create the age.'[9] *Adrastea* was to contain essays, plays and poetry – written, except for a few pieces by C.L. von Knebel by Herder himself – illustrating 'events and characters'[10] of the century that had just ended. It ranges from a discussion of Louis XIV and his contribution to arts and letters, to an account of the English achievements, of Locke, Shaftesbury, Addison, Swift and Pope; the third part discusses the literary forms current at the time, didactic, idyllic, poetry, fable, fairytale and novel – each section rich in critical insight. The forms and uses of dance, melodrama, drama and comedy are derived from their original Greek context and given significance for the present. Much of the discussion is interlarded with Herder's own poetry, and with examples drawn from fables, legend and allegory.

The third volume evokes models of eminence – statesmen as well as cultural entities such as Prussia – and a searching summary of the achievements of Leibnitz, Newton, Kepler and Swedenborg. The fragment of a 'Prometheus' play, more academic than inspired, interprets the figure that had for long represented the creative genius in rebellion. Prometheus appears as the great emancipator from darkness and ignorance, who shows the way to an earthly paradise: the divine can be translated into a generous humanity. Here and elsewhere Herder stresses the role of music in the making and receiving of poetry; different from Goethe, he experienced life and art in an auditory manner. The work that concludes *Adrastea*, for long Herder's most popular production, was a translation or adaptation from a French text of the Spanish romances composed under the title *Il Cid*: here Herder could, shortly before his death in 1803, return to his old enthusiasm for the tone and the imaginative sweep of folk poetry, rendered in modern terms by a mind of unexcelled intelligence and power.

Herder's achievement, and his role in the cultural life of the late eighteenth century, is not easy to assess. The scope, quality and energy of his critical work is beyond comparison. Explosive, aphoristic and superbly perceptive, his manner has often irritated those more systematically disposed; ready at every moment to defend his convictions, he could easily be disproved in his details or shown to be opinionated and inflexible. But his effect upon the subsequent two centuries has been powerful. German literary historians, generally dedicated to presenting the classical intermezzo as the pivotal achievement of German letters,

[9] Herder, *SW*, XXIII, p. 21.
[10] Ibid., XXIII, p. 25.

have construed Herder's differences with Goethe and Schiller as due to character and temperament, and have concluded from a certain cantankerousness in Herder's manner that animosity and resentment produced his demonstrative refusal to join the Weimar project. But this is a simplification. Herder was a man of remarkable integrity, intelligence, forcefulness and dedication to the life of the mind. He held fervently to two fundamental positions: a belief in the historical evidence of a reasoned and creative evolution towards a humane society, and in the feasibility of bringing the complex and fascinating energies of man into effective play. He was sure that no single culture could serve as a superior model; it is rather in the resonant, engaging and challenging varieties of culture, in their particular contributions to a common vision of happiness that life at its best becomes capable of interpretation and emulation.

There is another feature that distinguishes Herder's work from doctrinaíre classicism: the dynamism of his system is conveyed in an appropriate sort of prose. He is never interested in carefully particularizing shades of meaning or in precisely setting off one category against another. If Goethe and Schiller seek to inform and to analyse, Herder wants above all to move; if they had little respect for the amorphous reading public of the time, Herder, like Wieland and Hamann, speaks urgently to an audience he considers receptive and willing to become involved in the hermeneutical exercise. Against Schiller's exacting precepts, Herder consistently asserts the power of 'expression'. Beauty, harmonious or sublime, is in the classicist terminology a cluster of concepts logically arrived at; for Herder it is a state of grace, an experience of illumination, of happiness and of an awareness of the divine in the creative process.

It is not surprising that Schiller, in particular, could feel no sympathy for the basic tenor of Herder's philosophy; he thought it altogether wrong: 'His constant preoccupation with joining and connecting what others differentiate strikes me as destructive rather than useful.[11] And even more bitter: 'I seriously wonder,' he writes in March 1801, 'if a mind which shows himself so trivial, weak and inane can ever have been extraordinary.'[12] For Goethe, the old and close friendship could not be forgotten, even though their relationship was affected by Herder's insistence at the time of crisis on movement and change rather than the potential of order and stability. It was, indeed, Herder's belief in the power of history, of religion and the arts that enabled him, even after 1794 and throughout the last decade of his life, to maintain a far greater faith than either of the two classicist preceptors, in the capacities of the revolutionary, the republican and the anti-aristocratic convictions of

[11] Goethe *GA*, XX, p. 173.
[12] Goethe *GA*, XX, p. 848.

he German middle class. He had interpreted the early phases of the Revolution in pietistic terms as a religious event, 'we must almost believe in the apocalypse.'[13] Later, it was for him the strong pulse-beat of imagination and humane compassion even in a weak and frustrated body politic that offered the best hope of a creative community.

Wieland

While Herder felt increasing distaste for Goethe's and Schiller's narrow focusing upon Greek models, he remained on excellent terms with Wieland, that most durable and judicious advocate of a level-headed, at times ironic, but altogether happy sort of love of the classical world and of Greek and Roman virtues. As an eloquent and revered defender of the values of the Enlightenment, and of a civilized life, Wieland was uneasy equally among the fanatics of political change, the doctrinaire aesthetes and the spiritualists. In July 1794 he had published the third and final version of his *Geschichte des Agathon*, the novel that had 20 years earlier created a new type of philosophical fiction and that was now revised in detail but not in its essential intellectual premises. The conflict between the senses and a controlling capacity, whether of reason or of 'wisdom', is not in the new version conceptually sharpened by Wieland's sympathetic reading of Kant. Being convinced, like Herder, that man is decisively formed by his environment, and allowing a wide variety of behaviour rather than a single-minded response to idealistic precepts, he was inclined towards a pragmatic view of a future society and prepared to allow the incidents and coincidences of history to give direction to the enterprise of humanizing man.

He had followed the events of the Revolution, hopeful of its success but, after the execution of the king, restrained in his optimism. He continued to envisage a just society in which the three classes – the 'people', the potentially capable middle class, and an informed and liberal aristocracy – represented an harmonious team. He was thoroughly unwilling to believe in a strategy of violent confrontation between those in power and the obedient or exploited, in a radical struggle for freedom against oppression. The gradual elimination of arrogant interests and of economic oppression was bound, he thought, to follow the gradual maturing of the social partners. Progress, Wieland argued in his *Teutsche Merkur*, cannot be achieved by a utopian system, but only by individuals who have learned to master the negative impulses in man – egotism, greed and irrationality – and who understand and seize the historical opportunities of the age. Freedom and equality are, in any case, ideal conditions to be approximated in the slow progress of social

[13] J.G. Herder, *Briefe*, op. cit., VI, p. 292.

justice, and promoted most effectively by ensuring security and stabilit
rather than by inciting to violent change.

Among all the major German writers of the late eighteenth centur
Wieland was politically the most astute. In his early novels, the hellenisti
setting had proved remarkably useful as a fictional realm in which t
present his philosophy of a serene and disciplined life. Greece was for hir
not a world of immaculate perfection but a cosmos of attitudes, conflict
and resolutions, political alternatives and artistic accomplishmen
which should be considered and evoked urbanely and with due toleranc
and scepticism towards the claims of the past and the aspirations of th
present.

His last three novels, *Geheime Geschichte des Philosophen Peregrinu Proteus* (1791), *Agathodämon* (1799) and *Aristipp und einige seine Zeitgenossen* (1800–01) testify again to Wieland's unmatched talent as
novelist of ideas, and to his finely calibrated sense of style, language an
metaphor. By means of spacious and adventurous plots, enriched by well
deployed philosophical discourse, they restate the theme of Wieland'
earlier fiction: the unfolding of lives that move from instinctual an
irrational uncertainty to an achievement of assurance and happiness. I
Elysium Peregrinus Proteus tells the philosopher Lukian his story: th
passionate but passing seductions of love, the disappointments of magi
and mystery practiced by the order of the gnostics and the self-delusion
of Christianity persuade the susceptible young man to embrace the belie
of the cynics; he ends his life of unfulfilled striving for the highest forms o
Platonic beauty in an 'heroic' act of public death by fire.

Agathodämon, the 'good spirit', has dedicated his life to the philo
sophy of Pythagoras and Diogenes and founded an order that spread
across the vast Roman empire; he restores the faith in the ancient god
and assumes an important political role. Retired to Crete, he recognize
the rising power of Christianity but maintains an attitude of intellectua
detachment; he accepts Christ as the embodiment of a humane life and a
the respected founder of a religion which he fears will later be corrupte
by superstition and speculation.

Aristipp, though a contemporary of Sophocles, has decisive features i
common with Agathodämon: he is a wealthy young man who find
happiness in a rational and just frame of mind. As an eloquent critic o
the Platonic theory of the state he rejects, like many of Wieland's heroes
all blurring of the human capacities by seductive and deceptive impulses
Once more Wieland introduces a beautiful Greek hetaera, Wieland'
very ideal of the emancipated woman, whose ravishing personality is th
foil against which Aristipp's civilized philosophy can be given full scope

Lucid in their language, skillful in narrative technique and undimin
ished in intelligence, balanced judgement and trust in history and it

nstitutions, these late novels exemplify Wieland's genius as writer and preceptor. His classicism is infused with a delight in the abundance, the colour and the fragrance of Greece and Rome, a civilization richly reconstituted in the living present. That world supplied to the end the materials of Wieland's imagination: his last published work was a translation of Cicero's letters.

By affirming the ideals of the European Enlightenment Wieland was resolved to counter what he considered a false vision of Greece, the hypostatized image of it in Goethe's and Schiller's theory as much as in the Platonic idealism of the young romantics. He discredits these unacceptable attitudes not in Herder's polemical mood but with the sovereign gestures of a seasoned man of letters whose sensibility may to some have seemed antiquated, but who, on the contrary, remained remarkably alert to the intellectual currents of his time. He was eager to discover and encourage talent among the younger writers even if – as in the case of Heinrich von Kleist – they were far from congenial. His effect on Goethe and Schiller, both formal and intellectual, cannot be overstated: Schiller, in particular, learned much from Wieland's mastery of prosody, metrics and rhythm. In February 1813 Goethe honoured Wieland's memory in a generous and discerning address before the Weimar lodge to which they both belonged.

Fiction of Discontent

Wieland was shrewd enough to recognize that of all forms of current iterature the novel had the widest appeal. In his journal he devoted more and more space to critical reviews of this genre that was, as he saw it, the most telling medium of current social and political views. He knew only oo well that the level of intelligence in contemporary fiction was deplorably low. Since the mid 1770s its production and circulation had assumed unparalleled dimensions: sentimental and melodramatic narratives by a host of minor writers formed the bulk of this traffic, far removed from the elevated aura of the more 'serious' literature. Accounts of travel, authentic or fictional, were as much as ever in demand; tales of adventure met an insatiable market for historical costume pieces (C.G. Cramer, C.A. Vulpius, B. Naubert, F.C. Schlenkert); Gothic romances and mysteries shaped the popular imagination. The 21 volumes of H.A.O. Reichard's *Bibliothek der Romane* (1778–94) testify to the wide range of taste and topics.

When German novelists dealt with the contemporary scene, they produced at best moderately critical and mildly humorous accounts of the foibles and shortcomings of the middle class, cautious commentaries on aristocratic manners, prerogatives and indiscretions, journeys not much beyond the familiar horizon, barely motivated encounters between stereotyped representatives of life in the villages or small towns and of the haughty or boorish gentry. J.K. Wezel, whose *Lebensgeschichte Tobias Knauts* (1773–76) had been praised by Wieland for its satirical energy, and whose *Belphegor oder die wahrscheinlichste Geschichte unter der Sonne* (1776) attacked the dubious optimism of the age by exposing its cruelties and selfishness, showed himself in a 'comic novel' *Herrmann und Ulrike* (1780), to be the unflattering portraitist of an antagonistic society; 'The wit is poignant', F. Schlegel wrote in 1792, 'but bitter and cold'.[14] Wezel here defines the genre of the novel as a 'bürgerliche Epopöe'.[15] *Wilhelmine Arend* (1792), the last major work by this long-underrated writer, is an angry attack upon insipid effusiveness.

An admirable piece of domestic fiction, J.J. Engel's *Herr Lorenz Stark* (the most popular of all the contributions published, 1795–96, in Schiller's *Die Horen* and in 1801 enlarged and reissued to the delight of a large audience), still has a touch of that sentimental gentility of Diderot's *Père de Famille*; yet it is one of the few German novels of the time that is concerned with the world of business and commercial success or failure. Not many achieved the conversational ease of M.A. von Thümmel's *Reise in die mittäglichen Provinzen von Frankreich im Jahr 1785 bis 1786* (1791–1805), an account in 10 volumes of the travels from Berlin to Provence, undertaken by a hypochondriac, his servant and his dog, of their encounters with eccentric figures in more or less absurd circumstances and of his return to Berlin, only to feel confirmed in his melancholy dissatisfaction with the world. A. von Knigge's *Die Reise nach Braunschweig* (1792) unfolds scenes of provincial life, of comic confusion and deception, slapstick incidents and the mishaps of a group of stereotyped figures borrowed almost literally from Fielding.

Two of Friedrich Nicolai's novels; *Geschichte eines dicken Mannes* (1794) and *Leben und Meinungen Sempronius Gundibert's, eines deutschen Philosophen* (1798) attack Fichte and ridicule all 'modernist' speculation: as the uncompromising advocate of an empirical rationalism, Nicolai turned instinctively against the spirit of Jena and Weimar. Schiller's project of an 'aesthetic education' he considered only a fatal evasion of the social obligations of literature, a misguided and pointless effort without a feasible political concept. In J.H. Pestalozzi's *Lienhard und Gertrud* (1781–87), the work of a thoughtful social reformer, a pedantic but resolute plea is made for an improvement in the conditions of the poor, a strengthening of the threatened fabric of the family and an education for life in an increasingly industrialized society.

[14] *Friedrich Schlegels Briefe an seinen Bruder August Wilhelm*, op. cit., p. 39.

[15] J.K. Wezel, *Herrmann und Ulrike*, ed. G. Steiner, Leipzig, Insel, 1980 p. 5–6.

One of the most outspoken and resolute believers in enlightened
hilanthropist' pedagogy, C.G. Salzmann, points in his epistolary narra-
ve *Carl von Carlsberg, oder über das menschliche Elend* (1783–88), to
ıe unsatisfactory social conditions of the age, to corruption in the
dministrative and legal procedures, to the exploitation of the peasants,
ıe barbarous punishment of unmarried mothers and, importantly, the
ıadequate education of women.

The quality of female education is one of the recurring themes of
ublic debate and of contemporary fiction. T.G. von Hippel, a friend of
ant's, had in 1774 published a homespun tract *Über die Ehe*; some 20
ears later, in 1792, the year of Mary Wollstonecraft's 'A Vindication of
ıe Rights of Woman', he argued in *Über die bürgerliche Verbesserung
er Weiber* that the repression of women had led to social injustice and
ıequality; differences that are made between the sexes are entirely the
esult of social prejudice. A modern 'bourgeois' society, unless it is
shamed of its natural provenance' must demonstrate its commitment to
ıe postulates of justice by offering equal civil rights to women. It must
eturn to the important and noble half of its citizens the congenital rights
merit and honour, and must 'open to women halls of government and
ıw, lecture rooms, offices and workshops.'[16]

The Lutheran ethic is male-oriented and patriarchal; the role of
omen in the literary life was therefore peripheral. Sophie von LaRoche
as one of the few who appealed to devoted readers, men as well as
omen. After the success of her sentimental *Geschichte des Fräuleins von
ternheim* (1771), she produced a series of 'moral tales' in the manner of
larmontel, an entertaining fictionalized record of her son's experiences
ı America (*Erscheinungen am See Oneida*, 1798), and 10 or more thinly
isguised pieces of dainty, autobiographical fiction.

In the urbane society of the Weimar coterie, cultivated ladies con-
ributed an occasional novel (such as *Agnes von Lilien*, 1798, by Schiller's
ister-in-law, Karoline von Wolzogen – for some time taken to be a work
f Goethe's), and served the poets as elevated and idealized subjects or as
bjects of admiration and sentimental attachment.

ean Paul Richter

The quest for self pursued in such a curious fashion in *Wilhelm Meister*
ecomes, after 1796, and by no means in Goethe's spirit, the subject
natter of the intricate novels of the romantic writers. Tieck's *Geschichte
es Herrn William Lovell* (1795–96) and his *Franz Sternbalds Wander-
ıngen* (1798), F. Schlegel's *Lucinde* (1799), Brentano's *Godwi* (1801–02)

[16] T.G. von Hippel, *Über die bürgerliche Verbesserung der Weiber*, ed. R.-R.
Vuthenow, Frankfurt, Syndikat Autoren- und Verlagsgesellschaft, 1977, p. 207.

and Novalis's *Heinrich von Ofterdingen* (1802) could not have bee
written without the model of Goethe's *Bildungsroman*. F.H. Jacob
Woldemar (1779), dedicated to Goethe, a shapeless mixture of narrativ
letters, philosophical essays and dialogues, struck readers of the fin
version (1794) as tedious and absurdly old-fashioned: its unprinciple
and equivocating hero might well have seemed one of those romant
figures of radical, even nihilistic egocentricity if the novel were not at th
same time a document of almost puritanical sentimentality.

All these and their ingenuous imitations such as Ernst Wagner
Willibald's Ansichten des Lebens (1805), make it clear that in a worl
of petty courts and a bourgeoisie of severely limited power, the dissati
fied self turns inwards and develops in art and philosophy forms
life that transcend, at least emotionally or intellectually, its confine
social status. *Bildung*, that process of cultivation of the personali
through mental and imaginative growth, offers to the middle class th
semblance of equality with the landed aristocracy. In the absence of a
effective and reassuring political framework, the community that give
direction and confidence to the heroes of contemporary fiction is that
odd and eccentric quasi-societies, of secret associations, fraternities,
'orders' which are held together not by productive work and effort
social integration but by formal conventions or arcane ceremonies an
rituals.

The ablest recorder of German life at the turn of the century, middle
class as well as feudal, and at the same time the most original, gifted an
discerning among contemporary writers of fiction is Jean Paul Richter
known as Jean Paul. The strongest philosophical influence upon th
enormously popular novelist, especially in his early pieces, is the rationa
sensualism of Helvetius and Holbach. His avid reading of English fiction
of Swift and Sterne in particular, produced two collections of satirica
sketches, *Grönländische Prozesse* (1783–84) and *Auswahl aus de*
Teufels Papieren (1789).

A stupendous capacity for reading, excerpting and absorbing th
literature of the time and an extraordinary sensitivity for complex an
paradoxical relationships and states of mind are evident in Jean Paul'
first major work, *Die unsichtbare Loge* (1793). Here he establishes th
prototype of his narrative manner: the tracing of a network of mysteriou
connections between figures of great emotional intensity, and encounter
brought about by friendship or love, by coincidence or devious machina
tions. The plot gives an account of the education of a 'romantic' youth
the 'enthusiast' Gustav, his sentimental and political experiences and hi
gradual emancipation from a world of intrigue and deception.

Figures such as the gentle, loving Bertha and the schizophreni
Ottomar, and the interaction of bourgeois and aristocratic life remain i

one form or another recurring ingredients in Jean Paul's work. The narrator articulates himself more and more sharply, appears in a variety of roles and offers his public a wide range of appealing stylistic alternatives. By shifting from a discursive to a lyrical manner, from satire to introspection, from dream to sermon, from the grotesque to the factual, he attempts to bridge the gap that separates the critical analyst from readers who demand diversion and illusion; he creates visionary projections in order, obliquely, to achieve understanding and discriminating insight.

Attached to this novel is a short 'Leben des vergnügten Schulmeisterlein Wuz in Auenthal', an affectionate miniature portrait, coloured by the ever-present humorous reflections of a tolerant and compassionate narrator. The overflowing energies of the heart, often in comical disproportion to his frugal circumstances, enable the schoolmaster to transcend his pathetic life.

Hesperus (1795), Jean Paul's next novel, is a more fully developed account of the interaction of characteristic representatives of love, imagination, inwardness and self-questioning, joined in an intricate design of puzzling relationships and achieving a final resolution on the 'isle of reconciliation'. The lyrical power of the novel, its wealth of detail and, again, the compelling presence of an observant, imaginative and altogether reassuring narrator made *Hesperus* spectacularly successful. Goethe thought it something of a fabulous animal, 'a 'tragelaph'[17] – an odd term he later used to characterize the shape of his own *Faust*. Wieland was enchanted by the baroque and extravagant inventions of *Hesperus* and, with eyebrows slightly raised in the direction of his two Weimar friends, thought that 'to try to teach Greek taste to a mind like Jean Paul would be like whitewashing a Black'.[18] Certainly, no German novel since *Werther* had so deeply stirred readers on all levels of interest and judgement and no prose of equal imaginative and reflective intensity had been achieved by any living German writer.

Jean Paul's power to create and explore touching figures and their haunting, often bizarre interaction is confirmed in his next novel, with the extravagant title *Blumen- Frucht- und Dornenstükke oder Ehestand, Tod und Hochzeit des Armenadvokaten F. St. Siebenkäs im Reichsmarktflecken Kuhschnappel* (1796–97). This is the story of the liberation from a pedestrian marriage in a petty world through an elaborately organized exchange of identity between the hero, Siebenkäs, and his devoted friend, the sceptical and restless Leibgeber. By this substitution,

[17] Goethe *GA*, XX, p. 82.

[18] *Jean Pauls Sämtliche Werke*, (Historisch-Kritische Ausgabe), Ergänzungsband *Jean Pauls Persönlichkeit*, ed. E. Berend, Berlin, Akademie Verlag, 1956, p. 43.

Siebenkäs jeopardizes his inheritance and must eventually make enormous and absurd efforts to convince the authorities of his true identity. In the pursuit of his rights and his 'self', he becomes so desperately poor that his simple-minded wife must prevent him from selling her most treasured household goods.

Jean Paul's early admiration for Goethe and Schiller brought him to Weimar in 1796 and again from 1798 to 1800. There he was acknowledged as an exuberantly imaginative figure, demonstrative in his faith in an all-embracing emotional and spiritual community, yet clearly not comfortable in the exclusive company of the aesthetic purists, the idealistic philosophers and the young romantics. Wieland received him cordially, Herder at once extended his friendship and recognized in him an ally in his anti-classicist polemics. When it became clear to Schiller that Jean Paul was not to be a suitable contributor to *Die Horen*, he concluded that he was essentially a dilettante and a poet of the fantastic; in one of Goethe's epigrams (1796) the visitor appears much like a 'Chinese in Rome'[19]; for some time affably amused by Jean Paul's bizarre imagination; Goethe was in 1814 reported by Schopenhauer to have said that whenever he read a few pages of Jean Paul, he felt ill and had to put the book away.

Jean Paul, on his part, dissociated himself more and more openly from Goethe and Schiller; by the extravagant eccentricity of his work and with increasing confidence in the provincial substance of his imagination he attacked their neo-classical decorum. Fichte and Schelling became for him, like Kant himself, deplorable system-makers, subtle, perhaps, but ultimately producing only a 'murderous' vacuity'. The philosophical temper most attractive to him was that of F.H. Jacobi, who derived all knowledge from feeling and faith, and rejected any systematic and critical philosophy as atheistic and negative (*Über das Unternehmen des Kriticismus*, 1801).

Two works offer Jean Paul's reactions to his experiences in Weimar. The first is the 'humorous idyll', *Leben des Quintus Fixlein* (1796), a counter-statement to the exuberantly idealistic tone of *Hesperus*. In a preface characteristic of his pictorial imagination, of the cascades of images and sounds, of the fragrances of the immense associative power of his dream landscapes, he caricatures the Weimar aestheticism and speaks of three ways to happiness: the bird's lofty and sublime view of life, the idyllic and comic perspective of the frog, and the juxtaposition and interplay of the two in the disposition of the humorous writer. Fixlein's ridiculous ways of achieving bliss may be touching enough; they are ultimately absurd and evasive. The book is, in fact, a satire by a partisan of the

[19] Goethe *GA*, I, p. 353–4.

Revolution, on the withdrawal of the German intellectuals into provinciality and an acceptance of impotence in pursuit of the irrelevant.

The other and more searching commentary on the years Jean Paul spent in Weimar is a novel of extraordinary scope. Entitled laconically and ironically *Titan* (1800–03), it is meant to expose and reject the pretentions of greatness and nobility, of social and intellectual 'titanism' – 'Anti-Titan' might have been a more telling title.[20] What is here intended is not merely a caustic record of mediocrity, but an assessment of life 'on the chilly Mont Blanc of nobility',[21] of an aristocratic culture observed from the perspective of a middle-class hero who, as the result of dynastic stratagems (which include the exchange of newborn babies), turns out to be a 'secret prince'. In a plot of amazing intricacy, Jean Paul tells the story of Albano whose education is guided from a distance by Gaspard, his guardian and a perfect man of the world. Albano himself is conceived as the ideal of the cultivated aristocratic character, who achieves maturity through his encounters with men and women of archetypal qualities and interests. Dian, the Greek, introduces him to the cosmos of antiquity; in Rome Albano experiences the reality of historical greatness. Two women, Liane – delicate and sentimental – and Linda – passionate, demanding and egotistical – represent alternatives of love through which Albano grows in self-awareness.

Roquairol, Liane's brother, is a demonic superman, unbalanced, forever cynical, noncommital and spurious; in him Jean Paul creates one of his most arresting configurations, the child and the victim of the century, a pitiless projection of the appalling consequences, as he saw them, of the 'aesthetic education'. The theatre was an important element in Wilhelm Meister's maturing; for Roquairol it is the cause of self-destruction: his life is vitiated by a corroding excess of fantasy and subjectivity. The divorce of thought from the concrete realities of the world annihilates Albano's friend, the librarian Schoppe. In a fascinating but ultimately terrifying portrait, Jean Paul elucidates the fatal consequences of absolute, limitless questioning, that desperate and unrelieved preoccupation with the self which Fichte's philosophy seemed to extol and which here leads to Schoppe's end in isolation and madness.

This grand novel offered a design for *Bildung*, not through any commitment to a chimerical vision of Greece, but through the deployment of heart and mind in the contemporary world, accepted in its limitations and rendered in its inexhaustible wealth of feeling and imagination. *Titan* is not only Jean Paul's most accomplished and sustained fiction, it is a reckoning with the age and the intellectual and

[20] *Jean Pauls Sämtliche Werke*, Part III *Briefe*, IV, p. 236.
[21] Ibid., Part III, II, p. 278.

spiritual resolutions which a host of poets and philosophers offered to a society deeply at odds with itself, as rich in creative talent as it seemed divided in its political aspirations.

The fragment of a novel, *Flegeljahre* (1804–05), explores the double impulse that Jean Paul felt strongest within himself. Two brothers, Walt and Vult, one gentle, pensive and a dreamer happy in his simplicity, the other active and restless, represent the energies (beyond narrow classicist aestheticism or romantic abstract speculation) which it seemed important for him to encourage in the evolving German middle class. In his last work, *Der Komet* (1820–22), he intended to subject the new century to a scrutiny much like Goethe's *Wilhelm Meisters Wanderjahre*: was it an age of failing resolution or of momentous transition?

Jean Paul is a figure of singular interest, not only in the context of the time and place, but in European literary history altogether: widely read in the arts, in philosophy and criticism – his *Vorschule der Aesthetik* appeared in 1804 – he was a poetic genius of the most comprehensive modern sort. Deeply sceptical of the society which he uncompromisingly rendered in its most vulnerable and tragic features, he was yet inexhaustible in the use of his imaginative resources. Opposed to the formalism offered in Weimar, he was equally troubled by the cerebral philosophy of the younger romantics. The features of his poetic world are entirely original: it is a kaleidoscopic and reverberating cosmos, echoing and mirroring in every detail a universal presence and making that substance concrete in countless passing gestures, in glances, asides or tears. Jean Paul's fictional designs are allusive; they are indifferent to the pleasures of the clear line of definition and distinction that is the mark of the classical. Yet his subjectivity is not escapist, his lyricism is not a recourse to music at a moment of despair in the capabilities of speech. His work affirms, on the contrary, the power of language and its accretions in metaphor, to assess the strength of a politically unsatisfactory society and to testify to the abundance of life, to the felt cohesion among men and women at that historical moment of inestimable social and intellectual challenges between the Revolution and the uncertain prospects of the Napoleonic age.

8

A Society in Transition

The Conspectus of History

Throughout his life Goethe remained firm in rejecting any theory of history, secular or religious, that suggested indubitable progress in reason or happiness. But his careful weighing of the interdependence of all phenomena of life distinguished his thinking from Schiller's, which asserted the power of will and idea over circumstance. The morphological principle was central not merely to Goethe's scientific work but to his manner of comprehending the world: his method of understanding and articulating the structure and energy of a given *Gestalt* determined his historical judgement as well as his theory of science and his appraisal of the resources of art.

It was in the process of probing these three areas, history, science and art, that the stern features of his efforts of the 1790s were gradually transcended in critical attitudes and poetic productions that cannot readily be subsumed under either of the terms, 'classical' or 'romantic'. In that transformation an awareness of historical pressures is perhaps the most striking element. To establish the 'constellation' that determines the character of an event, a figure or a theory becomes more and more deliberately the purpose of Goethe's work.

His scientific studies, in particular, now appeared to him in need of justification within an historical context. Indeed, any given theory, he was now inclined to think, must be comprehended as a contribution to the precarious evolution of knowledge. It was for this reason that between 1798 and 1810 he organized his *Farbenlehre* in three distinct sections, one 'didactic', another 'polemical', and the third 'historical'. In the third of these he documents the discontinuous but progressive character of science by piecing together biographical vignettes of the major contributors to the field of optics, and instances of the institutional support which gave direction to that research. The somewhat miscellaneous but strenuously researched materials show his determination to discover in the history of scientific thought something like a 'filiation' of purposes and advances, but also of failures and accidents. It is for the historian to 'seek out the moral or political reasons for the preponderance of one theory over another, and to follow to the present time the succession and modifications of dominant theories.' Political history had seemed to him a haphazard sequence of events, to which a more or less persuasive but imposed scheme gave the semblance of continuity. The evolution of science was perhaps no less capricious: although opinions, ideological interests and the suppression of evidence can be objectively documented, their 'nexus' may ultimately permit an historical judgement that is discerning and imaginative, synoptic and critical at the same time.

The conspectus of history, he had come to realize, was clearly the premise of any attempt at understanding not merely specific events but the intricate texture, the achieved *Gestalt*, of a human life. Long before he attempted to narrate, in *Dichtung und Wahrheit* (1811–33), the discernable pattern of his own early years, he had been fascinated by the remarkable career of Cellini, and recognized in his *Vita* (which Goethe translated, partly from Thomas Nugent's English version, commented upon and published in full as *Leben des Benvenuto Cellini*, in 1803), the portrait of a contradictory yet marvelously coherent Renaissance figure, typical of his turbulent age, single-minded to the point of amorality in his pursuit of self-fulfillment and the realization of a vision of greatness.

In similar terms, the puzzling features of Diderot's 'Le Neveu de Rameau', the manuscript of which Schiller had asked Goethe to translate (1805), struck him as entirely intelligible in their historical setting. The scene of this absurd life was the *ancien régime*, offering a background which Goethe's preoccupation with the antecedents and effects of the French Revolution could further elucidate. That inexhaustible topic gave him the subject matter of several projects.

One of these, written between 1799 and 1803, *Die natürliche Tochter* (1804) is a poetic drama of an intensely metaphorical sort, based on Stephanie-Louise de Bourbon-Conti's *Mémoires historiques* (1798); it was evidence, as he put it, of his 'enormous efforts, to master in poetic terms, the causes and consequences of this most terrifying of events.'[1] The theme is now the feasibility of greatness in a society of opportunistic and devious power, 'greatness' here not, as in Schiller's *Wallenstein*, the result of ambition achieved, or tragically jeopardized, but one of ennobling ingredients in an ordered scheme of life. The play is a strictly contrapuntal composition in which symbolic figures, events and reflections

[1] Goethe *GA*, XVI, p. 881.

luminate the interdependence of self and the world, the assertion of ertain human capacities in a revolutionary situation and the movement f authentic characters from obscurity to light.

The heroine's almost fatal plunge from her horse at the beginning of ne play suggests, in a world of political corruption, the 'fall' from nnocence to consciousness. Her long-concealed identity and her noble irth are to be publicly acknowledged by the court; but her future is ıreatened by hatred and envy. Eugenie, the prototype of integrity, annot take her legitimate place in a confused age and a disoriented com-ıunity. Freedom of action is in that society determined by a pragmatic stem in which rank, happiness and coherence are no longer ensured by adition and inheritance. She saves her life by accepting the hand of a ommoner. It is Eugenie's task not merely to survive the dissolution of the oble order but to maintain the substance of that order in new 'bourgeois' orms of social life.

Planned as a trilogy, the work was to propose alternatives by which this ansformation might be accomplished; but Goethe found it possible to omplete only the first part. Except for *Herrmann und Dorothea*, it was ne single major poetic production to be published during the 'classical' ears. *Die natürliche Tochter* appeared in 1804. August Wilhelm chlegel had a few weeks earlier finished his public lectures in Berlin on ne history of European literature, that faith-sustaining record of Chris-an, medieval and modern energies, of language, myth and national nagination – the 'romantic' tradition, moving towards its fulfillment ı a universal kind of poetry, not in the spirit of Kant but of Schelling. hortly afterwards, Fichte – now also in Berlin – addressed much the ame distinguished audience on 'Grundzüge des gegenwärtigen Zeit-lters': he traced the progress of reason over instinct, and outlined the rospects of a modern state based on sovereign moral principles. These ectures were published in 1806. Napoleon was at Jena, about to destroy he Prussian army and to bring to an end the half-century of enlightened ationalism which, for all of Germany, Berlin had so eloquently epresented.

iberation and Legitimacy

n Napoleon Goethe had gradually come to accept the executor of what eemed to him the historical thrust of the French Revolution: he alone ppeared adequate to the enormous task of preparing Europe for a adical reorganization of political and social life. A few years after Napoleon's death he thought of him as a Prometheus, banished by the uropean powers to perish on the rocks of St Helena:

> And what did he have to atone for? Did he not, like Prometheus, bring light to mankind, moral enlightenment? He exposed the inadequacy of all the other

> rulers; he drew attention to the worth of every human being, to the role a
> citizen of each individual, his liberty, the danger of its loss, and the need of i
> assertion – all these Napoleon made the object of reflection and of person
> concern. He showed the people what they are capable of, as he himself unde
> took to lead them.[2]

While he had been deeply troubled by the revolutionary excesses of th
early 1790s and, at the turn of the century, the expansionist activities c
the republican army, he was, in 1807, ready to recognize the French a
the politically superior nation. By temperament inclined towards orde
as the precondition of change, he hoped that Napoleon's forced occupa
tion of German territories would compel modifications in their politica
and economic structure. In 1808, during the Congress of Erfurt, Goeth
and Wieland, the two conspicuous German men of letters, were briefl
received by the Emperor; four days later, during a second audience –
Talleyrand and the generals were present – Napoleon suggested tha
Goethe should come to Paris, to write a tragedy about Brutus.

It was by no means only admiration for an exceptional personality tha
coloured Goethe's respect for Napoleon; it was his profound disappoint
ment in the German princes who had lost the opportunity of a compre
hensive reassessment of their political role by stubbornly defending th
'legitimacy' of vested interests. The fiercely proclaimed 'wars of libera
tion' during the seven years between Napoleon's victory over Prussia a
Jena and his defeat in 1813 seemed to him essentially chauvinistic exer
cises, by which a narrow cultural and religious nationalism maintaine
itself. His analysis proved valid enough: the uprising against Napoleon
ostensibly the triumph of all-German idealism, served mainly to defen
the traditional order of the Prussian landed nobility, arch-conservativ
and reactionary, and eventually blocked all attempts at political reform
When in 1815 Goethe agreed to write a festive masque, *Des Epimenide
Erwachen*, to celebrate the entry into Berlin of the troops that ha
defeated the Emperor, it was without enthusiasm for the Prussian victory
The 'romantic', Christian and neo-feudal creed of such men as Adam
Müller (*Elemente der Staatskunst*, 1809) and Friedrich von Gentz (*An di
deutschen Fürsten*, 1814), soon to be reflected in the decisions of th
Congress of Vienna, was far from the tenor of hope that had sustaine
and given meaning to the classical project.

The experience of participating in an historical crisis without prece
dent led many German intellectuals to look back with some nostalgia or
the 'luciferous' age, the age of enlightened progress, that had change
the world intellectually and politically, and now to look anxiousl
towards the 'velociferous' future. In his *Briefe zu Beförderung de*

[2] *Goethes Gespräche*, ed. W. Herwig, Zurich, Artemis, 1972, III, Part 2, p. 22.

Humanität, Herder had reappraised and confirmed the aspirations of the Enlightenment; Fichte's Berlin lectures defined the characteristic features of past and present with obvious faith in his own subjective idealism.

Such abstracting summaries were, for Goethe, unattractive and arbitrary: historical constellations appeared intelligible only as 'natural' morphological patterns of growth and decline. His congenial mode of articulating and elaborating concepts and issues was now more than ever that of poetry. By 1808 he had recovered sufficient mobility and self-assurance to undertake a searching and comprehensive review of his own place. He had just finished another dramatic poem, *Pandora* (1810), set in a grand, Poussin-like landscape, in which the Titans Prometheus and Epimetheus, the one ('fore-thought') representing active and future power, the other ('after-thought') reflecting on the past, are shown in their separate and therefore insufficient existence. Epimetheus yearns for the return of Pandora, the 'all-gifted', living reality of beauty who has left him to descend to earth; one of her daughters, Elpore, the symbol of confident hope, she has taken with her, the other, Epimeleia, has remained with him as a witness of their former abundant life. The prospect of happiness and harmony is symbolized in a vision that joins the different resources of the gods, the titanic rebels and the representatives of human understanding.

Pandora was only one of several projects that occupied him. He completed his *Farbenlehre*, and once more returned to the form of the novel, now to be more complex in its allusiveness and more finely and polyphonically constructed than *Wilhelm Meister*. *Die Wahlverwandschaften* (1809) is the account of destructive involvements among a group of men and women where love jeopardizes the precarious framework of civilized living: the ominous power of impulsive and instinctual passion breaks into an order whose formal restraints prove inadequate. Ottilie, the central figure, in the end transcends this society by her uncompromising, absolute and ritualistic withdrawal, a state analogous in its severity to penitent sainthood. The novel is one of Goethe's most accomplished works, carefully paced, precisely figured and given tragic dimension by the narrator whose discreet compassion and whose unflagging attention to the telling gestures of the protagonists produces a narrative of peculiarly modern sensibility.

It is impossible to miss in this crystalline work Goethe's critical assessment of a sophisticated yet irresponsible and vulnerable aristocratic society. He shows us an effete nobility, urbane and charming, but obtuse in its manners, engaged in all sorts of dilettantish pottering, in haphazard gardening and silly charades, or in heroic posturing during brief spells of war. Inanity and susceptibility to pathological derangement seemed to

Goethe not far apart, and professions of religion and patriotism struck him as dubious substitutes for strength of character and intelligence.

Anguish of Uncertainty: Heinrich von Kleist

Goethe had on many occasions left no doubt of his distaste for the claims of eccentric genius: to the person and work of Heinrich von Kleist he felt a strong aversion. Kleist was an incomparably talented writer, closer to Schiller in his ambitions as a dramatist of the will and, in his apodictic temperament, the very antithesis of Goethe. For some months during 1802–03, Kleist had been Wieland's guest in Weimar, but the cast of his life was altogether outside the classicist orbit. The Kantian denial of an objectively definable truth may have had something to do with driving him into existential radicalism: he accepted the shocking conclusion that accident, coincidence and arbitrariness irreparably invalidate any considered scheme of life. The anguish of uncertainty shapes Kleist's work and signifies the end of an era of idealism. At the time of his death by his own hand in 1811 he had published only a few of his plays and two volumes of most concentrated and tautly structured narrative prose *Erzählungen* (1810–11). His first play, a comedy, *Der zerbrochene Krug* (published 1811), had toyed brilliantly with the ambiguity of personality, of the law, of truth; and in a second comedy (after Molière) *Amphytrion* (1807), he continued to explore the topic of the divided or double self.

Penthesilea (1808), a frenzied and utopian tragedy, wholly different from Winckelmann's notion of Greek poise, was to be his proud and anxious offering to Goethe. The passion of the heroine is here turned into a frantic desire to subjugate Achilles in love, and destroy him. Of this document of intense emotional and intellectual pathos, Goethe received in January 1808 the section that had appeared in Kleist's journal *Phoebus*. An accompanying letter desperately pleaded for understanding: with a poignant Biblical phrase Kleist offers the play to Goethe 'on the knees of my heart';[3] it was not written, he added, for the present unsatisfactory stage. There can be little doubt that Goethe recognized the extraordinary power of Kleist's talent; but his almost instant reply barely conceals his uneasiness at the radicalism of Kleist's vision.

> I cannot as yet [he writes], 'quite come to terms with your Penthesilea. She comes from such an astonishing ancestry and moves in such strange regions that I must take some time to get used to both. Permit me to add (and if I cannot be frank it would be better to keep silent) that I am always grieved and troubled to see young men of intelligence and talent waiting for a theatre that is yet to be. A Jew who waits for the Messiah, a Christian who waits for the new Jerusalem, a

[3] H. von Kleist, *Sämtliche Werke und Briefe*, ed. H. Sembdner, Munich, Hanser, 1961, II, p. 805.

Portuguese who waits for Don Sebastian could not displease me more. In front of every wooden platform I would say to the true genius: *hic Rhodus, hic salta!* I would myself venture, at any fair, with boards put across barrels, to give both learned and simple folk enormous pleasure, *mutatis mutandis*, with Calderon's plays.'[4]

Later that year he directed a disastrous performance of *Der zerbrochene Krug*, awkwardly reorganizing that interlocking sequence of scenes to conform to the conventional rhythm of three acts.

Kleist's last two plays, published posthumously, *Hermannsschlacht* (1821) and *Der Prinz von Homburg* (1821), may well have been written (1808–11) under the influence of Adam Müller's important Dresden lectures, *Vorlesungen über die deutsche Wissenschaft und Literatur* (1806), which declared that art and literature depend upon the historical, social and political energies of a nation and, in turn, urged the involvement of all men of letters in bringing about a resolution of the 'tension between opposites', in fact, between Prussia and Austria. *Der Prinz von Homburg*, perhaps Kleist's most luminous work, explicates the conflict between subjective imagination and the overriding authority of the law.

In 'Michael Kohlhaas' (1810), a singularly dramatic *novella*, Kleist probes the question that is forever at the centre of his thinking, the conflict between an unconditional and uncompromising personal integrity and the constraints of a given social order. It was an issue which was for Kleist beyond reconciliation; for Goethe it remained the challenge which any adequate and humane community must seek to meet.

Faust

The confrontation, since the Revolution, of political realities from which, in Germany, historical direction appeared at times to have vanished altogether, by a subjective ideology of almost pathological dimensions was the issue which the Weimar 'classicist' programme had anxiously recorded. In 1808 Goethe's misgivings were undiminished: the romantic proclamation of an arrogant self and the dubious prospects of a parochial sort of nationalism struck him as a betrayal of the most venerable traditions of European civilization.

This deeply disturbing experience may have had something to do with his resolution to turn once more to the myth of Faust, that archetypal figure, the great transgressor, that fascinating magus who had for more than 30 years almost continuously occupied Goethe's imagination. He was the subject matter of a few scenes impetuously sketched in the 1770s

[4] Goethe *GA*, XIX, p. 536.

at almost the same time as *Werther*; these he had put aside during the first 10 years in Weimar. The demonic scene of the Witches' Kitchen was added in Rome; a tentative version (*Faust. Ein Fragment*) was included in the 1790 edition of his works. Seven years later, at Schiller's urging, he turned once more to the topic and by April 1806 had produced a coherent dramatic poem which appeared during the Easter book-fair of 1808 under the title *Faust. Der Tragödie erster Teil.*

A lyrical, retrospective 'Dedication' and two somewhat baroque introductory scenes open the play, the one insisting on the fictional nature of what is to come, the other establishing the overarching, medieval order of a divine universe within which the tempting of modern man by Mephistopheles, the servant of the Lord, and the representative of a radically sceptical intelligence, is to be performed. The first few scenes of the action are reminiscent of the old chap-book on the life of Dr Faustus; they show the despair of a vastly learned scholar in the inadequacy of knowledge, his invocation of the spirit of nature in hopes of gaining access to the order of the universe, his disappointment and attempted suicide, and his recovery in a poetic act of rebirth and resurrection. He declares his desire for transcendent bliss despite a fervent affirmation of life, and in a series of encounters with Mephistopheles he is reminded that even the promise of a limitless experience will not enable him to free himself from the bondage of temporality.

The wager between Faust, the self that seeks universality, totality and synthesis, and Mephistopheles, the agile agent of duality, pragmatic relativism and a divided consciousness, is in the subsequent scenes rendered in all its ambivalence. Faust's rejuvenation in the Witches' Kitchen and the delirium of the Walpurgis-Night point to the absurdity and obscenity of Mephistopheles's project. Faust's accidental encounter with Margarete, the innocent young woman firmly committed to the order of her confined social sphere, seems to challenge Mephistopheles's confidence in his destructive element and points the way for Faust to happiness in love; but through Mephistopheles's intervention, that love turns into catastrophe: her mother, brother and child are killed and Margarete, alienated from her accustomed world, surrenders to divine judgement.

Faust is, in the first part, the tragedy of a mind turned against civilization; it is true that the order of the sustaining world, complex far beyond the orthodox frame of the original Faust biography, is in Goethe's play essentially coherent, dynamic and rich in religious and secular splendour. But precisely this order Faust feels compelled to reject: in the pact with the seducer Mephistopheles for whom chaos and the separate and warring aspirations of the universe are congenial elements, he renounces the defining and self-denying limits of civilization. Subjectivity and speculation, grand yet monstrous, have become absolute and, divorced from any objective private or social responsibility, are consumed in negativity and destruction.

As early as 1800 Goethe composed a fragment of what was in the later part to be the scene in which Faust – the restless northern spirit in quest of serenity and beauty – is to meet Helen. These verses, written at the height of Goethe's most explicit advocacy of the classical model, testify to his steady belief in the achieved dignity of Greek life, yet, a faith far from proclaiming ideal harmony, profoundly aware of the complexity of any evocation of past greatness. 'Greek' and 'modern' – these were for Goethe elements of an experienced polarity in which each condition challenged and elucidated the other.

The meeting between Faust and Helen, herself a figure ultimately ambiguous, self-conscious and far from tranquil, was to be fully explicated in the magnificent poetry of *Faust II*. It was only months before Goethe's death in March 1832 that the resolution of Faust's eccentric life within a grand universe of aspiration and failure, vision and blindness, the movement of mind towards a state of most lucid 'being', was completed. It was to be an epic of terror rather than grace. But even in the first part of this chronicle of tragic striving, Goethe offers the parable of an age in agonizing self-scrutiny, of the glory and despair of modern man. What began, in the so-called *Urfaust* version, as an intensely envisaged portrait of the defiant genius reaching and overreaching into a cosmos of the imagination beyond the sanction of medieval faith and science is now given a range of meaning far more intricate than in that Sturm und Drang document of Goethe's early infatuation with superlative greatness. The colourful historical setting is retained as the background against which an almost intolerable story of hubris, excess and delusion is unfolded.

Goethe's work on *Faust* was the indelible strand in the web of immeasurable literary, scientific and political activity: the fascination of the topic had created a magic circle into which his thinking and his poetic craft were again and again irresistibly drawn. As an account of modern man at once proud and unhappy, solitary yet craving community, in ceaseless pursuit of certainty and fulfillment beyond the consolation of traditional values and norms, the poem as a whole amounts to a summing-up of Goethe's own life and his craft, as well as of an age that had learned to recognize the burden of its role between endings and beginnings.

9

Retrospect

The half-century from the Seven Years' War to the defeat of Napoleon, between the publication of Lessing's early *Schriften* (1753–55) and A.W. Schlegel's lectures in Berlin (1801–04), had throughout Germany brought about inestimable changes. It was an epoch, perhaps the last in Europe, in which literature and the arts provided the central impulses towards the shaping of public opinion and served to define the self-consciousness of a disparate society. If Lessing and Herder, Goethe and Schiller ceaselessly urged the recognition of an articulating power in poetry, in fiction and the theatre, they knew that ideas and action are interdependent, that knowledge and imagination together provide the means of individual and collective maturity, without which, in a society deeply divided in its loyalties, the ideals of the European Enlightenment would remain only fragments of a noble vision.

The record of that flourishing of creativity and reflection in the conglomerate of provincial landscapes was at the time nowhere rendered more enthusiastically and with greater determination to discover unfamiliar forms of life, of philosophy and poetry, than in Mme de Staël's *De l'Allemagne*. The daughter of Jacques Necker, Louis XVI's minister of finance, she had in Paris maintained a fashionable salon but, because of her opposition to Napoleon's 'despotism', was forced to leave France. She travelled twice to Germany and Austria and visited the luminaries in Berlin, Weimar and Vienna. These journeys yielded a remarkable amount of information on the social divisions, the differences between the 'Christian' south and the 'pagan' north, the intricate systems of Kant, Jacobi and Fichte. She had enlisted the help of A.W. Schlegel who was, from 1804 until her death in 1817, her companion and adviser, and through him had formed a comprehensive view of the disjointed terrain of German life and letters. Her book, published in 1810 but confiscated and destroyed by Napoleon, was reissued in London in 1813.

De l'Allemagne is a rewarding, if opinionated survey, filled with admiration for the emotional and intellectual fervour she had detected in Germany. Determined to demonstrate to her countrymen that a culture of peculiar intensity existed *outre Rhin*, she was at the same time anxious to remind the Germans themselves of the enchanting diversity to be found in their ill-focused world. Her narrative suggested a concatenation of endeavour, a logic of growth and direction that seems, to a modern critical eye, however impressive, far from homogeneous; yet, within a horizon, certainly drawn by A.W. Schlegel, she undoubtedly recognized an historical phenomenon of considerable consequence.

What had occurred in Germany during the past half-century was the transformation of the canonical tenets of the European Enlightenment – its trust in the force of universal reason, its moral optimism, its restraining social prudence – within a cultural setting that had for long found strength and reassurance not in the achievement of urbanity but in religious fervour and sectarian idiosyncracy. The postulate of 'reason', in France, England and America the pragmatic premise of social and political progress, had in Germany become no less crucial an instrument of modern enquiry and action; but its understanding and its implications, its range of applicability to particular historical and local issues, had been made compatible with indigenous habits of life and faith.

If Mme de Staël was struck by curiously 'spiritual' and 'romantic' features in the chief writers, by their absorption in philosophical speculation as well as elemental or supernatural folklore, this was tantamount to discovering that essential ingredients of civilization (as the past half-century had come to understand it) had in Germany been profoundly modified. Native energies had produced literary and philosophical works of stirring originality. These and the manifold efforts at creating a self-confident and enlightened society were in large measure determined and justified by principles of conduct and by attitudes derived from a religious heritage as rich in imaginative energy as it was heterogeneous in its doctrinal allegiances.

That these impulses were not single-minded or pure, but mixed and complex, that Catholics and Protestants differed in the means of justifying their heritage, that they were bound to be combative in vision and strategies, does not diminish the reality, throughout the literature of the age, of a transcendent strain that seemed at times to evade concrete opportunities for immediate social action. The period as a whole testifies in its many extraordinary figures to a singularly pervasive sense of religious accountability. German philosophers, from Leibnitz to Kant, Fichte and Hegel never lost sight of the spiritual sanction without which even the most 'subjective' elaborations of rational system-making seemed spurious; for the great German epochal men of letters, Lessing Klopstock or Wieland, Herder, Goethe or Schiller, Hölderlin or Jean Paul – however different in the texture of their certainties – the enlightened mind was committed to the pursuit of critical reason shaped, tempered and illuminated by faith. 'Reason', we have seen in the preceding chapters, was in the German tradition never a tool of unbelief but, on the contrary, a divine gift that could not flourish without feeling without the presence of a pietistic 'inner light', of Herder's limitless 'Kraft', or Hölderlin's 'fire from Heaven'. However tinged with secular intelligence, these invocations of a redemptive idea lent to the serious works of the age an imaginative resonance, an awareness of the contingencies of life, a willingness to believe as well as to doubt.

Yet, the hope of justifying intellectual and social projections in critical or poetic writing, of bridging the gulf that seemed ever more forbidding between a growing confidence in the self and the compulsions of tentative forms of order, of unity or totality, carried within itself a reminder of its inherent elusiveness. What needed to be enunciated were the very preconditions of maturity, intellectual and political, the effort to turn indifference towards an unsatisfactory present into critical awareness, blindness into an open mind, obtuse obedience to the seductions of an unexamined life into an analytical view of contemporary culture.

It is the radical challenge of these alternatives that lends to German literature at a singularly impressive moment of its history a high degree of universal importance. What men of letters from Lessing to Schiller, Goethe, Kleist and Hölderlin hoped to achieve for a disparate and disaffected society was an intellectual and emotional willingness to confront the terror of knowledge, insight and feeling, rather than any yielding to serene consolation. Indeed, the signature of German letters between Lessing and the evolution of an incomparably demanding 'romantic' philosophy, is the rejection of conformity or untroubled harmony and the readiness to seek and accept the burden of questioning and challenge. The enlightened mind asserted its ability, within reason, to encompass a transparent structure of order. But the unity and coherence of that order could not be adequately derived from revelation or convention; towards its comprehension modern systems of understanding, logical, scientific, historical or, in Kant's term, aesthetic, must be brought into play. The variety of offered keys to meaning lends to German letters of that time an extraordinary kind of power, at once inspired, uncompromising and contentious. This diversity, often enough felt as a deeply disturbing charge, provides the themes and the particular formal energies of the most profound documents of the classical age.

Dissatisfaction with traditional aesthetic theory is, certainly, the impulse that produced in Germany a new kind of critical writing with its unmistakable historical thrust. For Lessing, Hamann and Herder, for Wieland, Moritz, Schiller and Goethe and, in its most exuberant and aggressive form in the young Friedrich Schlegel, criticism becomes an act of commitment to the wresting of significance not merely from a document but from a passionate encounter between antagonists. The new rhetoric of criticism is directed no longer at unambiguous reason but at the multivalent imagination; its purpose is to recognize variable criteria of understanding, to unfold unfamiliar perspectives of feeling and to captivate the mind by what is surprising and enigmatic. This inherently adversary kind of rhetoric bent on attacking sensibility and judgement rather than offering concurrence springs, first in the Sturm und Drang writers, from a deeply unsettling vision of the genius, the seer, the witness of grandeur.

Hamann and Herder, theologians close to the Hebrew tradition of faith, are the prime movers of the Sturm und Drang imagination, both intensely preoccupied with the redeeming power of language which uncovers, beneath the abused surface of contemporary speech, the 'original' body of divinely named objects and relationships. Hamann's anagogical mode is testimony to his contempt for secular, one-dimensional reason. 'There can be no "pure" reason,' he argues in his 'Metakritik über den Purismum der reinen Vernunft' (1784), because there is no pure language. 'Language is the sole, primary and ultimate organon and criterion of reason with no other justification but tradition and usage.'[1] Herder shared this distrust of rational constructions; the oblique and irregular seemed to him the truly compelling vehicle of the spirit; the voice of the poet as judge and prophet must be merciless, it must unsettle and attack rather than placate and accommodate.

But the rhetoric of conflict and negative fascination is no less the impulse that produced the peculiarly German mode of fiction in *Werther, Agathon, Wilhelm Meister* and *Titan*; it is the reason for the fragmentary nature of much of the literature of the time, grandest in Hölderlin's *Hyperion* and his hymns, for the unmediated endings of Goethe's plays, for his reluctance to provide straight-forward rather than allegorical endings to his fictions, and for the sense of failure of his dramatic characters, inescapably so in *Faust*. The most stirring documents of the age are Schiller's heroic tragedies: the precision and energy of their language is as disturbing as it is revealing of his hatred of a fatally flawed culture, of his fierce affirmation of a revolutionary will to destroy in order to lay bare the realities beneath a deceptively reassuring surface.

[1] J.G. Hamann, *Sämtliche Werke*, ed. J. Nadler, Vienna, Herder, 1951, III, p. 284.

We misinterpret the impulse that produced the polemical canon of Schiller's and Goethe's 'classicist' efforts if we take it as an injunction to escape from the disquieting present into a realm of harmony, to return to an idealism of balance and coherence. Their assessment of the Greek tradition was uncompromisingly critical and unsentimental, its object was to uncover the ceaseless play of creative tensions in works, concepts and forms that had, since the Renaissance, increasingly become the obtuse models of graceful stability and convention. The discovery of the classical world as an inexhaustible but disruptive challenge rather than as a conciliatory system to be imitated and appropriated, was for many of the best German writers a crucial experience in which religious, aesthetic, scientific and political anxieties and aspirations came together. The myths of greatness and beauty, and of despair and failure, were understood in their concrete bearing upon contemporary issues: they were reminders of the human capacity to think and feel in signs not yet made arbitrary or irrelevant by the dissociation of the imagination from reflection, from intellectual and social responsibility.

Insofar as current beliefs and habits were to be exploded, and judgement and perception clarified, the literature of the age is, in a most comprehensive sense, directed at the articulation of ideas, at demonstrating the interdependence between thought and action, the interlocking of concepts, images and symbols. The philosophical novel, the drama of ideas, and poetry intense in argument, vision and design, rhapsodic criticism – these were the forms and genres that best conveyed the provocative and protean temper of the age.

The range of purpose and motivation is, almost archetypically, exemplified by the distinct, yet superbly productive difference between Schiller's faith in a feasible order created heroically by obedience to the liberating power of the mind, and Goethe's in the patterned configuration of the observable natural world with its compelling consequences for a life alert and responsive to that inexhaustible universe. Meaning he perceived in its concreteness, whether in the palpable events of history and its accretions in deeds and myths, or in the radiant shapes of art and poetry, at their best the most clearly elucidating evidence of 'truth' made intelligible.

We can no longer share the confidence of that age in the alliance between beauty and truth and may, indeed, be unable to accept the efficacy of the kind of symbolic rendering of truth that is the very premise of classical as well as romantic art and poetry. In our world, signs, symbols and myths have too often been turned into powerful instruments of unreason rather than of critical judgement.

If the classical age seems in Germany to articulate its concerns preeminently in terms of literature and art, these are, at their most serious, never divorced from an awareness of political and social realities. The revolutionary experiences inevitably polarized the intellectual presuppositions of writers and readers and put the concept of an 'aesthetic' process of social maturing in serious doubt. Political tensions of a dynastic sort had for long been a characteristic feature of the German body politic; they were soon to be differentiated by doubts in the legitimacy, however benevolent, of autocratic government. Their force was for long spontaneous and prompted by humanitarian sentiments; they focused only gradually on the divergence of an evolving middle-class consciousness, its aspirations and its strengths, from established feudal forms of conduct. The importance of this political thread in the history of the classical age must not be underrated. Yet, it would be a dubious simplification to reduce the intricate texture of German social, intellectual and literary life in the late eighteenth century to a single dominant motif.

It was after all not, as in England, France or Holland, the radiance and glory of national power and pride that had in Germany given rise to literary and intellectual renown, but the sturdy if introverted energies of the small courts, the landed gentry and, above all, the Protestant parish. Parochial traditions and long-accustomed forms of life, now desperately tested in the crucible of the American and French Revolutions, were marshalled towards the prospects of a community of self-critical and self-confident minds. Beyond provincial horizons a shared awareness of purpose became unmistakable, the will to sharpen social, moral and intellectual sensibilities and, most strikingly of all, to give voice to all these in a chorus of extraordinary poetic genius. It was with disarming confidence that Mme de Staël could in 1802 enthusiastically assert: 'The human spirit, which seems to move from one country to another, at present resides in Germany.'[2]

[2] Mme de Staël, *Correspondance générale*, ed. B.W. Jasinski, Paris, Pauvert, 1978, IV, Part 2, p. 541.

Abbreviations

AGB	Archiv für Geschichte des Buchwesens.
DVjs	Deutsche Vierteljahrsschrift für Literaturwissenschaft und Geistesgeschichte.
GJb	Goethe Jahrbuch.
GLL	German Life and Letters.
Goethe-JbGG	Jahrbuch der Goethe Gesellschaft.
GRM	Germanisch-Romanisch Monatsschrift.
IASDL	Internationales Archiv f. d. Sozialgeschichte der deutschen Literatur.
JbDSG	Jahrbuch der deutschen Schiller-Gesellschaft.
JEGP	Journal of English and Germanic Philology.
JFDH	Jahrbuch des Freien Deutschen Hochstifts.
JIG	Jahrbuch für Internationale Germanistik.
MDU	Monatsheft für den deutschen Unterricht.
MLN	Modern Language Notes.
MLR	Modern Language Review.
PEGS	Publications of the English Goethe Society.
PMLA	Publications of the Modern Language Assoc. of America.
WW	Wirkendes Wort.
ZDP	Zeitschrift für deutsche Philologie.
ZFSL	Zeitschrift für französische Sprache und Literatur.

Bibliographical Guide

No period of German literary history has been so intensively subjected to critical scrutiny as the classical age. For most major writers there exist extensive bibliographies of recent scholarship; biographical information may be found in *Neue Deutsche Biographie*.

In the first section of this compilation, useful bibliographical resources and relevant works of reference are listed; the second section provides a selective survey of historical and critical scholarship dealing with various aspects of the material discussed in the book; the third suggests studies devoted to individual authors. Collected works or editions of individual texts are, with few exceptions, not included.

I Bibliographies and reference works

Annual Bibliographical Reports in: *Das Achtzehnte Jahrhundert*: Mitteilungen d. dt. Gesellschaft f. d. Erforschung des 18. Jahrhunderts. Wolfenbüttel, 1976f.

Aland, K., *et al.*, eds., *Bibliographien zur Geschichte des Pietismus*. Vol. I. G. Mälzer, ed., *Die Werke der württembergischen Pietisten des 17. und 18. Jahrhunderts. Verzeichnis der bis 1968 erschienenen Literatur*. Berlin and New York, de Gruyter, 1972, xvi, 415p.

Albrecht, Günter and Günther Dahlke, eds., *Internationale Bibliographie zur Geschichte der deutschen Literatur*. Teil 1–3 in 4 vols. Munich, Verlag Dokumentation, 1969–77.

Albrecht, Günter, *et al.*, eds., *Lexikon deutschsprachiger Schriftsteller von den Anfängen bis zur Gegenwart*. 2 vols. Leipzig, VEB Bibliographische Institut, 1972.

'Auswahlbibliographie zur Sozialgeschichte der deutschen Literatur', *IASDL* 1 (1976)ff.

Bartel, Klaus J., *German Literary History 1777 to 1835. An Annotated Bibliography*. German Studies in America, 22. Bern, Lang, 1976, 229p.

Frank, Horst J., *Handbuch der deutschen Strophenform*. Munich, Hanser, 1978, 888p.

Hempfer, Klaus W., 'Bibliographie zur Gattungspoetik (1). Allgemeine Gattungstheorie (1890–1971)', *ZFSL* 82 (1972) 53–66.

Hantsch, Ingrid, 'Bibliographie zur Gattungspoetik (2). Theorie der Satire (1900–1970)', *ZFSI* 82 (1972), 153–6.

Pfister, Manfred, 'Bibliographie zur Gattungspoetik (3), Theorie des Komischen, der Komödie und der Tragikomödie', *ZFSL* 83 (1973), 240–54.

Gebhardt, Helga, 'Bibliographie zur Gattungspoetik (4). Theorie des Tragischen und der Tragödie 1900–1972', *ZFSL* 84 (1974), 236–48.

Lindner, Hermann 'Bibliographie zur Gattungspoetik (5). Theorie und Geschichte der Fabel (1900–1974)', *ZFSL* 65 (1975) 247–59.

'Bibliographische Berichte'. In *Das achtzehnte Jahrhundert. Mitteilungen der Dt. Ges. f. d. Erforschung des 18. Jahrhunderts*. Wolfenbüttel, Herzog August Bibliothek, 1977ff.

Blume, Friedrich, ed., *Die Musik in Geschichte und Gegenwart*. 15 vols. Kassel, Bärenreiter Verlag, 1948–79.

Brunner, Otto, *et al.*, eds., *Geschichtliche Grundbegriffe. Historisches Lexikon zur politisch-sozialen Sprache in Deutschland*. 4 vols. Stuttgart, Klett–Cotta, 1979.

Dictionary of the History of Ideas: *Studies of Selected Pivotal Ideas*. 5 vols. New York, Scribner, 1973. Index 1974.

Dictionary of Scientific Biography. 14 vols. + 2 vols. Ed. Charles Gillispie. New York, Charles Scribner Sons, 1970–80.

The Encyclopedia of Philosophy. Ed. Paul Edwards. 8 vols. New York, Macmillan, 1967ff.

Encyclopedia of the Social Sciences. Ed. Edwin R. A. Seligman and Alvin Johnson. 15 vols. in 8. New York, Macmillan, 1962.

Faulhaber, Uwe K. and P. B. Goff, *German Literature. An Annotated Reference Guide*. New York, Garland Publ. Co., 1979, 398p.

Fischer, Heinz-Dietrich, ed., *Deutsche Zeitschriften des 17. bis 20. Jahrhunderts*. Munich, Saur/SUK, 1973, 445p.

Fischer, Heinz-Dietrich, ed., *Deutsche Zeitungen des 17. bis 20. Jahrhunderts*. Munich, Saur/SUK, 1973, 415p.

Friedrichs, Elizabeth, ed., *Die deutschsprachigen Schriftstellerinnen des 18. und 19. Jahrhunderts. Ein Lexikon*. Stuttgart, Metzler, 1981, xxiv, 388p.

Galling, Kurt, *et al.*, eds., *Die Religion in Geschichte und Gegenwart. Handwörterbuch für Theologie und Religionswissenschaft*. 7 vols. 3rd edn, Tübingen, Mohr, 1957–65.

Garland, Henry and Mary Garland, eds., *Oxford Companion to German Literature*. Oxford, Clarendon Press, 1976, 977p.

Germanistik. Internationales Referatenorgan mit biblographischen Hinweisen. Jhg. 1 (1960)–22f. (1981f.).

Germer, Helmut. *The German Novel of Education 1792–1805. A complete bibliography and analysis*. German Studies in America, No. 3. Bern, Lang, 1968, 280p.

Iadley, Michael, *The German Novel in 1790. A Descriptive Account and Critical Bibliography*. Bern/Frankfurt, Lang, 1973, viii, 291p.

Iadley, Michael, *Romanverzeichnis, Bibliographie der zwischen 1750 und 1800 erschienenen Erstausgaben*. Bern/Frankfurt/Las Vegas, Lang, 1977, xxii, 411p.

Iagen, Waltraud, *et al.*, eds., *Handbuch der Editionen*. Munich, Beck, 1979, 608p.

Iandbuch philosophischer Grundbegriffe. 3 vols., ed., H. Krings, H. M. Baumgartner, C. Wild, Munich, Kösel, 1973–74.

Iansel, Johannes. *Personalbibliographie zur deutschen Literaturgeschichte*. 2nd edn., Berlin, E. Schmidt, 1974, 258p.

Iarris, Kathleen, ed., *Goethezeit*. Vol. 7 of *Handbuch der Deutschen Literaturgeschichte. Zweite Abteilung: Bibliographien*. Bern, Francke, 1976, 80p.

Iistorisches Wörterbuch der Philosophie. Vols. 1–5ff., ed. Joachim Ritter Darmstadt: Wissenschaftliche Buchgesellschaft, 1971–80ff.

Iocks, Paul, *Bücherverzeichnis zur deutschen Literaturgeschichte*. Frankfurt, Ullstein, 1979, 159p.

Iocks, Paul and Peter Schmidt, *Literarische und politische Zeitschriften 1798–1805. Von der politischen Revolution zur Literaturrevolution*. Sammlung Metzler 121. Stuttgart, Metzler, 1975, 141p.

nternational Encyclopedia of the Social Sciences. 17 vols + 1 vol. *Biographical Supplement*. Ed. David L. Sills. Vols.. 1–17: New York, Macmillan, 1968–79. Vol. 18: New York, Free Press.

nternationale Bibliographie zur Deutschen Klassik 1750–1850. Ed. Hans Henning *et al.* Parts 1–10 in *Weimarer Beiträge*, 6–10. Parts 11ff. Weimar: Nationale Forschungs- und Gedenkstätten der Klassischen Deutschen Literatur in Weimar, 1964f.

irchner, Joachim. *Bibliographie der Zeitschriften des deutschen Sprachgebiets bis 1900*. Vol. I: *Von den Anfangen bis 1830*. Stuttgart, Hiersemann, 1969, xv, 489p.

irchner, Joachim, ed., *Lexikon des Buchwesens*. 4 vols. Stuttgart, Hiersemann, 1952–56.

öttelwesch, Clemens, ed., *Bibliographie der deutschen Literaturwissenschaft*. From Vol. 9: *Bibliographie der deutschen Sprach- und Literaturwissenschaft*. 16 vols. Frankfurt, Klostermann, 1957–77ff.

öttelwesch, Clemens, *Bibliographisches Handbuch der deutschen Literaturwissenschaft*. 3 vols. Frankfurt, Klostermann, 1945–79.

ohlschmidt, Werner and Wolfgang Mohr, eds., *Reallexikon der deutschen Literaturgeschichte*. 2nd edn, vols. 1–8f. Berlin, de Gruyter, 1958–81f.

osch, Wilhelm. *Deutsches Literatur-Lexikon. Biographisch-bibliographisches Handbuch*. 3rd edn, vols. 1–8f. B. Berger and H. Rupp, eds. Bern/Munich, Francke, 1968–81f.

öffler, Karl and Joachim Kirchner. *Lexikon des gesamten Buchwesens*. 2 vols. Leipzig, K.W. Hiersemann, 1935–37.

leyer, Reinhart. *Das deutsche Trauerspiel des 18. Jahrhunderts. Eine Bibliographie*. Munich, Fink, 1977, 226p.

ILA American Bibliography of Books and Articles on the Modern Languages and Literatures, PMLA 37 (1922)–84 (1969). Succeeded by *MLA International Bibliography of Books and Articles in Modern Languages 1969ff.* New York, Modern Language Association of America, 1970ff.

Neue Deutsche Biographie. Ed. Hist. Kommission bei der Bayr. Akad. d. Wissenschaften. Vols 1– Berlin, Duncker & Humblot, 1953ff.

The New Grove Dictionary of Music and Musicians. 20 vols. ed. S. Sadie. London, Macmillan, 1980.

O'Neill, Patrick. *German Literature in English Translation*. Toronto, Toronto Univ. Press, 1981, xii, 242p.

The Penguin Companion to European Literature. Ed. Anthony Thorlby. New York, McGraw–Hill, 1969–71, 907p.

The Phaidon Encyclopedia of Art and Artists. Oxford, Phaidon Press, 198[illegible] 704p.

Princeton Encyclopedia of Poetry and Poetics. 2nd edn, ed. Alex Preminger *et al.* Princeton, Princeton Univ. Press, 1974, xxiv, 992p.

Ruttkowski, Wolfgang Victor. *Bibliographie der Gattungspoetik*. Munich, Hueber, 1973, 246p.

Schindler, Otto G., ed., *Theaterliteratur. Ein bibliographischer Behelf für das Studium der Theaterwissenschaft*. Vienna, Wiener Gesellschaft für Theaterforschung, 1978, 194p.

Werwigg, Ferdinand, *Bibliographie Östereichischer Drucke während der 'erweiterten Pressefreiheit' (1781–1795*. Vienna and Munich, Jugend und Volk, 1973–79, 429p.

Wilke, Jürgen. *Literarische Zeitschriften des 18. Jahrhunderts*. 2 Parts. Sammlung Metzler 174, 175. Stuttgart, Metzler, 1978.

Wilpert, Gero von and Adolf Gühring. *Erstausgaben deutscher Dichtung. Eine Bibliographie zur deutsche Literatur 1600–1960*. Stuttgart, Kröner, 196[illegible] 1968.

The Year's Work in Modern Language Studies. Vols. 1–41f. Oxford/Cambridge/London, Modern Humanities Research Assoc., 1931–80f.

II General critical studies

Ackermann, James S., *et al., Rococo to Romanticism: Art and Architecture 1700–1850*. Garland Library of the History of Art, 10. London and New York, Garland, 1976, vii, 302p.

Albertsen, Leif L., *Das Lehrgedicht*. Aarhus, Akademisk Boghandel, 196[illegible] 409p.

Albrecht, Günter and Johannes Mittenzwei, eds., *Klassik*. 5th edn, Berlin, Volk und Wissen, 1967, 507p.

Ammermann, Monika, *Gemeines Leben. Gewandelter Naturbegriff und literarische Spätaufklärung. Lichtenberg, Wezel, Garve*. Bonn, Bouvier, 1978, 194p.

Anderson, Matthew Smith, *Europe in the Eighteenth Century 1713–1783*. 2nd edn, New York, Longman, 1976, 364p.

Anderson, Matthew Smith, *Historians and Eighteenth-Century Europe, 1715–1789*. Oxford, Clarendon Press, 1979, vi, 251p.

Anger, Alfred, 'Deutsche Rokoko-Dichtung. Ein Forschungsbericht'. *DVjs* 36 (1962), 430–479 and 614–648.

Anger, Alfred, *Literarisches Rokoko*. 2nd edn, Sammlung Metzler, 25. Stuttgart, Metzler, 1968, x, 115p.

Antal, Frederick, *Classicism and Romanticism. With other Studies in Art History*. London, Routledge & Kegan Paul, 1966, xvi, 198p.

Aretin, Karl Otmar von, *Der aufgeklärte Absolutismus*. Cologne, Kiepenheuer & Witsch, 1974, 392p.

Aris, Reinhold, *History of Political Thought in Germany from 1789–1815*. New York, Russell & Russell, 1965, 414p.

Arndt, Ingeborg, *Die seelische Welt im Roman des achtzehnten Jahrhunderts*. Diss. Giessen 1940. Tübingen, Bölzle, 1940, 83p.

Arntzen, H., *Die ernste Komödie. Das deutsche Lustspiel von Lessing bis Kleist*. Sammlung Dialog, 9. Munich, Nymphenburger Verlagshandlung, 1968, 303p.

The Arts Council of Great Britain, *The Age of Neo-Classicism. The Fourteenth Exhibition of the Council of Europe*. London, 1972, 1037p.

Ashton, T. S. *The Industrial Revolution*. Oxford, Oxford Univ. Press, 1969, 119p.

Baeumer, M. L., 'Der Begriff "Klassisch" bei Goethe und Schiller'. In *Die Klassiklegende*. Ed. Reinhold Grimm and Jost Hermand. Frankfurt/Main, Athenäum-Verlag, 1971, 17–49.

Bäumler, Alfred, *Das Irrationalitätsproblem in der Ästhetik und Logik des 18. Jahrhunderts bis zur Kritik der Urteilskraft*. Halle, 1923; rpt. Tübingen, Niemeyer, 1967, x, 354p.

Bahr, Erhard, ed., *Was ist Aufklärung? Thesen und Definitionen*. Stuttgart, Reclam, 1974.

Balet, Leo and Eberhard Gerhard, *Die Verbürgerlichung der deutschen Kunst, Literatur und Musik im 18. Jahrhundert*. Ed. Gerd Mattenklott. Frankfurt, Ullstein, 1973.

Barber, Giles and Bernhard Fabian, eds, *Buch und Buchhandel in Europe im 18. Jahrhundert/The Book and Book Trade in Eighteenth Century Europe*. Wolfenbüttler Symposium. Hamburg, Hauswedell, 1981, 364p.

Barth, Ilse Marie, *Literarisches Weimar. Kultur, Literatur, Sozialstruktur im 16.–20. Jahrhundert*. Sammlung Metzler, M93. Stuttgart, Metzler, 1971 xii, 164p.

Bauer, Bruno. *Geschichte der Politik, Kultur und Aufklärung des 18. Jahrhunderts*. Berlin, 1843–45; rpt. 4 vols. in 2. Aalen, Scientia Verlag, 1965.

Bauer, Roger, *La réalité, royaume de Dieu*. Munich, M. Hüber, 1965, 605p.

Bauer, Werner M., *Fiktion und Polemik. Studien zum Roman der Österreichischen Aufklärung*. Vienna, Österreichische Akad. der Wissenschaften, 1978, 395p.

Baumgart, Fritz, *Vom Klassizismus zur Romantik 1750–1832*. Cologne, M. DuMont, 1974, 246p.

Beaujean, Marion, 'Das Lesepublikum der Goethezeit. Die historischen und soziologischen Wurzeln des modernen Unterhaltungsromans'. In *Der Leser als Teil des literarischen Lebens*. Eds. Marion Beaujean *et al*. 2nd edn, Bonn, Bouvier, 1972, 5–32.

Beaujean, Marion, *Der Trivialroman in der zweiten Hälfte des 18. Jahrhunderts. Der Ursprung des modernen Unterhaltungsromans*. Bonn, Bouvier, 1964, 217p.

Bechtel, Heinrich. *Wirtschafts- und Sozialgeschichte Deutschlands. Wirtschaftsstile und Lebensformen von der Vorzeit bis zur Gegenwart*. 2nd edn, Munich, Callwey, 1967, 573p.

Beck, Adolf, *Griechisch–Deutsche Begegnung; Das deutsche Griechenerlebnis im Sturm und Drang*. Stuttgart, Cotta, 1947, 126p.

Beck, Lewis White, ed., *Eighteenth Century Philosophy*. New York, The Free Press, 1966, vi, 321p.

Becker, Eva, *Der deutsche Roman um 1780*. Stuttgart, Metzler, 1964, 231p.

Beissner, Friedrich, 'Studien zur Sprache des Sturms und Drangs. Eine stilistische Untersuchung der Klingerschen Jugenddramen'. *GRM*, 22 (1934), 417–29.

Beloff, Max, *The Age of Absolutism 1660–1815*. London and New York, Hutchinson's University Library, 1966, 187p.

Bennholdt-Thomsen, Anke and Alfredo Guzzoni, *Der 'Asoziale' in der Literatur um 1800*. Königstein, Athenäum, 1979, xi, 336p.

Bennett, Benjamin, *Modern Drama and German Classicism. Renaissance from Lessing to Brecht*. Ithaca, NY, Cornell Univ. Press, 1979, 359p.

Benz, Richard, *Die Zeit der deutschen Klassik; Kultur des achtzehnten Jahrhunderts 1750–1800*. Stuttgart, Reclam, 1953, 610p.

Berghahn, Klaus L., ed., *Die Weimarer Klassik. Paradigma des Methodenpluralismus in der Germanistik*, Kronberg, Scriptor, 1976, 300p.

Berlin, Isaiah, ed., *The Age of Enlightenment*. Selected with Introduction and Commentary. Oxford, Oxford Univ. Press, 1979, 284p.

Bernard, Paul, *Jesuits and Jacobins. Enlightenment and Enlightened Despotism in Austria*. Urbana, Univ. of Illinois Press, 1971, ix, 198p.

Bernard, Paul, *Joseph II*. New York, Twayne Publishers, 1968, 155p.

Bertram, Ernst, 'Möglichkeiten deutscher Klassik'. In his *Deutsche Gestalten: Fest- und Gedenkreden*. Leipzig: Insel, 1934, 278p.

Beutin, Wolfgang, *Das Weiterleben alter Wortbedeutungen in der neueren Literatur bis gegen 1800*. Hamburg, Lüdke, 1972, iv, 364p.

Beyer, Hans, *et al*., ed., *Aufklärung und Revolution*. Historia Mundi, 9. Bern and Munich, Francke, 1960, 560p.

Biedermann, Karl, *Deutschland im 18. Jahrhundert*. Leipzig, 1854–1880 rpt. 2 vols in 4. Aalen, Scientia Verlag, 1969.

Bjorklund, Beth, *A Study in Comparative Prosody: English and German Iambic Pentameter*. Stuttgart, Akademischer Verlag Heinz, 1978, 494p.

Blackall, Eric A., *The Emergence of German as a Literary Language 1700–1775*. 2nd edn, Ithaca, NY, Cornell Univ. Press, 1978, xi, 573p.

Bodi, Leslie, *Tauwetter in Wien. Zur Prosa der österreichischen Aufklärung 1781–1795*. Frankfurt, Fischer, 1977, 512p.

Boehn, Max von, *Deutschland im 18. Jahrhundert*. Berlin, Askanischer Verlag, 1921, vii, 610p.

Boening, John, ed., *The Reception of Classical German Literature in England*,

1760–1860. A Documentary History from Contemporary Periodicals. 10 vols. New York and London, Garland Publ. Co., 1977.

Boeschenstein, Bernhard, 'Die Transfiguration Rousseaus in der deutschen Dichtung um 1800: Hölderlin – Jean Paul – Kleist'. In his *Studien zur Dichtung des Absoluten.* Zürich, Atlantis, 1968, 11–24.

Boeschenstein, Hermann, *Deutsche Gefühlskultur.* Vol. I, *Die Grundlagen. 1770–1830.* Bern, Paul Haupt, 1954, 330p.

Boeschenstein-Schäfer, Renate. *Idylle.* 2nd edn, Stuttgart, Metzler, 1977, xii, 181p.

Boos, Heinrich, *Geschichte der Freimauerei. Ein Beitrag zur Kultur- und Literatur-Geschichte des 18. Jahrhunderts.* 2nd edn, Aarau, Sauerländer, 1906, 429p.

Borchmeyer, Dieter, *Höfische Gesellschaft und französische Revolution bei Goethe: Adliges und bürgerliches Wertsystem im Urteil der Weimarer Klassik.* Kronberg, Athenäum Verlag, 1977, 462p.

Borchmeyer, Dieter, *Die Weimarer Klassik. Eine Einführung.* 2 vols. Königstein/T., Athenäum Verlag, 1980.

Borkenau, Franz, *Der Übergang vom feudalen zum bürgerlichen Weltbild. Studien zur Geschichte der Philosophie der Manufakturperiode.* Paris, Alcan, 1934, xx, 559p.

Bormann, Alexander von, ed., *Vom Laienurteil zum Kunstgefühl.* Deutsche Texte, 30. Tübingen, M. Niemeyer, 1974, ix, 190p.

Boubia, Fawzi, *Theater der Politik: Politik des Theaters. Louis-Sebastien Mercier und die Dramaturgie des Sturm und Drang.* Frankfurt, Lang, 1978, 245p.

Boucher, Maurice, *La Révolution de 1789 vue par les écrivains allemands, ses contemporaines Klopstock, Wieland, Herder, Schiller, Kant, Fichte, Goethe* . . . Paris, M. Didier, 1954, 187p.

Bücken, Ernst, *Die Musik des Rokokos und der Klassik.* Wildpark Potsdam, Athenaion, 1928, 247p.

Bürger, Christa, Peter Bürger and Jochen Schulte-Sasse, *Aufklärung und literarische Öffentlichkeit.* Edition Suhrkamp, 1040, Frankfurt, Suhrkamp, 1980, 303p.

Bürger, Christa, *Der Ursprung der bürgerlichen Institution Kunst im höfischen Weimar.* Frankfurt, Suhrkamp, 1977, 212p.

Burger, Heinz Otto, ed., *Begriffsbestimmung der Klassik und des Klassischen.* Darmstadt, Wissenschaftliche Buchgesellschaft, 1972, 483p.

Burger, Heinz Otto, 'Europäisches Adelsideal und deutsche Klassik'. In his *Dasein heisst eine Rolle spielen.* Munich, C. Hanser, 1963, 211–32.

Burger, Heinz Otto, ed., *Studien zur Trivialliteratur.* Frankfurt, Klostermann, 1968, 270p.

Butler, Eliza M., *The Tyranny of Greece over Germany.* New York, Macmillan Co., 1935, 351p.

Buyssen, Andreas, *Drama des Sturm und Drang: Kommentar zu einer Epoche.* Munich, Winkler, 1980, 272p.

Braemer, Edith and Ursula Wertheim, *Studien zur deutschen Klassik.* Berlin, Rütten & Loening, 1960, 491p.

Brady, Patrick, 'The present state of studies on the Rococo', *Comparative Literature*, 27 (1975), 21–33.

Bray, René, *La Formation de la doctrine classique en France*. Paris, Nizet, 1951, 380p.

Brinker-Gabler, Gisela, ed., *Deutsche Dichterinnen vom 16. Jahrhundert bis zur Gegenwart. Gedichte und Lebensläufe*. Frankfurt, Fischer, 1978, 430p.

Brinkmann, Richard, *et al.*, ed., *Deutsche Literatur und Französische Revolution*. Göttingen, Vandenhoeck & Rupprecht, 1974, 191p.

Bruford, Walter H., *Culture and Society in Classical Weimar 1775–1806*. London, Cambridge Univ. Press, 1962, 465p.

Bruford, Walter H., *The German Tradition of Self-Cultivation. Bildung from Humboldt to Thomas Mann*. Cambridge, Cambridge Univ. Press, 1975, x, 290p.

Bruford, Walter H., *Germany in the 18th Century: The social background of the literary revival*. Cambridge, Cambridge Univ. Press, 1952, x, 354p.

Bruford. Walter H., *Theatre, Drama and Audience in Goethe's Germany*. London, Routledge & Kegan Paul, 1950, xi, 388p.

Brummack, Jürgen, 'Zu Begriff und Theorie der Satire', *DVjs*, 45 (1971), Sonderheft, 275–377.

Brunschwig, Henri, *Enlightenment and Romanticism in Eighteenth-Century Prussia*. Chicago, Univ. of Chicago Press, 1974, x, 323p.

Buch, Hans Christoph. *Ut pictura poesis: Die Beschreibungsliteratur und ihre Kritiker von Lessing bis Lukacs*. Munich, Hanser, 1972, 321p.

Campe, Joachim, *Der programmatische Roman. Von Wielands 'Agathon' zu Jean Pauls 'Hesperus'*. Bonn, Bouvier, 1979, 258p.

Carels, Peter E., *The Satiric Treatise in 18th-century Germany*. German Studies in America, 24. Bern, Herbert Lang, 1976, 169p.

Carlson, Anni, *Die deutsche Buchkritik von der Reformation bis zur Gegenwart*. Bern, Francke, 1969, 421p.

Carsten, F. L., *The Origins of Prussia*. Oxford, Clarendon Press, 1954, 309p.

Cassirer, Ernst, *The Philosophy of the Enlightenment*. Boston, Beacon Press, 1955, 366p.

Cloeter, Hermine, *Johann Thomas Trattner Ein Grossunternehmer im Theresianischen Wien*. Graz, Böhlau, 1952, 138p.

Cobban, Alfred, ed., *The Eighteenth Century. Europe in the Age of Enlightenment*. London, Thames & Hudson, 1969, 360p.

Commager, Henry Steele, *The Empire of Reason: how Europe imagined and America realized the Enlightenment*. London, Weidenfeld & Nicolson, 1978, xv, 342p.

Conrady, Karl Otto, ed., *Deutsche Literatur zur Zeit der Klassik*. Stuttgart, Reclam, 1977, 460p.

Critchley, John, S., *Feudalism*. London and Boston, Allen & Unwin, 1978, 210p.

Curtius, Ernst Robert, *Essays on European Literature*. Princeton, Princeton Univ. Press, 1973, 508p.

Dahnke, Hans-Dietrich, *Geschichte der deutschen Literatur von 1789 bis 1806*. 4th edn, Potsdam, Pädagogische Hochschule, 1965, 397p.

Dahnke, Hans-Dietrich, 'Klassik und Klassizismus: Zur Literaturgeschichtlichen Zuordnung der klassischen deutschen Literatur'. In *Akten des VI. Internationalen Germanisten-Kongresses, Basel 1980*, ed. Heinz Rupp and Hans-Gert Roloff. Bern, Lang, 1980, 334–8.

Dann, Otto, ed., *Lesegesellschaften und bürgerliche Emanzipation. Ein europäischer Vergleich*. Munich, Beck, 1981, 279p.

Danzel, Thomas W., *Zur Literatur und Philosophie der Goethezeit*. Stuttgart, Metzler, 1962, 351p.

Dedner, Burghard, *Topos, Ideal und Realitätspostulat. Studien zur Darstellung des Landlebens im Roman des 18. Jahrhunderts*. Tübingen, Niemeyer, 1969, 176p.

Dippel, Horst, *Deutschland und die amerikanische Revolution. Sozialgeschichtliche Untersuchungen zum politischen Bewusstsein im ausgehenden 18. Jahrhundert*. Diss. Cologne, 1972, 889p.

Doktor, Wolfgang, *Die Kritik der Empfindsamkeit*. Bern, Lang, 1975, xv, 535p.

Drewitz, Ingeborg, *Berliner Salons. Gesellschaft und Literatur zwischen Aufklärung und Industriezeitalter*. Berlin, Haude & Spener, 1965, 112p.

Droz, Jacques, *L'Allemagne et la Révolution française*. Paris, Presses Universitaires de France, 1949, 512p.

Dülmen, Richard von, *Der Geheimbund der Illuminaten. Darstellung, Analyse, Dokumentation*. Stuttgart, Frommann–Holzbug, 1975, 453p.

Einem, Herbert von, *Deutsche Malerei des Klassizismus und der Romantik 1760–1840*. Munich, Beck, 1978, 251p.

Eitner, Lorenz E. A., ed., *Neoclassicism and Romanticism 1750–1850. Sources and Documents*. 2 vols. Englewood Cliffs, NJ, Prentice–Hall, 1970.

Elias, Norbert, *Die höfische Gesellschaft*. 2nd edn, Soziologische Texte, 54. Neuwied, Luchterhand, 1975, 456p.

Elschenbroich, Adalbert, ed., *Deutsche Dichtung im 18. Jahrhundert*. Munich, C. Hanser, 1960, 742p.

Engell, James, *The Creative Imagination. Enlightenment to Romanticism*. Cambridge, Mass., Harvard Univ. Press, 1981, xix, 416p.

Engelsing, Rolf, *Analphabetentum und Lektüre: Zur Sozialgeschichte des Lesens in Deutschland zwischen feudaler und industrieller Gesellschaft*. Stuttgart, J. B. Metzler, 1973, xiv, 210p.

Engelsing, Rolf, *Der Bürger als Leser. Lesergeschichte in Deutschland 1500–1800*. Stuttgart, Metzler, 1974, 375p.

Epstein, Klaus, *The Genesis of German Conservatism*. Princeton, Princeton Univ. Press, 1966, xii, 733p.

Erning, Günter, *Das Lesen und die Lesewut. Beiträge zu Fragen der Lesergeschichte; dargestellt am Beispiel der schwäbischen Provinz*. Bad Heilbronn, Klinkhardt, 1974, 167p.

Ernst, Fritz, *Der Klassizismus in Italien, Frankreich und Deutschland*. Zürich, Amalthea Verlag, 1924, 135p.

Fabian, Bernhard, and Wilhelm Schmidt-Biggemann, eds., *Das achtzehnte Jahrhundert als Epoche*. Vol. I of *Studien zum 18. Jahrhundert*. Nendeln, KTO Press, 1978, 156p.

Fabian, Bernhard, 'English Books and the Eighteenth-Century German Reader'.

In *The Widening Circle*, ed. Paul J. Korshin. Philadelphia, Univ. o
Pennsylvania Press, 1976, 117–96.

Fabian, Bernhard, 'Der Naturwissenschaftler als Originalgenie'. In *Europäisch Aufklärung. Herbert Dieckmann zum 60. Geburtstag*, eds. Hugo Friedric and Fritz Schalk. Munich, Fink, 1967, 47–68.

Fambach, Oskar, *Das große Jahrzehnt in der Kritik seiner Zeit*. Berlin, Akademi Verlag, 1958, 684p.

Fertig, Ludwig, *Die Hofmeister. Ein Beitrag zur Geschichte des Lehrstandes un der bürgerliche Intelligenz*. Stuttgart, Metzler, 1979, vi, 392p.

Fetzer, G. and J. Schönert, 'Zur Trivialliteraturforschung. 1964–1976'. *IASL* (1977), 1–39.

Fink, Gonthier-Louis, ed., *L'Allemagne face au classicisme et la révolution* Paris, Didier, 1972, 319p.

Fink, Gonthier-Louis, 'Des privilèges nobiliaires aux privilèges bourgeois' *Recherches Germaniques* III (1973), 30–101.

Flaherty, Gloria, *Opera in the Development of German Critical Thought* Princeton, Princeton Univ. Press, 1978, xi, 382p.

Flessau, K. I., *Der moralische Roman. Studien zur gesellschaftskritischen Trivialliteratur der Goethezeit*. Cologne, Böhlau, 1968, 185p.

Forster, Robert and Elborg Forster, *European Society in the Eighteenth Century* New York, Walker, 1969, xi, 424p.

Fränzel, Walter, *Deutschland im Jahrhundert Friedrichs des Grossen und des jungen Goethe*. Gotha, Perthes, 1921, 161p.

Fränzel, Walter. *Geschichte des Übersetzens im 18. Jahrhundert*. Leipzig, R. Voigtländer, 1914, viii, 233p.

Frick, Karl R. H., *Die Erleuchteten. Gnostisch–theosophische und alchimistisch–rosenkreuzerische Geheimgesellschaften bis zum Ende des 18. Jahrhunderts*. Graz, Akademische Druck- und Verlagsgesellschaft, 1973, 635p.

Friedel, Ernst, *Zur Geschichte der Nicolaischen Buchhandlung und des Hauses Bruderstrasse 13 . . . in Berlin*. Berlin, Nicolaische Verlags-Buchhandlung, 1891, 55p.

Funke, Gerhard, ed., *Die Aufklärung: in ausgewählten Texten*. Stuttgart, K. F. Koehler, 1963, viii, 412p.

Garber, Klaus, 'Forschungen zur deutschen Schäfer- und Landlebendichtung des 17. und 18. Jahrhunderts'. *JIG* 3 (1971), 226–42.

Gay, Peter, *The Enlightenment: An Interpretation*. 2 vols. New York, Norton, 1977.

Gebhardt, Jürgen, ed., *Die Revolution des Geistes. Goethe, Kant, Fichte, Hegel, Humboldt*. Munich, List, 1968, 197p.

Geiger, Ludwig, *Berlin 1688–1840. Geschichte des geistigen Lebens der preussischen Hauptstadt*. 2 vols. Berlin, Gebrüder Paetel, 1893–95.

Gerteis, Klaus. 'Die deutschen Lesegesellschaften am Ende des 18. Jahrhunderts'. *Archiv für Kulturgeschichte* 53 (1971), 127–39.

Gerth, Hans H., *Bürgerliche Intelligenz um 1800. Zur Soziologie des deutschen Frühliberalismus*. Kritische Studien zur Geschichtswissenschaft, Vol. 19. Göttingen, Vandenhoeck & Rupprecht, 1976, 155p.

irnus, Wilhelm, 'Deutsche Klassik und literarische Tradition'. *Sinn und Form* 29 (1977), 377–89.

laser, Horst Albert. *Das bürgerliche Rührstuck*. Stuttgart, Metzler, 1969, 85p.

laser, Horst Albert, *Zwischen Revolution und Restauration: Klassik, Romantik 1786–1815*. Vol. 5 of *Deutsche Literatur. Eine Sozialgeschichte*. Reinbek, Rowohlt, 1980, 393p.

odechot, J. L., *The Napoleonic Era in Europe*. New York, Holt, Rinehart & Winston, 1971, 340p.

odechot, J. L. *La pensée révolutionaire en France et en Europe, 1780–1799*. Paris, Colin, 1964, 403p.

öhring, Martin, *Geschichte der grossen Revolution*. 2 vols. Tübingen, Mohr, 1950.

öpfert, Herbert G., ed., *Buch und Leser*. Schriften des Wolfenbüttler Arbeitskreis für Geschichte des Buchwesens; Bd. 1. Hamburg, Hauswedell, 1977, 229p.

öpfert, Herbert G. 'Lesegesellschaften im 18. Jahrhundert'. In *Dichtung, Sprache und Gesellschaft. Akten des IV. Internationalen Germanisten-Kongresses* Princeton, 1970, ed. Victor Lange and Hans-Gert Roloff. Frankfurt, Athenäum, 1971, 323–30

öres, Jörn, *Lesewut, Raubdruck und Bücherluxus. Das Buch in der Goethe-Zeit*. Düsseldorf, Goethe Museum A. und K. Kippenberg Stiftung, 1977, 349p.

örres, Johann Joseph von, *Europa und die Revolution*. Stuttgart: Metzler, 1821, 356p.

oldfriedrich, Johann, *Geschichte des deutschen Buchhandels vom Beginn der Klassischen Literaturperiode bis zum Beginn der Fremdherrschaft (1740–1804)*. Leipzig, Börsenverein der deutschen Buchhändler, 1909, 673p.

ooch, G. P., *Frederick the Great: the Ruler, the Writer, the Man*. London/New York, Longmans, Green & Co., 1947, 363p.

oodwin, Albert, ed., *The European Nobility in the Eighteenth Century*. London, A. & C. Black, 1953, vii, 201p.

rappin, Pierre, *La Théorie du génie dans le préclassicisme allemande*. Paris, Presses Universitaire de France, 1952, 329p.

reiner, Martin, *Die Entstehung der modernen Unterhaltungsliteratur. Studien zum Trivialroman des 18 Jahrhunderts*. Reinbek, Rowohlt, 1964, 153p.

rimm, Reinhold, ed., *Deutsche Dramentheorien*. 2 vols. Frankfurt, Athenäum-Verlag, 1971.

rimm, Reinhold, ed., *Deutsche Romantheorien*. Frankfurt, Athenäum-Verlag, 1968, 400p.

rimm, Reinhold, ed., *Die Klassik-Legende. Second Wisconsin Workshop*. Frankfurt, Athenäum-Verlag, 1971, 233p.

rimminger, Rolf, ed., *Deutsche Aufklärung bis zur Französischen Revolution 1680–1789*. Vol. 3 of *Hansers Sozialgeschichte der deutschen Literatur*. Munich, Deutscher Taschenbuch Verlag, 1980, 1099p.

roethuysen, Bernhard, *Die Entstehung der bürgerlichen Welt- und Lebensanschauung in Frankreich*. 2 vols. Halle/Saale, M. Niemeyer, 1927–30.

Grotegut, Eugene K. and Grant F. Leneaux, *Das Zeitalter der Aufklärung*. Ber Munich, Francke, 1974, 76p.

Gruenter, Rainer, ed., *Leser und Lesen im 18. Jahrhundert. Colloquium a Arbeitsstelle Achtzehntes Jahrhundert, Gesamthochschule Wuppert* Heidelberg, Winter, 1977, 190p.

Gulyga, Arseni W., *Der deutsche Materialismus am Ausgang des 1 Jahrhunderts*. Berlin, Akademie Verlag, 1966, 287p.

Guthke, Karl S., *Das deutsche bürgerliche Trauerspiel*. 3rd edn, Sammlu Metzler, 116. Stuttgart, Metzler, 1980, viii, 120p.

Guthke, Karl S., *Englische Vorromantik und deutscher Sturm und Dran* Göttingen, Vandenhoeck & Rupprecht, 1958, 231p.

Guthke, Karl, S., 'Gerstenberg und die Shakespeare Deutung der deutsch Klassik und Romantik'. *JEGP*, 58 (1959), 91–108.

Guthke, Karl S., *Geschichte und Poetik der deutschen Tragikomödie*. Göttinge Vandenhoeck & Rupprecht, 1961, 450p.

Guthke, Karl S., *Literarisches Leben im achtzehnten Jahrhundert in Deutsc land und in der Schweiz*. Bern/Munich, Francke, 1975, 423p.

Guthke, Karl S., *Wege zur Literatur*. Bern, Francke, 1967, 280p.

Hadley, Michael. *The Undiscovered Genre. A Search for the German Goth Novel*. Kanadische Studien zur deutschen Sprache und Literatur, 20. Ber Lang, 1979, 155p.

Haferkorn, H. J., 'Der freie Schriftsteller. Eine literatursoziologische Studie üb seine Entstehung and Lage in Deutschland zwischen 1750 und 1800'. *Archiv für Geschichte des Buchwesens* V (1964), 523–711.

Halbach, K., 'Zu Begriff und Wesen der Klassik'. In *Festschrift Paul Kluckho und Hermann Schneider*. Tübingen, J. C. B. Mohr, 1948, 539p.

Hammer, E., *Die Welt- und Lebensanschauung des Aufklärungsbürgers*. Dis Münster, 1943.

Hammer, Klaus, *Dramaturgische Schriften des 18. Jahrhunderts*. Berli Henschelverlag, 1968, 731p.

Hammermeyer, L., 'Die Illuminaten in Bayern'. In *Wittelsbach und Bayer* Vol. III, Part I/2: *Krone und Verfassung*, ed. Herbert Glaser. Munic Piper, 1980, 1256p.

Hanstein, Adalbert von, *Die Frauen in der Geschichte des deutsch Geisteslebens des 18. und 19. Jahrhunderts*. 2 vols. Leipzig, Freund & Witti 1900.

Harnack, Adolf von, *Geschichte der Königlich-Preussischen Akademie d Wissenschaften zu Berlin*. 2 vols. Berlin, Reichsdruckerei, 1900.

Hartmann, Nicolai, *Die Philosophie des Deutschen Idealismus*. Berlin, Gruyter, 1960, 575p.

Hartung, Fritz, *Enlightened Despotism*. Historical Association London Gener Series 36. London, Historical Association, 1957, 32p.

Hartung, Fritz, *Das Grossherzogtum Sachsen unter der Regierung Carl Augus 1775–1828*. Weimar, H. Böhlaus Nachfolger, 1923, x, 487p.

Haskell, Francis, *Rediscoveries in Art*. Ithaca, NY: Cornell Univ. Press, 198 234p.

Haskell, Francis and Nicholas Penny, *Taste and the Antique. The Lure of Classical Sculpture 1500–1900*. New Haven, Yale University Press, 1981, xvi, 376p.

Hatfield, Henry, *Aesthetic Paganism in German Literature. From Winckelmann to the Death of Goethe*. Cambridge, Mass., Harvard Univ. Press, 1964, 283p.

Hatzfeld, Helmut, *Rococo*. New York, Pegasus, 1972, 270p.

Hauser, Arnold, *Rococo, Classicism, Romanticism*. Vol. 3 of *The Social History of Art*. Vintage Books, V-114. 4 vols. New York, Random House, 1951.

Hausherr, Hans, *Wirtschaftsgeschichte der Neuzeit vom Ende des 14. bis zur Höhe des 19. Jahrhunderts*. Weimar, H. Böhlaus Nachfolger, 1954, xv, 543p.

Hazard, Paul, *European Thought in the Eighteenth Century. From Montesquieu to Lessing*. Glouster, Mass, Peter Smith, xx, 477p.

Heater, Derek Benjamin, *Order and Rebellion – A History of Europe in the 18th Century*. London, Harrap, 1964, 384p.

Heitner, Robert, *German Tragedy in the Age of Enlightenment. A Study in the Development of Original Tragedies. 1724–1768*. Berkeley, Univ. of California Press, 1963, xviii, 467p.

Hermand, Jost, ed., *Von deutscher Republik 1775–1795. Texte radikaler Demokraten*. Edition Suhrkamp, 793. Frankfurt, Suhrkamp, 1975, 360p.

Herrmann, Ulrich, 'Lesegesellschaften an der Wende des 18. Jahrhunderts'. *Archiv für Kulturgeschichte* 57 (1975), 475–84.

Heselhaus, Clemens, 'Die Wilhelm-Meister-Kritik der Romantiker und die romantische Romantheorie'. In *Nachahmung und Illusion*. Kolloquium Giessen 1963. Munich, Fink, 1969, 113–27.

Hettner, Hermann, *Geschichte der deutschen Literatur im achtzehnten Jahrhundert*. Ed. G. Witkowski, 4 parts. Leipzig, Paul List Verlag, 1928.

Heussler, Alexander, *Klassik und Klassizismus in der deutschen Literatur*. Sprache und Dichtung Heft 76. Bern, P. Haupt, 1952, 111p.

Hildebrand, Dorette, *Das kulturelle Leben Bayerns im letzten Viertel des 18. Jahrhunderts im Spiegel von drei bayrischen Zeitschriften*. Miscellanea Bavarica, No. 36. Munich, Wölfle, 1971, 185p.

Hillebrand, Bruno, *Theorie des Romans*. Munich, Deutscher Taschenbuch Verlag, 1980, 469p.

Hinck, Walter, *Das deutsche Lustspiel des 17. und 18. Jahrhunderts*. Stuttgart, Metzler, 1965, 467p.

Hinck, Walter, ed., *Handbuch des deutschen Dramas*. Düsseldorf, Basel, 1980, 610p.

Hinck, Walter, ed., *Neues Handbuch der Literaturwissenschaft: Europaische Aufklärung*. Frankfurt, Athenaion, 1974, 223p.

Hinck, Walter, ed., *Sturm und Drang. Ein literaturwissenschaftliches Studienbuch*. Kronberg/Ts., Athenäum Verlag, 1978, 270p.

Hinderer, Walter, 'Beiträge zur deutschen Klassik'. In his *Über deutsche Literatur und Rede*. Munich, Fink, 1981, 9–38.

Hinderer, Walter, ed., *Geschichte der politischen Lyrik in Deutschland*. Stuttgart, Reclam, 1979, 375p.

Hinske, Norbert, ed., *Was ist Aufklärung? Beiträge aus der Berlinischen*

Monatsschrift (*1783–1786*). 3rd edn, Darmstadt, Wissenschaftliche Buchgesellschaft, 1981, lxix, 578p.

Hohendahl, Peter Uwe, *Der europäische Roman der Empfindsamkeit*. Wiesbaden, Athenaion, 1977, 136p.

Hohendahl, Peter Uwe and Paul Michael Lützeler, eds., *Legitimationskrisen des deutschen Adels 1200–1900*. Literaturwissenschaft und Sozialwissenschaft, 11. Stuttgart, Metzler, 1979, xviii, 336p.

Holz, Harald, 'Das Problem des vollkommenen Menschen bei Kant und Schelling'. *Kant Studien*, lxiv (1973), 336–62.

Honour, Hugh, *Neo-Classicism*. Harmondsworth, Penguin Books, 1968, 221p.

Hubatsch, Walther, *Das Zeitalter des Absolutismus 1600–1789*. Braunschweig, Georg Westermann Verlag, 1965, xiii, 258p.

Huber, Thomas, *Studien zur Theorie des Ubersetzens im Zeitalter der deutschen Aufklärung*. Meisenheim, Anton Hain Verlag, 1968, 134p.

Hubrig, Hans, *Die patriotischen Gesellschaften des 18. Jahrhunderts*. Göttinger Studien zur Pedagogik, Heft 36. Weinheim/Bergstr.,/Berlin, Beltz, 1957, 199p.

Ide, Heinz and Bodo Lecke, eds., *Ökonomie und Literatur. Lesebuch zur Sozialgeschichte und literatursoziologie der Aufklärung und Klassik*. 2nd edn, Frankfurt, Diesterweg, 1975.

Ilgner, Richard M., *The Romantic Chivalrous Epic as a Phenomenon of the German Rococo*. Europäische Hochschulschriften I, 275. Bern/Frankfurt, Lang, 1979, 148p.

Irmscher, Johannes, ed., *Antikerezeption, deutsche Klassik und sozialistische Gegenwart*. Schriften der Winckelmann Gesellschaft, 5. Berlin, Akademie Verlag, 1979, vii. 84p.

Jacobs, Jürgen, ed., *Prosa der Aufklärung*: *moralische Wochenschriften. Autobiographie, Satire, Roman. Kommentar zu einer Epoche*. Munich, Winkler, 1976, 266p.

Jäger, Georg, *Empfindsamkeit und Roman. Wortgeschichte, Theorie und Kritik im 18. und frühen 19. Jahrhundert*. Stuttgart, Kohlhammer, 1969, 159p.

Jäger, Georg and Jörg Schönert, eds., *Die Leihbibliothek als Institution des literarischen Lebens im 18. und 19. Jahrhundert*. Hamburg, Hauswedell, 1980, 400p.

Jäger, Georg *et al.*, eds., *Die Leihbibliothek der Goethezeit*. Texte zum literarisches Leben um 1800, 6. Hildesheim, Gerstenberg, 1978.

Jäger, Hans-Wolf. 'Gegen die Revolution. Beobachtungen zur konservativen Dramatik in Deutschland um 1790'. *JbDSG* 22 (1979), 362–403.

Jäger, Hans-Wolf, *Politische Kategorien in Poetik und Rhetorik der zweiten Hälfte des 18. Jahrhunderts*. Texte Metzler, 10. Stuttgart, Metzler, 1970, 83p.

Jäger, Hella, *Naivität*: *eine kritisch-utopische Kategorie in der bürgerlichen Literatur und Ästhetik des 18. Jahrhunderts*. Skriptor Literaturwissenschaft, 19. Kronberg/Ts., Scriptor Verlag, 1975, 334p.

Das Jahrhundert Goethes. Kunst, Wissenschaft, Technik und Geschichte zwischen 1750 und 1850. Ed. von einem Autoren Kollektiv. Weimar, Nationale Forschungs-und Gedenkstätten, 1967, 221p.

Jenisch, Erich, *Die Entfaltung des Subjectivismus. Von der Aufklärung zur Romantik*. Königsberg, Gräfe & Unzer, 1929, ix, 145p.

Johnson, James William, *The Formation of English Neo-Classical Thought*. Princeton, Princeton Univ. Press, 1967, 359p.

Kahl-Pantis, Brigitte, *Bauformen des bürgerlichen Trauerspiels. Ein Beitrag zur Geschichte des deutschen Dramas im 18. Jahrhundert*. Frankfurt/Bern, Lang, 1977, 228p.

Kaiser, Gerhard, *Pietismus und Patriotismus im literarischen Deutschland. Ein Beitrag zum Problem der Säkularisation*. 2nd edn, Wiesbaden, Franz Steiner Verlag, 1973, viii, 302p.

Kaiser, Gerhard, ed., *Von der Aufklärung bis zum Sturm und Drang. 1730–1785*. 2nd edn, Munich, Francke Verlag, 1976, 363p.

Kann, Robert. *A Study of Austrian Intellectual History; from Late Baroque to Romanticism*. New York, Praeger, 1960, 367p.

Kapp, Friedrich and Johann Goldfriedrich. *Geschichte des deutschen Buchhandels*. 4 vols. in 5. 1886–1923. Rpt. Aalen, Scientia, 1970.

Kaufmann, Emil, *Architecture in the Age of Reason: Baroque and post-baroque in England, Italy and France*. Cambridge, Mass., Harvard Univ. Press, 1955, 298p.

Keller, Harald, *Die Kunst des 18. Jahrhunderts*. Vol. 10 of *Propyläen Kunstgeschichte*. Berlin, Propyläen Verlag, 1971, 479p.

Kelletat, Alfred, ed., *Der Göttinger Hain*. Reclams Universal-Bibliothek, 8789–93. Stuttgart, Reclam, 1967, 456p.

Kiener, Hans, *Die Baukunst des deutschen Klassizismus*. Die Kunst dem Volke, 83. München, Allgemeine Vereinigung 'Die Kunst dem Volke', 1935, 40p.

Kiesel, Helmut and Paul Münch, *Gesellschaft und Literatur im 18. Jahrhundert. Voraussetzungen und Entstehung des literarischen Marktes in Deutschland*. Munich, Beck, 1977, 245p.

Kimball, Sidney Fiske, *The Creation of the Rococo*. New York, Norton, 1964, xvii, 242p.

Kimpel, Dieter, *Der Roman der Aufklärung*. Stuttgart, Metzler, 1977, xv, 158p.

Kimpel, Dieter and Conrad Wiedemann, eds., *Theorie und Technik des Romans im 17. und 18. Jahrhundert*. 2 vols. Tübingen, H. Niemeyer, 1970.

Kirchner, Joachim, *Das deutsche Zeitschriftenwesen. Seine Geschichte und seine Probleme*. Part I: *Von den Anfängen bis zum Zeitalter der Romantik*. Wiesbaden, Harrassowitz, 1958, viii, 270p.

Klessmann, Eckart, *Deutschland unter Napoleon*. Düsseldorf, Rauch, 1965, 430p.

Köhn, Lothar, *Entwicklungs- und Bildungsroman. Ein Forschungsbericht*. Stuttgart, Metzler, 1969, viii, 115p.

Köpke, Wulf, 'Die emanzipierte Frau in der Goethezeit und ihre Darstellung in der Literatur'. In *Die Frau als Heldin und Autorin*, ed. Wolfgang Paulsen. Bern, Francke, 1979, 96–110.

Kohlschmidt, Werner, *Geschichte der deutschen Literatur von den Anfängen bis zur Gegenwart*. Vol. 2: *Vom Barock bis zur Klassik*. 2nd edn 1981. Vol. 3: *Von der Romantik bis zum späten Goethe*. 2nd edn 1979. Stuttgart, Reclam.

Konrad, G. 'Literatur des 18. Jahrhunderts als Objekt neuer Forschungen'. *Welt und Wort* 23 (1971), 566–73.

Koopmann, Helmut, *Drama der Aufklärung. Kommentar zu einer Epoche*. Munich, Winkler, 1979, 183p.

Kopitsch, Franklin, ed., *Aufklärung, Absolutismus und Bürgertum in Deutschland. 12 Aufsätze*. Munich, Nymphenburger Verlagsbuchhandlung, 1976. 440p.

Kopp, Bernhard, *Beiträge zur Kulturphilosophie der deutschen Klassik: Eine Untersuchung im Zusammenhang mit dem Bedeutungswandel des Wortes 'Kultur'*. Weisenheim am Glan, Hain, 1974, 118p.

Korff, Hermann August, *Geist der Goethezeit*. 5 vols. Leipzig, Koehler & Amelang, 1923–57.

Korff, Hermann August, *Voltaire im literarischen Deutschland des XVIII. Jahrhunderts*. 2 vols. Heidelberg, C. Winter, 1917.

Koselleck, Reinhardt, *Kritik und Krise. Eine Studie zur Pathogenese der bürgerlichen Welt*. Frankfurt, Suhrkamp, 1973, 250p.

Krauss, Werner, *Die französische Aufklärung im Spiegel der deutschen Literatur des 18. Jahrhunderts*. Berlin, Akademie-Verlag, 1963, 484p.

Kreuzer, Helmut. 'Trivialliteratur als Forschungsproblem. Zur Kritik des deutschen Trivialromans seit der Aufklärung'. *DVjs* 41 (1967), 173–91.

Krieger, Leonard, *The German Idea of Freedom. History of a Political Tradition*. Boston, Beacon Press, 1957, 540p.

Kruedener, Jürgen von, *Die Rolle des Hofes in Absolutismus*. Stuttgart, Gustav Fischer, 1973, 48p.

Krüger, Renate, *Das Zeitalter der Empfindsamkeit*. Vienna, Schroll, 1972, 207p.

Küntzel, Ulrich, *Die Finanzen grosser Männer*. Vienna/Düsseldorf, Econ-Verlag, 1964, 579p.

Küther, Carsten, *Räuber und Gauner in Deutschland. Das organisierte Bandenwesen im 18. und frühen 19. Jahrhundert*. Göttingen, Vandenhoeck & Rupprecht. 1976, 197p.

Kunz, Josef, *Die deutsche Novelle zwischen Klassik und Romantik*. Berlin, E. Schmidt, 1966, 164p.

Lämmert, Eberhard, *et al.*, eds., *Romantheorie. Dokumentation ihrer Geschichte in Deutschland 1620–1880*. Cologne, Kiepenheuer & Witsch, 1971, 407p.

Lanckoronska, Maria and A. Rümann, *Geschichte der deutschen Taschenbücher und Almanache aus der Klassisch-romantischen Zeit*. Munich, E. Heimeran, 1954, 215p.

Landsberger, Franz. *Die Kunst der Goethezeit. Kunst und Kunstanschauung von 1750 bis 1831*. Leipzig, Insel Verlag, 1931, 319p.

Lange, Erhard, ed., *Philosophie und Humanismus. Beiträge zum Menschenbild der deutschen Klassik*. Weimar, Böhlau, 1978, 239p.

Lange, Victor, 'Reflections on the "Classical Age" of German Literature'. *Studies in Eighteenth-Century Culture* VII (1978), 3–21.

Langen, August, *Anschauungsformen in der deutsche Dichtung des 18. Jahrhunderts*. 3rd edn, Darmstadt, Wissenschaftliche Buchgesellschaft, 1968, 131p.

Langen, August, 'Wechselbeziehungen zwischen Wort und Bildkunst in der Goethezeit'. In his *Gesammelte Studien zur neueren deutschen Sprache und Literatur*, ed. K. Richter *et al.* Berlin, E. Schmidt Verlag, 1978, 274–91.

Langen, August, *Der Wortschatz des deutschen Pietismus*. 2nd edn, Tübingen, Niemeyer, 1968, xlviii, 526p.

Lavedan, Pierre, *Moyen Âge et Temps Modernes*. Vol. II of *Histoire de l'Art*. Paris, Presses Univ. de France, 1949–50.

Leibfried, Erwin, *Fabel*. 3rd edn, Sammlung Metzler, 66. Stuttgart, Metzler, 1976, viii, 114.

Lenz, Georg, ed., *Deutsches Staatsdenken im 18. Jahrhundert*. Politica 23. Neuwied, Hermann Luchterhand Verlag, 1965, 436p.

Lepenies, Wolf, *Melancholie und Gesellschaft*. Frankfurt, Suhrkamp, 1969, 330p.

Levey, Michael, *Rococo to Revolution. Major Trends in Eighteenth Century Painting*. Praeger World Art Series. New York, Praeger, 1966, 252p.

De Levie, Dagobert, *Die Menschenliebe im Zeitalter der Aufklärung Säkularisation und Moral im 18. Jahrhundert*. Bern, Lang, 1976, 126p.

Liebel, Helen P., 'Enlightened Despotism and the Crisis of Society in Germany'. *Enlightenment Essays* I (1970), 151–68.

Lively, Jack, ed., *The Enlightenment*. London, Longman, 1967, xvi, 200p.

Ludz, P. C., ed., *Geheime Gesellschaften*. Wolfenbüttler Studien zur Aufklärung B5, 1, Heidelberg, Lambert Schneider, 1979, 462p.

Lühe, Irmela von der, *Natur und Nachahmung in der ästhetischen Theorie zwischen Aufklärung und Sturm und Drang. Untersuchungen zur Batteux-Rezeption in Deutschland*. Bonn, Bouvier, 1979, 451p.

Lütge, Friedrich Karl, *Deutsche Sozial- und Wirtschaftsgeschichte*. 3rd edn, Berlin/Hamburg/New York, Springer Verlag, 1966, xviii, 644p.

Lutz, Bernd, ed., *Deutsches Bürgertum und literarische Intelligenz 1750–1800*. Stuttgart, Metzler, 1974, 572p.

Mandelkow, Karl Robert, 'Der deutsche Briefroman'. *Neophilologus* 44 (1960). 200–8.

Mantoux, Paul Joseph, *The Industrial Revolution in the 18th Century*. New York, Harper & Row, 1962, 528p.

Marcuse, Herbert, *Eros and Civilization*. 2nd edn, Boston, Beacon Press, 1966, 277p.

Marcuse, Herbert, 'Uber den affirmativen Charakter der Kultur'. In his *Kultur und Gesellschaft*. Frankfurt, Suhrkamp, 1965, 56–101.

Markwardt, Bruno, *Geschichte der deutschen Poetik*. 5 vols. 3rd edn, Berlin: de Gruyter, 1956–66.

Martini, Fritz, 'Der Bildungsroman. Zur Geschichte des Wortes und der Theorie'. *DVjs* 35 (1961), 44–63.

Martini, Fritz, 'Geschichte und Poetik des Romans. Ein Literaturbericht'. *Deutschunterricht* 3 (1951), 3, 86–9.

Martini, Fritz, 'Die Poetik des Dramas im Sturm und Drang'. In *Deutsche Dramentheorie*, Reinhold Grimm, ed. 2 vols. Frankfurt, Athenäum, 1971, Vol. I, 123–66.

Martino, Alberto, *Geschichte der dramatischen Theorien in Deutschland im 18. Jahrhundert*. Tübingen, Niemeyer, 1972, x, 470p.

Mattenklott, Gert and Klaus Scherpe, *Grundkurs 18. Jahrhundert: die Funktion der Literatur bei der Formierung der bürgerlichen Klasse Deutschlands im 18. Jahrhundert*. 2 vols. Kronberg/Ts., Scriptor, 1974.

Mattenklott, Gert and Klaus Scherpe, eds., *Literatur der bürgerlichen Emanzipation im 18. Jahrhundert*. Kronberg/Ts., Scriptor, 1973, xiv, 216p.

Mattenklott, Gert, *Melancholie in der Dramatik des Sturm und Drang*. Stuttgart, Metzler, 1968, 185p.

May, Henry, *The Enlightenment in America*. New York: Oxford Univ. Press, 1976, xx, 419p.

May, Kurt, 'Beitrag sur Phänomenologie des Dramas im Sturm und Drang'. *GRM*, XVIII (1930), 260–8.

Mayer, Hans, ed., *Aufklärung, Klassik, Romantik*. Vol. 1 of *Meisterwerke Deutscher Literaturkritik*. Berlin, Rütten & Loening, 1954, 966p.

Mayer, Hans, *Zur deutschen Klassik und Romantik*. Pfullingen, Neske, 1963, 365p.

Mehring, Franz, *Die deutsche Klassik und die französische Revolution*. Ed. F. J. Raddatz. Darmstadt, Luchterhand, 1974, 329p.

Menhennet, Alan, *Order and Freedom: Literature and Society in Germany from 1720 to 1805*. London, Weidenfeld & Nicolson, 1973, 270p.

Metelmann, Ernst, *Zur Geschichte des Göttinger Dichterbundes 1772/1774*. Stuttgart, Metzler, 1965, 83p.

Meyer-Abich, Adolf, *Biologie der Goethezeit*. Stuttgart, Hypokrates-Verlag Marquardt, 1949, 302p.

Michelsen, Peter, *Laurence Sterne und der deutsche Roman des 18. Jahrhunderts*. Göttingen, Vandenhoeck & Rupprecht, 1962, 394p.

Miller, Norbert, *Der empfindsame Erzähler, Untersuchungen an Romananfängen des 18. Jahrhunderts*. Munich, C. Hanser, 1968, 479p.

Milstein, Barney M., *Eight Eighteenth Century Reading Societies. A Sociological Contribution to the History of German Literature*. Bern, Lang, 1972, 311p.

Minder, Robert, 'Mme de Staël entdeckt Deutschland'. In his *Kultur und Literatur in Frankreich und Deutschland*. Frankfurt, Insel Verlag, 1962, 94–105.

Mingay, G. E., *English Landed Society in the Eighteenth Century*. London, Routledge & Kegan Paul, 1963, x, 292p.

Möller, Helmut, *Die kleinbürgerliche Familie im 18. Jahrhundert. Verhalten und Gruppenkultur*. Berlin, de Gruyter, 1969, 341p.

Mortier, Roland, *Diderot in Deutschland 1750–1850*. Stuttgart, Metzler, 1967, 490p.

Mousnier, Roland and Ernest Labrousse, *Le XVIIIe siècle: Révolution intellectuelle, technique et politique. 1715–1815*. Paris, Presses Univ. de France, 1959, 573p.

Müller, Richard Matthias, *Die deutsche Klassik*. Abhandlungen zur Kunst-, Musik- und Literaturwissenschaft, 6. Bonn, Bouvier, 1959, 193p.

Müller-Seidel, Walter, 'Deutsche Klassik und Französische Revolution'. In

Deutsche Literatur und Französische Revolution, ed. Richard Brinkmann. Göttingen, Vandenhoeck & Rupprecht, 1974, 39–62.

.üller, Klaus-Detlev, *Autobiographie und Roman. Studien zur literarischen Autobiographie der Goethezeit*. Tübingen, Niemeyer, 1976, 392p.

'uschg, Walter, 'Die deutsche Klassik, tragisch gesehen'. Mainzer Akademie d. Wissenschaften u. d. Literatur. Klasse d. Literatur. Wiesbaden, F. Steiner, 1952, 19p.

amowicz, Tadeusz, 'Pietismus in der deutschen Kultur des 18. Jahrhunderts. Bemerkungen zur Pietismusforschung'. *Weimarer Beiträge* 13 (1967), 469–80.

aumann, Dietrich, *Aufklärung, Romantik, Idealismus*. Part I of *Literaturtheorie und Geschichtsphilosophie*. Sammlung Metzler, 184. Stuttgart, Metzler, 1979, xiii, 147p.

'eumeyer, Eva Marie, 'The Landscape Garden as a Symbol in Rousseau, Goethe and Flaubert'. *Journal of the History of Ideas* VIII (1947), 187–217.

ewald, Richard and Helmut de Boor, *Von Klopstock bis zu Goethes Tod. 1750–1832*. Vol. 6, 1 of *Geschichte der deutschen Literatur von den Anfängen bis zur Gegenwart*. München, Beck, 1973, ix, 438p.

'iggl, Günter, *Geschichte der deutschen Autobiographie im 18. Jahrhundert. Theoretische Grundlegung und literarische Entfaltung*. Stuttgart, Metzler, 1977, xv, 237p.

Iiklewski, Günter, *Versuch über Symbol und Allegorie* (*Winckelmann, Moritz, Schelling*). Erlanger Studien 21. Erlangen, Palm & Enke, 1979, v, 157p.

'ivelle, Armand, *Kunst- und Dichtungstheorien zwischen Aufklärung und Klassik*. 2nd edn, Berlin/New York, de Gruyter, 1971, vi, 266p.

Iivelle, Armand, *Literaturästhetik der europäischen Aufklärung*. Wiesbaden, Athenaion, 1977, 194p.

Iutz, Walter, *Der Trivialroman*. Kunst und Kommunikation, 12. Cologne und Opladen, Westdeutscher Verlag, 1962, 119p.

)elmüller, Willi, ed., *Die unbefriedigte Aufklärung. Beiträge zu einer Theorie der Moderne von Lessing, Kant und Hegel*. Frankfurt, Suhrkamp, 1978, 360p.

ppel, Horst. *Englisch-deutsche Literaturbeziehungen*. 2 vols. Berlin, E. Schmidt, 1971.

)sborne, John. *Romantik*. Bern and Munich, Francke, 1971, 166p.

)sterloh, Karl-Heinz, *Joseph von Sonnenfels und die Österreichische Reformbewegung im Zeitalter des aufgeklärten Absolutismus*. Lübeck/Hamburg, Matthiesen, 1970. 271p.

'agliaro, Harold E, ed., *Irrationalism in the 18th century*. Cleveland, Case Western Reserve Univ. 1972, XII, 393p.

'almer, Robert R., *The Age of the Democratic Revolution*. 2 vols. Princeton, Princeton Univ. Press, 1959–64.

'arry, G., 'Enlightened government and its critics in eighteenth-century Germany'. *Historical Journal* 6 (1963), 178–92.

'ascal, Roy, *Design and Truth in Autobiography*. London, Routledge & Kegan Paul, 1960, 202p.

Pascal, Roy, *The German Sturm und Drang*. Manchester, Manchester Uni
Press, 1963, 347p.

Pascal, Roy, *Shakespeare in Germany, 1740–1815*. New York, Octagon Book
1971, 190p.

Pauli, Gustav, *Die Kunst des Klassizismus und der Romantik*. Berli
Propyläenverlag, 1942, 533p,

Pauli, Gustav, *Die Kunst und die Revolution*. Berlin, B. Cassirer, 1921, 76p.

Paulsen, Wolfgang, *Der deutsche Roman und seine historischen und politische
Bedingungen*. Bern, Francke, 1977, 256p.

Pawel, Jaro, *Die literarischen Reformen des XVIII. Jahrhunderts in Wie*
Vienna, Konegen, 1881, 44p.

Perels, Christoph, *Studien zur Aufnahme und Kritik der Rokokolyrik zwische
1740 und 1760*. Göttingen, Vandenhoeck & Rupprecht, 1974, 220p.

Peacock, Ronald, *The Poet in the Theatre*. New York, Hill & Wang, 1960, 198p

Peyre, Henri, 'Le Classicisme'. In *Encyclopédie de la Pleiade. Histoire de
Littératures*. Vol. II. Paris, Gallimard, 1956, 110–39.

Pikulik, Lothar, *'Bürgerliches Trauerspiel' und Empfindsamkeit*. Cologne/Gra
Böhlau, 1966, vi, 200p.

Plumb, John Harold, *England in the 18th Century*. Vol. 7 in *The Pelican Histor
of England*. Harmondsworth, Penguin, 1963, 224p.

Praz, Mario, *On Neoclassicism*. Evanston, Northwestern Univ. Press, 1969, 100p

Price, Mary Bell and Lawrence Marsden Price, *The Publication of Englis
Literature in Germany in the 18th Century*. Berkeley, Univ. of Calif. Press
1934, 288p.

Price, Lawrence Marsden, *The Reception of English Literature in German*
Calif. Publications in Modern Philology, 37. Berkeley and Los Angeles
Univ. of Calif. Press, 1953, viii, 548p.

Promies, Wolfgang, *Der Bürger und der Narr oder Das Risiko der Phantasie
Sechs Kapitel über des Irrationale in der Literatur des Irrationalismus*
Munich, Hanser, 1966, 372p.

Prudhoe, John, *The Theatre of Goethe and Schiller*. Oxford, Blackwell, 1973
218p.

Prüsener, Marlies, *Lesegesellschaften im 18. Jahrhundert. Ein Beitrag zu
Lesergeschichte*. Archiv f. Gesch. d. Buchwesens. Sonderdruck. Frankfurt
Buchhandel. Vereinigung, 1972, 113p.

Pütz, Peter, ed., *Die deutsche Aufklärung. Erträge der Forschung* 81. Darmstadt
Wissenschaftliche Buchgesellschaft, 1978, vii, 204p.

Purdie, Edna, 'Some Problems of Translation in the 18th century in Germany'
English Studies, 30 (1949), 191–205.

Randall, Henry John, ed., *The Creative Centuries. A Study of Historica
Development*. London, Longmans, Green, 1947, xxix, 436p.

Raabe, Paul and Wilhelm Schmidt-Biggemann, eds., *Aufklärung in Deutsch
land*. Bonn, Hohwacht, 1979, 256p.

Raabe, Paul, 'Buchproduktion und Lesepublikum in Deutschland 1770–1780'
Philobiblon XXI (1977), 2–16.

Rasch, Wolfdietrich, 'Die Literatur der Aufklärungszeit'. *DVjs* 30 (1956)
533–60.

Rave, Paul Ortwin, *Das geistige Deutschland im Bildnis. Das Jahrhundert Goethes*. Berlin, Verlag Tempelhof, 1949, 390p.

Rehm, Walther, *Griechentum und Goethezeit Geschichte eines Glaubens*. 4th edn, Bern/Munich: Francke, 1969, xii, 436p.

Reiche, Adalbert, 'Der Pietismus und die deutsche Romanliteratur des achtzehnten Jahrhunderts'. Diss. Marbach 1948.

Reicke, Emil, *Der Gelehrte in der deutschen Vergangenheit*. Jena: Eugen Diederichs Verlag, 1924, 143p.

Reincke, Olaf, ed., *O Lust, allen alles zu sein. Deutsche Modelektüre um 1800*. Leipzig, Reclam, 1978, 417p.

Richter, Karl, 'Geselligkeit und Gesellschaft in Gedichten des Rokoko'. *JbDSG* 18 (1974), 245–67.

Roberts, J. M., *The Mythology of the Secret Societies*. London, Secker & Warburg, 1972, x, 370p.

Robertson, John George, *A History of German Literature*. 6th edn, Dorothy Reich, ed., Edinburgh/London, Blackwood, 1970, 817p.

Robson-Scott, William Douglas, *German Travellers in England. 1400–1800*. Modern Language Studies. Oxford, Blackwell, 1953, xi, 238p.

Røstwig, Maren-Sofie, *The Happy Man. Studies in the Metamorphosis of a Classical Ideal*. 2 vols. Oslo, Oslo Univ. Press, I^2 1962, II 1958.

Rose, Hans, *Klassik als künstlerische Denkform des Abendlandes*. Munich, C. H. Beck, 1937, viii, 167p.

Rosen, Charles, *The Classical Style*. New York, W. W. Norton, 1972, 467p.

Rosenberg, Hans, *Bureaucracy. Aristocracy and Autocracy. The Prussian Experience 1660–1815*. Cambridge, Mass., Harvard Univ. Press, 1968, ix, 247p.

Rosenblum, Robert, *Transformations in late 18th Century Art*. Princeton, Princeton Univ. Press, 1967, 203p.

Rosenfeld, Helmut, 'Zur Geschichte von Nachdruck und Plagiat. Mit einer chronologischen Bibliographie zum Nachdruck von 1733–1824'. *AGB* 11 (1970) Column 337–72.

Rosenstrauch-Königsberg, Edith, *Freimauerei im josephinischen Wien: Aloys Blumauers Weg vom Jesuiten zum Jacobiner*. Vienna/Stuttgart, W. Braumüller, 1975, viii, 376p.

Rosenthal, Bronishwa, *Der Geniebegriff des Aufklärungszeitalters*. Berlin, E. Ebering, 1933, 215p.

Rouché, Max, 'L'evolution du patriotisme allemand de 1750 à 1815'. *Études Germaniques* III (1948), 223–32.

Rousseau, George Sebastian, ed., *The Ferment of Knowledge. Studies in the Historiography of Eighteenth Century Science*. Cambridge, Cambridge Univ. Press, 1980, xiii, 500p.

Rowland, Benjamin, *The Classical Tradition in Western Art*. Cambridge, Mass, Harvard Univ. Press, 1963, xx, 379p.

Rudé, George, *Europe in the Eighteenth Century*. History of Civilization Series. London, Weidenfeld & Nicolson, 1972, 291p.

Rudé, George, *The Eighteenth Century*. New York, Free Press, 1966, vii, 248p.

Rumpf, Walther, 'Das literarische Publikum der sechziger Jahre des 18. Jahrhunderts in Deutschland'. *Euphorion* 28 (1927), 540–64.

Runge, Edith, *Primitivism and Related Ideas in Sturm und Drang Literature*. Baltimore, Johns Hopkins Press, 1946, xii, 305p.

Ruppert, Wolfgang, *Bürgerlicher Wandel. Studien zur Herausbildung einer nationalen deutschen Kultur im 18. Jahrhundert*. Frankfurt, Campus Verlag, 1981, 214p.

Ruttkowski, Wolfgang Victor. *Die literarischen Gattungen*. Munich, Francke, 1968, 155p.

Sashegyi, Oszkar, *Zensur und Geistesfreiheit unter Joseph II*. Budapest, Akademiai Kiado, 1958, 244p.

Saine, Thomas P., 'Natural Science and the Ideology of Nature in the German Enlightenment'. *Lessing Yearbook* 8 (1976), 61–88.

Saine, Thomas P., 'Was ist Aufklärung? Kulturgeschichtliche Überlegungen zu neuer Beschäftigung mit der deutschen Aufklärung'. *ZDP* 93 (1974), 522–45.

Sauder, Gerhard, *Empfindsamkeit*. Vol. I: *Voraussetzungen und Elemente*. Stuttgart, Metzler, 1974, xx, 341p. Vol. III: *Quellen und Dokumente*. Stuttgart, Metzler, 1980, xi, 386p.

Schaer, Wolfgang, *Die Gesellschaft im deutschen bürgerlichen Drama des 18. Jahrhunderts*. Bonner Arbeiten z. dt. Literatur. Vol. 7. Bonn, Bouvier, 1963, 255p.

Schalk, Fritz, 'Aufklärung' in: *Historisches Wörterbuch der Philosophie*. Vol. I. ed. J. Ritter. Basel, Schwabe, 1971, Column 620–33.

Schatzberg, Walter, *Scientific Themes in the Popular Literature of the German Enlightenment*. Bern, H. Lang, 1973, 349p.

Scheel, Heinrich, ed., *Jakobinische Flugschriften aus dem deutschen Süden Ende des 18. Jahrhunderts*. Berlin, Akademie-Verlag, 1965, xiii, 500p.

Schenda, Rudolf, *Volk ohne Buch. Studien zur Sozialgeschichte der populären Lesestoffe 1770–1910*. Frankfurt, V. Klostermann, 1970, 607p.

Scherpe, Klaus R., *Gattungspoetik im 18. Jahrhundert*. Stuttgart, Metzler, 1968, 300p.

Scheider, Thomas, ed., *Handbuch der europäischen Geschichte*. Vol. 4. and 5. Stuttgart, Union Verlag, 1968–79, 7 vols. in 8.

Schings, Hans-Jürgen, *Melancholie und Aufklärung. Melancholiker und ihre Kritiker in der Erfahrungsseelenkunde und Literatur des 18. Jahrhunderts*. Stuttgart, Metzler, 1977, 476p.

Schings, Hans-Jürgen, *Der mitleidigste Mensch ist der beste Mensch. Poetik des Mitleids von Lessing bis Büchner*. Munich, Beck, 1980, 116p.

Schlaffer, Heinz, *Der Bürger als Held: sozialgeschichtliche Auflösungen literarischer Widersprüche*. Frankfurt, Suhrkamp, 1973, 156p.

Schlenke, Manfred, *England und das Friderizanische Preussen. 1740–1763*. Munich, Karl Alber Verlag, 1963, 435p.

Schlumbohm, Jürgen, *Freiheit. Die Anfänge der bürgerlichen Emanzipationsbewegung im Spiegel ihres Leitwortes*. Geschichte und Gesellschaft, 12. Düsseldorf, Pädagogischer Verlag Schwann, 1975, 299p.

Schmidt, Martin, *Pietismus*. Stuttgart, Kohlhammer, 1978, 176p.

Schmidt, Martin Johann and Wilhelm Jannasch, eds., *Das Zeitalter des*

Pietismus. Klassiker des Protestantismus, vol. 6. Bremen, Schünemann, 1965, 480p.

Schmidt-Dengler, Wendelin, *Genius. Zur Wirkungsgeschichte antiker Mythologeme in der Goethezeit*. Munich, Beck, 1978, 323p.

Schmitz, Hermann, *Kunst und Kultur des 18. Jahrhunderts in Deutschland*. Munich, Bruckmann, 1922, 379p.

Schneider, Ferdinand Josef, *Die Freimauerei und ihr Einfluss auf die geistige Kultur in Deutschland am Ende des XVIII. Jahrhunderts*. Prague, Taussig & Taussig, 1909, 234p.

Schneider, Heinrich, *Quest for Mysteries. The Masonic Background of Literature in 18th Century Germany*. Ithaca, NY, Cornell Univ. Press, 1947, 178p.

Schöffler, Herbert, *Deutscher Geist im 18. Jahrhundert*. Göttingen, Vandenhoeck & Rupprecht. 1956, 317p.

Schöne, Albrecht, *Säkularisation als sprachbildende Kraft. Studien zur Dichtung deutscher Pfarrerssöhne*. Göttingen, Vandenhoeck & Rupprecht, 1958, 252p.

Schönert, Jörg, *Roman und Satire im 18. Jahrhundert*. Stuttgart, Metzler, 1969, 185p.

Schoeps, Hans, J., *et al.*, eds., *Zeitgeist der Aufklärung*. Paderborn, Schöningh, 1972, 199p.

Schrader, Monika, *Mimesis und Poesis: Poetologische Studien zum Bildungsroman*. Berlin, de Gruyter, 1975, xii, 367p.

Schrader, William C., 'Some Thoughts on Rococo and Enlightenment in 18th Century Germany'. *Enlightenment Essays* VI (1975), 52–65

Schrimpf, Hans Joachim, 'Komödie und Lustspiel. Zur terminologischen Problematik einer geschichtlich orientierten Gattungstypologie'. *ZDP* 97 (1979), Sonderheft, 152–82.

Schulte-Sasse, Jochen, *Die Kritik an der Trivialliteratur seit der Aufklärung. Studien zur Geschichte des modernen Kitschbegriffes*. 2nd edn, Munich: Fink, 1977, 162p.

Schulz, Franz, *Klassik und Romantik der Deutschen*. 2 vols. Stuttgart, Metzler, 1952.

Schumann, Detlev, 'Germany in the 18th Gentury'. *JEGP* 51 (1952), 259–75, 434–50.

Schumann, Detlev, 'Neuorientierung im 18. Jahrhundert'. *MLR* 9 (1948), 54–73, 135–45.

Schumann, Detlev, 'New Studies In German Literature of the 18th Century'. *JEGP* 54 (1955), 705–26.

Schwabe, Kurt, 'Die Entwicklung der Naturwissenschaften zwischen 1750 und 1850'. In *Das Jahrhundert Goethes. Kunst, Wissenschaft, Technik und Geschichte zwischen 1750 und 1850*. Ed. von einem Autoren Kollektiv. Weimar, Nationale Forschungs- und Gedenkstätten, 1967, 93–110.

Schweizer, Niklaus Rudolf, *The Ut Pictura Poesis Controversy in 18th Century England and Germany*. Bern, Lang, 1972, 123p.

Secretan, Dominique, *Classicism*. London, Methuen, 1973, 85p.

Sengle, Friedrich, 'Die Grundlagen der deutschen Klassik'. In his *Arbeiten zur deutschen Literatur 1750–1850*. Stuttgart, Metzler, 1965, 88–93.

Sengle, Friedrich, 'Die klassische Kultur von Weimar, sozialgeschichtlich gesehen'. *IASL* 3 (1978), 68–86.

Sichelschmidt, Gustav, *Liebe, Mord, Abenteuer. Geschichte der deutschen Unterhaltungsliteratur*. Berlin, Haude & Spener, 1969, 260p.

Siegrist, Christoph, *Das Lehrgedicht der Aufklärung*. Stuttgart, Metzler, 1974, ix, 323p.

Singer, Charles J., *et al.*, eds., *A History of Technology*. Vols. III and IV. New York, Oxford Univ. Press, 1954–78.

Singer, Gottfried Frank, *The Epistolary Novel*. Philadelphia, Univ. of Pennsylvania Press, 1933, 266p.

Skalweit, Stephan, 'Das Zeitalter des Absolutismus als Forschungsproblem'. *DVjs* 35 (1961), 298–315.

Sørensen, Bengt Algot, *Allegorie und Symbol. Texte zur Theorie des dichterischen Bildes im 18. und frühen 19. Jahrhundert*. Frankfurt, Athenäum, 1979, 268p.

Sørensen, Bengt Algot, 'Das deutsche Rokoko und die Verserzählung im 18. Jahrhundert'. *Euphorion* XLVIII (1954), 125–52.

Sørensen, Bengt Algot, *Symbol und Symbolismus in den ästhetischen Theorien des 18. Jahrhunderts und der deutschen Romantik*. Kopenhagen, Munksgaard, 1963, 332p.

Sommerfeld, Martin, 'Romantheorie und Romantypus der deutsche Aufklärung'. *DVjs* 4 (1926), 459–90.

Spiegel, Marianne, *Der Roman und sein Publikum im frühen 18. Jahrhundert. 1700–1767*. Bonn, Bouvier, 1967, 216p.

Stackelberg, Jürgen von, *Literarische Rezeptionsformen; Übersetzung, Supplement, Parodie*. Frankfurt, Athenäum, 1972, xv, 242p.

Stadelmann, Rudolf and Wolfram Fischer, *Die Bildungswelt des deutschen Handwerkers um 1800*. Berlin, Dunker & Humblot, 1955, 258p.

Stahl, Ernest and W. E. Yuill, *German Literature of the Eighteenth and Nineteenth Centuries*. London, Cressett Press, 1970, 510p.

Staiger, Emil, 'Deutsche Klassik'. In *Das Erbe der Antike*; ed. Fritz Wehrli. Zürich, Artemis, 1963, 238–51.

Staiger, Emil, *Stilwandel. Studien zur Vorgeschichte der Goethezeit*. Zürich/ Freiburg, Atlantis-Verlag, 1963, 204p.

Starck, Dietrich, 'Die idealistische Morphologie und ihre Nachwirkungen'. *Medizinhistorisches Journal* 15 (1980), 44–56.

Stein, Peter, *Politisches Bewusstsein und künstlerischer Gestaltungswille in der politischen Lyrik 1780–1848*. Hamburg, H. Lüdke, 1971, iii, 262p.

Steinmetz, Horst, *Die Komödie der Aufklärung*. 3rd edn, Stuttgart, Metzler, 1978, vii, 89p.

Stellmacher, Wolfgang, ed., *Auseinandersetzung mit Shakespeare. Texte zur deutschen Shakespeare-Aufnahme von 1740 bis zur französischen Revolution*. Berlin, Akademie Verlag, 1976, 216p.

Stellmacher, Wolfgang, ed., *Komödien und Satiren des Sturm und Drang. Goethe, Lenz, Klinger, Wagner, Maler Müller, Schiller*. Leipzig, Reclam, 1976, 463p.

Stephan, Inge, *Literarischer Jakobinismus in Deutschland 1789–1806.* Sammlung Metzler 150. Stuttgart, Metzler, 1976, vii, 202p.
Stewart, William E., *Die Reisebescheibung und ihre Theorie im Deutschland des 18. Jahrhunderts.* Bonn, Bouvier, 1978, 341p.
Stockley, Violet Annie, *German Literature as known in England 1750–1830.* London, G. Routledge & Sons, 1929, 339p.
Storz, Gerhard, *Klassik und Romantik. Eine Stilgeschichtliche Darstellung.* Stuttgart, Klett, 1972, 247p.
Strich, Fritz, *Deutsche Klassik und Romantik, oder Vollendung und Unendlichkeit.* 5th edn, Bern, Francke, 1962, 374p.
Sühnel, Rudolf, *Die Götter Griechenlands und die deutsche Klassik.* Diss. Leipzig 1935. Würzburg, K. Triltsch, 1935, 77p.
Swales, Martin. *The German Bildungsroman from Wieland to Hesse.* Princeton, Princeton Univ. Press, 1979, xi, 171p.
Swales, Martin, *Irony and the Novel. Reflexions on the German 'Bildungsroman'.* London, University College, 1979, 26p.
Sydow, Eckart von, *Die Kultur des deutschen Klassizismus.* Berlin, G. Grote, 1926, 264p.
Szabolcsi, Bence, *Aufstieg der klassischen Musik von Vivaldi bis Mozart.* Wiesbaden, Breifkopf & Härtel, 1970, 145p.
Szondi, Peter, 'Antike und Moderne in der Aesthetik der Goethezeit'. In his *Poetik und Geschichtsphilosophie* I, ed. S. Metz and H. H. Hildebrandt. Frankfurt, Suhrkamp, 1974, 11–265.
Szondi, Peter, *Die Theorie des bürgerlichen Trauerspiels im 18. Jahrhundert*, ed. Gert Mattenklott. Frankfurt, Suhrkamp, 1973, 297p.
Taminiaux, Jacques, *La nostalgie de la Grèce à l'aube de l'idealogisme allemand.* The Hague, M. Nijhoff, 1967, xii, 276p.
Tatar, Maria M., *Spellbound: Studies on Mesmerism and Literature.* Princeton, Princeton University Press 1978, xvi, 293p.
Tghart, Reinhard, *Weltliteratur. Die Lust am Übersetzen im Jahrhundert Goethes.* Marbacher Kataloge 37. Marbach, Deutsche Schillergesellschaft, 1982, 712p.
Thalheim, Hans-Günther, *Zur Literatur der Goethezeit.* Berlin, Rütten & Loening, 1969, 456p.
Thalmann, Marianne, *Der Trivialroman des 18. Jahrhunderts und der romantische Roman, ein Beitrag zur Entwicklungsgeschichte der Geheimbundmystik.* Nendeln/Liechtenstein, Kraus Reprint, 1967, 326p.
Thomas, Richard Hinton, 'The uses of "Bildung" '. *GLL* 30 (1977), 177–86.
Thurn, Hans Peter, *Der Roman der unaufgeklärten Gesellschaft: Untersuchungen zum Prosawerk Johann Karl Wezels.* Stuttgart, Kohlhammer, 1973, 144p:
Titzmann, Michael, *Strukturwandel der philosophischen Aesthetik, 1800–1880.* Munich, Fink, 1978, 357p.
Touaillon, Christine, *Der deutsche Frauenroman des 18. Jahrhunderts.* Vienna/Leipzig, W. Braummüller, 1919, 664p.
Träger, Claus, ed., *Die Französische Revolution im Spiegel der deutschen Literatur.* Frankfurt, M. Röderberg Verlag, 1975, 1134p.

Träger, Claus, ed., *Mainz zwischen Rot und Schwarz. Die Mainzer Revolution 1792–1793 in Schriften, Reden und Briefen*. Berlin, Rütten & Loening, 1963, 634p.

Träger, Claus, *Studien zur Literaturtheorie und vergleichenden Literaturgeschichte*. Leipzig, Reclam, 1972, 473p.

Träger, Claus, 'Über Historizität und Normativität des Klassik-Begriffs'. *Weimarer Beiträge* 75 (1979) 12, 5–20.

Treue, Wilhelm, *Wirtschaftsgeschichte der Neuzeit*. Vol. I, *18. und 19. Jahrhundert*. 3rd edn, Stuttgart, Kröner, 1973, 720p.

Tronskaja, Maria, *Die deutsche Prosasatire der Aufklärung*. Berlin, Rütten & Loening, 1969, 430p.

Trunz, Erich, *Fürstenberg, Fürstin Gallitzin und ihr Kreis*. Münster, Aschendorff, 1955, 108p.

Tubach, Frederic C., 'Die Naturnachahmungstheorie: Batteux und die Berliner Rationalisten'. *GRM* NFXIII (1963), 262–80.

Tümmler, Hans, *Das klassische Weimar und das grosse Zeitageschehen. Historische Studien*. Cologne, Böhlau, 1975, 241p.

Turk, Horst, 'Das "Klassische Zeitalter": Zur geschichtsphilosophischen Begründung der Weimarer Klassik'. In *Probleme der Literaturgeschichtsschreibung*, ed. Wolfgang Haubrichs. Göttingen, Vandenhoeck & Rupprecht, 1979, 155–74.

Uhlig, Ludwig, *Der Todesgenius in der deutschen Literatur: Von Winckelmann bis Thomas Mann*. Tübingen, Niemeyer, 1975, 118p.

Valjavec, Fritz, *Die Entstehung der politischen Strömungen in Deutschland. 1770–1815*. Munich, R. Oldenbourg, 1951, 542p.

Vaughan, William, *German Romanticism and English Art*. New Haven, Yale Univ. Press, 1979, x, 308p.

Venturi, Franco, *Italy and the Enlightenment*. London, Longman, 1972, xxi, 302p.

Venturi, Franco, *Utopia and Reform in the Enlightenment*. Cambridge, Cambridge Univ. Press, 1971, v, 160p.

Vierhaus, Rudolf, ed, *Der Adel vor der Revolution; zur sozialen und politischen Funktion des Adels im vorrevolutionären Europa*. Göttingen, Vandenhoeck & Rupprecht, 1971, 95p.

Vierhaus, Rudolf, ed., *Bürger und Bürgerlichkeit im Zeitalter der Aufklärung*. Wolfenbüttler Studien zur Aufklärung VII. Heidelberg, Lambert Schneider, 1981, 360p.

Vierhaus, Rudolf, 'Deutschland im 18. Jahrhundert; soziales Gefüge, politische Verfassung, geistige Bewegung'. In *Lessing und die Zeit der Aufklärung*. Joachim-Jungius Gesellschaft. Göttingen, Vandenhoeck & Rupprecht, 1968.

Vierhaus, Rudolf, *Deutschland im Zeitalter des Absolutismus 1648–1763*. Göttingen, Vandenhoeck & Rupprecht, 1978, 225p.

Voegt, Hedwig, *Die deutsche Jakobinische Literatur und Publizistik* 1789–1800. Berlin, Rutten & Loening, 1955, 244p.

Vossamp, Wilhelm. *Roman-Theorie in Deutschland; Von Martin Opitz bis Friedrich von Blankenburg*. Stuttgart, Metzler, 1973, 311p.

Voss, Ernst Theodor, *Erzählprobleme des Briefromans*. Bonn, Universität, 1960, 365p.

Wachsmuth, Andreas, *Geeinte Zweinatur. Aufsätze zu Goethes naturwissenschaftlichem Denken*. Berlin, Aufbau, 1976, 352p.

Wagner, Fritz, *Zur Apotheose Newtons: künstlerische Utopie und naturwissenschaftliches Weltbild im 18. Jahrhundert*. Bayr. Akad. d. Wiss. Phil-Hist. Klasse. Sitzungsberichte 1974, Heft 10. Munich, Becksche Verlagsbuchhandlung, 1974, 52p.

Wahrenburg, Fritz, *Funktionswandel des Romans und ästhetische Norm: die Entwicklung seiner Theorie in Deutschland bis zur Mitte des 18. Jahrhunderts*. Stuttgart, Metzler, 1976, 346p.

Wangerman, Ernst, *The Austrian Achievement 1700–1800*. New York, Harcourt Brace Jovanovich, 1973, 216p.

Wangerman, Ernst, *From Joseph II to the Jacobin Trials; Government Policy and Public Opinion in the Habsburg Dominions in the Period of the French Revolution*. 2nd edn, London: Oxford Univ. Press, 1969, 218p.

Ward, Albert, *Book Production, Fiction, and the German Reading Public, 1740–1800*. Oxford, Clarendon Press, 1974, vii, 214p.

Weber, Beat, *Die Kindsmörderin im deutschen Schrifttum von 1770–1795*. Bonn, Bouvier, 1974, v, 196p.

Weber, Ernst, *Die poetologische Selbstreflexion im deutschen Roman des 18. Jahrhunderts*. Stuttgart, Kohlhammer, 1974, 208p.

Weber, Peter, *Das Menschenbild des bürgerlichen Trauerspiels*. Berlin, Rütten & Loening, 1970, 272p.

Weis, Eberhard, *Der Durchburch des Bürgertums, 1776–1847. Propyläen Geschichte Europas*, Vol. 24. Frankfurt/Berlin, Propyläen Verlag, 1978, 538p.

Weissert, Gottfried, *Ballade*. Stuttgart, Metzler, 1980, vii, 134p.

Wellek, René, *A History of Modern Criticism 1750–1950*. Vol. I. *The Later Eighteenth Century*. New Haven, Yale Univ. Press, 1955.

Wellek, René, 'The Term and Concept of "Classicism" in Literary History'. In *Aspects of the Eighteenth Century*, ed. E. R. Wasserman, Baltimore, Johns Hopkins Press, 1965, 105–28.

Whaley, Joachim, 'Rediscovering the "Aufklärung" '. *GLL* N. S. 34 (1981), 183–95.

White, Reginald James, *Europe in the Eighteenth Century*. London, Macmillan; New York, St Martin's Press, 1965, xx, 300p.

Widmann, Hans, ed., *Der deutsche Buchhandel in Urkunden und Quellen*. 2 vols. Hamburg, Hauswedell, 1965.

Wierlacher, Alois, *Das bürgerliche Drama. Seine theoretische Begründung im 18. Jahrhundert*. Munich, Fink, 1968, 207p.

Wiese, Benno von, ed., *Deutsche Dichter des 18. Jahrhunderts. Ihr Leben und Werk*. Berlin, E. Schmidt, 1977, 1086p.

Wiese, Benno von, ed., *Das deutsche Drama vom Barock bis zur Gegenwart*. 2 vols. Düsseldorf, A. Bagel, 1958.

Wiese, Benno von, ed., *Deutsche Dramaturgie vom Barock bis zur Klassik*. Tübingen, Niemeyer, 1956, vii, 144p.

Wiese, Benno von, *Novelle*. Sammlg. Metzler 27, Stuttgart, Metzler. 1963, vi 89p.
Wieser, Max, *Der sentimentale Mensch*. Gotha/ Stuttgart, F. A. Perthes, 1924 325p.
Wilkinson, Elizabeth M. and Leonard Willoughby, 'Missing Links or Whateve Happened to Weimar Classicism?' *Erfahrung und Überlieferung. Festschrif für C. F. Magill*, ed. H. Siefken and A. Robinson. Cardiff, Trivium, 57–74
Willoughby, Leonard Ashley, *The Classical Age of German Literatur 1748–1805*. Oxford, Oxford University Press, 1926, 136p.
Windfuhr, Manfred, 'Kritik des Klassikbegriffs'. *Études Germaniques* 29 (1974) 302–18.
Winkler, Karl Tilman, 'Das revolutionäre Amerika im deutschen Schrifttum de 18. Jahrhunderts'. In *Börsenblatt für den deutschen Buchhandel* Frankfurter Ausgabe 32. Beilage: Aus dem Antiquariat. Frankfurt, 1976, 169–84
Wittkop, Justus Franz, *Die Welt des Empire*. Munich, M. Hueber, 1968, 375p.
Wolf, Abraham, *A History of Science, Technology and Philosophy in the 18th Century*. London, Allen & Unwin, 1952, 814p.
Wolffheim, Hans, *Die Entdeckung Shakespeares. Deutsche Zeugnisse des 18. Jahrhunderts*. Hamburg, Hoffman & Campe, 1959, 275p.
Wuthenow, Ralph-Rainer, *Das erinnerte Ich. Europäische Autobiographie und Selbstdarstellung im 18. Jahrhundert*. Munich, Beck, 1974, 248p.
Zeitler, Rudolf Walter, *Klassizismus und Utopia. Interpretationen zu Werken von David, Canova, Carstens, Thorvaldsen, Koch*. Stockholm, Almquist & Wiksell, 1954, 301p.
Zeman, Herbert, *Die deutsche anakreontische Dichtung*. Stuttgart, Metzler, 1972, 386p.
Zeman, Herbert, ed., *Die Österreichische Literatur. Ihr Profil an der Wende vom 18. bis zum 19. Jahrhundert (1750–1830)*. 2 vols. Graz, Akademische Druck- und Verlagsanstalt, 1979.
Zilsel, Edgar, *Die Entstehung des Geniebegriffes*. Tübingen, Mohr, 1926, viii, 346p.
Ziolkowski, Theodore, *The Classical German Elegy 1795–1950*. Princeton, Princeton Univ. Press, 1980, 344p.
Zmegac, Viktor, ed., *Geschichte der deutschen Literatur vom 18. Jahrhundert bis zur Gegenwart*. Vol. I/1, *1700–1848*. Königstein, Athenäum Verlag, 1979, 446p.

III Studies of individual authors

Bertuch

Heinemann, A. von, *Ein Kaufmann der Goethezeit. Friedrich Johann Justin Bertuchs Leben und Werk*. Weimar, Böhlau, 1955, 194p.

Bräker

Hinderer, Walter, 'Leben und Werk des Naturdichters Ulrich Bräker' in his *Über deutsche Literatur und Rede*. Munich, Fink, 1980, 39–65.

Mayer, Hans 'Aufklärer und Plebejer: Ulrich Bräker, der Arme Mann im Tockenburg' in his *Von Lessing bis Thomas Mann*. Pfullingen. Neske, 1959, 110–33.

Thalheim, Hans-Günther, 'Ulrich Bräker. Ein Naturdichter des 18. Jahrhunderts'. In his *Zur Literatur der Goethezeit*. Berlin, Rütten & Loening, 1969, 38–84.

Voellmy, Samuel, ed., *Leben und Schriften Ulrich Bräkers, des armen Mannes im Tockenburg*. 3 vols. Basel, Birkhäuser, 1945.

Diderot

Wilson, Arthur M., *Diderot*. New York, Oxford Univ. Press, 1972, 917p.

Fichte

Baumanns, Peter, *Fichtes Wissenschaftslehre*. Bonn, Bouvier, 1974, 283p.

Baumgartner, Hans Michael, *Fichte-Bibliographie*. Stuttgart, Frommann, 1968, 346p.

Buhr, Manfred, *Revolution und Philosophie. Die ursprüngliche Philosophie Johann Gottlieb Fichtes und die französische Revolution*. Berlin, Deutscher Verlag der Wissenschaften, 1965, 164p.

Willms, Bernard, ed., *Johann Gottlieb Fichte*: *Schriften zur Revolution*. Berlin, Ullstein, 1967, 393p.

Willms, Bernard. *Die totale Freiheit. Fichtes politische Philosophie*. Cologne, Westdeutscher Verlag 1967, x, 170p.

Forster

Gilli, Marita, *Georg Forster L'oeuvre d'un penseur allemand réaliste et révolutionnaire 1754–1794*. Paris, Champion, 1975, 701p.

Pütz, Peter, 'Zwischen Klassik und Romantik. Georg Forsters "Ansichten vom Niederrhein" '. *ZDP* 97 (1978), Sonderheft, 4–24.

Steiner, Gerhard, *Georg Forster*. Sammlung Metzler, 156. Stuttgart, Metzler, 1977, x, 136p.

Wuthenow, Ralph-Rainer, *Vernunft und Republik*; *Studien zu Georg Forsters Schriften*. Bad Homburg, H. Gehlen, 1970, 134p.

Fredrick The Great

Kästner, Erich. *Friedrich der Grosse und die deutsche Literatur*; *die Erwiderung auf seine Schrift 'De la littérature allemande*.' Stuttgart: Kohlhammer, 1972, 111p.

Füssli

Allentuck, Marcia, 'Fuseli and Lavater's "Physiognomic theory" ' in *Transactions of the 2nd Intern. Congress of the Enlightenment*. 1 (1967), 89–112.

Antal, Frederick, *Fuseli Studies*. London, Routledge & Kegan Paul, 1956, xxi, 176p.
Federmann, Arnold, *Johann Heinrich Füssli: Dichter und Maler 1741–1825*. Zurich, Orell Füssli Verlag, 1927, 180p.
Fuseli, Henry, *Sämtliche Gedichte*, ed. Martin Bircher and Karl S. Guthke. Zurich, Orell Füssli, 1973, 127p.
Mason, Eudo C., 'Heinrich Füssli und Winckelmann'. In *Unterscheidung und Bewahrung. Festschrift für Hermann Kunisch zum 60. Geburtstag*, ed. Klaus Lazarowicz and Wolfgang Kron. Berlin: de Gruyter, 1961, 232–58.
Mason, Eudo C., *The Mind of Henry Fuseli; Selections from his Writings*. London, Routledge & Kegan Paul, 1951, 374p.
Powell, Nicolas, *Fuseli: The Nightmare*. London, Penguin, 1973, 120p.
Pressly, Nancy L., *The Fuseli Circle in Rome*. New Haven, Yale Center for British Art, 1979, xiii, 145p.
Schiff, Gert and Werner Hofmann, *Henry Fuseli. 1741–1825 Exhibition*. London, Tate Gallery, 1975, 143p.
Schiff, Gert, *Johann Heinrich Füssli. 1741–1825*. 2 vols. Munich/Zürich, Prestel, 1973.
Starobinski, Jean, *Trois Fureurs*. Paris, Gallimard, 1974, 162p.
Tomory, Peter, *The Life and Art of Henry Fuseli*. New York, Praeger, 1972, 255p.

Gentz

Mann, Golo, *Secretary of Europe. The Life of Friedrich Gentz, enemy of Napoleon*. New Haven, Yale Univ. Press, 1946, xvi, 323p.
Sweet, Paul Robinson, *Friedrich Gentz. Defender of the Old Order*. Madison, Univ. of Wisconsin Press, 1941, viii, 326p.

Gellert

Hill, David, ' "Die Schwedische Gräfin". Notes on early bourgeois realism'. *Neophilologus* 65 (1981), 574–88.

Gessner

Hibbert, John, *Samuel Gessner. His creative achievement and influence*. Cambridge, Cambridge Univ. Press, 1976, vii, 183p.

Goethe

Adorno, Theodor, 'Zum Klassizismus von Goethes Iphigenie'. In his *Noten zur Literatur IV*, ed. R. Tiedemann. Frankfurt, Suhrkamp, 1974, 7–33.
Andreas, Willy, *Carl August von Weimar. Ein Leben mit Goethe 1757–1783*. Stuttgart, G. Killper, 1953, 612p.
Atkins, Stuart, *Goethe's Faust*. Cambridge (Mass.), Harvard Univ. Press, 1964, 283p.

Baioni, Giuliano, *Classicismo e Rivoluzione. Goethe e la Rivoluzione francese.* Naples, Guida, 1969, 349p.
Benjamin, Walter. 'Goethe'. In his *Gesammelte Schriften II, 2,* ed. R. Tiedemann. Frankfurt, Suhrkamp, 1972–77, 705–39.
Benn, Gottfried, 'Goethe und die Naturwissenschaften'. In his *Gesammelte Werke,* Bd. I, ed. Dieter Wellershoff. Wiesbaden, Limes-Verlag, 1960–68, 724–62.
Bergsträsser, Arnold, *Goethe's Image of Man and Society.* Chicago, Regnery, 1949, 361p.
Beutler, Ernst, *Essays um Goethe.* 7th edn, Zürich, Artemis Verlag, 1980, 887p.
Blackall, Eric, *Goethe and the Novel.* Ithaca, Cornell Univ. Press, 1976, 342p.
Bode, Wilhelm, *Goethes Ästhetik.* Berlin, E. S. Mittler & Sohn, 1901, 341p.
Bollacher, Martin, *Der junge Goethe und Spinoza. Studien zur Geschichte des Spinozismus in der Epoche des Sturms und Drangs.* Tübingen, Niemeyer, 1969, 253p.
Boyd, James, *Goethe's Knowledge of English Literature.* Oxford, Clarendon Press, 1932, 310p.
Braemer, Edith A., *Goethes Prometheus und die Grundpositionen des Sturm und Drang.* 3rd edn, Berlin/Weimar, Aufbau-Verlag, 1968, 435p.
Bräuning-Octavio, Hermann, 'Goethe und Johann Heinrich Merck. Die Geschichte einer Freundschaft'. *Goethe-JbGG* 12 (1950), 177–217; 14/15 (1952/3). 209–44.
Brown, Jane, 'Die Wahlverwandschaften and the English Novel of Manners'. *CL* XXVIII (1976), 97–108.
Bruford, Walter, 'Goethes "Literarischer Sanskulottismus". Classicism and Society'. In *Festgabe für L. L. Hammerich.* Kopenhagen, Naturmetodens Sproginstitut, 1962, 45–59.
Bubner, Rüdiger, *Goethe und Hegel.* Heidelberg, Winter, 1978, 51p.
Bürger, Christa, *Der Ursprung der bürgerlichen Institution Kunst im höfischen Weimar. Literatursoziologische Untersuchungen zum klassischen Goethe.* Frankfurt, Suhrkamp, 1977, 180p.
Carlson, Marvin A., *Goethe and the Weimar Theatre.* Ithaca, NY, Cornell Univ. Press, 1978, 328p.
Citati, Pietro, *Goethe,* trans. by Raymond Rosenthal. New York, Dial Press, 1974, xviii, 469p.
Corngold, Stanley, *et al.,* eds., *Aspekte der Goethezeit.* Göttingen, Vandenhoeck & Rupprecht, 1977, 311p.
David, Claude, 'Goethe und die französische Revolution'. In *Deutsche Literatur und Französische Revolution,* ed. Richard Brinkmann, Göttingen, Vandenhoeck & Rupprecht, 1974, 63–86.
Dédéyan, Charles, *Le thème de Faust dans la littérature européenne.* 4 vols. Paris, Lettres Modernes, 1954–1967.
Dickson, A. J., ed., 'Goethe in England. 1909–1949. A Bibliography'. *REGS* NS XIX, 1951, 48p.
Einem, Herbert von, *Goethe-Studien.* Munich, Fink, 1972, 192p.
Eissler, Kurt Robert, *Goethe. A psychoanalytic study. 1775–1786.* 2 vols. Detroit, Wayne State Univ. Press, 1963.

Emmel, Hildegard, *Was Goethe vom Roman der Zeitgenossen nahm. Zu Wilhelm Meisters Lehrjahre*. Bern/Munich, Francke, 1972, 47p.
Emrich, Wilhelm, 'Technisches und absolutes Bewusstsein in Goethes "Pandora" '. In his *Geist und Widergeist*. Frankfurt, Athenäum 1965, 117–28.
Fairley, Barker, *A Study of Goethe*. Oxford, Clarendon Press, 1950, vii, 280p.
Fambach, Oskar, *Goethe und seine Kritiker*. Düsseldorf, Ehlermann, 1953, xii, 460p.
Geerdts, Hans Jürgen, *Goethes Roman 'Die Wahlverwandschaften'*. Weimar, Arion Verlag, 1958, 222p.
Gögelein, Christoph, *Zu Goethes Begriff von Wissenschaft; auf dem Wege der Methodik seiner Farbstudien*. Munich, Hanser, 1972, 208p.
Goethe Bibliographie. Begründet von Hans Pyritz, fortgesetzt von Heinz Nicolai *et al.*, 2 vols. Heidelberg, Winter. 1965, 1968.
Graham, Ilse, *Goethe. Portrait of the Artist*. Berlin/New York, de Gruyter, 1977, 381p.
Graham, Ilse, *Goethe and Lessing. The Wellsprings of Creation*. London, Elek, 1973, xiii, 356p.
Gray, Ronald, *Goethe. A Critical Introduction*. London, Cambridge Univ. Press, 1969, ix, 288p.
Grumach, Ernst, *Goethe und die Antike*. 2 vols. Potsdam, Verlag Stichnote, 1949.
Hahn, Karl Heinz, 'Goethes Verhältnis zur Romantik'. *Goethe. N. F d. Jb. d. Goethe Gesellschaft* 29 (1967), 43–64.
Hamm, Heinz, *Der Theoretiker Goethe*. Kronberg/Ts., Scriptor, 1976, 268p.
Hass, Hans Egon, 'Wilhelm Meisters Lehrjahre'. In *Der deutsche Roman*. 2 vols., ed. Benno von Wiese. Düsseldorf, A. Bagel, 1963. Vol. I, 132–210, 425 f.
Hatfield, Henry, *Goethe. A Critical Introduction*. Cambridge, Mass., Harvard Univ. Press, 1964, 241p.
Heisenberg, Werner, 'Die Goethesche und die Newtonsche Farbenlehre im Lichte der modernen Physik'. In *Goethe im XX. Jahrhundert*, ed. Hans Meyer. Hamburg, Christian Wegner Verlag, 1967, 418–32.
Henning, Hans, Annual Goethe-Bibliography in: *Goethe-Jahrbuch* 89 (1972)–98 (1981).
Hetzer, Theodor, 'Goethe und die bildende Kunst'. In his *Aufsätze und Vorträge*. Leipzig, Seemann, 1957, II, 193–221.
Hinderer, Walter, ed., *Goethes Dramen. Neue Interpretationen*. Stuttgart, Reclam, 1980, 367p.
Hof, Walter, *Goethe und Charlotte von Stein*. Frankfurt, Insel, 1979, 315p.
Holtzhauer, Helmut, *Goethe-Museum: Werk, Leben und Zeit Goethes in Dokumenten*. Berlin, Aufbau Verlag, 1969, 715p.
Holtzhauer, Helmut, ed., *J. W. Goethe: Winckelmann und sein Jahrhundert*. Leipzig, Seemann, 1969, 370p.
Horton-Smith, N., 'The Anti-Romanticism of Goethe'. *Renaissance and Modern Studies* II (1958), 127–52.
Jacobs, Jürgen, *Wilhelm Meister und seine Brüder. Untersuchungen zum deutschen Bildungsroman*. Munich, Fink, 1972, 332p.

Jantz, Harold, *The Form of Faust*. Baltimore, Johns Hopkins Univ. Press, 1978, xxi, 201p.

Janz, Rolf-Peter, 'Zum sozialen Gehalt der "Lehrjahre" '. In *Literaturwissenschaft und Geschichtsphilosophie. Festschrift für Wilhelm Emrich*, ed. H. Arntzen. Berlin: de Gruyter, 1975, 320–40.

Jolles, Matthijs, *Goethes Kunstanschauung*. Bern, Francke, 1957, 342p.

Kayser, Wolfgang, 'Die Entstehung von Goethes "Werther" '. *DVjs* 19 (1941), 430–57.

Keller, Harald, *Goethes Hymnus auf das Strassburger Münster und die Wiedererweckung der Gotik im 18. Jahruhundert 1772–1972*. Bayr. Akad. d. Wiss. Philos.-Hist. Klasse. Sitzungsberichte 1974, 4. Munich, Beck, 1974, 83p.

Keller, Harald, *Goethe, Palladio und England*. Bayr. Akad. d. Wiss. Philos.-Hist. Klasse. Sitzungsberichte 1971, 6. Munich, Beck, 1971, 36p.

Keller, Heinz, *Goethe und das Laokoon Problem*. Frauenfeld, Huber, 1935, 120p.

Keller, Werner, ed., *Aufsätze zu Goethes* 'Faust I' Darmstadt, Wissenschaftliche Buchgesellschaft, 1974, xiv, 639p.

Keller, Werner, *Goethes dramatische Bildlichkeit. Eine Grundlegung*. Munich, Fink, 1972, 315p.

Keller, Werner, 'Der klassische Goethe und sein nicht-klassischer "Faust" '. *GJb* 95 (1978), 9–28.

Kindermann, Heinz, *Theatergeschichte der Goethezeit*. Vienna, A. Bauer, 1949, 931p.

Kolbe, Jürgen, *Goethes 'Wahlverwandschaften' und der Roman des 19. Jahruhunderts*. Stuttgart, Kohlhammer, 1968, 227p.

Korff, Hermann August, *Geist der Goethezeit*. Leipzig, J. J. Weber, 1930, xviii, 530p.

Krauss, Werner, 'Goethe und die französische Revolution'. *GJb* 94 (1977), 127–36.

Kreuzer, Ingrid, 'Strukturprinzipien in Goethes "Märchen" '. *JbDSG* XXI (1977), 221–35.

Kuhn, Dorothea, 'Grundzüge der Goetheschen Morphologie'. *GJb* 95 (1978), 199–211.

Lamport, Francis John, *A Student's Guide to Goethe*. London, Heinemann, 1971, 122p.

Landsberger, Franz, *Die Kunst der Goethezeit*. Leipzig, Insel, 1931, 320p.

Lange, Victor, ed., *Goethe. A Collection of Critical Essays*. Englewood Cliffs, NJ, Prentice Hall, 1968, 185p.

Lange, Victor, 'Goethe's Craft of Fiction'. *PEGS* N. S. 22 (1953), 33–63.

Lange, Victor, 'Nationalliteratur und Weltliteratur'. *GJb* 88 (1971), 15–30.

Leppmann, Wolfgang, *The German Image of Goethe*. Oxford, Clarendon Press, 1961, 220p.

Lewes, George Henry, *The Life of Goethe*. Intro. by Victor Lange. New York, Ungar, 1965, xxii, 578p.

Loram, Ian Craig, *Goethe and his Publishers*. Lawrence, Univ. of Kansas Press, 1963, 168p.

Lukacs, Georg, *Goethe and his Age*. London, Merlin Press, 1968, 260p.
Mandelkow, Karl Robert, ed., *Goethe im Urteil seiner Kritiker*. 3 Parts. Munich, Beck, 1975–79.
Mayer, Hans, *Goethe: ein Versuch über den Erfolg*. Frankfurt, Suhrkamp, 1973, 160p.
Mayer, Hans, ed., *Goethe im XX. Jahrhundert. Spiegelungen und Deutungen*. Hamburg, Wegner Verlag, 1967, 441p.
Mommsen, Wilhelm, *Die politischen Anschauungen Goethes*. Stuttgart, Deutsche Verlags-Anstalt, 1948, 313p.
Müller, Curt, 'Über den Symbolbegriff in Goethes Kunstanschauung'. (*Jb*) *Goethe* 8 (1943), 269–80.
Müller-Seidel, Walter, 'Naturforschung und deutsche Klassik. Die Jenaer Gespräche im Juli 1794'. In *Untersuchungen zur Literatur als Geschichte. Festgabe für Benno von Wiese*, ed. V. Günther *et al*. Berlin, Erich Schmidt, 1973, 61–78.
Nicolai, Heinz, Annual Goethe-Bibliography in *Goethe. NF des Jb. d. Goethe Gesellschaft* XIV/XV (1953)–XXXIII (1971).
Nicolai, Heinz, *Goethe und Jacobi. Studien zur Geschichte ihre Freundschaft*. Stuttgart, Metzler, 1965, viii, 364p.
Niederer, Heinrich, 'Goethes unzeitgemäße Reise nach Italien 1786–1788' in: *JFDH* 980, 55–107.
Nisbet, Hugh, *Goethe and the Scientific Tradition*. London, Institute of Germanic Studies, University of London, 1972, xi, 83p.
Øhrgaard, Per, *Die Genesung des Narzissus. Eine Studie zu Goethes 'Wilhelm Meisters Lehrjahre'*. Copenhagen, Institut for Germansk Filologi, 1978, 333p.
Peacock, Ronald, *Goethe's Major Plays*. Manchester, Manchester Univ. Press, 1966, 236p.
Petersen, Uwe, *Goethe und Euripides. Untersuchungen zur Euripides-Rezeption in der Goethezeit*. Heidelberg, Winter, 1974, 235p.
Prescher, Hans, ed., *Goethes Sammlungen zur Mineralogie, Geologie und Paläontologie*. Berlin, Akademie, 1978, 716p.
Rasch, Wolfdietrich, *Goethes 'Iphigenie auf Tauris' als Drama der Autonomie*. Munich, Beck, 1979, 205p.
Rasch, Wolfdietrich, 'Die Klassische Erzählkunst Goethes'. In *Formkräfte der deutschen Dichtung vom Barock bis zur Gegenwart*, ed. Hans Stefen. Göttingen, Vandenhoeck & Rupprecht, 1963, 81–99.
Reed, Terence James, *The Classical Centre. Goethe and Weimar 1775–1832*. London, Croom Helm, 1980, 271p.
Reiss, Hans, ed., *Goethe und die Tradition*. Frankfurt, Athenäum Verlag, 1972, 296p.
Reiss, Hans, *Goethe's Novels*. London, Macmillan, 1969, 309p.
Richter, Karl, 'Morphologie und Stilwandel. Ein Beitrag zu Goethes Lyrik'. *JbDSG* XX (1976), 387–401.
Robson-Scott, William Douglas, *The Younger Goethe and the Visual Arts*. Cambridge, Cambridge Univ. Press, 1981, xi, 175p.
Rösch, Ewald, ed., *Goethes Roman 'Die Wahlverwandschaften'*. Wege der

Forschung 113. Darmstadt, Wissenschaftliche Buchgesellschaft, 1975, v, 501p.

Rose, William, ed., *Essays on Goethe*. London, Cassells, 1949, 254p.

Rüdiger, Horst, 'Goethes "Römische Elegien" und die antike Tradition'. *GJb* 95 (1978), 174–98.

Schadewaldt, Wolfgang, *Goethestudien. Natur und Alter*. Zürich, Artemis Verlag, 1963, 531p.

Schäfer, Albert, ed., *Goethe und seine grossen Zeitgenossen*. Munich, Beck, 1968, 203p.

Scheidig, Walter, *Goethes Preisaufgaben für bildende Künstler*. Weimar, Böhlau, 1958, xi, 535p.

Scherpe, Klaus, *Werther und Wertherwirkung*. Bad Homburg, Gehlen 1970, 107p.

Schlaffer, Hannelore, *Wilhelm Meister: Das Ende der Kunst und die Wiederkehr des Mythos*. Stuttgart, Metzler, 1980, viii, 247p.

Schmiedt, Helmut, 'Woran scheitert Werther?' *Poetica* XI (1979), 83–104.

Sommerfeld, Martin, *Goethe. Umwelt und Folgezeit*. Leiden, Sijthoff, 1935, 283p.

Staiger, Emil, *Goethe*. 3 vols. Zürich, Atlantis Verlag, 1952–59.

Stammen, Theodor, *Goethe und die Französische Revolution. Eine Interpretation der 'Natürlichen Tochter'*. Munich, Beck, 1966, viii, 274p.

Steiner, Jacob, *Sprache und Stilwandel in Goethes 'Wilhelm Meister'*. Zürich, Atlantis Verlag, 1959, 190p.

Stellmacher, Wolfgang, 'Zur Entwicklung der Kunstauffassung Goethes'. *Weimarer Beiträge* 15 (1969), 6, 1229–51.

Stelzer, Otto, *Goethe und die bildende Kunst*. Braunschweig, Vieweg Verlag, 1949, 192p.

Stewart, Walter K., *Time Structure in Drama: Goethe's Sturm und Drang Plays*. Amsterdam: Rodopi, 1978, v, 308p.

Sudheimer, Hellmuth, *Der Geniebegriff des jungen Goethe*. 1935. Rpt. Nendeln/Liechentenstein, Kraus Reprint, 1967, viii, 652p.

Thalheim, Hans Günther, 'Zu den kunsthistorischen Schriften Goethes an der Wende vom 18. zum 19. Jahrhundert'. *Weimarer Beiträge* XXIII (1977), 5, 5–45.

Trevelyan, Humphry, *Goethe and the Greeks*. Intro. Hugh Lloyd-Jones. 2nd edn, Cambridge: Cambridge Univ. Press, 1981, 321p.

Trunz, Erich and Waltraud Loos, eds., *Goethe und der Kreis von Münster; zeitgenössische Briefe und Aufzeichnungen*. Münster/Westf., Aschendorff, 1971, 455p.

Tümmler, Hans, *Carl August von Weimar. Goethes Freund. Eine vorwiegend politische Biographie*. Stuttgart, Klett–Cotta, 1978, 430p.

Tümmler, Hans, *Goethe als Staatsmann*. Göttingen/Zürich/Frankfurt, Musterschmidt, 1976, 122p.

Tümmler, Hans, *Goethe in Staat und Politik*. Cologne, Böhlau, 1964, 279p.

Wegner, Max, *Goethes Anschauung antiker Kunst*. Berlin, Mann, 1944, 166p.

Wells, George A., 'Goethe'. In *Dictionary of Scientific Biography*. New York, Charles Scribner Sons, 1970–80, Vol. V, 442–7.

Wells, George A., *Goethe and the Development of Science*. Alphen, Sijthoff & Noordhoff, 1978, xii, 161p.

Wells, George A., 'Goethes qualitative Optics'. *Journal of the History of Ideas* 32 (1971), 617–26.

Wertheim, Ursula, *Goethe-Studien*. Berlin, Rütten & Loening, 1968, 242p.

Wilkinson, Elizabeth M. and Leonard Willoughby, *Goethe Poet and Thinker*. London, Edward Arnold, 1962, 248p.

Wilkinson, Elizabeth M. and Leonard Willoughby, 'Having and Being, or bourgeois versus nobility. Notes for a chapter on social and cultural history or for a commentary on 'Wilhelm Meister'. *GLL* 22 (1968/69) 101–5.

Wittich, Werner, 'Der soziale Gehalt von Goethes Roman "Wilhelm Meisters Lehrjahre" '. In *Hauptprobleme der Sociologie. Erinnerungsgabe fur Max Weber*, ed. Melchior Palyi. Munich/Leipzig, Duncker & Humblot, 1923, Vol II, 278–306.

Zimmermann, Rolf Christian, *Das Weltbild des jungen Goethe. Studien zur hermetischen Tradition des deutschen 18. Jahrhunderts. Erster Band: Elemente und Fundamente*. Munich, Fink, 1969, 368p.

Ziolkowski, Theodor, 'The imperial sanctuary. Towards a paradigm of Goethe's classical dramas'. In *Studies in the German Drama. Festschrfit in honor of Walter Silz*. Chapel Hill, Univ. of North Carolina Press, 1974, 71–87.

Haller

Balmer, Heinz, *Albrecht von Haller*. Bern. P. Haupt, 1977, 88p.

Guthke, Karl, *Haller und die Literatur*. Göttingen, Vandenhoeck & Rupprecht, 1962, 188p.

Heinzmann, Johann Georg, ed., *Albrecht von Haller, 1708–1777. Tagebuch seiner Beobachtungen über Schriftsteller und über sich selbst*. 1787. 2 vols. Rpt. Frankfurt, Athenäum, 1971.

Hamann

Alexander, W. M., *Johann Georg Hamann: Philosophy and Faith*. The Hague, Nijhoff, 1966, xii, 212p.

Dunning, Stephen Northrup, *The Tongues of Men*. Missoula, Mont., Scholars Press, 1979, xi, 260p.

Gajek, Bernhard, ed., *Acta des Internationalen Hamman-Colloquiums in Lüneburg 1976*. Frankfurt, Klostermann, 1979, ix, 348p.

Herde, Heinz, *Johann Georg Hamann: Zur Theologie der Sprache*. Bonn, Bouvier, 1971, 165p.

Hoffmann, Volker, *Johann Georg Hamanns Philologie. Hamanns Philologie zwischen enzyklopädischer Mikrologie und Hermeneutik*. Stuttgart, Kohlhammer, 1972, 256p.

Imendoerffer, Nora, *Johann Georg Hamann und seine Bücherei*. Schriften der Albertus Univ. 20, Königsberg/Berlin, Ost-Europa-Verlage, 1938, vii, 174p.

Jørgensen, Sven-Aage, *Johann Georg Hamann*. Sammlung Metzler 143. Stuttgart, Metzler, 1976, 106p.

Nebel, Gerhard, *Hamann*. Stuttgart, Klett, 1973, 352p.
O'Flaherty, James C., *Johann Georg Hamann*. Twayne's World Authors Series 527. Boston, Twayne, 1979, 199p.
O'Flaherty, James C., *Unity and Language: A Study in the Philosophy of Johann Georg Hamann*. New York, AMS Press, 1966, viii, 121p.
Salmony, Hansjörg Alfred, *Johann Georg Hamanns metakritische Philosophie*. Zollikon, Evangelischer Verlag, 1958, 338p.
Wessell, Leonard P., 'Hamann's Philosophy of Aesthetics: Its Meaning for the Storm and Stress Period'. *Journal of Aesthetics and Art Criticism* 27 (1969), 433–443.
Wild, Reiner, ed., *Johann Georg Hamann*. Wege der Forschung 511. Darmstadt, Wissenschaftliche Buchgesellschaft, 1978, vi, 452p.

Hegel

Findlay, John Niemeyer, *Hegel*. A Reexamination. London, Allen & Unwin; New York, Macmillan, 1958, 372p.
Koepsel, Werner, *Die Rezeption der Hegelschen Aesthetik im 20. Jahrhundert*. Bonn, Bouvier, 1975, vi. 381p.
Ritter, Joachim, *Hegel und die französische Revolution*. Frankfurt, Suhrkamp, 1965, 135p.

Heinse

Bäumer, Max L., *Heinse Studien*. Stuttgart, Metzler, 1966, v, 214p.
Bäumer, Max L., *Das Dionysische in den Werken Wilhelm Heinses*. Bonn, Bouvier, 1964, 168p.
Brecht, Walther, *Heinse und der ästhetische Immoralismus*. Berlin, Weidmannsche Buchhandlung, 1911, xvi, 195p.
Grappin, Pierre, 'Ardinghello und Hyperion'. *Weimarer Beiträge* 2 (1956), 165–81.
Horn, H., 'Heinses Stellung zur Klassik'. *Imprimatur* VII (1936–37), 49–59.
Keller, Otto, *Wilhelm Heinses Entwicklung zur Humanität. Zum Stilwandel des deutschen Romans im 18. Jahrhundert*. Bern/Munich, Francke, 1972, 267p.
Reiss, Edmund. *Wilhelm Heinses Romantechnik*. 1911. Rpt. Hildesheim, Gerstenberg, 1978, 108p.
Terras, Rita, *Wilhelm Heinses Aesthetik*. Munich, W. Fink, 1972, 192p.

Herder

Barnard, F. M., *Herder's Social and Political Thought. From Enlightenment to Nationalism*. Oxford, Clarendon Press, 1967, xxii, 189p.
Berlin, Isaiah, 'Herder and the Enlightenment'. In Aspects of the Eighteenth Century, ed. Earl R. Wassermann. Baltimore, Johns Hopkins Press, 1965, 47–104.
Berlin, Isaiah, *Vico and Herder. Two Studies in the History of Ideas*. New York, Viking Press, 1976, xxvii, 228p.

Clark, Robert Thomas, *Herder: His Life and Thought*. Berkeley, Univ. of California Press, 1955, vi, 501p.

Fugate, Joe K., *The Psychological Basis of Herder's Aesthetics*. The Hague, Mouton, 1966, 303p.

Gillies, Alexander, *Herder*. Oxford, Blackwell, 1945, vii, 152p.

Guthke, Karl S., 'Note on Herder and Rousseau'. *Modern Language Quarterly* 19 (1958), 303–6.

Günther, Gottfried, *et al.*, eds., *Herder Bibliographie*. Berlin, Aufbau Verlag, 1978, xii, 643p.

Gulyga, Arseni W., *Johann Gottfried Herder. Eine Einführung in seine Philosophie*. Frankfurt, Röderberg, 1979, 168p.

McEachran, Frank, *The Life and Philosophy of Johann Gottfried Herder*. Oxford, Clarendon Press, 1939, 98p.

Nisbet, Hugh, 'Herder and Francis Bacon'. *MLR* 62 (1967), 267–83.

Nisbet, Hugh, *Herder and the Philosophy and History of Science*. Cambridge, Modern Humanities Research Assoc. 1970, xi, 358p.

Richter, Lutz, ed., *J. G. Herder im Spiegel seiner Zeitgenossen*. Göttingen, Vandenhoeck & Rupprecht, 1978, 368p.

Schmidt, Royal J., 'Cultural Nationalism in Herder'. *Journal of the History of Ideas* 17 (1956) 407–7.

Stellmacher, Wolfgang, *Herders Shakespeare-Bild. Shakespeare-Rezeption im Sturm und Drang: dynamisches Weltbild und Bürgerliches Nationaldrama*. Berlin, Rütten und Loening, 1978, 322p.

Unterreitmeister, Hans, *Sprache als Zugang zur Geschichte; Untersuchungen zu Herders geschichtsphilosophischer Methode*. Bonn, Bouvier, 1971, 108p.

Wells, George A., 'Herder's Two Philosophies of History'. *Journal of the History of Ideas* 21 (1960), 527–7.

Hermes

Muskalla, Konstantin, *Die Romane von Johann Timotheus Hermes*. Breslau, F. Hirt, 1912, 87p.

Heyne

Bräuning-Oktavio, Hermann, *Christian Gottlob Heynes Vorlesungen über die Kunst der Antike und ihr Einfluss auf J. H. Merck, Herder und Goethe*. Darmstadt, Liebig, 1971, 109p.

Hippel

Greiner, Martin, *Theodor Gottlieb von Hippel. 1741–1796*. Giessen, Schmitz, 1958, 16p.

Hölderlin

Bertaux, Pierre, *Freiedrich Hölderlin*. Frankfurt, Suhrkamp, 1978, 663p.

Kohler, Maria and A. Kelletat, eds., *Hölderlin-Bibliographie 1938–1960*, Stuttgart, Landesbibliothek, 195, vii, 103p.
Mason, Eudo C., *Hölderlin and Goethe*, ed. Peter Howard Gaskill. Foreword by Hans Reiss. Bern/Frankfurt, Lang, 1975, 145p.
Montgomery, Marshall, *Friedrich Hölderlin and the German Neo-Hellenic Movement*. Oxford, Oxford Univ. Press, 1923.
Miller, Ronald Duncan, *A study of Hölderlin*. Harrogate, Duchy Press, 1959, 96p.
Nägele, Rainer, *Literatur und Utopie. Versuche zu Hölderlin*. Heidelberg, Stiehm, 1978, 222p.
Peacock, Ronald, *Hölderlin*. London, Methuen; New York, Barnes & Noble, 1938, xiii, 179p.
Ryan, Lawrence, *Hölderlins 'Hyperion'. Exzentrische Bahn und Dichterberuf*. Stuttgart, Metzler, 1965, 244p.
Shelton, Roy C., *The Young Hölderlin*. Bern/Frankfurt, Lang, 1973, 282p.
Szondi, Peter, *Hölderlin-Studien* Frankfurt, Insel Verlag 1970, 377p.
Unger, Richard, *Hölderlin's Major Poetry. The dialectics of unity*. Bloomington, Indiana Univ. Press, 1975, xiv, 267p.

Hölty

Oberlin-Kaiser, Thymiane, *Ludwig Christoph Heinrich Hölty*. Zürich, Juris Verlag, 1964, 137p.

W. V. Humboldt

Müller-Vollmer, Kurt, *Poesie und Einbildungskraft. Zur Dichtungstheorie Wilhelm von Humboldts*. Stuttgart, Metzler, 1967, vi, 248p.
Novak, Richey A., *Wilhelm von Humboldt as a Literary Critic*. Bern, Herbert Lang, 1972, 142p.
Scurla, Herbert, *Wilhelm von Humboldt. Leben und Werken*. Düsseldorf, Claasen 1976, 660p.
Sweet, Paul Robinson, *Wilhelm von Humboldt. A Biography*. 2 vols. Columbus, Ohio State Univ. Press, 1978, 1980.

Iffland, Kotzebue

Klingenberg, K. H., *Iffland und Kotzebue als Dramatiker*. Weimar, Arion, 1962, 189p.

Jacobi

Hammacher, Klaus, ed., *Friedrich Heinrich Jacobi. Philosoph und Literat der Goethezeit*. Frankfurt, Klostermann, 1971, xii, 380p.
Homann, Karl, *F. H. Jacobis Philosophie der Freiheit*. Freiburg, Karl Alber, 1973, 304p.

Pascal, Roy, 'The Novels of F. H. Jacobi and Goethe's early Classicism'. *PEGS* n.s. XVI (1947) 54–89.

Terpstra. Jan Ulbe, *Friedrich Heinrich Jacobis* 'Allwill'. Groningen, Wolters, 1957, 365p.

Jung-Stilling

Günther, Hans R. G., *Jung-Stilling Ein Beitrag zur Psychologie des Pietismus.* 2nd edn, Munich, Federmann, 1948, 190p.

Kant

Bäumler, Alfred, *Kants Kritik der Urteilskraft, ihr Geschichte und Systematik.* Vol. I. Halle, M. Niemeyer, 1923, 352p.

Galston, William Arthur, *Kant and the Problem of History*. Chicago, Univ. of Chicago Press, 1975, xiv, 290p.

Gulyga, Arseni, *Kant*. Frankfurt, Insel Verlag, 1981, 420p.

Koerner, Stephan, *Kant*. Harmondsworth, Penguin, 1960, 230p.

Meredith, James Creed, transl. *Critique of Judgment*. Oxford, Clarendon Press, 1961, 426p.

Schultz, Uwe, *Immanuel Kant in Selbstzeugnissen und Bilddokumenten.* Hamburg, Rowohlt, 1971, 184p.

Kleist

Gall, Ulrich, *Philosophie bei Heinrich von Kleist. Untersuchung zu Herkunft und Bestimmung des philosophischen Gehalts seiner Schriften*. Bonn, Bouvier, 1977, 275p.

Graham, Ilse, *Heinrich von Kleist. Word into Flesh*. Berlin/New York, de Gruyter, 1977, 296p.

Helbling, Robert E., *The Major Works of Heinrich von Kleist*. New York, New Directions, 1975, 275p.

Mommsen, Katharina, *Kleists Kampf mit Goethe*. Frankfurt, Suhrkamp, 1979, 274p.

Silz, Walter, *Heinrich von Kleist; studies in his work and literary character.* Philadelphia, Univ. of Pennsylvania Press, 1961, 313p.

Klinger

Geerdts, Hans Jürgen, 'Über die Romane F. M. Klingers'. *Zeitschrift der Friedrich Schiller Universität Jena. Ges.- Sprachwissensch. Reihe* 3, 1953/4, 456–70.

Hering, Christian, *Friedrich Maximilian Klinger. Weltman als Dichter*. Berlin, de Gruyter, 1966, viii, 389p.

Osterwalder, Fritz, *Die Überwindung des Sturm und Drang im Werk F. M. Klingers. Die Entwicklung der republikanischen Dichtung in der Zeit der französischen Revolution*. Berlin, Schmidt, 1979, 253p.

egeberg, Harro, *Friedrich Maximilian Klingers Romandichtung. Untersuchungen zum Roman der Spätaufklärung*. Heidelberg, Winter, 1974, 213p.
'olhard, Ewald. *Klingers philosophische Romane. Der Einzelne und die Gesellschaft*. Halle, Niemeyer, 1930, xv, 158p.

Klopstock

Alewyn, Richard, 'Klopstocks Leser'. In *Festschrift für Rainer Grünter*, ed. Bernhard Fabian. Heidelberg, Winter, 1979, 100–121.
Boeschenstein, Bernhard, 'Klopstock als Lehrer Hölderlins'. *Hölderlin Jahrbuch* 17 (1971–72), 30–42.
Burkhardt, Gerhard and Heinz Nicolai. *Klopstock-Bibliographie* In: F. G. Klopstock *Werke und Briefe. Historisch-Kritische Ausgabe*. Abt. Addenda: Bd. I. Berlin/New York, de Gruyter, 1975, 340p.
Grosse, Wilhelm. *Studien zu Klopstocks Poetik*. Munich: Fink, 1977, 240p.
Kaiser, Gerhard, *Klopstock. Religion und Dichtung*. Gütersloh, G. Mohn, 1977, 370p.
Langen, August, 'Klopstocks Sprachgeschichtliche Bedeutung'. In his *Gesammelte Studien zur neueren deutsche Sprache und Literatur*, ed. Karl Richter *et al.* Berlin, E. Schmidt, 1978, 87–108.
Murat, Jean, *Klopstock. Les Thèmes principaux de son oeuvre*. Paris, Les Belles Lettres, 1959, xi, 386p.
Schneider, Karl Ludwig, *Klopstock und die Erneuerung der deutschen Dichtersprache*. Heidelberg, Winter, 1960, 142p.
Werner, Hans-Georg, 'Klopstock und sein Dichterberuf'. *Weimarer Beitrage* 20 (1974) 11, 5–38.
Werner, Hans-Georg, *F. G. Klopstock. Werk und Wirkung. Wiseenschaftliche Konferenz der Martin-Luther-Universität Halle-Wittenberg im Juli 1974*. Berlin, Akademie Verlag, 1978, 307p.

Knigge

Kogel, Jörg-Dieter, *Knigges ungewöhnliche Empfehlungen zu Aufklärung und Revolution*. Berlin, Oberbaum, 1979, 121p.
Yuill, William Edward, 'A Genteel Jacobin: Adolf Freiherr von Knigge'. In *Erfahrung und überlieferung: Festschrift for C. P. Magill*. Cardiff, Univ. of Wales Press, 1974, 42–56.

Kotzebue

Maurer, Doris, *August von Kotzebue. Ursachen seines Erfolgs. Konstante Elemente der unterhaltenden Dramatik*. Bonn, Bouvier, 1979, 329p.
Stock, Frithjof, *Kotzebue im literarischen Leben der Goethezeit Polemik, Kritik, Publikum*. Düsseldorf, Bertelsmann, 1971, 224p.

LaRoche

Milch, Werner, *Sophie LaRoche die Grossmutter der Brentanos*. Frankfurt Societäts-Verlag, 1935, 269p.

Lavater

Janentzky, Christian, *Johann Caspar Lavater*. Frauenfeld, Huber, 1928, 127p.

Lenz

Benseler, David P., 'Jakob Michael Reinhold Lenz. An indexed bibliography wit an introduction on the history of the mss. and editions'. Diss. Univ. o Oregon, 1971, 302p.

Burger, Heinz Otto, 'J. M. R. Lenz: "Der Hofmeister" '. In *Das deutsch Lustspiel*, ed. Hans Steffen. Göttingen, Vandenhoeck & Rupprecht, 1968 48–67.

Harris, Edward P., 'Structural Unity in J. M. R. Lenz.' *Seminar* 8 (1972), 77–87

Hohoff, Curt, *J. M. R. Lenz in Selbstzeugnissen und Bilddokumenten*. Reinbek Rowohlt, 1977, iv, 152p.

Osborne, John, *J. M. R. Lenz. The Renunciation of Heroism*. Göttingen Vandenhoeck & Rupprecht, 1975, 173p.

Lessing

Allison, Henry E., *Lessing and the Enlightenment*. Ann Arbor, Univ. of Michiga Press, 1966, ix, 216p.

Althaus, H., *Laokoon. Stoff und Form*. Bern/Munichen, Francke, 1968, 132p

Aner, Karl, *Die Theologie der Lessingzeit*. Halle, M. Niemeyer, 1929, xi, 376p

Barner, Wilfried, *Lessing. Epoche – Werk – Wirkung*. Munich, Beck, 1981 453.

Batley, E. M., 'Lessing's Dramatic Technique as a Catalyst of the Enlighten ment'. *GLL* N. S. 33 (1979), 9–23.

Bieber, Margarete, *Laocoon, The Influence of the Group since its Rediscovery* 2nd edn, Detroit, Wayne State Univ. Press, 1967, 41p.

Birus, Hendrick, *Poetische Namengebung. Zur Bedeutung der Namen in Lessings 'Nathan der Weise'*. Göttingen, Vandenhoeck & Rupprecht, 1976, 268p.

Bollacher, Martin, *Lessing; Vernunft und Geschichte. Untersuchungen zum Problem religiöser Aufklärung in den Spätschriften*. Tübingen, Niemeyer, 1979, x, 361p.

Brown, F. Andrew, *Gotthold Ephraim Lessing*. Twayne's World Authors Series 113. New York, Twayne, 1971, 205p.

Daunicht, Richard. *Lessing im Gespräch*. Munich, Fink, 1971, 701p.

Demetz, Peter. *Gotthold Ephraim Lessing. 'Nathan der Weise'*. Frankfurt, Ullstein, 1966, 236p.

Garland, Henry Burnand, *Lessing, The Founder of Modern German Literature*. 2nd edn, London, Macmillan; New York, St Martin's Press, 1962, 202p.

öpfert, Herbert G., *Das Bild Lessings in der Geschichte*. Wolfenbüttler Studien z. Aufklärung IX. Heidelberg, Lambert Schneider, 1981.

ombrich, Ernst, *Lessing*. Proceedings of the British Academy, Vol. 43. London, Oxford Univ. Press, 1957, 133–56.

uthke, Karl S., *Gotthold Ephraim Lessing*. 3rd edn, Stuttgart, Metzler, 1979, ix, 108p.

uthke, Karl S., 'Grundlagen der Lessingforschung. Neuere Ergebnisse, Probleme, Aufgaben'. In *Wolfenbüttler Studien zur Aufklärung* II (1975), 10–46.

uthke, Karl S., *Der Stand der Lessing-Forschung*. Stuttgart, Metzler, 1965, 108p.

arris, Edward P. and Richard E. Schade, *Lessing im heutiger Sicht. Beiträge zur Internationalen Lessing Konferenz, Cincinnati, Ohio, 1976*. Bremen, Jacobi, 1977, 348p.

eftrich, Eckhard, *Lessings Aufklärung. Zu den theologisch-philosophischen Spätschriften*. Frankfurt, Klostermann, 1979, 81p.

ertl, Michael and Renate Hertl, *Laokoon. Ausdruck des Schmerzes durch zwei Jahrtausende*. Munich, Thiemig Verlag, 1968, 64p.

illen, Gerd, *Lessing Chronik. Daten zu Leben und Werk*. Munich, Hanser, 1979, 144p.

oensbroech, Marion, *Die List der Kritik. Lessings kritische Schriften und Dramen*. Munich, Fink, 1976, 230p.

üskens-Hasselbeck, Karin, *Stil und Kritik. Dialogische Argumentation in Lessings philosophischen Schriften*. Munich, Fink, 1978, 150p.

ommerell, Max, *Lessing und Aristoteles*. 3rd edn, Frankfurt, Klostermann, 1960, 315p.

amport, Francis John, *Lessing and the Drama*. Oxford, Clarendon Press, 1981, 247.

essing und die Zeit der Aufklärung. Joachim-Jungius Gesellschaft der Wissenschaften, Hamburg. Göttingen, Vandenhoeck & Rupprecht, 1968, 204p.

iepert, Anita, 'Lessing-Bilder. Zur Metamorphose der bürgerlichen Lessingforschung'. *Deutsche Zeitschrift für Philosophie* 19 (1971), 1318–30.

lay, Kurt, *Lessings und Herders kunsttheoretische Gedanken*. Germanische-Studien 25. Berlin, E. Ebering, 1923, 159p.

lehring, Franz, *Die Lessing Legende*. Intro. by Rainer Gruenter. 2nd edn, Ullstein Buch 2854. Frankfurt, Ullstein, 1972, xviii, 621p.

lortier, Roland, 'Lessing und die französische Aufklärung des 18. Jahrhunderts'. *Zeitschrift für Germanistik* 2 (1980), 201–10.

ellegrini, Alessandro, 'Lessing e l'Illuminismo', *Studi Germanici* Series 2, no. 2 (1964), 5–21.

illa, Paul, *Lessing und sein Zeitalter*. 2nd edn, Munich, Beck, 1977, 464p.

obertson, John George, *Lessing's Dramatic Theory*. 1939. rpt. New York, B. Blom, 1965, x, 544p.

chröder, Jürgen, *Gotthold Ephraim Lessing; Sprache und Drama*. Munich, Wilhelm Fink Verlag, 1972, 416p.

chulte-Sasse, Jochen, ed., *Lessing, Mendelssohn, Nicolai. Briefwechsel über das Trauerspiel*. Munich, Winkler, 1972, 250p.

Seifert, Siegfried, *Lessing-Bibliographie*. Berlin, Aufbau Verlag, 1973, ix, 857p
Steinmetz, Horst, ed., *G. E. Lessings 'Minna von Barnhelm'. Dokumente zu Rezeptions- und Interpretationsgeschichte*. Königstein, Athenäum, xxvi 230p.
Steinmetz, Horst, ed., *Lessing – ein unpoetischer Dichter*. Frankfurt Athenäum, 1969, 598p.
Strohschneider, Ingrid, *Vom Prinzip des Masses in Lessings Kritik*. Stuttgart Metzler, 1969, 43p.
Szarota, Elida Maria, *Lessings Laokoon*. Weimar, Arion-Verlag, 1959, 273p.
Thalheim, Hans-Günther, 'Zu Lessings Fabeln'. In his *Zur Literatur de Goethezeit*. Berlin, Rütten & Loening, 1969, 9–37.
Weber, Peter, *Das Menschenbild des bürgerlichen Trauerspiels. Entstehung un Funktion von Lessings 'Miss Sara Sampson'*. Berlin, Rütten & Loening, 1970 272p.
Wessels, Hans-Friedrich, *Lessings 'Nathan der Weise'. Seine Wirkungsgeschicht bis zum Ende der Goethezeit*. Königstein, Athenäum, 1979, xi, 460.

Lichtenberg

Gumbert, Hans Ludwig, ed., *Lichtenberg in England. Dokumente eine Begegnung*. 2 vols. Wiesbaden, Harrassowitz, 1977.
Mautner, Franz H. and Henry Hatfield, eds., *The Lichtenberg Reader*. Boston Beacon, 1959, x, 196p.
Promies, Wolfgang, ed., *Aufklärung über Lichtenberg*. Göttingen, Vanden hoeck & Rupprecht, 1974, 93p.
Promies, Wolfgang, *Georg Christoph Lichtenberg 1742–1799*. Reinbek Rowohlt, 1972, 175p.
Schöffler, Herbert, *Lichtenberg. Studien zu sein Wesen und Geist*. Göttingen Vandenhoeck & Rupprecht 1956, 91p.
Stern, Joseph P., *Lichtenberg: A Doctrine of Scattered Occcasions*. London Thames & Hudson, 1963, 381p.

Mendelssohn

Altmann, Alexander, *Moses Mendelssohn; a biographical study*. University University of Alabama Press, 1972, xvi, 900p.
Altmann, Alexander, *Moses Mendelssohns Frühschriften zur Metaphysik* Tübingen, Mohr (Paul Siebeck), 1969, xii, 396.
Pfeideler, Martin, ed., *Moses Mendelssohn. Selbstzeugnisse*. Tübingen Erdmann, 1979, 214p.
Richter, Lieselotte, *Philosophie der Dichtkunst. Moses Mendelssohns Aesthetik zwischen Aufklärung und Sturm und Drang*. Berlin, Chronos Verlag, 1948 58p.

Merck

Haas, Norbert, *Spätaufklärung. J. H. Merck zwischen Sturm und Drang und französische Revolution*. Kronberg, Scriptor, 1975, 218.

Prang, Helmut, 'Johann Heinrich Merck – Bibliographie'. *Merckische Familien-Zeitschrift* 19 (1953–54), Heft 1/2, 5–59.

Vaget, Hans Rudolf, 'Johann Heinrich Merck über den Roman'. *PMLA* 83 (1968), 347–56.

Möser

Berger, Friedemann, ed., *Anwalt des Vaterlands*. Leipzig, Kiepenheuer Verlag, 1978, 604p.

Flaherty, Marie Gloria, 'Justus Möser. Pre-romantic literary Historian, Critic and Theorist'. In *Traditions and Transitions. Studies in Honor of Harold Jantz*, ed. Lieselotte Kurth *et al.* Munich, Delp, 1972, 87–104.

Moritz.

Boulby, Mark. *Karl Philipp Moritz. At the Fringe of Genius.* Toronto/Buffalo, Toronto Univ. Press, 1979, xii, 308p.

Dell 'Orto, Vincent J. 'Karl Philipp Moritz in England: a psychological study of the traveller'. *MLN* 91 (1976), 453–66.

Grolimund, Josef, *Das Menschenbild in den autobiographischen Schriften Karl Philipp Moritz*. Zürich, Juris-Verlag, 1967, 104p.

Fürnkäs, Josef, *Der Ursprung des psychologischen Romans, Karl Philipp Moritz "Anton Reiser"* '. Stuttgart, Metzler, 1977, 160p.

Minder, Robert, *Glaube, Skepsis und Rationalismus. Dargestellt auf Grund der autobiographischen Schriften von Karl Philipp Moritz.* Frankfurt, Suhrkamp, 1974, 294p.

Saine, Thomas, *Die ästhetische Theodizee. Karl Philipp Moritz und die Philosophie des 18. Jahrhunderts.* Munich, Fink, 1971, 244p.

Schrimpf, Hans Joachim, *Karl Philipp Moritz.* Stuttgart, Metzler, 1980, 151p.

Schrimpf, Hans Joachim, ed., *Karl Philipp Mortiz Schriften zur Aesthetik und Poetik.* Tübingen, Niemeyer, 1962, 411p.

Nicolai

Aner, Karl, *Der Aufklärer Friedrich Nicolai.* Giessen, Töpelmann 1912, iv, 196p.

Martens, Wolfgang, 'Ein Burger auf Reisen. Bürgerliche Gesichtspunkte in Nicolais "Beschreibung einer Reise durch Deutschland und die Schweiz im Jahre 1781" '. *ZDP* 97 (1978), 561–85.

Möller, Horst, *Aufklärer in Preussen. Der Verleger, Publizist und Geschichtsschreiber Friedrich Nicolai.* Berlin, Colloquium Verlag, 1974, viii, 629p.

Ost, Günther, *Friedrich Nicolais Allgemeine Deutsche Bibliothek.* Germanische Studien 63. 1928. Rpt. Nendeln/Liechtenstein, Kraus Reprints, 1967, viii, 118p.

Philips, Franz Carl August, *Friedrich Nicolais literarische Bestrebungen.* The Hague, W. P. van Stocken & Sohn, 1926, ix, 320p.

Sichelschmidt, Gustav, *Friedrich Nicolai. Geschichte seines Lebens.* Herford, Nicolai, 1971, 187p.

Sonnenfeld, Martin, *Friedrich Nicolai und der Sturm und Drang. Ein Beitrag zur Geschichte der deutschen Aufklärung*. Halle, Niemeyer, 1921, 400p.

Novalis

Hamburger, Michael, *Reason and Energy*. London, Routledge, 1957, 71–104.
Haywood, Bruce, *The Veil of Imagery. A Study of the poetic work of Friedrich von Novalis (1772–1801)*. Cambridge, Mass. Harvard Univ. Press, 1959, 159p.
Janz, Rolf-Peter, *Autonomie und soziale Funktion der Kunst. Studien zur Ästhetik von Schiller und Novalis*. Stuttgart, Metzler, 1973, vi, 157p.
Mähl, Hans-Joachim, *Die Idee des goldenen Zeitalters im Werk des Novalis*. Heidelberg, Winter, 1965, viii, 496p.
Mason, Eudo, 'Hölderlin und Novalis' in *Hölderlin Jhb. 1958–1960*. 72–119.
Schanze, Helmut, *Romantik und Aufklärung. Untersuchungen zu Friedrich Schlegel und Novalis*. Nürnberg, Hans Carl, 1966, xiii, 172p.
Schulz, Gerhard, 'Die Poetik des Romans bei Novalis', *JFDH* 1964, 120–57.
Schulz, Gerhard, *Novalis*. Darmstadt, Wissenschaftliche Buchgesellschaft, 1970, xx, 423p.
Schulz, Gerhard, *Novalis in Selbstzeugnissen und Bilddokumenten*. Reinbek, Rowohlt, 1969, 189p.

Oeser

Schulze, Friedrich, *Adam Friedrich Oeser, der Vorläufer des Klassizismus*. Leipzig, Koehler & Amelang, 1944, 66p.

Ramler

de Capua, A. G. 'K. W. Ramler. Anthologist and editor'. *JEGP* 55 (1956), 355–72.

Raspe

Carswell, John, *The Prospector: Being the Life and Times of Rudolf Erich Raspe (1737–1794)*. London, Cresset Press, 1950, vi, 277p.

Rebmann

Schneider, Falko. *Aufklärung und Politik. Studien zur Politisierung der deutschen Spätaufklärung am Beispiel A. G. F. Rebmanns*. Wiesbaden, Athenaion, 1978, 107p.

Reichardt

Salmen, Walter, *Johann Friedrich Reichardt*. Freiburg, Atlantis Verlag, 1963, 364p.

Jean Paul Richter

Arnold, Heinz Ludwig, ed., *Text und Kritik. Sonderheft Jean Paul.* 2nd edn, Munich, Boorberg, 1974, 145p.
Baumann, Gerhart, *Jean Paul: zum Verstehensprozess der Dichtung.* Göttingen, Vandenhoeck & Rupprecht, 1967, 47p.
Berend, Marion, 'Die Erzählformen in den Romanen Jean Pauls.' Diss. Göttingen, 1952.
Berend, Eduard, 'Jean Paul – der meistgelesene Schriftsteller seiner Zeit'. *Imprimatur* N. F. 2 (1958–60), 172 ff.
Boeschenstein, Bernhard, 'Jean Pauls Romankonzeption'. In his *Studien zur Dichtung des Absoluten.* Zürich, Atlantis Verlag, 1968, 25–44.
Fuhrmann, Eike, 'Jean Paul Bibliographie'. *Jahrbuch der Jean-Paul-Gesellschaft* I (1966), 163–79.
Koepke, Wulf, *Erfolglosigkeit. Zum Frühwerk Jean Pauls.* Munich, Fink, 1977, 426p.
Merwald, Renate, 'Jean Paul Bibliographie'. *Jahrbuch der Jean-Paul-Gesellschaft* V (1970), 185–219.
Petersen, Julius, 'Jean Paul und die Klassiker'. *JFDH*, 1929, 234–52.
Profitlich, Ulrich, *Der selige Leser. Untersuchungen zur Dichtungstheorie Jean Pauls.* Bonn, Bouvier, 1968, 198p.
Rasch, Wolf-Dietrich, *Die Erzählweise Jean Pauls.* Munich, Hanser, 1961, 57p.
Schweikert, Uwe, *Jean Paul.* Sammlung Metzler 91. Stuttgart, Metzler, 1970, vi, 109p.
Schweikert, Uwe, *Jean Paul Chronik. Daten zu Leben und Werk.* Munich, Hanser, 1975, 201p.
Sprengel, Peter, ed., *Jean Paul im Urteil seiner Kritiker: Dokumente zur Wirkungsgeschichte Jean Pauls in Deutschland.* Munich, Beck, 1980, xcii, 400p.
Wöfel, Kurt, ed., 'Sammlung der Zeitgenössischen Rezensionen von Jean Pauls Werken'. *Jahrbuch der Jean-Paul-Gesellschaft* 13 (1978), 5–184; 16 (1981), 5–179.

Ritter

McRae Robert J., 'Johann Wilhelm Ritter'. In: *Dictionary of Scientific Biography.* New York, Charles Scribner's Sons, 1970–80, Vol. XI. 473–75.
Wezels, Walter D., *Johann Wilhelm Ritter: Physik im Wirkungsfeld der deutschen Romantik.* Berlin, de Gruyter, 1973, 135p.

Runge

Mathieu, Stella Wega, ed., *Philipp Otto Runge. Leben und Werk in Daten und Bildern.* Frankfurt, Insel Verlag, 1977, 181p.
Träger, Jörg, *Philipp Otto Runge und sein Werk.* Munich, Prestel, 1975, 556p.

Schelling

Frank, Manfred and Gerhard Kurz, eds., *Materialien zu Schellings Philosophischen Anfängen*. Frankfurt, Suhrkamp, 1975, 475p.
Jähnig, Dieter, *Schelling: Die Kunst in der Philosophie*. 2 vols. Pfullingen, Neska, 1966–69.
Sandkühler, Hans Jörg, *F. W. J. Schelling*. Sammlg. Metzler 87. Stuttgart, Metzler, 1970, viii 108p.
Szondi, Peter, 'Schellings Gattungspoetik'. In his *Poetik und Geschichtsphilosophie*, II, Frankfurt, Suhrkamp, 1974, 185–307.
Tilliette, Xavier, *Schelling im Spiegel seiner Zeitgenossen*. Turion, Bottega d'Erasmo, 1974, 657p.
Zeltner, Hermann, *Schelling*. Stuttgart, Fromman. 1954, xii, 335p.

Schiller

Barnouw, Jeffrey, 'Das "Problem der Aktion" und "Wallenstein" '. *JbDSG* 16 (1972), 330–408.
Beaujean, Marion, 'Zweimal Prinzenerziehung: "Don Carlos" und "Geisterseher": Schillers Reaktion auf Illuminaten und Rosenkreuzer'. *Poetica* X (1978), 217–35.
Berghahn, Klaus L., 'Asthetik und Politik im Werke Schillers. Zur jüngsten Forschung'. *MDU* 66 (1974), 410–21.
Berghahn, Klaus L., *Friedrich Schiller: zur Geschichtlichkeit seines Werkes*. Kronberg/Ts., Scriptor-Verlag, 1975, 397p.
Berghahn, Klaus L. and Reinhold Grimm, eds., *Schiller. Zur Theorie und Praxis der Dramen*. Darmstadt, Wissenschaftliche Buchgesellschaft, 1972, 524p.
Bode, Ingrid, *Schiller-Bibliographie 1962–1965*. *JbDSG* 10 (1966) 465–505.
Bode, Ingrid, *Schiller-Bibliography 1966–1969*, *JbDSG* 14 (1970), 584–636.
Böckmann, Paul, 'Politik und Dichtung im Werk Friedrich Schillers'. In his *Formensprache*. Hamburg, Hoffmann & Campe, 1966, 268–82.
Borchmeyer, Dieter, *Tragödie und Offentlichkeit; Schillers Dramaturgie im Zusammenhang seiner ästhetisch-politischen Theorie und die rhetorische Tradition*. Munich, Fink, 1973, 328p.
Borchmeyer, Dieter, 'Über eine ästhetische Aporie in Schillers Theorie der modernen Dichtung. Zu seinen "sentimentalischen Forderungen" an Goethes "Wilhelm Meister" und "Faust" '. *JbDSG* 22 (1978), 303–54.
Cassirer, Ernst, 'Schiller and Shaftesbury'. *PEGS* NS XI (1935).
Dewhurst, Kenneth and Nigel Reeves, *Friedrich Schiller: Medicine, Psychology and Literature*. Oxford, Sandford Publications, 1978, xii, 413p.
Doppler, Alfred, 'Schiller und die Frühromantik'. *Jahrbuch des Wiener Goethe-Vereins* 64 (1960), 71–91.
Forster, Leonard, 'A cool fresh look at Schiller's "Das Lied von der Glocke" ' *PEGS* N. S. 42 (1972), 90–115.
Garland, Henry Burnand, *Schiller The Dramatic Writer. A Study of Style in the Plays*. Oxford, Clarendon Press, 1969, 301p.
Garland, Henry Burnand, *Schiller*. London, Harrap, 1949, 280p.

Graham, Ilse, *Schiller. A Master of the Tragic Form. His theory in his practice.* Pittsburgh, Duquesne Univ. Press, 1975, xiv, 185.

Graham, Ilse, *Schiller's Drama: Talent and Integrity.* London, Methuen, 1974, xii, 406p.

Graham, Ilse, 'Zweiheit im Einklang. Der Briefwechsel zwischen Schiller und Goethe'. *GJb* 95 (1978), 29–64.

Hamburger, Käthe, 'Schiller und die Lyrik'. In her *Kleine Schriften.* Stuttgart, Akademischer Verlag, 1976, 137–69.

Hamburger, Käthe, ed., *Über die aesthetische Erziehung des Menschen.* Stuttgart, Reclam, 1973, 150p.

Hannich-Bode, Ingrid, *Schiller-Bibliographie 1970–1973. JbSG* 18 (1974), 642–701.

Hannich-Bode, Ingrid, *Schiller Bibliographie 1974–1979 und Nachträge. JbDSG* 23 (1979), 551–

Henrich, Dieter, 'Der Begriff der Schönheit in Schillers Aesthetik'. *Zeitschrift für philosophische Forschung* 11 (1957), 527–47.

Hermand, Jost, 'Schillers Abhandlung "Uber naive und sentimentalische Dichtung" im Lichte der Popularphilosophie des 18. Jahrhunderts'. In *Friedrich Schiller: zur Geschichtlichkeit seines Werkes.* Kronberg/Ts., Scriptor Verlag, 1975, 253–79.

Heuer, Fritz und Werner Keller, eds., *Schillers 'Wallenstein'.* Darmstadt, Wissenschaftliche Buchgesellschaft, 1977, xi, 429p.

Hinderer, Walter, *Der Mensch in der Geschichte. Ein Versuch über Schillers 'Wallenstein'.* Königstein/Ts.: Athenäum Verlag, 1980, 140p.

Hinderer, Walter, ed., *Schillers Dramen. Neue Interpretationen.* Stuttgart, Reclam, 1979, 390p.

Janz, Rolf-Peter, 'Schillers "Kabale und Liebe" als bürgerliches Trauerspiel'. *JbDSG* 20 (1976), 208–28.

Kaiser, Gerhard, *Von Arkadien nach Elysium: Schiller-Studien.* Göttingen, Vandenhoeck & Rupprecht, 1978, 218p.

Koopmann, Helmut, *Friedrich Schiller.* 2 vols. Sammlung Metzler M 51. Stuttgart, Metzler, 1977.

Koopmann, Helmut, *Schiller-Forschung 1970–1980. Ein Bericht,* Marbach, Deutsches Literaturarchiv, 1981, 208p.

Liepe, Wolfgang, 'Der junge Schiller und Rousseau'. In his *Beiträge zur Literatur- und Geistesgeschichte.* Neumünster, Wachholtz. 1963. 29–64.

Lohner, Edgar, *Schiller und die moderne Lyrik.* Göttingen, Akademie Verlages-Athenaion, 1964, 80p.

Lukacs, George, 'Der Briefwechsel zwischen Schiller und Goethe'. In his *Goethe und seine Zeit.* Berlin, Aufbau Verlag, 1953, 266p.

Meyer, Herman, 'Schillers Philosophische Rhetorik'. *Euphorion* 53 (1959), 313–50.

Müller-Seidel, Walter, 'Episches im Theater der deutschen Klassik: Ein Betrachtung über Schillers "Wallenstein" '. *JbDSG* 20 (1976) 333–86.

Oellers, Norbert, ed., *Schiller-Zeitgenosse aller Epochen.* 2 Parts. Munich, Beck, 1970–76.

Pick, Robert, ed., 'Schiller in England 1787–1960'. *PEGS* N. S. XXX (1961), 1–123.
Pott, Hans-Georg, *Die schöne Freiheit: eine Interpretation zu Schillers Schrift Über die ästhetische Erziehung des Menschen in einer Reihe von Briefen.* Munich, Fink, 1980, 160p.
Raabe, Paul and Ingrid Bode, *Schiller-Bibliographie 1959-1961. JbDSG* 6 (1962), 465–553.
Regin, Deric, *Freedom and Dignity The Historical and Philosophical Thought of Schiller.* The Hague, W. Nijhoff, 1965, 153p.
Stahl, Ernest, *Friedrich Schiller's Drama.* Oxford, Clarendon Press, 1954, 172p.
Staiger, Emil, *Friedrich Schiller.* Zürich, Artemis Verlag, 1967, 452p.
Szondi, Peter, 'Das Naive ist das Sentimentalische. Zur Begriffsdialektik in Schillers Abhandlung. In his *Lektüren und Lektionen*, ed. Henriette Beese *et al.* Frankfurt, Suhrkamp, 1972, 47–99.
Thalheim, Hans-Günther, 'Schillers Stellung zur französischen Revolution und zum Revolutionsproblem'. In his *Zur Literatur der Goethezeit.* Berlin, Rütten & Loening, 1969, 118–45.
Ueding, Gert, *Schillers Rhetorik; idealistische Wirkungsästhetik und rhetorische Tradition.* Tübingen, M. Niemeyer, 1971, viii, 204p.
Vulpius, Wolfgang, *Schiller-Bibliographie 1893–1958.* Weimar, Arion Verlag, 1959, xviii, 569p.
Vulpius, Wolfgang, *Schiller-Bibliographie 1959–1963.* Berlin/Weimar, Aufbau Verlag, 1967, vii, 204p.
Wacker, Manfred, *Schillers 'Räuber' und der Sturm und Drang; stilkritische und typologische Überprüfung eines Epochenbegriffs.* Göppingen, A. Kümmerle, 1973, 209p.
Wentzlaff-Eggebert, Friedrich, *Schillers Weg zu Goethe.* Berlin, de Gruyter, 1963, xi, 338p.
Wersig, Peter, *Schiller Bibliographie 1964–1974.* Berlin, Aufbau Verlag, 1977, vii, 254p.
Wiese, Benno von, 'Schiller-Forschung und Schiller-Deutung von 1937–1953'. *DVjs* 27 (1953) 452–83.
Wiese, Benno von, *Friedrich Schiller.* 4th edn, Stuttgart, Metzler, 1978, xxv, 868p.
Wilkinson, Elizabeth M. and Leonard A. Willoughby, eds., *Friedrich Schiller. On the Aesthetic Education of Man.* Oxford, Clarendon Press, 1967, 372p.
Wilkinson, Elizabeth M. and Leonard Willoughby. ' "The Whole Man" in Schiller's Theory of Culture and Society'. In *Essays in German Language, Culture and Society*, ed. S. Prawer. London: Univ. of London, 1969, 177–210.
Witte, William, *Schiller.* Oxford, Blackwell, 1949, xvii, 211p.
Wittkowski, Wolfgang, ed., *Friedrich Schiller. Kunst, Humanität und Politik in der späten Aufklärung* Tübingen, Niemeyer, 1982.

A. W. Schlegel

Ewton, Ralph W., *The Literary Theories of August Wilhelm Schlegel.* The Hague, Mouton, 1972, 120p.

F. Schlegel

Behler, Ernst, *Friedrich Schlegel in Selbstzeugnissen und Bilddokumenten*. Reinbek, Rowohlt, 1966, 183p.
Deubel, Volker, 'Die Friedrich-Schlegel-Forschung 1945–1972'. *DVs* xlvii (1973), Sonderheft, 48–181.
Eichner, Hans, *Friedrich Schlegel*. New York, Twayne, 1970, 176p.
Lange, Victor, 'Friedrich Schlegel's Literary Criticism'. *Comparative Literature* VII (1955) 289–305.
Mennemeier, Franz Norbert, *Friedrich Schlegels Poesiebegriff*. Munich, Fink, 1971, 414p.
Menze, Clemens, *Der Bildungsbegriff des jungen Friedrich Schlegel*. Ratingen, Henn 1964, 37p.
Peter, Klaus, *Friedrich Schlegel*. Sammlung Metzler M171. Stuttgart, Metzler, 1978, vii, 93p.
Polheim, Karl Konrad, *Die Arabeske. Ansichten und Ideen aus Friedrich Schlegels Poetik*. Paderborn, Schöningh, 1966, 406p.
Schillemeit, Jost, 'Systematische Prinzipien in Friedrich Schlegels Literaturtheorie'. *JFDH* (1972), 137–62.
Stoljar, Margaret, *Athenäum: a Critical Commentary*. Bern, Lang, 1973, 152p.

Thümmel

Windfuhr, Manfred, 'Empirie und Fiktion in August von Thümmels "Reise in die mittäglichen Provinzen von Frankreich" '. *Poetica* 3 (1970), 115–26.

Tieck

Lillyman, William J., *Reality's Dark Dream. The Narrative Fiction of Ludwig Tieck*. Berlin/New York, de Gruyter, 1979, 159p.
Minder, Robert, *Un poete romantique allemand: Ludwig Tieck*. Paris, Les Belles Lettres, 1936, viii, 516p.
Segebrecht, Wulf, ed., *Ludwig Tieck*. Darmstadt, Wissenshaftliche Buchgesellschaft, 1976, xxx. 417p.

Unger

Biedermann, Flodoard v., *Johann Friedrich Unger im Verkehr mit Goethe und Schiller*. Berlin, Berthold, 1927, xl, 204p.

Voss

Häntzschel, Günter, *Johann Heinrich Voss. Seine Homer-Übersetzung als sprachschöpferische Leistung*. Munich, Beck, 1977, xvii, 283p.

Wagner

Lange, Victor, 'Ernst Wagners Roman "Willibalds Ansichten des Lebens" ', in *Festschrift für Rainer Grünter*. Heidelberg, 1979, 70–85.

Wezel

Adel, Kurt, *Johann Karl Wezel. Ein Beitrag zur Geistesgeschichte der Goethezeit*. Vienna, Verlag Notring, 1968, 217p.

Holzehey-Pfenniger, Elizabeth, *Der desavouierte Erzähler: Studien zu J. C. Wezels 'Lebensgeschichte Tobias Knauts'*. Frankfurt, Lang, 1976, 99p.

Jansen, Wolfgang, *Das Groteske in der deutschen Dichtung der Spätaufklärung. Ein Versuch über das Erzählwerk Johann Carl Wezels*. Bonn, Bouvier, 1980, 256p.

McKnight, Philipps., *The Novels of Johann Karl Wezel. Satire, Realism and Social Criticism in Late 18th Century Literature*. Bern, Lang, 1981, 312p.

McKnight, Philipps., 'Versuch einer Gesamtbibliographie über Johann Carl Wezel'. In *J. C. Wezel. Kritische Schriften*. Vol. 2., ed. A. R. Schmitt. Stuttgart, Metzler, 1971, 815–36.

Steiner, Gerhard, 'Zerstörung einer Legende oder Das wirkliche Leben des Johannes Karl Wezel'. *Sinn und Form* 31 (1979), 699–710.

Wieland

Abbe, Derek Maurice. Van, *Christoph Martin Wieland (1733–1813)*. London, Harrap, 1961, 191p.

Benjamin, Walter, 'Christoph Martin Wieland'. In his *Schriften*, II. ed. Theodor Adorno *et al.* Frankfurt, Suhrkamp, 1955, 330–42.

Campe, Joachim, *Der programmatische Roman. Von Wielands 'Agathon' zu Jean Pauls 'Hesperus'*. Bonn, Bouvier, 1979, 258p.

Elson, Charles, *Wieland and Shaftesbury*. New York, Columbia Univ. Press, 1913, xii, 143p.

Hemmerich, Gerd, *Christoph Martin Wielands 'Geschichte des Agathon'. Eine kritische Werkinterpretation*. Nürnberg, Carl, 1979, 105p.

Hinderer, Walter, 'Beiträge Wielands zu Schillers ästhetischer Erziehung'. *JbDSG* XVIII (1974), 348–87.

Kurth-Voigt, Lieselotte E., *Perspectives and Points of View: The early works of Wieland and their background*. Baltimore, Johns Hopkins Univ. Press, 1974, x, 189p.

Lohmeyer, Dieter, ed., *Christoph Martin Wieland. Aufsätze zu Literatur and Politik*. Reinbek, Rowohlt, 1970, 347p.

McCarthy, John, *Fantasy and Reality. An Epistemological Approach to Wieland*. Bern, H. Lang 1974, 166p.

Müller, Jan-Dirk, *Wielands späte Romane*. Munich, Fink, 1971, 207p.

Paulsen, Wolfgang, *Christoph Martin Wieland: Der Mensch und sein Werk in psychologischen Perspektiven*. Bern, Francke, 1975, 268p.

Preisendanz, Wolfgang, 'Wieland und die Verserzählung des 18. Jahrhunderts'. *GRM* N. F. 12 (1962), 17–31.

Schelle, Hansjörg, *Christoph Martin Wieland*. Darmstadt, Wissenschaftliche Buchgesellschaft, 1981, 493p.

Sengle, Friedrich, *Wieland*. Stuttgart, Metzler, 1949, 612p.

Sommer, Cornelius, *Christoph Martin Wieland*. Sammlung Metzler M 95. Stuttgart, Metzler, 1971, vi, 67p.

Sommer, Cornelius, 'Europäische Tradition und individuelles Stilideal. Zur Versgestalt von Wielands späteren Dichtungen'. *Arcadia* 4 (1969), 247–73.

Stoll, Karin, *Christoph Martin Wieland. Journalistik und Kritik: Bedingungen und Massstab politischen und ästhetischen Raisonnements im 'Teutschen Merkur' vor der französische Revolution*. Bonn, Bouvier, 1978, ix, 196p.

Swales, Martin, 'An unreadable novel? Some observations on Wieland's "Agathon" and the "Bildungsroman" tradition'. *PEGS* N. S. 45 (1976), 101–30.

Ungern-Sternberg, Wolfgang von, *C. M. Wieland und das Verlagswesen seiner Zeit*. Frankfurt, Buchhändler-Vereinigung, 1974, Columns 1211–534.

Walzel, Oskar, 'Wielands Versepik'. *Jahrbuch für Philologie* II (1927), 8–34.

Wieland: Vier Biberacher Vorträge 1953. Wiesbaden, Insel Verlag, 1954, 104p.

Wolffheim, Hans. *Wielands Begriff der Humanität*. Hamburg, Hoffmann & Campe, 1949, 335p.

Winckelmann

Flavell, M. Kay, 'Winckelmann and the German Enlightenment: On the recovery and uses of the past'. *MLR* 74 (1979), 77–96.

Gerstenberg, Kurt, *Johann Joachim Winckelmann und Anton Raphael Mengs*. Halle/Saale, M. Niemeyer, 1929, 39p.

Häsler, Berthold, ed., *Beiträge zu einem neuen Winckelmannbild*. Schriften der Winckelmann Gesellschaft, Vol. 1. Berlin, Akademie Verlag, 1973, 117p.

Hatfield, Henry, *Winckelmann and his German Critics. 1755–1781*. New York, Kings Cross Press, 1943, 169p.

Kunze, Max and Johann Irmscher, *Johann Joachim Winckelmann. Leben und Wirkung*. Schriften der Winckelmann Gesellschaft. Berlin, Akademie Verlag, 1974.

Irwin, David, *Winckelmann. Writings on Art*. London, Phaidon, 1972, x, 166p.

Leppmann, Wolfgang, *Winckelmann*. New York, Knopf, 1970, xx, 312p.

Rehm, Walter, 'Winckelmann und Lessing'. In his *Götterstille und Göttertrauer*. Salzburg, Das Bergland Buch, 1951, 183–201.

Rüdiger, Horst, *Winckelmann und Italien; Sprache, Dichtung, Menschen*. Krefeld, Scherpe, 1959, 44p.

Uhlig, Ludwig, 'Kunst und Dichtung bei Winckelmann'. *ZDP* 98 (1979), 161–76.

Uhlig, Ludwig, ed., *J. J. Winckelmann. Gedanken über die Nachahmung der griechischen Werke in Malerei und Bildhauerkunst*. Stuttgart, Reclam, 1969, 156p.

Index